From 'Stone-Age' to 'Real-Time'

Exploring Papuan Temporalities, Mobilities and Religiosities

From 'Stone-Age' to 'Real-Time'

Exploring Papuan Temporalities, Mobilities and Religiosities

Edited by Martin Slama and Jenny Munro

MONOGRAPHS IN
ANTHROPOLOGY SERIES

Australian
National
University

PRESS

ANU PRESS

Published by ANU Press
The Australian National University
Canberra ACT 0200, Australia
Email: anupress@anu.edu.au
This title is also available online at http://press.anu.edu.au

National Library of Australia Cataloguing-in-Publication entry

Title:	From 'stone-age' to 'real-time' : exploring Papuan temporalities, mobilities and religiosities / Martin Slama and Jenny Munro (editors).
ISBN:	9781925022421 (paperback) 9781925022438 (ebook)
Subjects:	Migration, Internal--Indonesia--Papua. Religion and culture--Indonesia--Papua. Papua (Indonesia)--Social life and customs. Papua (Indonesia)--Civilization. Papua (Indonesia)--History.
Other Creators/Contributors:	
	Slama, Martin, editor.
	Munro, Jenny, editor.
Dewey Number:	995.1

Cover design and layout by ANU Press

Cover illustration: An indigenous woman walking up a road in Tiom, a rapidly developing town in the central Papuan highlands, photographed in 2013 by Carole Reckinger.

Contents

List of Contributors

Leslie Butt is Associate Professor in the Department of Anthropology at the University of Victoria, Canada. She is a medical anthropologist with extensive experience conducting research in Eastern Indonesia on families, HIV/AIDS, reproduction and health care. Her current research focuses on the impact of international migration on the experiences of eastern Indonesian families. She has co-edited two volumes: *Troubling Natural Categories: Engaging the Medical Anthropology of Margaret Lock* (2013, McGill-Queens University Press, with N. Adelson and K. Kielmann); and *Making Sense of AIDS: Culture, Sexuality, and Power in Melanesia* (2008, University of Hawai'i Press, with R. Eves). She has also written numerous papers about Papua, including 'Sexual Tensions: HIV-positive Women in Papua', in *Sex and Sexualities in Contemporary Indonesia: Sexual Politics, Health, Diversity and Representations,* L.R. Bennett and S.G. Davies (eds) (2014); and 'Local Biologies and HIV/AIDS in Highlands Papua, Indonesia', in *Culture, Medicine and Psychiatry* 37 (1) (2013).

Budi Hernawan is a research fellow at the Abdurrahman Wahid Centre for Inter-Faith Dialogue and Peace at the University of Indonesia and a research associate at Franciscans International, an international NGO accredited with the United Nations based in Geneva and New York. He has done extensive research and professional work in Papua, Indonesia, from 1997–2009. His PhD thesis, entitled 'From the Theatre of Torture to the Theatre of Peace: The Politics of Torture and Reimagining Peacebuilding in Papua', reflects his research interests in the anthropology of state violence, human rights, and peacebuilding in Indonesia and the Pacific. He was a guest lecturer at Parahyangan Catholic University in Bandung, Atma Jaya University in Yogyakarta, The Australian National University in Canberra, the University of Sydney, and the University of Wellington.

Jenny Munro is a research fellow in the State, Society and Governance in Melanesia Program at The Australian National University. She is a cultural anthropologist who works in Papua and other regions of eastern Indonesia. Her doctoral research followed a group of indigenous university students from the central highlands of Papua to North Sulawesi and back home again to examine the social, cultural and political impacts of schooling. Since completing her PhD in 2010, Jenny has conducted five collaborative ethnographic research projects in the domains of HIV/AIDS, sexuality, education and alcohol-related violence. Her research reflects a broader interest in understanding emerging and enduring inequalities that are reshaping daily life in Papua. She has published articles on racial stigma and premarital pregnancy experiences (*Journal of Youth Studies*), the politics of HIV research and policy formation (*The Asia Pacific*

Journal of Anthropology), and indigenous experiences of the value of education in highlands Papua (*Indonesia*). She is currently writing about HIV, gender and mobility in Papua.

Henri Myrttinen is a Senior Researcher on Gender in Peacebuilding at the London-based NGO International Alert. Prior to this, he has worked and researched extensively in and on Papua and eastern Indonesia more generally, as well as on Timor-Leste, which was also the focus of his PhD research, which he completed at the University of KwaZulu-Natal, South Africa. Recent publications include 'Resistance, Symbolism and the Language of Stateness in Timor-Leste', in *Oceania* 83 (3) (2013); 'Phantom Menaces: The Politics of Rumour, Securitisation and Masculine Identities in the Shadows of the Ninjas', in *The Asia Pacific Journal of Anthropology* 14 (5) (2013); 'Claiming the Dead, Defining the Nation – Contested Narratives of the Independence Struggle in Post-Conflict Timor-Leste', in *Governing the Dead*, F. Stepputat (ed) (2014).

Sarah Richards is a PhD candidate at the University of Melbourne. She has six years of fieldwork experience in Tanah Papua (Wamena and Manokwari) and Papua New Guinea (Bougainville). With a background in psychology (BA Hons.), her research interests involve morality, gender, youth, emotion, HIV and sexuality. Prior to embarking on a PhD, Sarah worked as a subject coordinator for Medical Anthropology at the Centre for Health and Society (Melbourne University), a research assistant and in community development with Indonesian and international NGOs. Her dissertation inquires into the meanings and motivations of avoiding sex before marriage amongst young Papuan women in Manokwari. As well as indexing trends in West Papuan social and political life, this study relies on Papuan experiences of sexual morality to rethink Durkheim for the anthropology of morality and ethics.

Danilyn Rutherford received her doctorate in anthropology with a minor in Southeast Asian Studies from Cornell University in 1997. She is the author of two books: *Raiding the Land of the Foreigners: The Limits of the Nation on an Indonesian Frontier* (Princeton, 2003) and *Laughing at Leviathan: Sovereignty and Audience in West Papua* (Chicago, 2012). She has taught at Goldsmiths College, the University of Chicago, and, most recently, the University of California, Santa Cruz, where she is professor and chair. She is a past president of the Society for Cultural Anthropology. Her research has long focused on the disputed Indonesian half of New Guinea and has involved fieldwork and archival research in West Papua, the Netherlands and the United States. She is currently finishing a book provisionally entitled *Sympathy, Technology, and the Making of the Stone Age in Dutch New Guinea*. She is taking small steps towards her next project, which will focus on belief, secularism, speech and disability in Indonesia and the United States.

Martin Slama is a postdoctoral researcher at the Institute for Social Anthropology, Austrian Academy of Sciences. He has conducted extensive fieldwork in Indonesia (Java, Bali, Sulawesi, the Moluccas, West Papua) and was guest researcher at The Australian National University in Canberra, State Islamic University Syarif Hidayatullah in Jakarta and Gajah Mada University in Yogyakarta. His main research topics include the Hadhrami diaspora, Islam in Indonesia, and the uses of social media and mobile communication technologies in Southeast Asian contexts. Recent publications: 'Marriage as Crisis: Revisiting a Major Dispute among Hadhramis in Indonesia', in *Cambridge Anthropology* 32 (2) (2014); 'From Wali Songo to Wali Pitu: The Travelling of Islamic Saint Veneration to Bali', in *Between Harmony and Discrimination: Negotiating Religious Identities within Majority-Minority Relationships in Bali and Lombok*, B. Hauser-Schäublin and D. Harnish (eds) (2014); 'Hadhrami Moderns: Recurrent Dynamics as Historical Rhymes of Indonesia's Reformist Islamic Organization Al-Irsyad', in *Dynamics of Religion in Southeast Asia: Magic and Modernity*, V. Gottowik (ed.) (2014).

Rupert Stasch is a lecturer in the Division of Social Anthropology at the University of Cambridge, and has carried out fieldwork with Korowai of Papua since 1995. He is the author of *Society of Others: Kinship and Mourning in a West Papuan Place* (University of California Press, 2009). This and many of his other publications have examined how Korowai take up qualities of separation and otherness as a central, productive basis of social relating. He is working on a book about interactions between Korowai and international tourists, and he has edited a special issue of *Ethnos* on the subject of 'Primitivist Tourism' scheduled for publication in 2015.

Jaap Timmer is Senior Lecturer and Director of the Master of Applied Anthropology at Macquarie University, Sydney. He is the author of *Living with Intricate Futures* (2000) and numerous articles on cultural change, millenarianism and political developments in Papua, and on political ecology and access to justice in East Kalimantan. Recently, he is also focusing on the anthropology of the state, alternative constitutions, religion and lost tribes in the Asia-Pacific region. His recent publications include 'Justice in Indonesia: The Social Life of a Momentous Concept', in *The Asia-Pacific Journal of Anthropology* 15 (4) (2014) (with Laurens Bakker); 'The Threefold Logic of Papua-Melanesia: Constitution-writing in the Margins of the Indonesian Nation-State', in *Oceania* 83 (3) (2013); 'Straightening the Path from the Ends of the Earth: The Deep Sea Canoe Movement in Solomon Islands', in *Flows of Faith: Religious reach and community in Asia and the Pacific*, L. Manderson, W. Smith and M. Tomlinson (eds) (2012); and 'Being Seen Like the State: Emulations of Legal Culture in Customary Labor and Tenure Arrangements in East Kalimantan, Indonesia', in *American Ethnologist* 37 (4) (2010).

Illustrations

130°E 135°E 140°E

PACIFIC OCEAN

0   kilometers   300

---- Province border
---- Regency border

Halmahera

Segun River

Tidore

Kaibus River

Mansinam Island

Insumbabi Island
Aiburanbondi Island

0°

Raja Ampat Islands

Sorong

Bird's Head Peninsula

Manokwari

Dorey Bay

Biak

Biak-Numfor Regency

Kapeso

Cape Sele

Teminabuan

Ransiki

Baimla

WEST PAPUA

Bintuni

Serui

Jayapura

Kokoda

Berau Bay

Bintuni Bay

Cenderwasih Bay

Babo

Mamberamo

Onin Peninsula

Wondama

Keerom Regency

Seram

Fak-Fak

Bomberai Peninsula

Arguni Bay

PAPUA

Swart Valley

Mulia

River

Ambon

Kaimana

Wisselmeren (Wissel Lakes)

Enarotali

Tiom

Wamena

Geser-Gorom archipelago

Banda Islands

Timika

Yahukimo Regency

Baliem Valley

5°S

Banda Sea

Kei Islands

Aru Islands

Arafura Sea

Tanimbar Islands

Merauke

© Australian National University
CartoGIS CAP 14-212_JS

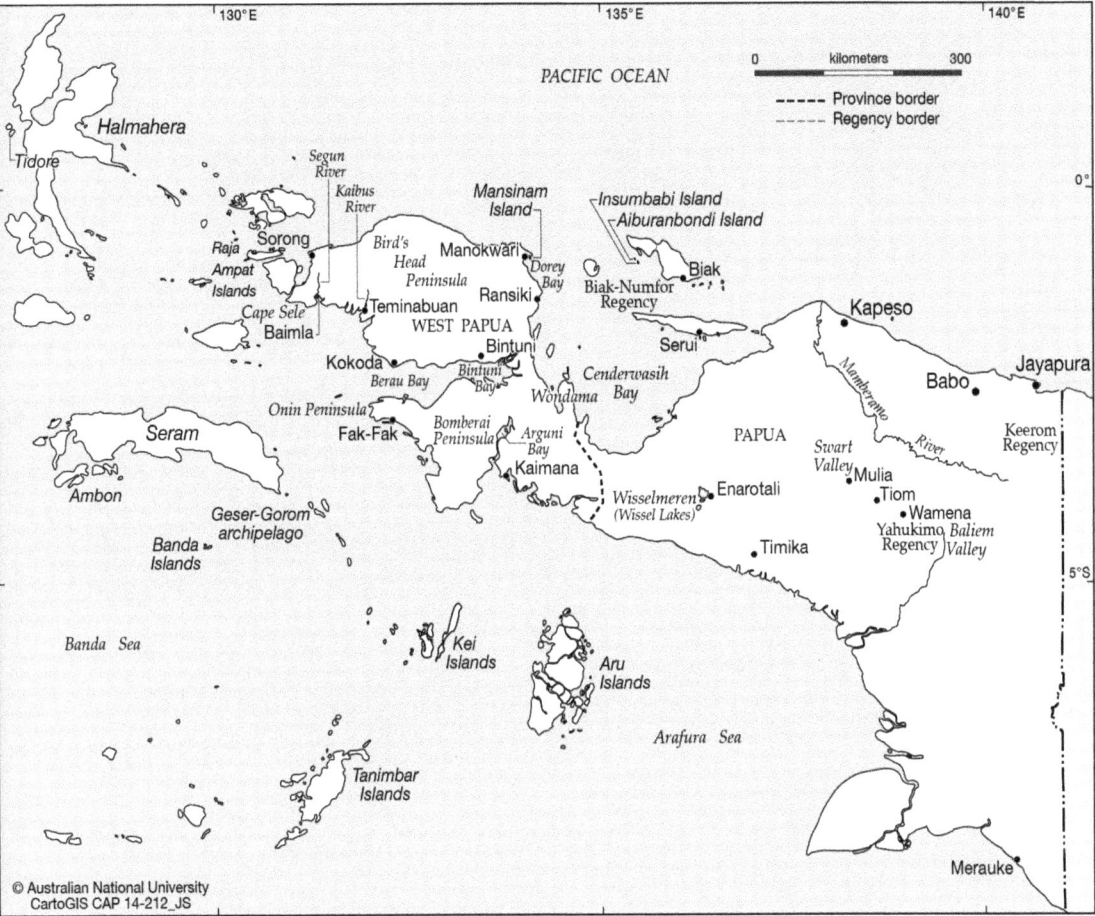

Map of Papua and West Papua showing places referenced in the volume.

Source: The Australian National University, CartoGIS CAP 14-212.

1. From 'Stone-Age' to 'Real-Time': Exploring Papuan Temporalities, Mobilities and Religiosities – An Introduction

Martin Slama and Jenny Munro

There are probably no other people on earth to whom the image of the 'stone-age' is so persistently attached than the inhabitants of the island of New Guinea, which is divided into independent Papua New Guinea and the western part of the island, known today under the names of Papua and West Papua. This volume focuses on the latter region, which took its own trajectory since the colonial division of the island and especially since its controversial incorporation into the Indonesian nation-state in the 1960s. In Papua, stone-age imagery has motivated missions to 'pacify', 'civilise', 'modernise', 'Christianise' and 'Islamise' the local population, and mobilised a proliferation of hierarchical relations, locally and regionally. These projects of frontier transformation became particularly invasive during the authoritarian Suharto regime (1966–98), but are continuing today under different guises.

Today, many Papuans are connected in 'real-time' through Facebook, YouTube and other social networking sites and are increasingly mobile within and beyond Indonesia, certainly belying the old images of isolated stone-agers. At the same time, technologies and mobilities offer certain freedoms while constraining others; novel trajectories may meet familiar challenges. This volume explores the real-time, mobile, social and cultural aspects of contemporary Papua, including historical trajectories that collapse notions of the past with visions of the future. It is concerned with the genealogy of the image of the stone-ager as well as with its current transformations by Papuan, regional and (inter)national agents. In this interconnected age, Papuans may position themselves anew offline and online, as they explore often heterodox religious and political visions, engage in Christian and Muslim networks, renegotiate intra-Papuan relations as well as their relations with non-Papuans, develop forms of resistance in a highly militarised space, and critically question prejudices directed against them. In short, Papua is being remade.

Grappling with today's globalised modernities, indigenous agents are reworking inherited ideas, institutions and technologies according to their own interests, but also coming up against palpable limits on what can be imagined or achieved, secured or defended. This volume investigates some of these trajectories of innovation for the cultural logics and social or political structures that shape them, and examines in detail ways that Papuan efforts and aspirations may equally go awry. It attends to the circulation of particular images, technologies and ideas among Papuans and interrogates what they mean for emerging and ongoing inequalities. The volume analyses the scope of Papuan actions, and reactions, that have been generated and curtailed at the intersection of new (trans)national connections and routes of mobility. At the same time, it also illuminates how new mobilities shape power dynamics in situations that are variously intimate, interactive or publicly visible.

Most of the chapters in this volume are highly ethnographic, based on first-hand research with Papuans, conducted in various spaces within and beyond Papua.[1] We present perspectives from diverse sites – lowland, highland, coastal, rural and urban – around the territory of *Tanah Papua* (the Land of Papua). These contributions explore topics ranging from hip hop to historicity, filling much-needed conceptual and ethnographic lacunae in West Papuan studies. In this volume, we have assembled papers that foreground current social, cultural and religious experiences, processes and conditions in Papua. At the same time, the volume explores historical genealogies that reach back to Dutch colonial times, notably the stone-age image itself, which cannot be ignored when analysing current social and political dynamics. In this regard we want to stress that, in some ways, political conditions in Papua are well-documented and the subject of much impressive scholarship (Chauvel 2005, 2011; Chauvel and Bhakti 2004; McGibbon 2004; Braithwaite et al. 2010; Widjojo et al. 2008; King et al. 2011). In other ways, the political tends to be revealed as extraneous to the social and cultural machinations of everyday life. By depicting ethnographic complexity and everyday entanglements, the contributors to this volume show us a different side of politics in Papua, a politics that is deeply embedded in social change, cultural tensions and economic inequalities and is sometimes less straightforwardly 'separatist' or 'nationalist' than we might assume.

Following the subtitle of the volume, this introduction reflects on the chapters via the themes of temporalities, mobilities and religiosities. It is not that one cannot find other categories to guide the reader through the rich material and analyses presented in the chapters, but we think that the chapters are particularly connected through these three concepts and that these concepts elicit particular intersections that generate novel perspectives for understanding current Papuan conditions. We start with 'temporalities', a theme reflected in the main title of the volume, as the image of the stone-age as well as the notion of the real-time

---

1   The origins of this volume go back to a panel held at the Annual Meeting of the American Anthropological Association in November 2012 in San Francisco. It was organised by Martin Slama and Christian Warta and bore the title 'From "Stone-Age" to "Real-Time": Temporalities and Mobilities in and beyond Papua', including papers by Leslie Butt, Budi Hernawan, Eben Kirksey, Jenny Munro, Jacob Nerenberg, Danilyn Rutherford, Martin Slama, Rupert Stasch, Jaap Timmer and Christian Warta. Andrew Willford was so kind as to discuss the papers.

imply particular conceptions of time that are intrinsic to so many contemporary Papuan issues. Given the emphasis of this volume on the everyday, intimate and interactive, we find it appropriate to introduce the theme of temporalities through ethnographic accounts in the first place.

Temporalities

In today's Indonesia one can encounter representations of Papuans in unexpected and at the same time familiar ways – for example, by way of a picture shown on the display of an Indonesian businessman's smartphone depicting a Papuan man who sits, dressed in his penis sheath (*koteka*), on a chair in front of a bank counter in one of Indonesia's neatly air-conditioned bank buildings being served by a female Indonesian bank employee dressed in her professional business attire. Allured by this blatant juxtaposition of 'primitiveness' and 'modernity' at a frontier that is obviously promising wealth, the businessman explained that this picture was recently sent to him by a friend who got 'a project' (*proyek*) in Timika, and that he is hoping to join him soon.[2] Whereas one might be struck to find such a picture on the smartphone of a Javanese businessman, the representation of a Papuan man as primitive in the context of Indonesian manifestations of modernity is less surprising.[3] Yet this volume is not only occupied with the remarkably persistent association of Papuans with primitivism, especially with the stone-age as the ultimate realm of the primitive other, but also with the question how this stone-age image surfaces in the current era, in which so much emphasis is put on the 'real-time', an expression that popularly alludes to immediate digital communication that is free of delays. People communicate, transmit all kinds of data, as it *really* happens – at least this is the ideal. As such, 'real-time' functions as a synonym for the present, for participating in the present, for being part of today's globalising modernity, and certainly not for belonging to a bygone age. The real-time thus signifies a global digital modernity in which 'cyber'-citizens, i.e. potentially everybody who is not confined to the offline, occupy the same spatio-temporal realm. And in light of current user numbers of social media it becomes apparent that the real-time is very appealing to Indonesians.[4]

---

2   This is an episode from Martin Slama's fieldwork in Yogyakarta in June 2012.

3   See for example Michael Cookson's analysis of Indonesian post stamps from the year 2002 dedicated to 'modern communication devices' (*alat komunikasi* modern). One stamp depicts a female Indonesian office worker and a Papuan man both holding mobile phones in their hands. Cookson (2008: 124) writes: 'The Papuan's exaggerated facial features and naked black skin contrast sharply with the elegantly dressed, pale female office worker and despite possibilities to the contrary, this stamp issue powerfully reinforces popular imaginary of Papuans as tribal, traditional and perhaps even primitive in a modern world.'

4   For example, with more than 48 million users Indonesia boasts the world's fourth-largest Facebook community. See: http://www.clicktop10.com/2013/04/top-10-countries-with-most-facebook-users-in-2013/ (accessed 1 June 2014). 1. United States 165 million. 2. Brazil 65.6 million. 3. India 61.7 million. 4. Indonesia 48.8 million.

Similarly to the appeal of the real-time today, in the Dutch colonial era officials were occupied with what they regarded as 'real' or as belonging to 'the real world', notions that implied already a sense of coevalness as well as its denial. Most importantly, it was the world of Papuans that was not granted this status of being 'real'. Michael Cookson (2008: 389) quotes in his dissertation Jan van Baal, a key figure of the colonial regime, who lamented in the 1950s about the state of education in Papua:

> Their knowledge of arithmetic may be very unsatisfactory and that of reading and writing only slightly better, but they will all come to understand that the world of their fathers, that small and mysterious little world, is not the real world after all. There is only one real world that matters: it is the world of schools, of big ships and planes, of trade and films, of motor-cars, luxury and prosperity. That real world, however, is not theirs.

In the meantime, conditions in Papua have changed considerably and one might argue that 'the real world' as described by van Baal has, at least in some of its aspects, become part of Papuan daily life. Moreover, Papuans participate not only in what van Baal characterised as 'real' but in realms of the real-time he was not able to imagine in the 1950s. Given this contemporary emphasis on contemporaneity this volume asks what consequences, frictions and anxieties the current moment generates, when the persistency of the stone-age image meets the practices and ideologies of the real-time, and when different conceptions of time collide in ways that potentially endanger Indonesian-Papuan hierarchies. A first answer to that question may be that in the age of the real-time, considerably more effort has to be invested in denying Papuans a role in the present, and in relegating them to a past time by identifying them with stone-age images. Again, consider the case of the circulating picture of the Papuan in the bank. The Javanese businessman's friend, or whoever has taken the picture, could easily have portrayed Papuans dressed in trousers and not a *koteka*. In fact, there were probably more trouser-wearing Papuans than *koteka*-wearing Papuans in the bank. Yet such a representation would grant Papuans a status of contemporaneity, of being part of Indonesia's modern economy as bank customers or even businessmen. Instead, this picture from the Papuan frontier, circulating among Javanese businessmen in contact with each other via social media, exhibits the Papuan as a curiosity in the modern space of a bank. It imputes the opportunities that Papua apparently has to offer to those who are *really* part of the real-time, i.e. smartphone-owning Javanese businessmen who feel themselves compelled to document outsiders-cum-stone-agers who are intruding into the spatio-temporal realm of the contemporary.

Digital files sometimes take widely ramified trajectories, and this has also been the case with the '*koteka*-wearing Papuan in a bank' picture. A quick search on

Google Images reveals that the picture has made it onto the Indonesian online portal indowebster, which boasts around 1.6 million members. Discussed in the portal's forum section, comments range from sensationalist remarks about a 'naked' (*bugil*) man in a bank wearing, besides his *koteka*, only a 'cool wrist watch' (*jam tangan keren*) to expressions of sympathy and understanding that his attire should be regarded as part of his 'tradition' (*adat*) and that one should respect people who 'still love their culture' (*masih cinta terhadap budayanya*).[5] Though not centred on an interest in business opportunities, these interpretations follow a similar logic of denying the contemporary contemporaneity, as, in the first instance, they suggest that the 'naked' Papuan does not belong in the bank just like the 'cool watch' does not belong to such a 'primitive' man and, in the second case, they grant the Papuan a place in the bank only as a personification of tradition, as the 'noble savage' who still loves his culture in contrast to, as is suggested, those modern Indonesians who are active in the online forum.

As our interpretations of these examples indicate, the volume builds on a tradition of scholarship in anthropology that critically reflects temporal and spatial hierarchisations as they appear within the discipline and beyond. This scholarship is characterised by critical (self-)reflexivity, i.e. following Edward Said's seminal *Orientalism* (1978) it is concerned with strategies of representing non-Western people in temporally remote forms and with the construction of 'cultural, temporal, and geographical distance' (ibid. 222) at large. We thus find the 'denial of coevalness', which Johannes Fabian (1983) sees constitutive for classic anthropological accounts, as having transcended the realms of Western scholarship and cultural production. Seeking to contribute to an anthropology of temporal representations, this volume demonstrates that this denial can decisively inform not only ideological categories and government policies but also everyday encounters, practice and performance, offline and online – in a country like Indonesia and, due to the spread of evolutionist and developmentalist ideologies, in many other places in the world as well (for Africa see e.g. Ferguson 2006).

Another important aspect of the spread of temporal hierarchisations in the current era is that representations, such as exemplified by the digital files discussed above, are likely to reach new audiences. The importance of audiences for political projects in Papua, especially for notions of sovereignty, is emphasised by Danilyn Rutherford (2012: 2), who asserts that 'audience infects the very concept of sovereignty: audience is sovereignty's basis and its bane'. And it can indeed become its bane when files reach audiences for which they were not intended. The chapter by Budi Hernawan exemplifies such a case. Hernawan examines 'torture as a mode of governance' in Papua. His chapter is based on 431 codified cases of torture in Papua over the period of 1963–2010 and

---

5 See: http://forum.indowebster.com/showthread.php?t=77666 (last accessed 12 December 2013).

214 interviews in five countries, which formed the basis of his doctoral research (Hernawan 2013). His analysis suggests that the most distinct pattern of torture in West Papua is that it takes place in public spaces, i.e. torture is practiced in public with a particular audience in mind, namely the family members and fellow villagers of the torture victim. However, in 2010 videos of Papuans being tortured by Indonesian military personnel were published on YouTube and spurred international reactions. The audience of Papuan villagers, which the perpetrators might have perceived as being spatially and temporally too distant from the interconnected world, suddenly gained support from the realm of the real-time, in which the videos were watched, shared and discussed.

We consider this example significant because, unlike the Papuan bank customer, the tortured Papuans were impossible to relegate to the stone-age. As torture victims they became subject to contemporary state practices, to one means that Indonesia employs to assert its sovereignty over Papua today. In sharp contrast to evolutionist and developmentalist projects that find international recognition as well as reinforce stone-age discourses, torture is irreconcilable with such attempts. When it is represented online, torture is part of the real-time and, tragically, one of its effects is that Papuans become part of the real-time as well. However, this occurs through mediatisation, whereas the act of torture is attended with discourses of dehumanisation, as the chapter by Hernawan also reveals, that resort to evolutionist and racist ideologies finding their expression in name-calling (e.g. *monyet*, meaning 'monkey'). In fact, many of the chapters assembled in this volume give accounts of such practices of humiliation in which the 'monkey' referent features as a particularly evolutionist example derived from popular representations of apes as precursors of human beings, i.e. the early stone-agers. So these derogatory discourses place Papuans one evolutionary stage downwards, even below humankind.

But let us turn now to another example for stone-age/real-time dynamics that differs considerably from the ones above, since here we can observe Papuan-Indonesian encounters that have dialogic features and thus also represent the views of Papuans. This time our source is not to be found on digital social media but was recently published in an academic journal article. 'A note on Jayapura' is written by an Indonesian student, Inaya Rakhmani (2012: 151), who visited Papua with the attempt 'to identify the threads that weave Indonesia together now'. In the course of her PhD research on 'television, religion and national identity in Indonesia', supervised at Murdoch University, Inaya had visited six cities in Indonesia, among which Jayapura 'left the deepest impression personally and professionally' (ibid.). As her visit in October 2011 coincided with the Third Papua Congress and its violent suspension by the Indonesian security apparatus, it was Inaya's 'driver [who] mapped out, based on his real-time communication with local officials, which areas would be more dangerous to travel through and [he] expertly avoided them' (Rakhmani 2012: 152). Thus, in the first instance, modern real-time communication was used to keep a safe distance from the 'rebelling' Papuans, emphasising cultural distance between Indonesian modernity and Papuan primitiveness, similar to the circulating picture of the *koteka*-wearing Papuan man in the bank. But as a PhD student and researcher, Ina came to Jayapura not at all with the intention of shunning Papuans; she actually wanted to meet them, which she eventually did, choosing high school students as her respondents. From her conversations with them she learned that the 'students showed great concern over how they are being stereotyped by people in Java, especially how they are being represented as "*koteka*-wearing-primitives" (as one respondent put it) by Jakarta-centred, nationally broadcast television programmes' (ibid. 154). She was asked whether she expected them to wear *koteka*, and she was told by students who visited 'Java with their family, [that] many people had been surprised that they were fully-clothed and articulate' (ibid. 155). The students were also amazed that she wanted to talk with them, as one of her interlocutors said to her: 'It is not common for a Javanese Muslim to have such an interest in us' (ibid. 156).

Inaya's approach was indeed uncommon, and it was not in accordance with how the Papuan students expected her to see them based on what some of them had experienced in Java, and certainly not based on the exemplary views of the Javanese businessmen discussed above. Perhaps related to her status as a well-educated young woman pursuing her tertiary education at an Australian university, she did not regard the young Papuans she met as somehow belonging to another age. Since she was interested in 'the threads that weave Indonesia together now', i.e. *now*, she treated her interlocutors as contemporaries – much to their astonishment. Nevertheless, her account includes the short reference to the real-time in the form of mobile phone communication that was used to avoid areas where Papuans could clash with Indonesian security forces – understandable from the perspective of personal safety. This is, of course, a very different use of real-time communication compared to the picture-sending Javanese businessmen with their smartphones. Yet both represent examples of the ambivalence of the real-time when it comes to Papua, where thanks to the real-time one can find a 'secure' way through a conflict-prone frontier or from where one can send pictures to confirm its inhabitants' alleged primitivity. Although Papuans, like other citizens of the Indonesian Republic, are active participants in online spheres, as is also reflected in many chapters of this volume, Indonesian representations leave the impression that Papuans remain offline, reinforcing the stone-age identity.

Given the persistency of the stone-age image, mobile and techno-savvy Papuans who visit Java thus can become a source of surprise, as one of Inaya's interlocutors pointed out, and also a source of anxiety – primitives who are no longer primitive anymore spur reactions. Unfortunately, one popular reaction is to deny them contemporaneity despite all empirical counter-evidence. So how do Indonesians and others reconcile modern, mobile and 'articulate' Papuans with their stone-age image? What attempts are made to reinstall a hierarchy, structurally and in personal encounters, that is based on temporal inequality? The chapters in this volume comprise instructive examples of how in Indonesia today, on different levels and in different settings, much effort is put into upholding this stone-age image and its attendant social hierarchy. Contributors also reveal how Papuans are taking up these ideas and for what reasons, and what cultural logics are invoked or dispelled in the process.

By doing so, they build on the first chapter of this volume written by Danilyn Rutherford, who is occupied with the Dutch colonial period when 'expeditions' into the interior of West Papua took place. Rutherford reveals that demonstrations of technology, from firearms to gramophones, were a crucial means of asserting colonial authority and structuring relations with Papuans between the 1930s and 1950s. Intrinsic to these performances was the need to demonstrate not only one's own mastery of technology but also the stone-age condition of Papuans, and in doing so establishing relationships based on this hierarchy. It was not enough to conceptualise the Papuans as stone-agers according to certain evolutionist criteria; rather, the Dutch felt the need to visibly enact their evolutionist ideology in face-to-face activities. After the Second World War, when many Papuans had already acquainted themselves with the technologies demonstrated and introduced by the Dutch, the colonial authorities invited anthropologists to document the alleged primitivism of the Papuans through films. According to Kirsch (2010: 8) the Papuans were depicted as 'living in a state of nature and ... as representatives of our collective human past. As members of a Stone Age society, they are not regarded as coevals but survivors of another era who must be brought into the present, thereby legitimating a variety of state interventions' – and colonial presence, we might add. In fact, when the Dutch era came to an end, it was the stone-age image that featured in international discourse and was used to deny Papuan self-determination. After all, it was no less a person than John F. Kennedy who stated that 'those inhabitants of West New Guinea are living, as it were, in the Stone Age' (see Rutherford 2013; Webster 2013).

Referring to the late Dutch colonial period, Rutherford reveals another crucial aspect of the stone-age discourse that helps to understand current dynamics in Papua. In her chapter, she discusses a case where a Biak woman was brought to the highlands to work in the Dutch household of the head of the post's health department where she encountered a local houseboy. In their first encounter it became apparent, as Rutherford writes, 'how this coastal Papuan internalised the Dutch view that made Stone Age tribes out of people who had once used stone tools', although the houseboy presented himself to the Biak woman as someone who receives formal education. For Rutherford, this example shows that even if Papuans 'mastered modern instruments, the Stone Age stuck to their identities, like glue from a label they couldn't peel off' – all the more so if Papuans themselves view other Papuans as stone-agers. This example of the hierarchisation of relations between coastal and highlands Papuans based on colonial discourses anticipates current tensions among Papuans that often run along these coastal–highland lines, with Papuans from the coast still resorting to claims of superiority over highland populations.

However, this picture is complicated by Rupert Stasch's chapter on the Korowai of the southern lowlands, where in fact highland Dani missionaries (among other actors) are engaged in the project of bringing the Korowai into the realm of the real-time, which the Korowai themselves very much desire. As Stasch shows, this project and its opposite, namely selling the Korowai as the ultimate stone-agers to international 'alternative' and 'adventure' tourists, is characterised by a set of highly ambiguous relationships: 'Korowai take up the category of the primitive as a self-understanding, acting toward and through this category in their relations with outsiders [mainly tourists and government officials] newly central to their world.' Stasch also shows how the Korowai appropriate the notion of the primitive according to their own concept of unequal human relations, although the inequality they are confronted with today is unprecedented in their history, in which 'strategies of self-lowering as a way to elicit relations are … cultural patterns with deep regional resonance'. So what we see here is a very particular way of dealing with the stone-age image: Korowai are occupied less with getting rid of it and finding recognition as contemporary moderns, as many Papuans attempt today, but rather are actively using the stone-age image to obtain funds, services and consumer goods, and thus to become part of the real-time world as well. Moreover, Stasch sharpens our awareness that 'in the Indonesian and Dutch colonial eras alike, church workers, government functionaries, schoolteachers, and other outsiders who introduce primitivist ideas to local populations have been themselves Papuan'.

From the above examples we can see that Papuan engagements with the real-time necessitate grappling with complex internalisations of the gaze of others; an affective experience with unpredictable results. In the central highlands, the perceived epicentre of Papuan primitivity and certainly the homeland of the *koteka*, growing towns and urban settlements are sites where the stone-age stigma shapes real-time highlander experiences, encounters and ambitions. Wamena is one seat of local government, a site of rowdy markets and a fluorescence of shops, where tall buildings are going up, and the new Wamena Mall, a shopping complex that could have been built in any other small Indonesian city, is awaiting merchants and customers (see also Sugandi 2013).

Dani and other locals engage in compelling practices of impression management when preparing for a jaunt into this town, entering a different social, political and economic space that is now home to as many non-Papuans as highlanders. For instance, it is seen as important to put on footwear, minimally sandals, and ideal to remove garden boots and leave those at home. In general, the more layers of clothes and accessories the better, preferably on a freshly bathed and perfumed body. Activities like visiting a doctor or a government office require long pants (for men), as well as an accomplice with sufficient education or experience to avoid possible discomfort or embarrassment over not knowing the correct procedure, not understanding the lingo, feeling shy amidst powerful outsiders – or becoming the 'primitive' subject of a picture taken by a Javanese businessman and proliferated across Indonesia in real-time. A notebook in a netbag is essential for those women or men who want to be seen as having a genuine purpose in town, perhaps linked to a church activity, an NGO, or a project team. Walking is to be avoided at all costs because it implies that one does not have money (or a friend) for a ride. Mobile phones should be on display as much as possible, along with USB drives dangling from lanyards and laptops (or laptop bags, if a laptop is lacking).

These activities suggest ways people are recognising, while also devising, certain expectations related to modern, urban, multi-ethnic space, and in doing so seeming to accept, or at least know intimately, the gaze of others upon which judgments of their character and capacity are likely to be made. It is hard not to see the layers of clothing, the hats, jackets, socks and other accessories, in juxtaposition to the traditional *koteka* or the hip-hugging grass skirt that hold a significant place in so many conceptualisations of Papuans' identity, but it is also possible to see an ongoing cultural form of adornment with traditional roots. We can read the recognition of unequal positioning in Indonesian modernity brought to the fore in a small, rapidly growing town. But, we would also encounter staunch and articulate resistance to many (but not all) expressions of alleged Papuan primitivity. What often confounds the stone-age designation in contemporary Papua is in fact Papuans' confident critiques, creative expressions, thoughtful histories and bold moves. These scenes, flush perhaps with emotions of discomfort, anger, pride and concern, also remind us of the importance of looking at affective experiences of the current moment, as well as past and present mobilisations of affect in cross-cultural encounters.

Given the long-lasting association of the highlands with primitivism and more recent Papuan strategies to counter this image, it does not come as a surprise that desires of becoming part of the real-time world are particularly pronounced there, especially in the last few years when the lifestyles of Indonesian modernity have become more and more accessible, at least for some Papuans, spurring the dreams of those who have been merely bystanders. When we were in the phase of completing this introduction a 'letter from the field' reached us, i.e. an email and not a traditional letter of course. It was written by Jacob Nerenberg, a doctoral student in anthropology at the University of Toronto, who is currently 'embedded in a small-scale mobile phone network pilot project, designed by foreign scientists, in a district centre that lies beyond the reach of the major national mobile phone networks, at the end of the main road from Wamena'.[6] We want to include our colleague's account here, as he illustrates so vividly the concerns of many Papuans with their spatial and temporal position in the world:

> While conducting fieldwork in the Central Highlands I have heard many different forecasts and aspirations for changes that people anticipate happening in the region. One day, after a rally to promote the formation of a new regency in what is now a mere district centre, I asked a retired local politician what changes he hoped the new regency would bring. This man explained that new roads would link the village market to surrounding villages so that farmers could transport their produce efficiently; and that more new roads would allow the regency to sell its produce all over Papua, becoming the region's breadbasket. I was also told that the national carrier would extend mobile phone network coverage, so that 'the voice of the people would be heard' in power centres far away; and that these changes would make this place more 'advanced'. I have heard other, seemingly very different projects – providing improved education, training women to market handicrafts, or changing Papua's political status – get framed in surprisingly similar terms of enhancing forms of wide-ranging connection.[7]

Nerenberg's reflections on his fieldwork are worth quoting here as well:

> It becomes difficult to decide if transcending space and time is seen as a means to an end, or an end in itself [...] Sometimes I think about this situation as a kind of laboratory, where I am to determine how new network access transforms people's reality. The stories I collect remind me of these transformations' complicated trajectories. Families scatter from this 'remote' district to Wamena, Jayapura, Timika, Yogyakarta; young people travel around Papua living and working as miners, stereo salesmen, teachers, drivers, airplane ticket hawkers, before coming back home; some end up assisting foreign researchers, only realizing later that they appear in internationally-published books. The transition to 'modern' network connection has never been discrete – 'rural' life in Papua has long been about relocation, dislocation, migration, seeking out new knowledge and technologies. The story of real-time connection

---

6   Email from Jacob Nerenberg, 29 January 2014.
7   ibid.

is also one where high-tech infrastructures try to catch up to existing patterns of connection and mobility. It is about disconnection, network failure and lack – busy signals, weak network reception, phones dying in the rain, trucks stuck in the mud, SIM cards that stop working because there is no cash to buy airtime. So much of life in Papua unfolds in this space between anticipated connections, experiences of breakdown, and realities of uncertainty and impermanence.[8]

Nerenberg addresses here the less pleasant side of the introduction of real-time connection in highlands Papua, namely that hopes and desires can be destroyed as connections break down or do not function the way they should. Yet being connected, having access to the real-time circles of Indonesian modernity, does not mean that one has automatically gained secure status, since this social space is characterised by its own particular risks. We remain in the highlands to exemplify this point with the following story.[9]

In 2013, Jeremiah,[10] a Dani campaign manager and senior public servant, was released from prison after four years of detention and subsequent house arrest. The circumstances that led to his arrest are not entirely clear. In one version of the story, Jeremiah borrowed a vast sum of money from an Indonesian police officer to help a Dani candidate, who was also Jeremiah's relative, advance in local elections. Jeremiah went to jail when the candidate did not advance and the money could not be repaid. The expectation was that if the campaign was successful the money would be returned through contracts or cash once the candidate was in office. In another version, the one that officially explains his imprisonment, Jeremiah is alleged to have corrupted public funds using his position as District (*Kabupaten*) Treasurer to secure funds for the election campaign of his relative. The rumour behind this official story is that the District Head (also an indigenous man) and the police wanted to expel Jeremiah from his position in the government due to disagreements over budgetary resources, including the extent of government corruption that the Treasurer was willing to cover up (and potentially, inevitably, take the blame for), and the fact that Jeremiah was supporting another man's campaign in an effort to depose the District Head. Another version insists that the alleged embezzlement and subsequent imprisonment had nothing to do with an election campaign, but rather that Jeremiah used public funds to buy a project (*proyek*, probably a construction contract or an order for infrastructure) from officials in Jakarta, described as typical practice. In this case, he handed over the money, but the officials did not deliver the project as promised. Felix, an indigenous informant, himself a civil servant, explained this as a common way that the Indonesian

---

8   ibid.

9   This is an episode recounted during Jenny Munro's fieldwork in Wamena in August 2013.

10   All names in this scenario are pseudonyms.

government continues to control, manipulate and oppress Papuans. The big business players and government ministers in Jakarta (where Jeremiah travelled to buy the project), Felix said, bring Papuans into business networks only to turn on them, to cheat them, and to expose them in compromising positions.

A great deal of shame and hardship was experienced by Jeremiah's relatives, who spent the better part of 18 months after he went to jail pooling their very limited resources (by holding community pig feasts, donating garden produce and cash) in an attempt to repay a small percentage of the 500 million rupiah (about AU$50,000) he borrowed/embezzled. Jeremiah had been one of the most senior Dani government officials ever, with more years in the public service than the District Head. He was disgraced and his wife left him. Unfortunately, in Wamena it was not possible to hear his version of events, as his relatives and other informants said he was still suffering from 'stress' and it could be emotionally damaging for him to recount the events that led to his imprisonment.

Here we see some of the tested connections, challenging undercurrents and personal impacts of Papuan engagements in real-time, where money, politics and development evince new ambiguity. Especially after the government's decentralisation policy of 'Special Autonomy' was introduced in Papua in 2001 (see Timmer 2007; McWilliam 2011; Suryawan 2011), more Papuans have reached higher positions in the bureaucracy and financial flows between Jakarta and Papua have increased. New opportunities – a 'proyek' or an election – bring to the fore untested alliances coupled with high stakes. There is the chance to win big or lose very badly – with the risks mainly being borne by Papuans such as Jeremiah. Highlanders' narrations of Jeremiah's experience also illustrate that there are no longer clear lines between indigenous and Indonesian interests or allegiances, but deep mistrust of Indonesian intentions remains obvious. The acts and decisions of government players are deeply entangled with 'community' or family, and new demands are made on kinship systems.

In Jeremiah's story it is his trip to Jakarta that indicates the close correlation between being connected and being mobile. Since Special Autonomy, such 'official' trips to Indonesia's capital are certainly on the rise, and within Papua they are replicated by travel to provincial and district centres. At the same time, there is a heightened desire for being mobile, as hopes are invested in mobility as a way to become part of the contemporary age. Thus, for many Papuans today, exploring new mobilities is tantamount to attempting to locate oneself anew in the complex landscape of temporal hierarchisations. It is thus expedient to focus our attention on emerging forms of mobility, bearing in mind the intrinsic relationships between mobilities and temporalities.

Mobilities

Contemporary Papuan mobilities are certainly not isolated phenomena but are embedded in wider developments within and beyond Indonesia. New opportunities of travel, communication and meaning production are part of what one of the editors of this volume has called 'globalisation within Indonesia' (Slama 2011), referring to the fact that phenomena that hitherto have mainly been described and analysed in their transnational guise, such as accelerated and intensified flows of people, capital and images (e.g. Appadurai 1996; Hannerz 1996; Eriksen 2007), occur to a large extent *within* Indonesia given its sheer size, its cultural diversity and its notable domestic inequalities. Especially since the fall of Suharto and the introduction of Special Autonomy, these inner-Indonesian flows have affected more and more Papuans, and more Papuans have become active participants in these mobile circles. However, this has been hardly acknowledged in the literature, as Leslie Butt aptly puts it in her contribution to this volume: 'The lure of Papua as a discrete, politically distinct space has curtailed the study of Papuan mobility, or the impacts of the mobile technologies, peoples, objects and ideas that flow in and out of the province on the indigenous men and women who live there.'

In fact, mobility, of Papuans around and outside of Papua, and of Indonesians into Papua, is creating more opportunities for face-to-face encounters and personal evaluations than ever before. Although these encounters, due to new forms of mobility, might open channels for Papuans that hitherto were not available for them, the chapters in this volume hardly suggest that we can celebrate this 'globalisation within Indonesia' as mainly generating 'win-win situations' that are to the advantage of all parties involved. Rather, the new mobilities may evoke confrontations with Indonesians, or conjure tension amongst Papuans, even within families. For example, young people increasingly leave home, often for schooling, with the hopes of the family, clan and nation on their shoulders. These are mobilities of opportunity and privilege, but often fraught with risk and hardship. Mobilities away from home can result in lost connections, lost property and lost status. When mobilities intersect with the very real threats to life that are prevalent in Papua, including political violence, HIV and interpersonal conflict, the outcomes are unpredictable.

In her chapter, Butt explores the critical role of mobility for a particular group of highlands men – HIV-positive men – whose personal trajectories intersect with the mobile flows of viruses, drugs and technologies. As Butt asserts: 'Upon his return the mobile HIV-positive man finds that the mechanisms of discrimination within the nation get replicated in the machinery of HIV health care.' Indeed, in some cases mobility outside Papua is less problematic than the return to kin, territory and community – with empty hands and possibly in a state of weakness.

Butt's chapter thus makes clear that mobility and migration can become sites of anxiety where flows from outside are perceived as threat, such as in the case of HIV, and formerly mobile Papuan men are forced to become immobile due to the treatment requirements of their illness (see also Butt 2014; for 'the anxieties of mobility' in another Indonesian setting see Lindquist 2009). Exploring the ways mobility is gendered in Papua, Butt shows that her interlocutors, being unable to assume standard masculine roles in their home region, also cannot continue to explore the new masculinities that their mobility once offered them.

By contrast, as Munro shows in her chapter, university students who leave Papua may be drawn back to the attractive emotional space of Wamena. There, belonging is less of a struggle than in North Sulawesi where Papuan students have to deal with prejudices anchored in the evolutionist and racist discourses referred to above. This is particularly disappointing for Papuan students, since in Indonesia the category of 'student' (*mahasiswa*) implies occupying a respected position in Indonesian society, i.e. taking part in the real-time connections and mobile circles. However, this is not acknowledged by the locals in North Sulawesi, who do not consider the national image of the student appropriate for Papuans. As a result, assertiveness among students can cause conflict with locals who are heavily invested in ideologies that not only confine Papuans to stereotypes of primitive and uncouth but expect them to quietly acquiesce to these roles.

Munro's research in North Sulawesi suggests itself to be associated with Inaya Rakhmani's 'note on Jayapura', which comprises the account of a Papuan high school student who visited Java and met people there that were surprised that she and her family members 'were fully clothed and articulate'. In both cases, the (high school and university) students – *due to* their mobility – were exposed to stone-age discourses prevalent in Indonesian society at large. But, as Munro also suggests in her chapter, the return of Dani graduates to the central highlands does not automatically mean that they will gain the positions they desire. In fact, the results that educated Dani women and men are able to achieve in the central highlands are severely limited by political conditions that continue to favour Indonesian settlers and migrants, but circumstances may allow for activities that nonetheless garner some status and positive reactions in the family (Munro 2013).

Mobility for educational purposes brings us to Rupert Stasch's chapter. Stasch emphasises that 'extreme parental enthusiasm and self-sacrificial striving in relation to children's education is common throughout rural Papua'. In the case of the Korowai, 'bootstrapping out of the primitive' is closely associated with strategies of mobility such as making trips to administrative centres and sending boys to school in places outside Korowai land. Whereas in the first instance Korowai 'primitivity' is displayed in order to attract the attention of government officials, in the second instance it is hoped that the educated Korowai children will become civil servants themselves and thus will have access to funds and goods that will benefit the community at home. As in the case of Butt's chapter, the mobility here is also highly gendered. Almost exclusively boys are sent to school in faraway places, whereas the girls are subject to parental control at home. However, what the boys experience in their new places is often hardship, as Stasch asserts, and adds to the chapter by Munro in exemplifying the difficulties of Papuan migration: 'Boys themselves are often hungry in town, and may stay out of school for long periods there due to lack of money for fees or uniforms. Their relatives send them the little money they ever scrape together through income opportunities arising back home. Persons on all sides suffer painful separations, including during crises of illness or death.' Contemporary Korowai experiences differ greatly from 'the circulation of children to improve family circumstances' on Java where we find a tradition of child adoption along kin and patron–client relations based on the principle of upward social mobility (Newberry 2014: 70).

As these Dani and Korowai examples suggest, by drawing attention to mobilities we refer not just to movement in space and time but to efforts to reposition oneself in social terms, in hierarchical relations, and how these actions evoke self-representations and self-definitions. In this, our contributors reveal some deep ironies of life in Papua related to the emergence of certain apparent liberties of expression, interpretation and assertiveness among Papuans. Henri Myrttinen sketches the multiple Papuan narratives linking *Tanah Papua* with Israel and the Holy Land; narratives that invoke different voices, local mythology, understandings of Christianity, political aspirations and readings of global politics (see also Kirksey 2012). Expressions of affinity with Israel take diverse forms, including Star of David graffiti in the streets of the provincial capital Jayapura, indigenous Papuans sporting pro-Israel t-shirts, and functionaries of the Christian congregations using Israeli and Jewish symbols as wallpaper on their laptops and smartphones. Some of these expressions are meant to invoke Papuan nationalism. However, this proliferation of Israeli symbols in Papuan public space occurs in a political context where freedom of expression on the streets is otherwise limited and expressive liberties are increasingly acted out on the internet.[11] In 2013, 537 Papuans were arrested on political charges, such as flying the Papuan independence flag, the Morning Star, an increase of 165 per cent over 2012.[12] In contrast, Israeli symbols can be regarded as 'safe', since they are not interpreted as representing Papuan nationalism by Indonesian authorities.

---

11   At date of publication, it seems that surveillance of the internet by the Indonesian state is rather weak and, to our knowledge, so far no Papuan bloggers or webmasters have been arrested.

12   http://www.papuansbehindbars.org/?p=2326 (accessed 22 February 2014).

If we assert that Papua is currently being remade, limits to Papuan agency appear to be a major topic – not only with regard to the political sphere. Transformations are taking place at an accelerated pace and expanded breadth in spaces that were once considered off limits or beyond reach. It is fair to say that most Papuans have little power to determine what developments take place where, or in what manner. Mobilities thus evokes another theme, that of mobile capital, its 'quick and dirty' extractive approach to development in resource-rich Papua, and what it means to live in the shadow of these enterprises (Ballard 2002; Kennedy and Abrash 2001), or to try to engage from the margins. Other scholars have explored current economic conditions directly (Resosudarmo et al. 2009a, 2009b; King 2004). Rather than following them, the contributors in this volume illuminate everyday life in the frontier economy, and expose how economic inequalities are ingrained in social interactions and perceptions of the present. In exploring the affinity for American hip hop among Papuans in Manokwari, Sarah Richards considers the role of images of black affluence that stand in contrast to what Papuans usually see of themselves and other peoples of black heritage: poverty, sickness, hardship and being stuck on the fringes of 'progress'. In other instances, university students' ambitions for taking up the cause of development in their home areas are shaped by the perception that Freeport and other companies are extracting Papua's natural wealth and leaving Papuans in the 'stone-age', even when on occasion their education is funded directly or indirectly via such endeavours. And, as noted above, the chapter by Rupert Stasch on the Korowai documents strategies of coping with extreme economic inequalities through mobilities aiming at access to circulating goods and capital, which are perceived according to indigenous concepts of social inequality.

Papuan concepts and symbols are examined in many chapters of this volume, and we can only agree with Myrttinen, who argues in his chapter that 'in order to gain a better understanding of Papuan aspirations and dreams of a better future, one needs not to merely look at socio-economic statistics but also to investigate symbolic offerings'. He asserts that symbols – often with a heavily religious/mythological overtone – play a central role in Papuan nationalist politics. Moreover, Timmer, who brings forward a similar argument, writes that 'the producers of Papuan histories are a diverse crowd, including intellectuals, philosophers, bureaucrats, church ministers and local leaders'; they are mobile figures residing in different places. The chapters indeed show that Papuan forms of expression are much more diverse than either Indonesian or Papuan nationalists would have us believe. Deep ethnographic exploration into local affinities, hierarchies and histories reveals surprising forms and content related to Papuan nationalism. Thus, when Timmer examines how nationalist narratives unfold, he comes to the conclusion that they often 'turn the unpredictable succession of events into retroactive proof of a glorious predestination'. In a similar vein, these local-cum-national(ist) narratives point to translocal connections and mobilities as part of Papua's predesigned destiny.

In light of the research presented in this volume, and in particular with regard to Rutherford's seminal book *Raiding the Land of the Foreigners* (2003), we want to adopt an argument put forward by Noel Salazar (2010) about 'cultural mobilities' or 'culturally rooted imaginaries of mobility'. We argue that in Papua one can discern particular mobilities that are difficult to comprehend without taking into account Papuan cosmologies (in all their entanglements with the Abrahamic religions and nationalism). Myrttinen reports that after Special Autonomy, pilgrimages to the Holy Land became more and more popular, and suggests that these new relations to Israel might also be read through the lens of Papuan mythology where people travel to engage with foreign beings who are in possession of goods that must be returned to Papua. In addition to such Koreri-like (imaginations of) mobilities that reach out to the foreign,[13] one can encounter variations of mobility that spur travels within Papua, such as pilgrimages by Papuan Muslims to the 'mountain of the prophet' (*gunung nabi*), which is located close to Kaimana. In this case, the foreign, i.e. Mecca, is substituted by or relocated to a local site (Wanggai 2008: 59–60; see also next section, and Slama in this volume).

Particularly interesting examples of Papuan conceptions of mobility can also be found in Timmer's chapter on Papuan historiography. In the histories he analyses, Papua is not only imagined as a place of origin from which people spread across the globe, an attempt to (re)localise Genesis in Papua, but also as having been in close contact with Sriwijaya and Majapahit, the great precolonial kingdoms so important in Indonesian historiography. Some of these histories that stem from the Bird's Head Peninsula go even so far as to locate the origin of groups of Papuans in Java, from which they had to flee due to a 'religious war' between Islam and Buddhism. Without discussing the local contexts of and interests involved in these Papuan histories, which Timmer examines in detail in his contribution, one can conclude that what is emphasised in these narratives is a mobility that lets Papuans appear as having travelled across the archipelago for ages, i.e. as being a constitutive part of the archipelago's, if not of the world's, history, running counter to any discourses that only grant them a role as marginalised 'primitives' being stuck in remote lands while history unfolds elsewhere.

---

13   Koreri is a central Papuan myth originating from Biak which spread to coastal Papuan regions, especially the northern coast of the Bird's Head Peninsula, due to the mobility and migration flows of the people from Biak. The myth tells of a messiah-like figure called Manarmakeri who returns from a foreign place in a millennial event dissolving the dichotomy of the foreign and the self and thus rendering 'raiding the land of the foreigners' to bring back goods that initially belonged to the people of Biak unnecessary (Kamma 1972; Rutherford 2003; Kirksey 2012).

As this section has described, due to mobilities great contrasts in experience abound: Papuans are unpredictably jostled about, dislodging themselves from kin and land, or being dislocated by more powerful social actors and economic processes. Yet they also venture on undertakings that bring them to new places within and outside Papua based on their particular imaginaries rooted in Papuan cosmologies. Thus, in this volume, we have the young HIV sufferer in Wamena who, despite his efforts to live up to expectations of the mobile educated generation of which he is a part, is totally shunned and shamed because of HIV, or the young Korowai schoolchild who is struggling for education and for having enough food for the day. This contrasts with the hip hop dancer in Manokwari who finds pride in bodily expression and hope in images of black wealth and power, or the university students in North Sulawesi who may literally fight with Indonesians over recognition and equal treatment. And this contrasts again with Papuans who imagine their people as a mobile force in the archipelago, or with those who go on pilgrimages to Israel or to the 'mountain of the prophet'. It is not a coincidence that among these diverse examples of contemporary Papuan mobilities religious aspects are prominent. In the next section we will discuss them in greater detail.

Religiosities

As particular concepts of time are constitutive for both the image of the stone-age and contemporary assertions of the real-time, they also cannot be separated from another theme that runs through this volume, namely the centrality of religious imaginations, expressions and practices. Similarly, as demonstrated above, the mobilities that the chapters of this volume discuss are often closely linked to Papuan religious life. When Papuans reflect on their history, their relations to non-Papuans, current political conditions and projects etc., they often resort to symbols and narratives that are rooted in major religious traditions such as Christianity as well as Papuan mythology. They do so in ways that often creatively combine and reconfigure these traditions so that one can discern the logic of local myths in interpretations of Christianity and Islam or find myth and monotheistic doctrine reconciled in novel ways. Moreover, as we have also already alluded to in the preceding section, there are strong links between religious thought and Papuan nationalism.

Following Kapferer, Telle and Eriksen (2010: 1), who assert that 'many nationalisms implicated religious or cosmo-ontological orientations embedded in religious practice', Papua features as a particularly salient example of a nationalism that employs religious symbols and logics for interpreting events and 'history' itself. For example, defining Papua as a Christian land, as opposed to Indonesia which is identified with Islam, is a theme that has its roots in the late Dutch colonial period (Rutherford 2012: 168). The popular labelling of Manokwari as the 'Gospel City' (*kota injil*) in the post-Suharto period indicates to what extent Papuan political thought continues to be informed by religious, especially Christian, concepts. Jaap Timmer, in his contribution to the volume, observes that 'people do not read the Bible as a disparate set of texts but instead as a cohesive whole that reveals the nature of local history, the unfolding of time and the purpose of history'. Analysing nationalist texts and Papuan conceptualisations of history, Timmer suggests that the coming of Christianity marks Papua's 'coming of age', i.e. when the hierarchy between adolescents and adults, between the 'junior' stone-agers and the 'mature' moderns, is dissolved by becoming part of the spatio-temporal realm of global Christianity. In this enchanted, equalising realm, according to some interpretations, Papua features as 'holy land' and Papuans as 'chosen people'. These discourses spur analogies with Israel (see especially Myrttinen's chapter) while fuelling the nationalist imagination. Timmer is inspired by Ballard, who asserts in his 'Oceanic Historicities' (2014: 111) that 'our enquiry must centre on the ways in which historicities transform with the adoption of new religions, with incorporation into colonial or post-colonial states, and with the emergence of bureaucratic and professional elites'.

The coming of Christianity to Papua indeed transformed Papuan historicities, but it did not do so in a uniform way. The multiple uses and (re)interpretations of religious symbols, as the chapters also indicate, point to 'limits of meaning' (Engelke and Tomlinson 2006) in the Papuan realm, since what for some Papuans seems to be highly significant has for others no meaning at all. We find such an example in the contribution of Henri Myrttinen where one can see that the rather recent emergence of uses of 'Israel' in Papuan nationalist circles, including ample references to the Old Testament, can be decoded by some Papuans, whereas for others they remain a riddle. The significance of religiosities in this volume, i.e. religion understood as source of dynamics of meaning and practice, thus leads us directly to the complexities of the production of meaning in today's Papua. Instead of associating Papua with 'the jungle' in an evolutionist fashion, as Indonesian Islamic preachers (see Slama's chapter) or Western travel agencies (see the chapter by Stasch) do, Papua is better approached as a 'forest of symbols', a rather free adoption of the title of one of Victor Turner's (1967) classic books. This forest of symbols can be observed in various Papuan domains, not only in rituals where strict followers of Turner would look for it, and its analysis must take into account a wide range of sources, intersections and assemblages of meaning. But the point we want to make in this introductory chapter is that in most cases, meaning production, in all its complexity, relies in one way or the other on religious symbols (of transnational and local origins). From this observation follows the question: Why do Papuans find religious idioms so attractive for expressing their concerns and hopes?

Let us try to answer this question by referring to an example in Timmer's chapter where Papuans employ a range of Christian concepts, including identifying Papua as the Garden of Eden, and in doing so, turn evolutionist regimes of value on their heads – instead of representing the 'stone-age' and 'backwardness' Papua appears as the paradisiacal place of the origin of mankind. Indeed, we think that the attractiveness of Christianity to Christian Papuans as well as Islam to Muslim Papuans is to a considerable extent rooted in the fact that Christian and Islamic concepts offer an alternative to evolutionist and racist devaluations (see also Warta 2011: 44). However, this promise of equality that one can find in Christianity and Islam, namely that everybody is the same before God, can easily lead to disappointments when experiences in everyday life are a far cry from the ideal. This volume comprises such cases when Papuan ways of imagining and practicing Christianity meet, inside and outside Papua, the harsh reality of Indonesian hierarchisations. In Jenny Munro's chapter, we find a telling example where she describes the celebration of the 88th birthday of a Catholic priest in North Sulawesi. A group of Papuan students honoured the priest by staging a dance for him, which did not deter key members of the community from treating them derogatively.

When Papuans become part of church congregations abroad, Munro's ethnography suggests, they are not automatically seen as fellow members of the church being on one level with anybody else. In contrast, there is a high chance that they are treated as second-class believers and are confronted with stereotypes and prejudice that, ironically, often rest upon (or are at least informed by) the very evolutionist concepts that these denominations officially reject. Current conditions thus differ greatly from how Dutch colonial officials imagined the future integration of Papuans into wider society. To illustrate this, let us again quote the colonial official Jan van Baal (in Cookson 2008: 389) who, after stating that Papuans are not part of 'the real world', saw 'only one narrow sphere where the Papuan may enter and where he is even welcome without being reminded of his inferiority: that is the church, where he is called a brother and acknowledged to have a place of his own'.

Van Baal would certainly be disappointed to see that many Christian Papuans today, particularly those in diaspora, have to deal with the condition of not being fully accepted in the social universe of official religion, the social realm where they would most expect to find recognition in Indonesia's multi-ethnic society. This must also be viewed against the backdrop of the importance of church congregations as major fora of sociality and social support in Papua and Indonesia at large. The social role of churches, particularly as significant sources of status for Papuan men, becomes apparent in Leslie Butt's chapter about HIV-positive Papuan men. She describes cases that reveal not only the effects of HIV on the mobility of Papuan men (referred to above) but also notices the severe consequences for their social life once their HIV seropositivity has become public. Being barred from the church congregation is among the most hurtful consequences for HIV positive men. One of Butt's interlocutors told her that nobody visits him anymore, 'not people from our church and not people from my family'. Whether it is a coincidence that he mentioned church first and then family remains undecided, but what this quote and other examples in Butt's chapter indicate is that in celebrating a collective spirituality, the church, with its public forms of religiosity, such as church going, participating in church committees etc., assigns public roles to men in everyday life as well as rituals. Those HIV-positive men who were excluded from church sociality and have lost all their status thus have to develop their religiosity anew, as they are isolated not only socially but also spiritually. As Butt shows, people not only do not want to meet them anymore but also do not want to pray for them anymore. It is this double isolation, or even the threat of it, that may lead to a religiosity that becomes centred on an individualised human–God relationship. As a consequence, HIV-positive men associate their seropositivity with sin, but feel guilty only to God, not to the community which, for obvious reasons, is not supposed to know. This reflects a very personal(ised), unmediated relationship to God, which we find telling because it is rather untypical for Papua, where religiosity is so closely connected to local sociality, imaginations of a global community of believers and national identity.

But let us come back to the question of the attractiveness of religious symbols for Papuans. As noted above, Papuan mythology, like the Abrahamic religions, offers alternative ways to imagine Papua in the world and world history than the evolutionist paradigm. Moreover, one can discern similar temporal logics in the ideologies of Christian denominations, especially Pentecostal and evangelical ones that have become popular in Papua in the last decades, and Papuan millennial movements. In this regard, our reading of Papuan religiosities is inspired by Joel Robbins (2007: 12) who has argued that 'scholars have not ... fully recognized or attended to similarities between the rupturing of temporal continuity in conversion and in millennial imaginings or tied these to the similar rupture that, in Christian understandings, lies at the origin of Christian history'. What Robbins characterises here as rupture concerns the personal as well as the collective levels on which radical breaks with the past are intrinsic to both Christianity and millenarianism (for Christianity see also Keane 2007). The coming of Christ or the coming of Manarmakeri, the central figure of the Koreri myth, often becomes interchangeable, and, as Rutherford (2012: 158) has pointed out, some Papuans indeed identify Jesus Christ with Manarmakeri. Myrttinen (this volume) discerns another Koreri theme: that Papua is a place of origin from which foreigners have taken objects that Papuans must recuperate. In this case, Myrttinen describes the view that 'the Star of David is actually the Morning Star which was taken by Israel from Papua'.

In Papua, Abrahamic narratives are 'grounded in landscapes' and 'privilege the performative and sensory,' features that Ballard (2014: 105, 107) sees as typical for vernacular histories in the Pacific. Indeed, Myrttinen found that it 'was not always possible in all my interviews to draw a distinct line between when events in Papua were merely being compared to those occurring in the Bible and when Biblical events were actually considered to have happened *in* Papua'. Taking the landscape theme seriously, it does not come as a surprise that we find, as briefly noted above, a 'mountain of the prophet' (*gunung nabi*) close to Kaimana as a pilgrimage site for Papuan Muslims (see Slama in this volume). As for the performative and the sensory themes in Papuan religious histories, in the Fakfak region we find an oral tradition that asserts particular origins of Christianity as well as Islam in Papua. According to this tradition, close to Fakfak there are two springs, a saltwater and a sweet water spring, that were watched over by guards. The guards each owned a book. The guard of the saltwater spring owned the Qur'an, and the guard of the sweet water spring the Bible. They then spread the teachings of the books, with the people living on the coast following the Qur'an (from the saltwater spring), and the people of the interior following the Bible (from the sweet water spring) (Onim 2006: 53–54; Warta 2011: 334). Thus, this self-empowering narrative assigns Papua a special place in Christianity and Islam and does not identify it with an inferior evolutionary stage or a remote geographical region.

As Myrttinen and Slama note in their chapters, the question of the coming of Christianity and Islam to Papua, especially the question of which religion came first, is a topic that is not only treated in mythological narratives but also quite openly debated – in Papua and in Indonesia at large, in online fora and offline. Whereas Western scholarship has a clear answer to this question, namely that some Papuans of the coastal regions of the Bird's Head Peninsula adopted Islam in the course of tributary trade relations with the Sultan of Tidore in the 17th century, if not earlier (see Warnk 2010, and Slama in this volume), many Papuans imagine Papua as a Christian land and equate the coming of Islam with the arrival of the Indonesian state.[14] The question 'Who came first?' has, as in so many other parts of the world, highly political connotations and its relevance is certainly not confined to the academic field. At the same time, such discourses are challenged from within Papua, not only by heterodox interpretations of Christianity and Islam or civil society groups that seek to ease interreligious tensions, but also by the emergence of a Muslim Papuan identity, as it is advocated by the Council of Papuan Muslims (*Majelis Muslim Papua*)

---

14   One should not underestimate the extent to which this undifferentiated view has entered the work of international NGOs and engaged scholarship. For example, in an otherwise interesting article about land grabbing in Papua, Ginting and Pye (2013: 165) write: 'The national government in Jakarta wanted to change the demographic character of key lowland areas and build up a political base of Muslim Javanese to counter the Christian Papuans.'

(Pamungkas 2008, 2011). This relatively new organisation has to navigate Papua's political landscape by asserting that being Muslim does not automatically mean adopting the positions or interests of Indonesian Muslims, including religious authorities from Java who share particular Islamic perceptions of Papua as a marginal frontier (analysed by Slama in detail), or becoming disloyal to the land of Papua. At the same time, the presence of an increasing number of Islamic proselytisers of various organisational backgrounds (see e.g. Noor 2010), some of whom also attract Papuan Muslims to study Islam in other parts of Indonesia, is further diversifying Papua's Islamic field, and it remains to be seen what consequences these new inner-Indonesian connections will have for forging a Muslim Papuan identity. Yet what becomes apparent in Slama's chapter is that the presence of Islamic preachers from outside Papua add to the spatio-temporal hierarchisations with which Papuans have to deal, as their Islamic frontier notions are inflected by evolutionist and developmentalist discourses.

How different Christian and Islamic configurations of identity will inform Papuan assertions of identity at large is a question that is only touched upon in this volume and will certainly occupy researchers in the future. Similarly, we think, researchers will attend to orthodox versions of religion that, as it seems, will become more influential not only with regard to religious practice and doctrine but also concerning everyday cultural life. We consider Sarah Richards' chapter as anticipating trends in this regard, as her work shows that the hip hop cultural scene in Manokwari, a self-empowering subculture that enables young Papuans to connect with global trends – to become part of a global 'real-time' – without abandoning their Papuanness, could develop without major ideological obstacles except versions of orthodox Christianity. In fact, as Richards' chapter makes clear, orthodox Christianity can be seen as the only source of counter-discourse to hip hop in the 'Gospel City'. Furthermore, her chapter indicates that when we place broad, singular notions such as Papuan identity in specific local contexts, we are able to shed light on some of the dynamics that give rise to a heightened sense of Papuanness in some places, but test this idea in others.

As we wanted to point out in this section, looking at Papuan religiosities brings to light various aspects of being Papuan today and of engaging with forces – symbolic and material – from outside Papua that point to a range of ambiguities and contradictions. Whereas Christianity informs Papuan nationalist expressions to a great extent, Christianity – itself being of transnational nature – can also emerge as counter-force to other global influences. It can be a source on which Papuan histories build, and at the same time its history can be reinterpreted according to the logics of Papuan mythology. Similarly, Christianity as well as Islam can offer an alternative to evolutionist perceptions. Papuans might find a great deal of social support through religious institutions, yet in the very realms of these religions deprecatory attitudes might prevail in everyday encounters. Moreover, the very identification of Papua or a Papuan city such as Manokwari with a particular religion raises issues not only of historical trajectories and Dutch colonial reverberations but also of the very possibility of an encompassing Papuanness that can transcend religious boundaries. Having said this, and having explored Papuan conditions in their mobile and temporal dynamics, we want to highlight additional aspects of the volume, especially by embedding contemporary Papuan experiences in wider regional settings.

Regional trends and experiences

With this volume we hope to position conversations about cultural change, religion, gender, technologies, mobilities, economic inequalities, colonialism and everyday politics in Papua in relation to regional trends and experiences – Melanesian as well as Southeast Asian. For instance, a particular thread that runs through many of the chapters indicates ways that Papuan experiences of colonial hierarchies and ideologies of diminishment invoke contestations familiar in other cultural and historical contexts (Robbins 2004, 2005; Rosaldo 2003). Contestations are related to ways of being seen and being known, and negotiating the frameworks that each party brings to the encounter (Balme 2007; Jolly et al. 2009). In thinking about how Papuans are responding to encounters, even how and when they may also produce and evoke primitivist identities, contributors are building on widely discussed experiences of encounter in Melanesian contexts (for Papua, see Ploeg 1995; Ballard 2009; for elsewhere in Melanesia see Clark 2000; Douglas and Ballard 2008; Bashkow 2006). There are many different sorts of 'outsiders' to whom Papuans may present themselves, including Indonesian and Papuan (local or non-local) government officials and *proyek* (project – see Aspinall 2013) personnel, international and domestic tourists and ethnic neighbours within or beyond Papua (see Stasch 2009, 2011; Silverman 2013).

Authors are also pursuing explorations of contemporary racial formulations in relation to development priorities and mentalities, and in doing so build on earlier work that sketches racial ideas in historical context in Papua (Ballard 2008; Giay and Ballard 2003). Butt's analysis of HIV among Papuan men notes: 'The political conditions whereby endemic racism and colonial mentalities make their way into health care regimens exacerbate the challenges of getting on drugs and staying on them.' And Stasch (in this volume) highlights the close connections between racism and developmentalism:

> Global metropolitan publics today widely hold a model of a Manichaean contrast of 'primitive' and 'civilized' poles of humanity. This model is indebted to 19th century anthropological theories of social evolution

for its sense that the 'civilized' pole is history's telos. Additionally, this globally dominant primitivist model has strong if submerged overlaps with histories of racism and racial theory, as well as connections to the crypto-evolutionism of 'development'. Although ideological structures of 'primitivism' are my main focus across this chapter, one effect of looking at stereotyped people's own uptake of such ideologies is that the inter-implication of primitivist, evolutionary, racial, and developmentalist models are made more explicit than usual.

Melanesianist scholars thus may find that Papua provides insights into the complex formulation of new racial identities and new antagonisms in the region, especially related to Asian settlement and immigration, labour migration, and tensions formed in the shadows of extractive industries.

In this volume, several contributors shed light on how Papuans are engaging with exogenous orders, practices and values (Rumsey 2006; Robbins and Wardlow 2005) that are a prominent part of life in a society characterised by high levels of in-migration by Indonesians as well as high levels of internal mobility. Political authority is increasingly dependent on bureaucratic know-how, networks that include Indonesians, and educational qualifications that confer status. As Melanesians engage with contemporary practices and ideologies of capitalism and neoliberal development (Jacka 2007; Cox 2013; Bainton and Cox 2009), a formulation Robert Foster (1999: 143; see also Lash and Urry 1994) refers to as 'hypermodernity', in this volume we shed light on Papuans' affective experiences with notions and practices of Indonesian modernity, such as *kemajuan* (progress) and *pembangunan* (development), as well as globalised capital. In fact, Papuans are not alone in their positioning on the 'fringes' of Indonesian modernity, as other frontier inhabitants have also been the subject of spatio-temporal degradation (Li 2001; Tsing 2005). In this context, desire, humiliation, shame and pride are just a few of the affective dimensions of Papuan experiences explored in this volume.

In the region, profound shifts in gender relations and constructions of masculinity and femininity are taking place at the interface of cultural change, capitalism and colonialism (Ford and Lyons 2012; Nilan et al. 2014; Lipset and Roscoe 2011; Wardlow 2006). Papuans are grappling with an influx of new gender ideals, norms and expectations, including those that prioritise more individualistic pursuits and evaluations. Indonesians in Papua are seen as closely linked to national cultural and religious norms and state power, giving their gender models added weight (Butt 2005). State practices, including, for example, the torture activities described by Hernawan, clearly treat men and women differently, raising questions about how gender asymmetries and the spatio-temporal hierarchisations discussed in this volume reinforce each other, such as more strongly associating Papuan men with the perceived dangers of 'the wild' and 'primitive' and thus with 'insecurity', as well as Papuan women with 'underdevelopment' and thus with not being able to assume public roles.

The volume thus also sheds light on the ways that gender identities and practices of gender relate to, embrace, resist and otherwise engage with primitivist and evolutionist ideologies in the region, for these ideologies position men and women differently in spaces of development, education, culture and politics. A close examination of the chapters reveals that Papuan men and women are positioned differently with respect to their ability to engage in mobilities and modern pursuits and the ways in which they are burdened with primitivist symbolism and stereotypes (Munro, this volume). Papuan men may be criticised for not reflecting modern aims of mobility, education and employment, whereas women are judged negatively for engaging too much in these initiatives, which in local ideologies ought to come second to marital and child-rearing duties. Gendered interests are also revealed in relation to disclosure of HIV-positive status (Butt, this volume), with women employing secrecy to maintain comfortable domestic relations, while men are keeping their status a secret to maintain their public social roles. Anxieties typically identified with Melanesian men, such as around gender and masculinity, do not surface in these accounts (see Knauft 1997). Instead, the stories of HIV-positive men in Papua tell us that mobility and migration are sites of anxiety, and mobility affects how these men experience their masculinity.

Another line of inquiry reflects on Papuan engagements with religion, nationalism and historiography, which we discussed extensively above. Just as questions are being asked about nation-building and collective identity in other regional cultural contexts (Leach et al. 2012; Otto and Thomas 1997; Foster 1997; Robbins 2004), chapters in this volume explore religion, memory and contemporary music in relation to Papuan understandings of identity and sovereignty. Christianity (alongside a few feelers of Baha'i, Islam and Judaism) thoroughly suffuses Melanesian societies at both national and community levels (Tomlinson and MacDougall 2012). What a regional comparison (Gingrich 2012) reveals here is that in Papua religion frequently enters the domain of political strategising for self-determination and for the purposes of differentiating 'Papuans' from 'Indonesians', of drawing boundaries between 'Christianity' and 'Islam'. However, as it can be observed throughout Melanesia, in Papua the domains of the state and religion, as well as custom, are in most contexts hard to conceptually separate (Timmer 2013; and Timmer in this volume). Moreover, a diverse set of linkages are mapped out connecting Papuan self-understandings to arguably 'foreign' content and imagery – Israel, American hip hop and ancient Javanese kingdoms, as we have seen above. Thus, regional comparison points also to Papuan particularities or to unexpected Papuan expressions of broader patterns that one can observe in other Melanesian and Indonesian/Southeast Asian settings.

Among these broader patterns, another theme informs the chapters of this volume, revolving around the question of how Papuans are engaging with and imagining the state as a material and symbolic institution (see also Timmer 2013), and how the state positions Papuans in stone-age or real-time imaginaries. Stasch opens his chapter with a Korowai encounter with a new (if familiar) expression of state power, an official delegation from the Unit for Accelerated Development in Papua, not the first nor the last intervention of this sort, but an intervention that asks Korowai to once again suspend their prior knowledge and experience with the Indonesian state and to invest in this new iteration of the perpetual promise of development. He also explores how the civil service features in Korowai engagements with notions and expressions of primitivity, both as an aspiration that positions Korowai as less successful than other Papuans, in terms of obtaining jobs in the civil service, and how encounters with bureaucrats and Papuan government officials are managed from a Korowai point of view. How the state presents itself to Papuans is considered by Rutherford and Hernawan (see also Kirksey 2012), who are both concerned with the delivery of powerful messages, albeit in different ways, times and contexts. Hernawan reflects on direct and indirect forms of state violence occurring in the case of torture (and its public display), while less overt forms of state violence, manifested as threats, accusations, intimidation and surveillance, feature in Munro's account of highlander students in North Sulawesi.

It continues to be the case that the stone-age is invoked in Papuan encounters with the state, in one way or another, and that the state puts forward particular visions of how Papuans ought to be incorporated into real-time. These struggles are highlighted in the current era of decentralisation, as competing voices attempt to define and shape the modernisation agenda of the future. Tensions in state–society relations are being played out throughout the broader region, yet in Papua in particular ethnic inequalities continue to be expressed in and through structures of governance, which have historically been dominated by Indonesians. Indeed, it is the role of Papuans (and, which Papuans) in the state, and the rights of Papuans (and, which Papuans) vis-à-vis the state, that is currently the subject of much debate linked to the Special Autonomy revisions (the so-called 'Otsus Plus'). It is certainly possible to read in these debates views that promulgate Papuans' alleged incapabilities and unsuitabilities in the realm of governance, as well as views that deny longstanding Papuan engagements with the real-time.

(No) future of the stone-age

This volume demonstrates that the stone-age image in its various manifestations shapes Papuan encounters and imaginaries. It is constitutive for representations of Papuans in Indonesia and internationally, and it heavily influences, often by its active negation, Papuans' own constructions of their place in the world and their history. Putting the stone-age in the context of the real-time, as this volume does, has the effect of illuminating the very contestedness of the concept in the current age as well as the multiple ways of using and engaging with it. The volume is thus essentially occupied with questions of hierarchy and possibilities for equality expressed in spatio-temporal idioms. It shows how 'ideologies of unequal human worth', as Rupert Stasch put it, are enacted in face-to-face encounters, and how they find their expression in symbolic production in a time of heightened translocal mobility and communication. As such, the volume first of all aims to provide insights into contemporary Papuan dynamics that have so far been largely unrecognised, and to deliver new understandings on topics that are already on the agenda of researchers. Yet, more than this, and despite the fact that the chapters examine ongoing processes, we also want to discuss to what extent the work assembled in this volume can provide the basis for drawing more general conclusions. This discussion comprises considerations probably of relevance for formulating future research agendas, including future research on the stone-age image.

A conclusion that this volume evidently supports is that conceptions of time are critically ingrained in contemporary processes in Papua. Starting from the hegemonic evolutionist concepts epitomised by the stone-age image to their anti-evolutionist counterparts of Christian, Islamic and Papuan ancestry, these concepts and discourses mediate power asymmetries among different groups and persons within and beyond Papua. When the Papuan student pursues his studies in Manado, the Javanese health worker treats Papuans in Wamena, the coastal Papuan civil servant is stationed in the highlands, the highland Papuan preacher spreads the word of God in the Korowai lowlands, or the Islamic preacher from Jakarta tours the Bird's Head Peninsula – their endeavours are framed by concepts that locate their interlocutors and themselves in time or, as it is often the case, in different times. These concepts might be consciously contested or concealed in particular circumstances, but as such they are present in a seemingly inescapable way; and they have already been there for quite a long time now, as reflected in the colonial accounts examined in Rutherford's chapter.

This brings us to another conclusion inspired by the chapters, especially Rutherford's contribution. It is based on the observation that technologies need to be demonstrated to convey certain messages, especially messages that emphasise power asymmetries. In the early Dutch colonial era that meant that the colonial masters were also the masters of technology. In the age of real-time communication, where the possession and usage of technologies is much more widely distributed, expressing social hierarchy through technological demonstrations becomes more complex. However, as the hopes and desires associated with communication technologies show, in today's Papua becoming a user of these technologies is a major source of status, not least because it offers the possibility to demonstrate that one has left the stone-age behind: demonstrating the real-time, not the stone-age. To this realm of the real-time belong mobilities and religiosities as well as cultural expressions that distinguish Papuans as being part of wider networks and socialities, of sharing the world with other moderns, spurring reactions among those who still perceive them through the prism of the stone-age image. Such reactions range from spontaneous wonder that Papuans are 'fully clothed and articulate' to reiterating assertions of Papuan inferiority in everyday life that re-establish a hierarchy that has lost its alleged obviousness. Thus, demonstrations of the real-time can exacerbate emphasis on social hierarchies, as they can be used to dismantle them.

Finally, let us emphasise that the emotional experiences, affective affinities and repulsions that are exposed and imposed by Papuan mobilities, religiosities and self-expressions are structured by these very tensions at the interface of 'stone-age' and 'real-time', as are Papuan efforts to re-enact, change and reinterpret contemporary ways of being. And we think that in this complex sphere of tensions many encounters within and beyond Papua will also take place in the future. However, as the realm of the real-time is irreversibly expanding, the future of the stone-age will be an increasingly contested one, as it is today. But even if we close with the optimistic note that the notion of the stone-age per se will lose its strength and influence, it is rather unlikely that spatio-temporal hierarchisations in general will cease to exist. As this volume also shows, the dynamics of the real-time imply temporal others, and it is not unlikely that Papuans will personify some kind of past and remoteness for still quite a long time in the eyes of those who consider themselves as having seized the present and the centre. At the same time, Papuans increasingly mobilise against being relegated to a bygone age, be it the stone-age or another yesteryear. We thus would like to see that this volume will not be the last one that considers these dynamics, which we find crucial for understanding current Papuan conditions.

References

Appadurai, Arjun 1996. *Modernity at Large. Cultural Dimensions of Globalization*. Minneapolis: University of Minnesota Press.

Aspinall, Edward 2013. 'A Nation in Fragments: Patronage and Neoliberalism in Contemporary Indonesia'. *Critical Asian Studies* 45(1): 27–54.

Bainton, Nick and Cox, John 2009. 'Parallel States, Parallel Economies: Legitimacy and Prosperity in Papua New Guinea. SSGM Discussion Paper 2009/5'. Canberra: The Australian National University, State, Society and Governance in Melanesia Program.

Ballard, Chris 2002. 'The Signature of Terror: Violence, Memory and Landscape at Freeport'. In David, Bruno and Wilson, Meredith (eds), *Inscribed Landscapes: Marking and Making Place*. Honolulu: University of Hawaii Press, 13–26.

Ballard, Chris 2008. '"Oceanic Negroes": British anthropology of Papuans, 1820–1869'. In Douglas, Bronwen and Ballard, Chris (eds), *Foreign Bodies: Oceania and the Science of Race 1750-1940*. Canberra: ANU E Press, 157–201.

Ballard, Chris 2009. 'The Art of Encounter: Verisimilitude in the Imaginary Exploration of Interior New Guinea, 1725–1876'. In Jolly, Margaret, Tcherkezoff, Serge and Tryon, Darrell (eds), *Oceanic Encounters: Exchange, Desire, Violence*. ANU E Press, 221–258.

Ballard, Chris 2014. 'Oceanic Historicities'. *The Contemporary Pacific* 26(1): 95–154.

Balme, Christopher 2007. *Pacific Performances: Theatricality and Cross-cultural Encounter in the South Seas*. New York: Palgrave Macmillan.

Bashkow, Ira 2006. *The Meaning of Whitemen: Race and Modernity in the Orokaiva Cultural World*. Chicago: University of Chicago Press.

Braithwaite, John, Braithwaite, Valerie, Cookson, Michael, and Dunn, Leah 2010. *Anomie and Violence: Non-truth and Reconciliation in Indonesian Peacebuilding*. Canberra: ANU E Press.

Butt, Leslie 2005. 'Sexuality, the State, and the Runaway Wives of Highlands Papua, Indonesia'. In Adams, Vincanne and Pigg, Stacy Leigh, *Sex in Development: Science, Sexuality, and Morality in Global Perspective*. Durham NC: Duke University Press, 163–185.

Butt, Leslie 2014. 'Sexual Tensions: HIV-positive Women in Papua'. In Bennett, Linda Rae and Davies, Sharyn Graham (eds), *Sex and Sexualities in Contemporary Indonesia: Sexual Politics, Health, Diversity and Representations*. London: Routledge, 109–120.

Chauvel, Richard 2005. *Constructing Papuan Nationalism: History, Ethnicity, and Adaptation*. Policy Studies 14. Washington, D.C.: East-West Center Washington.

Chauvel, Richard 2011. 'Policy Failure and Political Impasse: Papua and Jakarta a Decade after the "Papuan Spring"'. In King, Peter, Elmslie, Jim and Webb-Gannon, Camellia (eds), *Comprehending West Papua*. Sydney, NSW: Centre of Peace and Conflict Studies, University of Sydney, 105–115.

Chauvel, Richard and Bhakti, Ikrar Nusa 2004. *The Papua Conflict: Jakarta's Perceptions and Policies*. Policy Studies 5. Washington, D.C.: East-West Center Washington.

Clark, Jeffrey 2000. *Steel to Stone: A Chronicle of Colonialism in the Southern Highlands of Papua New Guinea*. Oxford: Oxford University Press.

Cookson, Michael Benedict 2008. *Batik Irian: Imprints of Indonesian Papua*. PhD thesis, The Australian National University.

Cox, John 2013. 'The Magic of Money and the Magic of the State: Fast Money Schemes in Papua New Guinea'. *Oceania* 83: 175–191.

Douglas, Bronwen and Ballard, Chris (eds) 2008. *Foreign Bodies: Oceania and the Science of Race 1750-1940*. Canberra: ANU E Press.

Engelke, Matthew and Tomlinson, Matt (eds) 2006. *The Limits of Meaning: Case Studies in the Anthropology of Christianity*. New York and Oxford: Berghahn.

Eriksen, Thomas Hylland 2007. *Globalization: The Key Concepts*. Oxford: Berg.

Fabian, Johannes 1983. *Time and the Other: How Anthropology Makes Its Object*. New York: Columbia University Press.

Ferguson, James 2006. *Global Shadows: Africa in the Neoliberal World Order*. Durham and London: Duke University Press.

Foster, Robert J. (ed.) 1997. *Nation Making: Emergent Identities in Postcolonial Melanesia*. Ann Arbor: University of Michigan Press.

Foster, Robert J. 1999. 'Melanesianist Anthropology in the Era of Globalization'. *The Contemporary Pacific* 11(1): 140–159.

Ford, Michele and Lyons, Lenore (eds) 2012. *Men and Masculinities in Southeast Asia*. New York: Routledge.

Giay, Benny and Ballard, Chris 2003. 'Becoming Papuans: Notes towards a History of Racism in Tanah Papua'. Paper presented at the annual meeting of the American Anthropological Association, 19–23 November, Chicago.

Gingrich, Andre 2012. 'Comparative Methods in Socio-cultural Anthropology'. In Fardon, Richard et al. (eds), *The Sage Handbook of Social Anthropology*. London: Sage, 211–221.

Ginting, Longgena and Pye, Oliver 2013. 'Resisting Agribusiness Development: The Merauke Integrated Food and Energy Estate in West Papua, Indonesia'. *ASEAS – Austrian Journal of South-East Asian Studies* 6(1): 160–182.

Hannerz, Ulf 1996. *Transnational Connections. Culture, People, Places*. London: Routledge.

Hernawan, Budi 2013. *From the Theatre of Torture to the Theatre of Peace: The Politics of Torture and Re-imagining Peacebuilding in Papua, Indonesia*. PhD thesis, The Australian National University.

Jacka, Jerry K. 2007. 'Whitemen, the Ipili, and the City of Gold: A History of the Politics of Race and Development in Highlands New Guinea'. *Ethnohistory* 54(3): 445–472.

Jolly, Margaret, Tcherkezoff, Serge and Tryon, Darrell (eds) 2009. *Oceanic Encounters: Exchange, Desire, Violence*. Canberra: ANU E Press.

Kamma, Freerk C. 1972. *Koreri: Messianic Movements in the Biak-Numfor Culture Area*. The Hague: Martinus Nijhoff.

Kapferer, Bruce, Kari, Telle and Eriksen, Annelin (eds) 2010. *Contemporary Religiosities: Emergent Socialities and the Post-Nation-State*. New York and Oxford: Berghahn.

Keane, Webb 2007. *Christian Moderns. Freedom and Fetish in the Mission Encounter*. Berkeley: University of California Press.

Kennedy, Danny and Abrash, Abigail 2001. 'Repressive Mining in West Papua'. In Evans, Geoffrey, Goodman, James and Lansbury, Nina (eds), *Moving Mountains: Communities Confront Mining and Globalisation*. Sydney: Mineral Policy Institute, 59–74.

King, Peter 2004. *West Papua and Indonesia since Suharto: Independence, Autonomy or Chaos?* Sydney: University of New South Wales.

King, Peter, Elmslie, Jim and Webb-Gannon, Camellia 2011. *Comprehending West Papua*. Centre for Peace and Conflict Studies, University of Sydney.

Kirksey, Eben 2012. *Freedom in Entangled Worlds: West Papua and the Architecture of Global Power*. Durham and London: Duke University Press.

Kirsch, Stuart 2010. 'Ethnographic Representation and the Politics of Violence in West Papua'. *Critique of Anthropology* 30(1): 3–22.

Knauft, Bruce M. 1997. 'Gender Identity, Political Economy and Modernity in Melanesia and Amazonia'. *Journal of the Royal Anthropological Institute* 3(2): 233–259.

Lash, Scott and Urry, John 1994. *Economies of Signs and Space*. London: Sage.

Leach, Michael, Scambary, James, Clarke, Matthew, Feeny, Simon and Wallace, Heather 2012. 'Attitudes to National Identity Among Tertiary Students in Melanesia and Timor Leste: A Comparative Analysis'. *SSGM Discussion Paper* 2012/8. Canberra: The Australian National University, State, Society and Governance in Melanesia Program.

Li, Tania Murray 2001. 'Relational Histories and the Production of Difference on Sulawesi's Upland Frontier', *Journal of Asian Studies* 60(1): 41–66.

Lindquist, Johan A. 2009. *The Anxieties of Mobility: Migration and Tourism in the Indonesian Borderlands*. Honolulu: University of Hawai'i Press.

Lipset, David and Roscoe, Paul (eds) 2011. *Echoes of the Tambaran: Masculinity, History and the Subject in the Work of Donald F. Tuzin*. Canberra: ANU E Press.

McGibbon, Rodd 2004. *Plural Society in Peril: Migration, Economic Change, and the Papua Conflict*. Washington DC: East-West Center.

McWilliam, Andrew 2011. 'Marginal Governance in the Time of Pemekaran: Case Studies from Sulawesi and West Papua'. *Asian Journal of Social Science* 39: 150–170.

Munro, Jenny 2013. 'The Violence of Inflated Possibilities: Education, Transformation, and Diminishment in Wamena, Papua'. *Indonesia* 95: 25–46.

Newberry, Jan 2014. 'Class Mobil: Circulation of Children in the Making of Middle Indonesia'. In Klinken, Gerry van and Berenschot, Ward (eds), *In Search of Middle Indonesia: Middle Classes in Provincial Towns*. Leiden: KITLV, 69–88.

Nilan, Pam, Demartoto, Argyo and Wibowo, Agung 2014. 'Youthful Warrior Masculinities in Indonesia'. In Gelfer, Joseph (ed.), *Masculinities in a Global Era*. New York: Springer, 69–84.

Noor, Farish A. 2010. 'The Arrival and Spread of the Tablighi Jama'at in West Papua (Irian Jaya), Indonesia', *RSIS Working Paper* No. 191. Singapore: S. Rajaratnam School of International Studies.

Onim, Jusuf Fredrik 2006. *Islam and Kristen di Tanah Papua. Meniti Jalan Bersama Hubungan Islam-Kristen Dalam Sejarah Penyebaran dan Perjumpaannya di Wilayah Semenanjung Onin Fakfak*. Bandung: Jurnal Info Media.

Otto, Ton and Thomas, Nicholas (eds) 1997. *Narratives of Nation in the South Pacific*. Amsterdam: Harwood Academic Publishers.

Pamungkas, Cahyo 2008. *Papua Islam dan Otonomi Khusus: Kontestasi Identitas di Kalangan Orang Papua*. Tesis Program Paskasarjana Sosiologi, Universitas Indonesia.

Pamungkas, Cahyo 2011. 'Muslim Papua and Special Autonomy: The Identity Contest in Papua'. *Journal of Indonesian Social Sciences and Humanities* 4: 133–155.

Ploeg, Anton 1995. 'First Contact, in the Highlands of Irian Jaya'. *The Journal of Pacific History* 30(2): 227–239.

Rakhmani, Inaya 2012. 'A Note on Jayapura'. *Review of Indonesian and Malaysian Affairs* 46(1): 151–157.

Rosaldo, Renato (ed.) 2003. *Cultural Citizenship in Island Southeast Asia: Nation and Belonging in the Hinterlands*. Berkeley: University of California Press.

Resosudarmo, Budi, Napitupulu, Lydia, Manning, Chris and Wanggai, Velix 2009a. 'Papua I: Challenges of Economic Development in an Era of Political and Economic Change'. In Resosudarmo, Budi and Jotzo, Frank (eds), *Working with Nature against Poverty: Development, Resources and the Environment in Eastern Indonesia*. Singapore: Institute for Southeast Asian Studies, 21–58.

Resosudarmo, Budi, Manning, Chris, and Napitupulu, Lydia 2009b. 'Papua II: Challenges for Public Administration and Economic Policy under Special Autonomy'. In Resosudarmo, Budi and Jotzo, Frank (eds), *Working with Nature against Poverty: Development, Resources and the Environment in Eastern Indonesia*. Singapore: Institute for Southeast Asian Studies, 59–73.

Robbins, Joel 1994. 'Equality as a Value: Ideology in Dumont, Melanesia and the West'. *Social Analysis* 36: 21–70.

Robbins, Joel 2004. *Becoming Sinners: Christianity and Moral Torment in a Papua New Guinea Society*. Berkeley: University of California Press.

Robbins, Joel 2005. 'Humiliation and Transformation: Marshall Sahlins and the Study of Cultural Change in Melanesia'. In Robbins, Joel and Wardlow, Holly (eds), *The Making of Global and Local Modernities in Melanesia: Humiliation, Transformation, and the Nature of Cultural Change*. Aldershot, Burlington: Ashgate, 3–21.

Robbins, Joel 2007. 'Continuity Thinking and the Problem of Christian Culture: Belief, Time, and the Anthropology of Christianity'. *Current Anthropology* 48(1): 5–38.

Robbins, Joel and Wardlow, Holly (eds) 2005. *The Making of Global and Local Modernities in Melanesia: Humiliation, Transformation and the Nature of Cultural Change*. Aldershot, Burlington: Ashgate.

Rumsey, Alan 2006. 'The Articulation of Indigenous and Exogenous Orders in Highland New Guinea and Beyond'. *The Australian Journal of Anthropology* 17(1): 47–69.

Rutherford, Danilyn 2003. *Raiding the Land of the Foreigners. The Limits of the Nation on an Indonesian Frontier*. Princeton: Princeton University Press.

Rutherford, Danilyn 2012. *Laughing at Leviathan. Sovereignty and Audience in West Papua*. Chicago and London: The University of Chicago Press.

Rutherford, Danilyn 2013. 'Living, as it were, in the Stone Age'. *Indonesia* 95: 1–7.

Said, Edward 1978. *Orientalism: Western Conceptions of the Orient*. New York: Vintage Books.

Salazar, Noel 2010. 'Towards an Anthropology of Cultural Mobilities'. *Crossings: Journal of Migration and Culture* 1(1): 53–68.

Silverman, Eric K. 2013. 'After Cannibal Tours: Cargoism and Marginality in a Post-touristic Sepik River Society'. *The Contemporary Pacific* 25(2): 221–257.

Slama, Martin 2011. 'Translocal Networks and Globalisation within Indonesia: Exploring the Hadhrami Diaspora from the Archipelago's North-East'. *Asian Journal of Social Science* 39(3): 238–257.

Stasch, Rupert 2009. *Society of Others. Kinship and Mourning in a West Papuan Place*. Berkeley: University of California Press.

Stasch, Rupert 2011. 'Textual Iconicity and the Primitivist Cosmos: Chronotopes of Desire in Travel Writing about Korowai of West Papua'. *Journal of Linguistic Anthropology* 21: 1–21.

Sugandi, Yulia 2013. *The Notion of Collective Dignity among Hubula in Palim Valley, Papua*. PhD thesis, University of Münster.

Suryawan, I Ngurah (ed.) 2011. *Tanah Papua di Garis Batas: Perspektif, Refleksi, dan Tantangan*. Malang: Setara Press.

Timmer, Jaap 2007. 'Erring Decentralisation and Elite Politics in Papua'. In Schulte Nordholt, Henk and Klinken, Gerry van (eds), *Renegotiating Boundaries: Local Politics in Post-Suharto Indonesia*. Leiden: KITLV Press, 459–482.

Timmer, Jaap 2013. 'The Threefold Logic of Papua-Melanesia: Constitution-writing in the Margins of the Indonesian Nation-State'. *Oceania* 83(3): 158–174.

Tomlinson, Matt and McDougall, Debra L. (eds) 2012. *Christian Politics in Oceania* (Vol. 2). Oxford and New York: Berghahn.

Tsing, Anna Lowenhaupt 2005. *Friction. An Ethnography of Global Connection.* Princeton and Oxford: Princeton University Press.

Turner, Victor 1967. *The Forest of Symbols: Aspects of Ndembu Ritual.* Ithaca/New York: Cornell University Press.

Wanggai, Toni Victor M. 2008. *Rekonstruksi Sejarah Umat Islam di Tanah Papua.* Disertasi Sekolah Pascasarjana, Universitas Islam Negeri Syarif Hidayatullah Jakarta.

Wardlow, Holly 2006. *Wayward women: Sexuality and Agency in a New Guinea Society.* Berkeley: University of California Press.

Warnk, Holger 2010. 'The Coming of Islam and Moluccan-Malay Culture to New Guinea c.1500–1920'. *Indonesia and the Malay World* 38(110): 109–134.

Warta, Christian 2011. *Religiositäten in Bewegung: Adat, Schriftreligionen und Nationalismen in Papua, Indonesien.* PhD thesis, University of Vienna.

Webster, David 2013. 'Self-Determination Abandoned: The Road to the New York Agreement on West New Guinea (Papua)', 1960–62. *Indonesia* 95: 9–24.

Widjojo, Muridan S., Elisabeth, Adriana, Amiruddin, Pamungkas, Cahyo and Dewi, Rosita 2008. *Papua Road Map: Negotiating the Past, Improving the Present and Securing the Future.* Jakarta: Indonesian Institute of Sciences, Jakarta.

2. Demonstrating the Stone-Age in Dutch New Guinea

Danilyn Rutherford

What is a colonial officer to do? When the radio he has been waiting for to begin his expedition into uncharted land arrives only to break the first time it is used? When the coolies he has recruited from a nearby coastal settlement announce they are going on strike? When his superiors suddenly decide he should head for an entirely different region than the one he was planning for – a region for which he has no maps and has read no reports? When the scientist along for the expedition, who has never been to this island, changes the route under the mistaken assumption that it is harder to travel by water than to walk? When it becomes apparent that the erstwhile commander of the expedition has little control over its components – and little reason to think that the natives he meets will be impressed by his government's supposed sovereignty over their land?

Police commissioner Jan van Eechoud faced all these challenges, and pondered them grimly, while waiting at Pioneer Bivak to begin his third expedition up the Mamberamo River into the Dutch New Guinea highlands, in the hinterland of what was then the Netherlands Indies. What's a colonial officer to do? Here's what van Eechoud did: he built a machine. To pass the time and make himself useful, van Eechoud gathered ethnological data from members of the surrounding tribes, inviting the Papuans into his tent to be interviewed in a mixture of Malay and the little he had picked up of the local tongue. With a crowd of Papuans watching, the individual providing information sat on a petroleum drum, answering questions on kinship, religion and politics in exchange for tobacco and food. Some 'lecturers' as van Eechoud called them, enjoyed the refreshments so much that they rambled on and on. Afraid of offending his informants, he used 'indirect means to end a discussion' (1953: 181). At first, he tricked the entire group into following him outside, then jumped back into the tent and locked the door. Then he came up with a more ingenious solution:

> The petroleum drum was placed on a plank, so that it was separated from the ground. Attached to the plank was an insulated wire that ran in a wide arc along the wall then outside to where it was attached to the spark plug of a Delco motor [DR: a battery-operated starter motor, presumably from one of the motor boats used by the expedition]. When I wanted a lecturer to go away, without interrupting the discussion or looking up I said under my breath to Dr. Koppeschaar, 'Doc, run it!' After a minute, the doctor vanished outside and pressed the Delco

motor's start knob. All of a sudden, the lecturer sat up with a grimace on his face, convulsively waving his arms and legs until he had a chance to get off. After that, he stood there, looking around, asking himself what had happened to him. (van Eechoud 1953: 181)

They never grasped the connection between the drum, wire, and Delco motor, but when the trick had been played several times, they very well got wind of one coincidence: if someone was invited to sit down, he squinted at the drum, looked at me suspiciously, and asked anxiously, 'Doc, run it?' After my comforting declaration that there would be no 'Doc, run it' he would take a seat and light up a cigarette. (van Eechoud 1953: 181)

Unable to command the Stone-Age Papuans directly, van Eechoud managed to dominate them through a proxy. He bent them to his will through the words by which he commanded a modern machine.

Van Eechoud didn't stage a technology demonstration in the typical way, which would have involved producing what Erving Goffman called a 'theatrical frame' by using conventional signals (such as a sideshow barker's 'Step right up!') to attract an audience and focus its attention on the action about to unfold (1986 [1974]: 124–155). Yet this scene contains many of the ingredients that will detain us in the pages that follow: a machine unfamiliar to local people produced an action that elicited fear, surprise, amusement and curiosity. And, in the hopeful imaginations of colonial impresarios, these performances elicited respect for Dutch visitors and the regimes they represent.

In this essay, which forms part of a larger project, I focus on technology demonstrations staged in the Wisselmeren region of Dutch New Guinea between 1936 and 1953. This part of present-day Papua launched the careers of influential officials, including van Eechoud, who promoted the policy that led to Dutch New Guinea's continued colonisation following World War II (see Derix 1987; Drooglever 2005). Van Eechoud and his colleagues led expeditions into the territory's interior in the 1930s. Daily life on these journeys blurred the boundaries between colonisers and colonised, not to mention New Guinea's erstwhile rulers and their tools. The technological performances I explore in this paper intervene to redraw a sharp line. At the same time, they staged a meeting between the Stone-Age and modernity, they opened a gulf that kept these times apart.

In making this argument, I draw on snapshots from three authors: Dr H.J.T. Bijlmer, who wrote a book on his 1936 journey to the Wisselmeren (n.d.); Jan van Eechoud, who wrote reports and a memoir on his experiences in the same region (1938, 1953; see also de Bruijn 1939a, 1939b, 1939c, 1941); and Dr K.W.J. Boelen's memoir depicting a later moment of colonial state building, when the

Dutch returned to the Wissel Lakes after the war (1955; see also Meijer Ranneft 1952; van Emmerik 1953). These snapshots enable me to track the progress of state building in the highlands as the Dutch consolidated their hold on the region and established an apparatus with a growing number of the elements associated with modern rule. They also offer glimpses of Papuan perspectives on this changing scene. Over the period I cover, the Wisselmeren's inhabitants, and Papuans elsewhere in Dutch New Guinea, became increasingly nimble in appropriating the authority and status they came to associate with motors, gramophones, magnets and other modern instruments. At the same time, they grappled with and sometimes reproduced the view that made Stone-Age primitives out of people who used stone axes and knives.

The authors I consider didn't invent the idea of the Stone-Age; that was the work of the Danish curator, Christian Jürgensen Thomsen, who in 1816 came up with the idea of dividing artifacts among galleries representing eras defined by the materials used for tools.[1] Nor did they invent the idea that present-day 'non-metallic savages' could serve as proxies for Europeans' own Stone-Age ancestors. For that, we can thank Sir John Lubbock, who wrote what some call the most influential archaeological textbook of the 19th century, *Pre-Historic Times* (1865).[2] They weren't even the first to import Lubbock's proposition to Dutch New Guinea. Earlier in the 20th century, when English and Dutch explorers ventured into the territory's mountainous interior in what Ballard, Vink, and Ploeg (2002) call 'the race to the snows', the notion that the people they encountered were throwbacks to an earlier stage in human development was ready to hand. The record of one such expedition, A.F. Wollaston's *Pygmies and Papuans: The Stone Age Today in Dutch New Guinea* (1912), was a popular bestseller in its day. What these authors did to this conceit was to give it political purchase and staying power in the waning years of the Netherlands Indies, when Dutch colonials and Indo-European activists hatched the first plans to administer New Guinea separately from the rest of the colony (see Rutherford 2012). They helped to turn the Papuans' positioning in this particular version of what Michel-Rolph Trouillot (1991) called 'the savage slot' into an excuse for Dutch New Guinea's prolonged colonisation and the denial of Papuans' political rights.

But that's skipping to the end of the story. The first step is to scrutinise how the Stone-Age became palpable for these adventurers. To grasp how technology

---

1   Thomsen, who organised what was to become the Danish National Museum on this basis, is credited with inventing stratigraphy, a dating method central to modern archaeological research. See http://en.wikipedia. org/wiki/Three-age_system, accessed 19 February 2013.
2   See http://en.wikipedia.org/wiki/John_Lubbock,_1st_Baron_Avebury.

demonstrations helped to consolidate the Stone-Age image of New Guinea, we must approach them as performances – performances that both acted out claims to sovereignty and put it at risk.

Demonstrate, perform, or, how to do things with things

We have all been there. We're watching television. Steve Jobs stands at a podium introducing the latest Apple product. An enormous screen lights up behind him, and he puts the device through its paces. Or we're at the movies. Hugh Jackman walks onto a stage and steps into a wire cage. Lights flash, the wires shoot off sparks and he disappears, only to reappear at the back of the hall. Demonstrations of technology: they entertain and sometimes dazzle, but they also create the impression of a consolidated kind of agency. Apple's founder both borrowed power from and lent power to the iPad. His technology demonstrations invited shareholders to buy into the premise that the creative power of a man and a brand, not a network of people and previous inventions, found expression in a machine's novel actions. A magician does the same thing when he performs a technological trick. His performance constitutes a massive disavowal of the distributed nature of agency: the networks of people, artifacts, and histories of practice gathered together in every technique (see Heidegger 1977; Hutchins 1995; Stiegler 1998; Riddington 1999; Mauss 2006). 'The Real Transported Man', not the transporter, appears on the marquis in *The Prestige*: the transporter's agency becomes the magician's own.

These examples reveal the performative nature of technology demonstrations. The philosopher John Austin (1976) defined performatives as phrases, like 'I promise', 'I deny', 'I swear' or 'I declare', that do what they say they are doing in the very act of being said. What Austin called a 'speech act' creates the impression of willful agency, attesting to a speaker's capacity to change the world. In the case of technology demonstrations, people achieve a similar outcome – only not, as Austin puts it, by doing with words but also by doing things with things. In colonial settings, this aspect of technology demonstrations becomes obvious. Greg Dening (1980) writes of the 'shows of force' that 18th- and 19th-century ship captains felt compelled to stage in order to control the Marquesan islanders who swarmed onto their decks. To stop the islanders from stealing, the sailors sometimes shot a few. The others learned to flee, and to appreciate the power of firearms, which they soon began acquiring by trading local goods. On the Australian half of New Guinea, 20th-century patrol officers and prospectors sometimes staged brutally direct shows of force, as when some Yonki men attacked Jim Taylor, and his police opened fire, or when Mick and Dan Leahy shot a handful of Papuans in a village where they found gold (Gammage 1998: 11, 12). But they also staged technology demonstrations as a way of putting their capacities on display. One sees such a scene at the end of the documentary *First Contact*, when the Leahy brothers line up some Papuans to show them how a rifle can kill a pig (see e.g. YouTube 2008).[3]

On the Dutch side of the island, the administration avoided open conflict, and there were far fewer killings of either locals or their guests in the encounters that accompanied state building in the interior. Officials like van Eechoud were tasked with establishing peaceful contact with 'our' authority and making the Papuans' behavior more 'predictable', 'according to our concepts' (see Rutherford 2009). Technology demonstrations, especially involving firearms, proved a favourite method for trying to ensure that the Papuans would recognise 'our authority' as authority – especially when the guns were wielded by bedraggled and hungry hikers who scarcely seemed capable of caring for themselves. Repeatedly seeing a rifle or gramophone in action would make Papuans better able to predict the behavior of modern weapons and devices. Their own behavior would become more predictable as a result. Somehow, the shooting of pigs – and, as we will see, the playing of gramophones – would constitute a Dutch 'I' and a Papuan 'you' – the agent and patient of colonial sovereignty. The Papuans would come to recognise technological supremacy as an attribute of Dutch personhood; something that these 'white men' naturally had. In insisting on the range of human and non-human agents involved in every act of thinking, Edwin Hutchins has criticised the idea that primitive technologies are the product of primitive minds (1995: 355). The technology demonstrations staged by Dutch officials had the effect of perpetuating this mistake. Van Eechoud could not always control the trekking machine; he could rarely tell the primitives what to do. Technology demonstrations enabled him to persuade himself and others, however fleetingly, that machines were the measure of men.

Another way to put this is that Dutch officials staged these performances in order to cultivate particular inferences among the Papuans (see Hume 1988

---

3   This is not to say rifle demonstrations always worked to instill respect for Australian authority. Gammage quotes Patrol Officer Jim Taylor writing of his earliest patrols in the eastern New Guinea highlands, where, in the company of the Leahy brothers, who first discovered gold in the region, he explored the Baiyer and Jimi valleys and climbed Mt Hagen in 1932. One way home, the men faced frequent attacks and found the 'attitude of the natives ... entirely different from that on our first trip through':

> Then they imagined us gods or spirits but on reflection they realized their mistake apparently and so a revulsion of feeling took place ... Our peaceful behaviour they regarded as being due to us not being warriors – and to an absence of weapons. Rifles they imagined were sticks and though they saw them shoot through trees and kill pigs they still could not connect them with their concept of war. Day after day we encountered large numbers of hostile or contemptuous people who shouted insults at us and howled with derisive laughter when told to desist. They appeared to think that they had us in their power ... One fellow actually brought rope to tie up his share of the loot.

See Gammage 1998: 13.

[1748]; Rutherford 2009). Technology demonstrations invited Papuan audience members to trace an effect to a cause, a cause residing in the body of a human actor and, by extension, others like him. The concept of personal or group identity arguably results from just such acts of inference (see Hume 1988 [1748]: 50–66). People do things, we presume, because they are the sorts of people prone to behaving in just this way. Speech acts offer a particularly powerful way to link an identity and an action. The power of a performative resides in a speaker's ability to refer to the fact that he or she is speaking (see Lee 1997; see also Rutherford 2012). The relationship between our words and the world may be arbitrary, and our statements may be erroneous. But when I say, 'I am saying', I can't help but speak the truth.[4] This utterance enables me to believe, if only for an instant, that the power to speak belongs to the speaker alone, instead of stemming from multiple sources: from the qualities of sound waves to the evolutionary processes that gave us our tongues, ears and brains to the habits and expectations we have acquired from living in settings where people use signs in particular ways. What Austin (1976) calls speech acts are technology demonstrations, to the extent that language is a tool, a prosthetic device made by humans that in turn makes humans what they are (see Mumford 1967; Stiegler 1998). Rifle demonstrations and wedding vows both focus attention on the fiction of a cause: the officer who pulls the trigger, the bride who says 'I do'.

Figure 2.1. Expedition member S. van der Groot demonstrates the workings of a magnifying glass to a group of Ekari Papuans, 1936.

Source: Tropenmuseum Collection 10032903, http://papuacollectie.ab-c.nl.

---

4   What's more, the person 'I' become in articulating this phrase takes on an unassailable-seeming reality as the agent of this speech act. The pronoun itself already refers to the event of its utterance: 'I' is defined as the individual uttering 'I' (See Benveniste 1971).

Paying heed to this function of technology demonstrations not only helps us better understand their appeal for colonial officials. It also helps us understand how these performances could run astray. Speech acts only work because they are conventional, which means they are repeatable – or 'iterable', to use the philosopher Jacques Derrida's (1982, 1986) term – and detachable from any particular context of use. 'I promise' may lose some of its 'felicity' – its 'happy' effect – when uttered in jest or onstage. This question of iterability bears in two ways on the efficacy of the technology demonstrations I consider. On the one hand, this was not a setting where one could presume that what one took to be conventions were, in fact, conventions: colonial officials had to repeat their experiments, as it were, engineering experiences that created expectations in order for a demonstration to have its desired effect. On the other hand, the iterability of technology demonstrations gave Papuans a chance to engage in their own experiments, which sometimes had subversive effects. Suffice to say that local notions of personhood, agency and authority loomed large in their performances, in ways I can only gesture towards here.[5] To get a sense of the powers and dangers of these colonial performances, let's turn to our first snapshot, which portrays a performance staged by Dr H.J.T. Bijlmer, who had a particularly keen desire to use modern technology to reveal the nature of primitive selves.

Snapshot 1: The circus comes to town

Dr. H.J.T. Bijlmer was a medical doctor and an 'anthropologist', a term that in his day referred to a specialist in the study of the racial types that made up the human species. He arrived in the southern part of the Wisselmeren in 1935–36 at the end of an expedition to investigate the so-called Tapiro Pygmies, a small-statured group of Papuans first encountered by Europeans in 1910.[6] He reached

---

5 Some of the Papuans involved might well have had little trouble understanding what Austin was talking about when he described how performatives work. During the early 1950s, Leopold Pospisil (1963) interviewed a number of philosophically inclined Kapauku in the 'uncontacted' Kamu Valley. They explained that persons were composed of two parts: bodies and souls. 'To live' was *ami-tou*, 'to sleep, referring to the separate existence of the soul, and to stay in place, referring to the material existence of the body.' 'My body stays in place, my soul dreams, and I live,' one man explained (Pospisil 1963: 87). For the Kapauku, Pospisil elaborated, '"I" means consciousness; it means the thinking process is the cooperative effort of the body and soul' (ibid.). This model of the person, which valorised the unified action of an uttered word or enacted gesture and a body staged in space, may well account for the appeal of technology demonstrations and the eagerness of Kapauku to repeat them.

6 Bjilmer undertook this trip at the behest of the Maatschappij ter Bevordering van het Natuurkundig Onderzoek der Nederlands Kolonien (Corporation for the Advance of Natural Scientific Research in the Dutch Colonies) and the support of then Governor General B.C. de Jonge and his boss, the Minister of Colonies and New Guinea enthusiast, Dr H. Colijn (see Biljmer n.d.). Twenty companions came along, including a local government official, Civiel Gezaghebber S. van der Groot, and the Catholic priest, Father Tillemans, whom Bijlmer had met in 1931, when he served as medical officer on a British expedition to the top of Mt Carstens (ibid; see also Ballard et al. 2002). (The British expedition had passed through the Tapiro pygmies' homeland, and Bijlmer and Tillemans met individuals who still remembered them – and, no doubt, their loot, which took the form of metal knives, axes, shells, mirrors and beads [Bijlmer n.d.: 49].)

the Wisselmeren by way of Mimika, the coastal region that was the entryway to the region for van Eechoud as well. Biljmer was no novice; during an even earlier expedition in 1920, Bijlmer had visited the Swart Valley, the first densely populated area of the highlands that Dutch explorers reached by foot. Bijlmer called his book on the journey *To the Ends of the Earth*, and, as this title makes clear, New Guinea had lost none of its charm for Bijlmer in the intervening years. Framed as fodder for the popular imagination, Biljmer's account of his adventure shows how technology demonstrations gave Dutch travellers a sense of superiority at moments when their mastery seemed in doubt.

For Bijlmer, stone tools and Stone-Age selves went together in a way that made New Guinea's present a mirror onto the Netherlands' past. In the Swart Valley, Bijlmer found himself in

> ...a world from past ages! Because weaving and pottery appeared unknown, and people felled the forest and cut planks with stone axes! Not a scrap of metal was to be seen; the Stone-Age, sunk deep in the mists of prehistory in Europe, was here in full bloom ... The extant stone axe is the sign that this folk still pass their days untouched by civilization. That is why studying them is so extraordinarily important. (Bijlmer n.d.: 17)

For Bijlmer, the continued use of stone axes in the Swart Valley and elsewhere was a sign of the mountain Papuans' isolation: this was a land forgotten by time, a land that 'brought nothing' from the civilised world. This characterisation is, of course, debatable. Given the lengthy trade routes that crossed the highlands, its inhabitants' multilingualism, and the delight so many of them took in travelling and trading, it seems unlikely that highlands Papuans waited passively for imports to arrive (see e.g. Pospisil 1963; Haenen 1992; Timmer 2000). Yet it is illuminating of the fantasy that Bijlmer experienced technology demonstrations as affirming – a fantasy in which the Dutch explorer reached across the eons to touch the lives of the mountain Papuans and was exhilarated to discover that these living ancestors were just like him.

Bijlmer's experiences in the Wisselmeren fed this fantasy. After taking biometric measurements among the Tapiro, Bijlmer returned to the coast and made his way into the region, where the first community he reached was in the densely populated Pogi Valley. The inhabitants were Kapauku, members of the ethnolinguistic group that made up the lion's share of the population in the vicinity of the lakes. While the coolies made camp, Bjilmer and the Dutch officers sat among curious onlookers; gradually a dozen men gathered. With the delicacy of a nature lover coaxing a wild animal, Bijlmer managed to lure several women and a child close enough to put a string of beads around the little girl's neck.

Figure 2.2. Portrait of H.J.T. Bijlmer with an Ekari Papuan, 1936.

Source: Tropenmuseum Collection 10032847, http://papuacollectie.ab-c.nl.

But the real excitement came after a larger crowd had gathered.

> We decided to do a demonstration with the gramophone. We had brought this instrument along in the first place to observe the effect it would have on primitives, but I will happily admit I also got much pleasure out of it.

> A score of men pressed up close to the table; the six women sat at a safer distance.

> We chose Sarie Marijs, sung by a deep male voice, as the first record. Upon first hearing the music, the listeners rubbed their ears in wonder, but when the male voice resonated their amazement knew no bounds. Ten faces – the women had taken flight – stared in dumb amazement at the fantastic instrument … and now these were human faces in full form! They may actually have been primitive, somewhat foolish faces, but now they exuded spirit and effervescent life. Each reacted in his manner. There appeared tense attention on the face of one; straightforward wonder on that of another; paranoid fear, cheerful joy, dumb ecstasy, an investigative gaze on the rest! There were those who, without showing any fear, took up the matter seriously and sank into a reverie; there

were others who, after they overcame their hesitation, examined the device from all angles and didn't recoil from a bold investigation. Next to peaceful thinkers, one noticed clever investigators in the making … No, it's not like we found anything different than what is to be expected by every student of humanity. But such an experience at what one might say is the source is always worth mentioning. As if in a fantasy, we discovered in the end ourselves: we are here within our own prehistory! (Bijlmer n.d.: 137–138)

Our own prehistoric circus: 'The Papuans' stance towards us was scarcely different from that of a spectacle hungry crowd at a fairground back home' (ibid.). The demonstration brought familiar passions into focus by wiping the 'foolishness' off the villagers' primitive faces. Bijlmer took the most pleasure in the 'clever scientists' in the making; those who shared Bijlmer's own 'investigative gaze'. That's not to say that the Papuan researchers were capable of penetrating the mystery. They gave up when Bijlmer played a second record, which featured a female singer and destroyed their theory that Bijlmer or one of his colleagues was throwing his voice.

Bijlmer had this happy scene to remember during episodes that called his competence into doubt. In another passage, Bijlmer described huddling, wet and cold, on a rugged trail, waiting for his coolies to build a shelter. His Kapauku guides looked on with pity and scorn, but there was no reason to worry about their reactions. The Dutch could afford to be 'friendly' with the Papuans, Bjilmer noted, given that 'the respect that our arrival, our appearance, and all our doings inspired was so great' (n.d. 157). This is a fantasy of superiority, but, if we follow Rupert Stasch (2009), then we can see that it tamed otherness as much as it created it. The Stone-Age Papuan did not appear as our father, someone who shared the current moment, but whose death the Dutch would survive. Rather he appeared as a younger version of 'ourselves'; someone whom, outside of science fiction, the Dutch could never meet. A temporal wall divided the Dutch from the Papuans. A trick with a record player was all it took.

But the gramophone was not the only machine Bijlmer relied upon to affirm his superiority. The expedition's leaders might have been friendly, but they weren't foolish: they insisted that the party should travel with armed guards. Van Eechoud, who came to the Wisselmeren to govern, not measure heads, could not be quite as confident in the outcome of these performances. Let's turn now to our second snapshot and the multiple ways a rifle could misfire.

Snapshot 2: Performing sovereignty

Police Commissioner Jan van Eechoud passed through the same region where Bijlmer had conducted measurements on his way with a long line of coolies and police agents to establish a post in Enarotali, a lakeside village in the heart of the Wisselmeren. Elsewhere I have described the logistical difficulties van Eechoud faced in carrying out this mission (Rutherford 2009). When it came to recruiting the support of local Papuans, challenges raised their head right from the start. Van Eechould wasn't sure that the first group of Kapaukus he met would be as friendly as they had been with earlier visitors. So he decided to make a show of force 'to get rid of any unpleasant ideas that might have found their way into their heads' (1953: 103).

> Behind a twenty-centimeter tree, an empty trekking drum was set. Five meters in front of the tree, I positioned myself with a carbine. Through gestures and by making noise, I tried to make it clear that the tree as well as the can would be bored through with a loud report. Full of tension, the group watched. I aimed, shot, and looked triumphantly to see the effect on their faces – but there were no more faces. With great leaps, some of the group had vanished into the forest, while others raced at full sped to the other side of the garden running, or so they thought, for their lives.
>
> If another shot had been fired, then the poor devils in their panic would have climbed over Mt Carsten. But we began to call reassuringly – at least it seemed to us reassuringly. Meanwhile, at least a half an hour went by before a couple of them dared to return, wavering and reluctant. Fear was again in their eyes when they looked at either me or the carbine. (van Eechoud 1953: 103)

Van Eechoud began the demonstration with a prophecy: gestures and noise meant to mimic the shooting of the carbine. He used a drum and a tree as targets; later he used pigs, which provided him with an even better way of demonstrating his weapons' – and his government's – power. The demonstration displayed the sovereign's grip on what Agamben called the 'mere fact of living', which is what pigs and, in a different way, trees share with people. But sovereignty needs more than 'bare life'; it needs an audience as well (Rutherford 2012). The Kapauku had to fear van Eechoud enough to remove any 'unpleasant ideas' from their heads. But they had to trust him enough to feed him, given his difficulties with the supply line. To balance these imperatives, van Eechoud had to display the state's capacity for violence without scaring the Papuans off.

As it turned out, firearm demonstrations did help to sustain van Eechoud's security and food supply. But not for the reasons he presumed they would. When news of van Eechoud's expedition reached Timiela, the inhabitants of this village brought the colonial officer a piglet and asked him to shoot it (van Eechoud 1953: 114). Like the audience at a tightrope act, the Kapauku found these 'executions' unnerving; and yet they enjoyed the show. Van Eechoud's successor, Jan Victor de Bruijn, gained enough of a sense of local life to understand that the appeal of these performances: pigs were publicly slaughtered at the elaborate pig feasts where Kapauku gathered to dance and trade shells for pork (see Pospisil 1963: 270). The shooting of a pig with a revolver intended to scare hostile villagers also served as a familiar way of making 'friends' (Van Eechoud 1953: 138).

These Dutch travelers were able to assure themselves of the 'deep respect' – and even 'affection' – that 'our arrival, our appearance, and all our doings' had inspired (Bijlmer n.d.: 178) in the Kapauku. Yet their writings bear witness to what potentially could become disturbing appropriations of the power the Dutch seemed to wield when they played a record or shot a pig. Bijlmer tells of young Kapauku repeating the experiment with the magnet, showing off their own agency to their friends. De Bruijn describes how some villagers chanted 'So! So!' whenever he shot a pig, repeating the expression the colonial officer always uttered when the deed was done (1939a: 80). After the war, when the Dutch re-established a colonial presence in New Guinea, some Kapauku rebelled and lost their lives. But even as Papuans learned more radical ways of appropriating the machinery of state building, they found it increasingly difficult to leave the Stone-Age behind.

Snapshot 3: Our demonstrations, their demonstrations

Dutch officials returned to Wisselmeren in 1948 to reopen the post in Enarotali. Assigned to head up the health department, the author of our third snapshot, Dr K.J.W. Boelen, arrived several years later with his pregnant wife. Technology demonstrations of a routine sort had become the order of the day: those that made up the work of the growing corps of Kapauku teachers, nurses and clerks. But even as they mastered modern instruments, the Stone-Age stuck to their identities, like glue from a label they couldn't peel off.

Boelen, like other chroniclers of this period, spilled much ink describing typical Kapauku technology: houses, fire starters and net bags, but above all clothes (see also Meijer Ranneft 1952; van Emmerick 1953). He found the attire of new Kapauku police recruits particularly arresting:

> The corps follows military order. The Kapauku recruits take part in the force in local clothing, and it is a funny sight to see them, in full gravity, under the command of the Agent First Class, performing drills dressed only in penis gourds. But they quickly get their uniforms, and one can see an impeccably clad help agent, with his wife in her fiber skirt, off to church on a Sunday morning, both fully aware of their importance. (Boelen 1955: 22)

Boelen goes on to note that the Kapauku agents could prove very helpful as guides or interpreters. They were less adept in the main responsibility of the police force, which was to lead the locals 'to accustom themselves to having a higher authority above them. Instead they remained in the thick of local things, using 'the authority of their uniform' to win their own family disputes' (ibid.). We don't often think of wearing an outfit as demonstrating a technology, but Boelen's remarks are legible in these terms: the uniform becomes a tool the agents turn toward their own ends.

But in making this point, Boelen also points to the mismatch between Papuans and modern technology: the clothing never quite fits these men. In another passage, Boelen describes how the 'old customs ... came again to the surface during tours'.

> During rainstorms, one sometimes sees the Kapauku agents putting back on their penis gourds, although they keep the American helmets with the initials 'A.P.' (Algemeen Politie) [DR: General Police] on their heads and their rifles on their shoulders as a sign of their dignity. Also at feasts, the awkward clothing is set aside and the penis gourd takes its place. (Boelen 1955: 22)

From the depths of Papuan identity, Stone-Age tendencies can't help but resurface: you can take the Papuan out of the penis gourd, but you can't take the penis gourd out of the Papuan. When Stone-Age bodies meet modern garments, the effect is both amusing and ephemeral – modernity doesn't sit well, and it is easily cast off. Boelen's memoir partakes of a fantasy that creates a tight bond between the essential traits of Europeans and the capacities of modern equipment. The essential traits of Papuans, by contrast, are at odds with modern technology. Their technological performances are inherently infelicitous: theatrical spoofs rather than serious enactments of an agency that cleaves to an instrument like a hand slipped into a glove. This is a conceit purpose-built for what Homi Bhabha (1994) described as the ambivalence of colonial discourse (see also Spyer 1998). On the one hand, natives had to have the capacity to become like their colonisers for the civilising mission to have meaning. Yet they couldn't actually achieve this goal, or the civilising mission would have to end.[7]

More disturbing appropriations of modern things and ways also preoccupied the small Dutch community. Officials wrote extensively about the rebellion members of the Pakage clan mounted against the Dutch government and its proxies. The violence against persons and property that took place during this conflict merely confirmed the intractability of Stone-Age practices; in all but a

---

7   As I have suggested, the appeal of New Guinea for the Dutch during this period rested on its primitive character. No matter how civilised, dignified or respectable they appeared, the Stone-Age Papuans would remain primitive beneath the surface for generations to come.

few regions, the Dutch gave up on stopping local wars. Less easy to put out of mind was Zacheus Pakage, a Kapauku convert sent by American missionaries to Makassar for training (see Giay 1995; see also Boelen 1955: 22–23; van Emmerik 1953: 36–39).[8] Upon his return in 1950, Pakage insisted on being posted in his own home region, where he used his influence to begin a movement using Christian ritual and doctrine against the colonial regime.[9] The power of coastal Papuans also became the target of capture. A man and his wife who had lived in Kokonau, a town on the southern coast, unsettled Dutch officials when they returned to the Wisselmeren to open a 'school'. They modeled loincloths, a coastal garment, and demonstrated fire walking, a coastal custom, to prove they had access to supernatural powers (van Emmerik 1953: 36). Here were examples of mimicry gone too far.

And yet, even as the Kapauku learned more and more radical ways of appropriating others' technologies, they also were forced to recognise, and sometimes even internalise, the racial hierarchy on which Dutch self-assurance rested. However subversive they might have seemed, Papuan technology demonstrations could not help but affirm the conceit underlying the Stone-Age fantasy. In using the same tricks as the Dutch did to demonstrate their superiority, Kapauku leaders strengthened the opposition that divided modern and Stone-Age bodies and things. This opposition had the potential to poison relationships among Papuans with different histories of colonial contact. Boelen relates the following incident involving his Kapauku houseboy, Marcus.

> The wife of a colleague from Biak offered to find a Biak girl. Marcus helped us set up the small room next to the kitchen. We put in a bed and laid an earthen floor. When Jacomina arrived with the Catalina, she was exuberant from her first flight and found everything lovely. Marcus, in a clean, pretty shirt, carried her bag with an aggrieved look. She found him a most amusing boy and spoke to him in rapid Malay, so that he could barely follow her. She nearly choked when she saw her first mountain Papuan walking by in a penis gourd. She found our house pretty, was taken by her room, and asked my wife a hundred things. Marcus deported himself very shyly, but within an hour he found that the women's chatter must come to an end, and it was time for more scientific pursuits. He put his slate under his arm and said firmly, 'Mama, I'm going to school'. This did not impress Jacomina in the least. In Biak, most children start school at the normal age and have already

---

8   This was against the better judgment of I.J.R. Meijer Ranneft, who at the time was the head of government in the Wisselmeren.

9   Zacheus threatened to quit if the missionaries refused. By a gentleman's agreement, the Roman Catholics split the region with the Christian and Missionary Alliance, an American Protestant group. Tigi was officially a Catholic mission field; the missionaries wanted Zacheus to go to Wandai, three days walk to the east.

finished by the time they are twelve. She began to laugh and asked him bluntly: 'Such a big boy already, and you are still going to school? How funny. How old are you, and what grade are you in?' (Boelen 1955: 70)

Marcus 'slinked off' with an offended sniff; 'things were never in order between him and Jacomina'. Note how this coastal Papuan internalised the Dutch view that made Stone-Age tribes out of people who had once used stone tools. Marcus' performance with the books and slate could not make him seem 'civilised' to Jacomina. *This* technology demonstration's failure justified continued colonisation. The Stone-Age was becoming a prison that was hard to escape.

Conclusion: 'Paper's power'

A Dutch official sets up a gramophone and turns it on. His finger pulls a trigger and a bullet leaves a barrel, speeding towards a hapless pig. We can trace these events to an endless series of causes: from the supplier who sold these devices, to the government coffers that paid for them, to the experiences that shaped the official's habits and expectations so he could operate these machines. This is not to mention the histories that gave rise to the gramophone and the rifle, which include the moments of memory and anticipation that are inscribed in every technical thing (see Stiegler 1998). All these possibilities are put out of mind as the official sets these machines in motion. Of course, a clever Papuan could well have asked the colonial official, 'Did he himself understand how a gramophone or a rifle works?' No one ever grasps, no one ever masters, the workings of their own minds and bodies, let alone all the other things of which social persons are composed.

Among these things is the technology of writing: the paper, pens, typewriters, filing cabinets, printing presses, archives and libraries that made these officials' stories available to me and through me to you.[10] 'The Papuan is not conscious that the paper's power lies in the words written on it,' Bijlmer wrote of a Kapauku messenger who loudly announced the instructions he had been given instead of simply handing over the letter (1938: 174). In fact, the messenger was right: paper doesn't speak by itself. Its power lies not merely in the words written upon it, but in how it is handled – how it enters circulation and with what effects. Paper played a central role in fueling the Stone-Age fantasy that continues to dog the people of today's West Papua. The texts I have considered reached a broad Dutch audience. And the effects on West Papua's people were great.

---

10   On the power of paper to shape colonial encounters like the ones described in this essay, see Mueggler (2011).

Figure 2.3. Father Tillemans points out the presence of a camera to an Ekari Papuan, 1936.

Source: Tropenmuseum Collection 10032916, http://papuacollectie.ab-c.nl.

In the decades following the period described in these snapshots, the idea that Papuans were living in the Stone-Age persisted. John F. Kennedy referred to the fact that the Papuans were 'living, as it were, in the Stone-Age' to justify the United State's refusal to intervene on behalf of their right to self-determination when the Dutch lobbied his administration to oppose the territory's transfer to Indonesia in 1962. Even today, Jared Diamond (2012) is still writing of West Papuans as a modern day version of 'non-metallic savages' who can tell us what the 'world until yesterday' looked like for the entire human race. This is not to mention the Stone-Age tribes, Stone-Age dogs, Stone-Age diets and Stone-Age climbing gyms that a quick Google search turns up. It is hard to imagine another colonial conceit that has had such staying power. Only by attending to the power of paper – and the fraught encounters that left their traces in these texts – can we grasp how the Stone-Age gained its grip and came to have the implications the other essays in this volume describe so well.

Essays are technology demonstrations, and while our status as their authors is fictive, our responsibilities are real. How should today's anthropologists of West Papua be mobilising paper's power? What should we make of our own deployment of all this machinery and the pleasures and anxieties it provokes? With what habits and passions should we be handling our words? Contending with the Stone-Age fantasy that has dogged West Papuans may be the right place to begin.

References

Austin, John Langshaw 1976. *How to Do Things with Words*. London: Oxford University Press.

Ballard, Chris, Vink, Steven and Ploeg, Anton 2002. *Race to the Snow: Photography and the Exploration of Dutch New Guinea, 1907–1938*. Leiden: KITLV Press.

Benveniste, Émile 1971. *Problems in General Linguistics*. Coral Gables (Florida): University of Miami Press.

Bhabha, Homi 1994. 'Of Mimicry and Man: The Ambivalence of Colonial Discourse'. In Bhabha, Homi (ed.), *The Location of Culture*. London: Routledge, 121–131.

Bijlmer, Dr. H.J.T. n.d. *Naar de Achterhoek der Aarde*. Amsterdam: Scheltens and Giltay.

Boelen, K.W.J. 1955. *Dokter aan de Wisselmeren*. Baarn: Bosch and Keuning N.V.

De Bruijn, Jan Victor 1939a. *Verslag van een tocht naar Kemandora in Centraal Nieuw-Guinea door den Adspirant-Controleur der Wisselmeren Dr. J.V. de Bruijn van 20 Februari 1939 tot 10 Maart 1939*. ARA Min van Kol. Kantor Bevolkingszaken Hollandia Rapportarchief 2.10.25, inv. 253.

De Bruijn, Jan Victor 1939b. *Verslag van een tocht van Enarotali via Itodah, Janopa, Obaja, Kamere naar Orawja door den Adspirant-Controleur der Wisselmeren Dr. J.V. de Bruijn van 4 Mei 1939–14 Mei 1939*. ARA 2.10.25, inv. 254.

De Bruijn, Jan Victor 1939c. *Verslag van een tocht naar het brongebied van de Edere of Elegeboe-rivier in Centraal Nieuw Guinea door den Adspirant-Controleur der Wisselmeren Dr. J.V. de Bruijn van 29 Juli 1939 tot 7 Augustus 1939*. ARA 2.10.25, inv. 255.

De Bruijn, Jan Victor 1941. *Verslag van een tocht naar Beura, het stroomgebied van de Beurong en Ielop, het stroomgebied van de Ielorong in Centraal Nieuw Guinea door den Controleur der Wisselmeren Dr. J.V. de Bruijn van 9 juni 1941 tot 7 augustus 1941.* ARA 2.10.25, inv. 256.

Dening, Greg 1980. *Islands and Beaches: Discourse on a Silent Land.* Honolulu: University of Hawaii Press.

Derix, Jan 1987. *Bapa Papoea; Jan P.K. van Eechoud, Een Biografie.* Venlo: Van Spijk.

Derrida, Jacques 1982. 'Signature, Event, Context'. Trans. Weber, Samuel, *Margins of Philosophy.* Chicago: University of Chicago Press, 307–330.

Derrida, Jacques 1986. 'Declarations of Independence'. Trans. Keenan, Thomas and Pepper, T. *New Political Science* 15: 11.

Diamond, Jared 2012. *The World Until Yesterday: What Can We Learn from Traditional Societies?* New York: Viking.

Drooglever, Pieter J. 2005. *Een Daad van Vrije Keuze: De Papoea's van Westelijk Nieuw-Guinea en de Grenzen van het Zelfbeschikkingsrecht.* Instituut voor Nederlandse Geschiedenis. Amsterdam: Boom.

Gammage, Bill 1998. *The Sky Travellers: Journeys in New Guinea 1938-1939.* Melbourne: Melbourne University Press.

Giay, Benny 1995. *Zacheus Pakage and His Communities: Indigenous Religious Discourse, Socio-Political Resistance, and Ethnohistory of the Me of Irian Jaya.* PhD thesis, Free University, Amsterdam.

Goffman, Erving 1986 [1974]. *Frame Analysis: An Essay on the Organization of Experience.* Cambridge: Harvard University Press.

Haenen, Paul 1992. *Weefsels van Wederkerigheid: Sociale Structuur bij de Moi van Irian Jaya.* PhD thesis, University of Nijmegen.

Heidegger, Martin 1977. 'The Question Concerning Technology'. In Heidegger, Martin, *The Question Concerning Technology and Other Essays.* New York: Harper and Row, 3–35.

Hume, David 1988 [1748]. *An Enquiry Concerning Human Understanding.* Amherst: Prometheus Books.

Hutchins, Edwin 1995. *Cognition in the Wild.* Boston: MIT Press.

Lee, Benjamin 1997. *Talking Heads: Language, Metalanguage and the Semiotics of Subjectivity.* Durham: Duke University Press.

Lubbock, John 1865. *Pre-Historic Times, As Illustrated by Ancient Remains, and the Manners and Customs of Modern Savages*. London and Edinburgh: Williams and Norgate.

Mauss, Marcel and Schlanger, Nathan (eds) 2006. *Techniques, Technology, and Civilisation*. Oxford: Berghahn Books.

Meijer Ranneft and Johan Everhard 1952. 'Memorie van Overgave van de Onderafdeling Wisselmeren, 1 November 1948 t/m 19 September 1952'. ARA 2.10.25, inv. 257.

Mueggler, Eric 2011. *The Paper Road: Archive and Experience in the Botanical Exploration of West China and Tibet*. Berkeley: University of California Press.

Mumford, Lewis 1967. *Technics and Human Development. The Myth of the Machine* Vol. 1. New York: Harvest Books.

Pospisil, Leopold 1963. *The Kapauku Papuans of West New Guinea*. New York: Rinehart and Wilson.

Riddington, Robin 1999. 'Dogs, Snares, and Cartridge Belts: The Poetics of a Northern Athapaskan Narrative Technology'. In Dobres, M.-A. and Hoffman, C.R. (eds), *The Social Dynamics of Technology: Practice, Politics and World Views*. Washington: Smithsonian Institution, 167–118.

Rutherford, Danilyn 2009. 'Sympathy, State-building, and the Experience of Empire'. *Cultural Anthropology* 24(1): 1–32.

Rutherford, Danilyn 2012. *Laughing at Leviathan: Sovereignty and Audience in West Papua*. Chicago: University of Chicago Press.

Spyer, Patricia 1998. 'The Tooth of Time, or, Taking a Look at the "Look" of Clothing in Late Nineteen-Century Aru'. In Spyer, Patricia (ed.), *Border Fetishisms: Objects in Unstable Places*. London: Routledge, 150–182.

Stiegler, Bernard 1998. *Technics and Time, I: The Fault of Epimetheus*. Stanford: Stanford University Press.

Timmer, Jaap 2000. *Living with Intricate Futures: Order and Confusion in Imyan Worlds, Irian Jaya, Indonesia*. Nijmegen: Centre for Pacific and Asian Studies, University of Nijmegen.

Trouillot, Michel-Rolph 1991. 'Anthropology and the Savage Slot'. In Fox, Richard G. (ed.), *Recapturing Anthropology: Working in the Present*. Santa Fe: School for American Research Press, 17–44.

van Eechoud, Jan Piet Karel 1938. 'Verslag van de Exploratie naar het Wisselmerengebied van 14 Mei – 14 November 1938 en Doorsteek van Paniai/Wisselmeer naar de Monding van de Siriwo van 15 November tot 1 December 1938. Onderleiding van J.P.K. van Eechoud, Commissaris van Politie 2e-Klasse'. ARA Min van Kol. Kantor Bevolkingszaken Hollandia Rapportarchief 2.10.25, inv. 246.

van Eechoud, Jan Piet Karel 1953. *Met Kapmes en Kompas Door Nieuw-Guinea*. Amsterdam: Uitgeverij van H.C. de Boer, Jr.

van Emmerik, E.M. 1953. 'Rapport over de Kapaukoe'. ARA 2.10.25, inv. 258.

Wollaston, Alexander Frederick Richmond 1912. *Pygmies and Papuans: The Stone Age Today in Dutch New Guinea*. London: Smith and Elder.

YouTube 2008. *First Contact (Highlands Trilogy) – PREVIEW*. http://www.youtube.com/watch?v=2Y5rC7kDx3o (accessed 23 August 2012).

3. From Primitive Other to Papuan Self: Korowai Engagement with Ideologies of Unequal Human Worth in Encounters with Tourists, State Officials and Education

Rupert Stasch

On 12 December 2012, an Indonesian Air Force helicopter flew 230 miles north from the coastal city of Merauke to an unfinished dirt airstrip in the middle of the forested territory of Korowai people of Papua's southern lowlands. Korowai number only about 4,000 persons, but from among the many different peoples of Papua they have become uniquely prominent in the global mass media, where they are known for their 'treehouse' architecture and their supposed 'Stone Age' isolation from markets and the state. Their location, spread across the upper lowland watersheds of several rivers, and the lack of extractive resources there, have indeed meant that the Indonesian state has little direct administrative presence on their land. The helicopter expedition at the end of 2012 was unusual.

The aircraft carried the head of a government agency known as UP4B, or the Unit for the Acceleration of Development in the Provinces of Papua and West Papua. Indonesian president Susilo Bambang Yudhoyono created this agency in 2011, with the charge of rectifying the fact that most Papuans' lives had not actually been improved by the US$3 billion in 'Special Autonomy' supplementary funding sent to Papua since 2001. At the helicopter's destination, meanwhile, airstrip construction had been underway for two years. The project was led by Western Dani men of a highland church called GIDI (Ipenburg 2008: 372; Pagawak 2007), who started missionising this part of the Korowai area in 2005. One of the highlanders had brokered the government visit from his office in town, and sent word by radio a day in advance about the helicopter's arrival. When the aircraft landed, the agency head and his entourage were met by 200 Korowai in a martial dance formation. Korowai men performed cycles of synchronised ululation and snapping of bowstrings, a dance genre normally enacted during ceremonial feasting or feuds. Most Korowai on the scene wore no clothing except traditional-dress genital coverings and festive adornments, though the government party did not know that the performers had only removed their shirts and shorts earlier that morning.

The encounter soon transitioned into an exchange of objects and talk between spokesmen from each side, who earnestly stated how important the others were to themselves. The Javanese head of UP4B, a retired army Lieutenant General named Bambang Darmono, stated: 'I am so truly sad I am almost crying, that this nation has existed for almost seventy years and it turns out there are people who still live naked … I thank God that I have had the opportunity to visit the Stone Korowai tribe who live as though in the Stone Age'.[1] A senior Korowai man gave Darmono a series of emblematic artifacts, including a stone axe, a bow and arrow, house thatch, a wild yam, a palm leaf base, an animal tooth necklace, a bamboo tobacco pipe, a fire-saw, a bird-of-paradise skin headdress and a string bag. Via a younger man who translated into Indonesian, the elder explained the gifts' significance, namely that Darmono would 'join in experiencing our people's hardships' and be moved to give Korowai better substitutes. Handing over the stone axe, the man said, 'I now present this to Mr Boss [Bapak Kepala] so it can be replaced with cutting tools that are easier to use for felling trees and splitting logs.' Giving the palm leaf base, the man explained, 'This palm leaf base is used for eating sago. We present it to Sir, so Sir can replace it with plates.' He characterised the bow and arrow as signs of endemic violence and cannibalism, and their handover as an act of self-pacification:

This is for hunting, for shooting pigs and shooting cassowaries, and for killing people. If someone elopes with someone's daughter, this is for fighting. And regularly when people want to eat someone, need to kill a witch, I routinely use this to kill. And feuding, here in the Korowai area, [we] use this all the time. What this arrow here is for is, I go on killing people and eating them. Up until now, when I give it up. I want to give it to Sir.[2]

---

1   Sungguh saya sedih dan mau menangis, hampir 70 tahun negara ini ada ternyata masih ada yang hidup telanjang …Saya bersyukur kepada Tuhan telah mendapat kesempatan bisa datang di kelompok Suku Korowai Batu yang hidup layaknya zaman batu (www.up4b.go.id/index.php/prioritas-p4b/10-sosial-budaya/item/108-suku-korowai-batu-bangun-lapangan-terbang-dengan-kapak-batu). Across this chapter, I distinguish Indonesian speech in underlining from Korowai speech in italics. All URLs about the Darmono visit cited in this and later notes were accessed 28 February 2013.

2   The first three of the senior Korowai man's statements are from UP4B publicity reports, where it is the younger Korowai man's translation into Indonesian that is written down (altered by dialect features of the standard Indonesian spoken by agency staff). The phrase 'join in experiencing our people's hardships' (agar bapak bisa ikut merasakan bagaimana susahnya rakyat kami) is from www.up4b.go.id/index.php/prioritas-p4b/10-sosial-budaya/item/116-pertemuan-dua-kepala-yang-sarat-dengan-pesan-perubahan. The statement about the stone axe was Sekarang saya serahkan ke Bapak Kepala agar diganti dengan alat tebang lebih mudah untuk digunakan tebang pohon dan belah kayu (www.up4b.go.id/index.php/prioritas-p4b/10-sosial-budaya/item/100-kunjungan-kepala-up4b-dan-sebuah-ketelanjangan-kehidupan-suku-korowai). The statement about the leaf base was Pelepah ini, biasa digunakan untuk alas makan sagu, kami serahkan kepada bapak, agar bapak mengganti ini dengan piring (www.up4b.go.id/index.php/prioritas-p4b/10-sosial-budaya/item/116-pertemuan-dua-kepala-yang-sarat-dengan-pesan-perubahan). The block quotation comes from a recording of the translator's speech in a news segment about Darmono's visit available at www.youtube.com/watch?v=q1uNZiiKEJ4, originally broadcast on the Papuan regional station of state-owned TVRI. The translator's words, at 5:30, were: Ini busur. Panah. Ini, pakai ini berburu, panah kasuari, dan pakai ini bunuh orang. Bawa lari orang punya anak dan merontak, pakai ini bunuh orang. Ya, biasa orang suka makan orang, suangi, bunuh, biasa pakai ini saya bunuh. Dan berperang, di daerah Korowai ini, pakai ini

Figure 3.1. Danuwage village, July 2011. The airstrip is out of frame to the right. Aerial photos in UP4B's press release cropped out the large missionary residence at left.

Source: R. Stasch.

Figure 3.2. Ten Western Dani evangelists at the Danuwage airstrip, July 2011, with six Korowai in the distant background and at right.

Source: R. Stasch.

---

terus. Yang pakai panah ini, saya bunuh orang makan, terus. Sampai sekarang, saya lepas, mau kasih Bapak. His discourse reflects interference from Korowai grammar and pragmatics. On Korowai bilingualism in Indonesian, see Stasch (2007).

Accepting the gifts, Darmono elaborated on the same transactional logic: 'My brothers and sisters whom I deeply love, all this that the Tribal Chief has given me is a symbol that the Tribal Chief has given to me the responsibility to ensure that this Stone Korowai community experiences and obtains development in future days.'[3] He listed infrastructure projects Korowai would receive, such as asphalting of the airstrip and construction of a school and clinic. Then his group flew away, without having walked the quarter-mile to Danuwage village, where in addition to houses of Korowai and Dani residents they would have seen the dwelling of an American missionary family who had lived there part-time since 2008, and who had coincidentally flown out by floatplane the previous day to evacuate an acutely ill Korowai woman (Figures 3.1 and 3.2). In the following weeks, UP4B staff publicised details of the visit via television and newspaper. Twenty months later, in August 2014, a government helicopter flew heavy equipment to the airstrip and a work crew began the asphalting job, as one of UP4B's showcase development projects.

What is most striking about the December 2012 encounter is its high degree of impromptu coordination between people who understood little about the wider background to each other's involvement. Central to this harmonisation was the category 'primitive', functioning within an overall logic of theatricalised exchange of 'primitivity' for 'development'. The category 'primitive' was signified not only through linguistic terms like 'Stone Age' (Zaman Batu) but also through more-than-linguistic signifiers such as material artifacts and bodily violence.

My topic in this chapter is how Korowai take up the category of the primitive as a self-understanding, acting toward and through this category in their relations with outsiders newly central to their world. Power imbalances between Korowai and outsiders mean that it would be valuable to analyse the category of the primitive as it functions for those who project it onto others in the first place (something partly addressed by Stasch 2011b and 2014a). We have already seen that Darmono understands civilising of primitives to be a national imperative and a measure of Indonesia's true existence.[4] He invests great significance in

---

3   Saudara-saudaraku yang sangat saya cintai, apa yang diberikan Kepala Suku kepada saya, ini adalah lambang bahwa Kepala Suku memberikan tanggung jawab kepada saya untuk membuat masyarakat Korowai Batu ini merasakan dan mendapatkan pembangunan di hari-hari yang akan datang (at 8:10 in the video cited in note 2).

4   The theme of primitivity as a foundational site of the nation is further exemplified in Darmono's statement that 'I repeat, the nation has to be present here to lift up the lives of Stone Korowai to become a good community' (Sekali lagi negara, harus hadir di tempat ini untuk mengangkat kehidupan Korowai Batu menjadi masyarakat yang baik, www.up4b.go.id/index.php/prioritas-p4b/10-sosial-budaya/item/100-kunjungan-kepala-up4b-dan-sebuah-ketelanjangan-kehidupan-suku-korowai). See also a PR officer's formulation that 'Among the Stone Korowai community we may encounter the original people of Papua in the true sense. Unblemished and without artifice. Truly authentic. In the aforementioned image of authenticity we encounter a different face of Indonesia' (Di komunitas Korowai Batu kita bisa menjumpai makna orang asli Papua. Tanpa noda, tanpa rekayasa. Sunguh asli. Dalam pancaran keasliannya tersebut kita menjumpai wajah Indonesia yang

nudity, stone tool technology and 'tribal chiefs' (kepala suku), stereotypes deserving analysis. Also deserving analysis is how the figure of the primitive gives officials a role of paternalistic benefactor, obscuring harm done to Papuan people by actual state policies and practices. Yet in my fieldwork, I have been struck by the importance of the primitive as a *self-understanding* taken up by those to whom it is applied. While there is much scholarship on primitivist thought as projected onto others by those who see themselves as 'civilised', relatively little ethnographic attention has been given to reception of primitivist frameworks among people whom the frameworks are about (but see Gow 1993; Albert and Ramos 2000; Knauft 2002, 2007; Causey 2003; Pandian 2009). What the story of Darmono's visit to Korowai makes clear is that primitivist ideology is an important path of actual relating *between* stereotypers and the people stereotyped, thanks to Korowai perceiving and adopting outsiders' stereotypy of them, and actively performing in its terms.

Yet the idea of the primitive may differ between those who project it onto others, and those who hold it as a self-understanding. As part of my analysis, I also trace distinctive sensibilities structuring emergent Korowai concepts of the primitive. This is one level on which the comparative relevance of my discussion extends beyond the issue of primitivist ideology alone (important enough as it is), to take in more general questions of interethnic hierarchy and state formation. Ideas of primitivity are centred on claims about human otherness and unequal human worth. What has most heavily organised Korowai people's adoption of ideas of the primitive is their own sensibilities about social inequality, and about transacting with others across disparities of history and value.

The fluidity with which Korowai and state actors today relate is theoretically surprising, because Korowai in their own social relations uphold a radically egalitarian political ethos that could be described as 'anti-state' or 'anarchist' (following Clastres 1977; Scott 2009). For example, they previously had no named roles of political leadership, and they are very quick to rebuke anyone among themselves who tells others what to do, has more possessions than others, or claims to be better than others. Like other egalitarians, Korowai 'vote with their feet'. Their past extreme residential dispersion was motivated by the idea that dwelling apart allows people to live by their own wills (*xul-melun*, lit. 'thoughts'), whereas aggregating in one place would lead to conflicts over adultery, theft or other acts of one person unduly imposing on another (Stasch 2008, 2009, 2013).

---

beda, www.jurnas.com/halaman/12/2012-12-26/230221). Numerous publicity documents paint Darmono and the Korowai 'tribal chief' as analogous figures within their respective communities, and emphasise Korowai people's instant embrace of Darmono as a patriarchal authority. This suggests that the fantasy of an archaic hierarchical polity ruled by a 'tribal chief' embodying exceptional masculine virtue is a projection of modern bureaucratic authority's own wishful self-understanding.

This chapter thus addresses a paradoxical question of how deep commitment to an anti-state political ethos can lead people toward the state rather than away from it. In the Korowai case, a first part of the answer lies in specific structural features of the state they are engaged with. Under Suharto, the Indonesian state was pervasively clientelistic (Aspinall 2013). But recent transformations have meant that in Papua specifically, the conditions for clientelism have greatly intensified. In all of Papua's immigrant-dominated towns, there are still hardly any Papuan-owned shops, service establishments, construction or transport companies, or other commercial enterprises involving fixed assets. Immigrants also dominate economically across the network of smaller administrative and commercial centres stretching out to the rural, gardening-based hinterland where Papuans are an overwhelming demographic majority. Alongside continued marginalisation from private enterprise, though, Papuans' situation with respect to *state* resources has shifted. The Special Autonomy law of 2001 required that high-tier civil offices be filled by Papuans, and that tax revenues from Freeport's Grasberg mine and BP's Tangguh gas project be primarily returned to regional coffers rather than absorbed in Jakarta. Meanwhile, Papua has also seen an extraordinary proliferation of new civil territorial units, at nested levels of 'province', 'regency', 'subdistrict' and 'village'. For example, the former total of nine regencies has now been remade into 40, with a further 30 soon to be instituted. This trend has followed an Indonesia-wide decentralisation policy, but subdivision in Papua has specifically functioned to counteract separatism and the power shifts entailed in Special Autonomy. It does so by dividing Papuan blocs from each other and by increasing civil servant jobs. In Papua these jobs already accounted for 30 per cent of non-gardening employment, but in the first years of the subdivision process they tripled in number, from 37,000 to 114,419 (Booth 2011: 44; Institute for Policy Analysis of Conflict 2013: 5). Even more prominent has been the proliferation and localisation of high offices such as 'Regent' (Bupati) and 'subdistrict head' (Camat or Distrik). The new offices are lucratively funded, but have little established bureaucratic infrastructure beneath them and receive no effective capacity-building guidance. Thus decentralisation and increased financial resources have led not to improved delivery of state services, but to intensified corruption and clientelism, such as in the form of locally ascended civil leaders giving cash and consumables to outlying rural constituents in direct exchange for electoral support. As McWilliam (2011: 163) puts it,

> For the majority of the population in these areas [on Papua's administrative periphery], engagement with formal government is severely constrained by its practical invisibility and inaction for much of the time. Occasionally, there are flurries of performative symbolism when officialdom is on show or election campaigns are in the air, but the presence of everyday government in action is patchy and inconsistent

at best. Formal government on the margins, therefore, appears to be as much about the projection and regulatory intent of state power as it is about its practical implementation and tangible benefits.

Or as Anderson (2013) observes, 'district proliferation and the creation of new government offices often have nothing to do with the provision of services', with 'many local governments … essentially functioning as nothing but distribution systems for cash, favours, and no-show jobs' (see also Timmer 2007; Widjojo 2014: 513).

Whatever the motives of central state actors, the goal of having new administrative units is now endorsed by most Papuan politicians and by local rural populations. The puzzle of Korowai people's active embrace of state power is in this way partly explained by top-down transformations in the nature of the state they are meeting. The new clientelistic and locally accessible state is a transactional other whom Korowai can more recognisably find their way to, through their own logics of exchange-based kinship.

But the preceding sketch of the structural context to what is today happening in the Korowai lands is only a preliminary to my main topic, the Korowai side of the 'working misunderstanding' that unfolds in scenes of encounter like what took place at the Danuwage airstrip. There are three ethnographic areas I examine in the rest of this chapter to give evidence that Korowai uptake of ideas of the primitive are driven and shaped by their own egalitarian political order. These areas are performance of primitivity for international tourists, performances for government heads, and migration to town for education.

Performing the primitive toward tourists

There is no such thing as 'primitive' people, except as created by other people's *primitivism*. Primitivism is any cultural framework that typifies a set of others as incarnating an archaic condition of humanity radically different from the condition of the stereotypers themselves. Global metropolitan publics today widely hold a model of a Manichaean contrast of 'primitive' and 'civilised' poles of humanity. This model is indebted to 19th-century anthropological theories of social evolution for its sense that the 'civilised' pole is history's telos. Additionally, this globally dominant primitivist model has strong if submerged overlaps with histories of racism and racial theory, as well as connections to the crypto-evolutionism of 'development'. Although ideological structures of 'primitivism' are my main focus across this chapter, one effect of looking at stereotyped people's own uptake of such ideologies is that the inter-implication of primitivist, evolutionary, racial and developmentalist models are made more explicit than usual.

Figure 3.3. House of Melanux Waüop and her relatives, 2007.

Source: R. Stasch.

Korowai over the last 25 years have been the focus of a boom in primitivist tourism. They have been visited by thousands of travellers, coming from virtually all European states and most European settler colonies, as well as many East and Southeast Asian countries. Engagement with tourists has, for many Korowai, been more direct than engagement with state actors. It has been through tourism that ideas of the primitive have initially grown to importance in their social world.

Because the primitive is defined as a quality of authenticity and purity relative to something else that is corrupt, it is in the category's own logic to elicit a fractal subdivision of that to which it is applied. Metonymic parts are constantly hived off as *true* paragons of the primitive type. This is what has led to the boom in tourism to the Korowai area specifically. At least since the Cook voyages, Pacific peoples have had special standing as civilised Europe's radical others. Across the 1800s, the somewhat open intellectual foment provoked by Pacific cultural diversity hardened into fixed taxonomies of inferiority and superiority, and a new racialising distinction between Melanesia and Polynesia helped stabilise southwest Pacific peoples' status as the truly archaic pole of humankind (Smith

1985, 1992; Douglas 1999, 2011; Douglas and Ballard 2008). An idea of New Guineans as the ultimate primitives deepened across the 20th century. Within travel discourse of the last several decades, there has been a tendency for the Indonesian-controlled western half of the island to be portrayed as the ultimate paragon of primitivity even relative to the island's eastern half, independent Papua New Guinea. And within Papua, treehouse-building Korowai have now become famous as the ultimate of the ultimate, possibly the most iconic figures of the primitive globally today (Figure 3). Tourists' meetings with Korowai have an aura of deep meaningfulness, because they experience Korowai as embodying the cosmological type of 'primitive humanity' on a world historical scale.

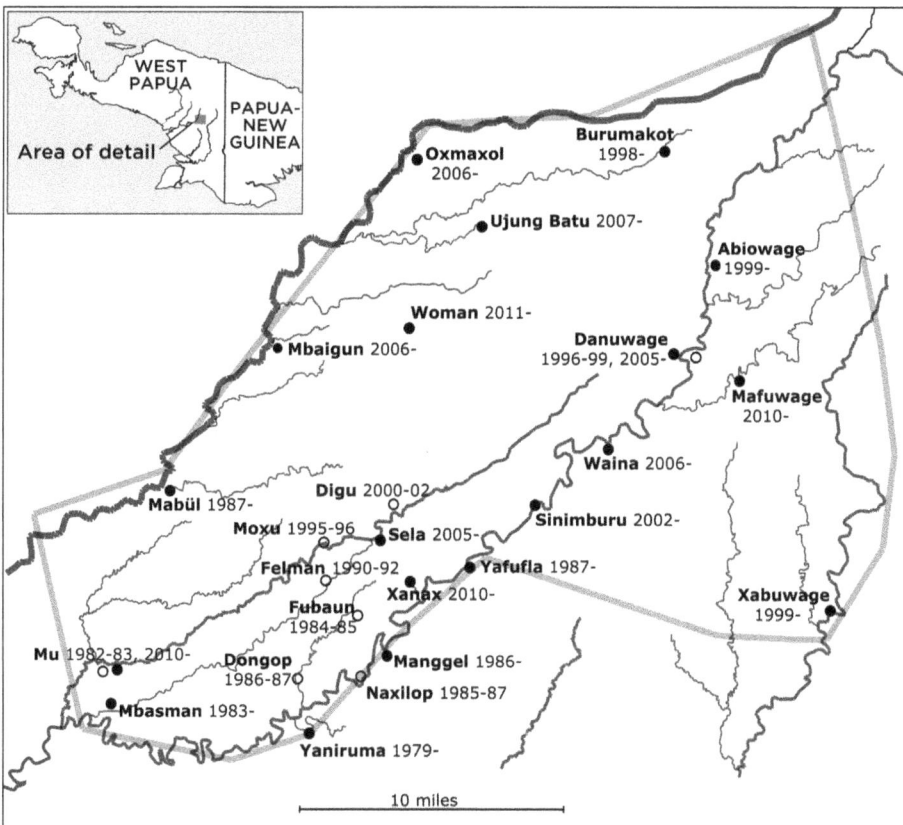

Figure 3.4. Korowai lands in West Papua, showing villages created since the founding of Yaniruma. Extant villages shown by solid dots, abandoned ones by circles.

Source: R. Stasch.

Tour guides started bringing groups by boat to the southwestern edge of the Korowai area in the mid-1980s. Until 1978, when Dutch missionaries established the post of Yaniruma, Korowai had had no regular interaction with long-distance strangers. It was around 1990, at the beginning of a 10-year hiatus in missionary presence, that international tour groups began steadily travelling to the Korowai area, including by Cessna flights to the Yaniruma airstrip. Also in the 1990s, Korowai began to be featured in international mass media representations, such as the *Outside Magazine* story 'No Cannibal Jokes, Please: Upriver into the Swamps of Irian Jaya, and Back in Time' (Cahill 1992) and the *Arts & Entertainment Channel* film 'Treehouse People: Cannibal Justice' (also distributed as 'Lords of the Garden', Hallet 1994). The most consequential media event was *National Geographic*'s photo essay 'Irian Jaya's People of the Trees' (Steinmetz 1996), which shaped the expectations of many later visitors. Passages about how to visit Korowai and their Kombai neighbours began appearing in editions of *Indonesia Handbook* and *New Guinea: Journey into the Stone Age*, and later in the Indonesia guidebooks of *Rough Guide* and *Lonely Planet* (e.g. Dalton 1991: 1016–17; Müller 1990: 46; Backshall et al. 1999: 926; Berkmoes et al. 2010: 816). Professional guides recall that during tourism's peak around 1997, they would routinely cross paths with each other at the Yaniruma airstrip, bringing their groups in and out of the region. The 1990s also saw continuation of a process of village formation earlier initiated by the missionaries, in a downstream to upstream direction (Figure 4). The earlier pattern of dispersed residence on patriclan-owned forest territories gave way to a new practice of alternation between lone forest houses and the new centralised settlements (Stasch 2013).

Wider geopolitical events meant that few tourists visited from 1998 to 2002, and the flow of visitors has been erratic even since this temporary crash, limited above all by the high cost of airplane or boat charters to the area. Trips by media professionals, though, have increased in quantity, with a total of about 50 professional films now having been made about Korowai or Kombai. Film production particularly intensified with the global rise in popularity of reality TV shows in which home-country presenters 'go native' in a primitivism-marked destination. Two productions in this genre that were widely seen in English-language television markets, for example, were a 2005 Kombai episode of the wider series *Tribe* (also titled *Going Tribal*), and the 2007 series *Living with the Kombai Tribe: The Adventures of Mark and Olly* (BBC/Discovery Channel 2005; Cicada Productions/Travel Channel 2007; see also Hoesterey 2012). Similar programs have since been made by crews from Finland, France, Germany, Italy, Slovakia, Australia, Switzerland, Brazil, Vietnam, Japan, Denmark, Korea, Spain, Vietnam, Hungary and Slovenia. Korowai treehouse construction was the culminating sequence in the 'Jungles' episode of the 2011 BBC blockbuster series *Human Planet*. Photos of Korowai are featured in Sebastião Salgado's *Genesis* project that has been circulating internationally in prominent exhibition venues since 2013, and in the heavily publicised Curtis-style project of Jimmy Nelson titled *Before They Pass Away* (Salgado 2013: 136–49; Nelson 2013).

The power of foreigners' experience of Korowai as primitive flows from an array of attributes that they project onto Korowai or selectively emphasise about them, and that reinforce each other in an overall feeling of coherence. One focus is treehouses, which activate more general primitivist ideas of animality, closeness to nature, childhood innocence and cultural primevalness (Stasch 2011a). Media representations especially play up cannibalism, while tourists at large dwell on themes of violence and danger. Above all, visitors are concerned with the idea that Korowai are isolated from the global consumer economy, produce their livelihood directly from their forest surroundings, and have not previously seen whites. All these motifs intertwine with an idea that Korowai have not changed across time, and incarnate a deep past of humanity at large. Many of the different motifs are concretely summed up in nudity. Absence of imported clothes is the most prominent issue tourists attend to in judging specific Korowai people's match to a primitivist ideal (Stasch 2014b).

The character of the primitive as a collective representation with a life of its own in tourists' societies is particularly clear from regularities of their discourse that poorly match actual Korowai lives. Tourists and media professionals regularly identify Korowai as 'hunter-gatherers', even though there are domesticated pigs and large banana gardens right beneath their houses, and the sago stands providing their staple food are anthropogenic. Tourists commonly describe specific elderly men as 'chiefs', just as Darmono used the Indonesian expression kepala suku 'tribal chief'. Yet there are no endogenous-named leadership roles in Korowai life and no tendencies of gerontocratic authority. A more complex example is the rise of the English-language phrase 'Stone Korowai' and its Indonesian analog Korowai Batu, used as ethnic designations for Korowai who live in an upstream direction. During the 1990s and early 2000s, upstream Korowai were understood to be less contacted by outsiders than their downstream counterparts. There is no Korowai-language expression meaning 'Stone Korowai' that is used to designate a subpart of the Korowai population. But in the 1990s when tourists repeatedly asked to meet Korowai who use stone axes, Indonesian and international tour guides, along with certain Korowai intermediaries, innovated the Indonesian-language expression meaning 'Stone Korowai', to talk about Korowai who live to the northeast. The expression took off as a floating designation that could be used for any Korowai whom tourists were seeking to meet, and who lived farther upstream than the downstream villages where tourists first arrived in the area. The expression is used by tourists and guides as if it is the proper name of a definite Korowai ethnic subgroup, but the category only exists in tourism and other new contexts of interaction with radical foreigners (like Darmono) in which there is pressure to identify a metonymic subpart more truly exemplifying the primitive type. The attraction of 'Stone Korowai' for outsiders is boosted by the way this label makes the iconic primitivist attribute of stone tool technology the very *name* of the people the outsiders seek to encounter.

Across the above-outlined tourism history, meanwhile, Korowai have acquired and performed an idea of their own primitiveness that is cognate to tourist primitivism, but that reflects distinctive Korowai cultural sensibilities about issues of social inferiority and superiority. Two patterns I will first explore are a cultural emphasis on material objects as the truth of relations, and an emphasis on meeting others on their own transactional terms. These are both exemplified, for example, in a response to tourists that Korowai widely report themselves as having, namely a desire to create exchange relations with the wealthy foreigners. As one woman said: 'When Whites first came, people were scared and took off. Now they say, "What will we give?" If we get money, we'll be happy. If we bring them produce and they buy it, then the sellers are happy'. This reaction of 'What will we give?' reflects feelings that exchange of material objects is the main question of social relations in general, and that the appropriate response to an encounter with people possessed of wealth is to try to get into the transactional stream with them by meeting their desires.

This pattern of seeking to meet tourists on their own transactional terms goes beyond objects to the staging of performances. A revealing detail here is widespread Korowai knowledge of the word asli, which in standard Indonesian means 'authentic, original, indigenous, primitive'. Through tour guides, Korowai have learned this word as a description of the people tourists seek to meet, but what Korowai understand asli to mean is simply 'nude', in the sense of not wearing imported clothing. Korowai say that tourists come to visit them because they want to see people who do not have clothing but instead wear fibre skirts, rattan waistbands and leaf penis wrappers, since the tourists have never experienced such conditions before. The Korowai focus on material objects here is parallel to tourists' own material focus: tourists actually are intensely scanning Korowai bodies for the material signs on them. And yet for tourists, material objects and the visible condition of nudity are penumbral to a larger spiritual or metaphysical presence that primitive humans are thought to incarnate, while Korowai are disarmingly direct in locating the significance in the material conditions themselves.

The most common way Korowai seek to meet tourists on their own transactional terms is to hide away factory-made clothing and other imported manufactured goods shortly before tourists arrive, much as in the Gary Larson 'Far Side' cartoon showing two islanders hiding away their TV and VCR while anthropologists approach. This staging of an appearance of primitivity would be morally disturbing to tourists and their compatriots, who interpret actions through a cultural obsession with 'authenticity' or 'sincerity' (Trilling 1972). The staging does not trouble Korowai, who instead say that what would be immoral is *not* presenting tourists with the experience they have been led to expect. Hosting tourists, Korowai also allow the visitors' desires to organise what activities the Korowai hosts will carry out for the time the tourists are present. Yet these ways of relating to tourists' presence are not radically different from Korowai people's strong concern in relations among themselves with solicitousness to the other's distance. For example, feast transactions involve elaborate work of feast owners managing appearances and communications with invitees, to try to bring about an eventual exchange of food for dance performances, across gaps of geography and political independence (Stasch 2003). The transactional outcome of the feast process *is* the truth of that process, rather than the relation being riven by anxieties of authentic meaning different from appearances.

Running through the 'What will we give?' response to tourists is a more basic stereotype of tourists as wealthy, which is also a good illustration of the Korowai focus on material articles as the truth of persons and their relations. The stereotype of tourist wealth is based partly on direct observation of tourists' objects and money during their visits. But the stereotype also plays out in the further form of a model of tourists' home country lives, according to which the foreigners consume piles of food and money that are 'just there' (*xondüp*) in their houses. This is a canny long-distance insight into the organisation of capitalist consumer culture, but also an inverted projection of Korowai people's object-led focus in understanding social relations, and their ambivalent sense of the defining centrality of outdoor toil in their own lives.

Fantasising the tourist other as living in an unalienated material utopia of ready-to-hand consumables, Korowai also reverse the evaluative hierarchy of their past first categorisations of foreigners. In a common cross-cultural pattern, Korowai refer to themselves ethnically by two synonymous words meaning 'human' (*yanop* and *mayox*). Prior to new foreigners' intrusion over recent decades, these words stood in relations of paradigmatic contrast with proper names for neighbouring ethnolinguistic groups, but also with the term *laleo*, which designates a non-human demonic monster people are thought to become after death. Korowai conceive these monsters as an ethnic population. They think the demonic dead are repulsive and dangerous, and they regularly experience these monstrous dead as intruding into living people's lives. When Whites, Indonesians and strange Papuans started intruding in the 1970s and 1980s, Korowai called them all the 'demonic dead', and initially thought of the intruders as non-human, by contrast with Korowai people's own resolutely 'human' selves. This 'human' versus 'demon' ethnic polarity was highly pejorative toward the foreigners. But with the rise of discourses of foreigners' utopian material conditions, Korowai have gone from being a superior 'human' centre in contrast to an inferior periphery of the demonic dead, to the reverse situation of even referring to themselves as 'not human', in contrast to a superior centre elsewhere. The fact that 'human' and 'demon' already existed as a hierarchical framework for thinking about ethnic difference helped make this primitivist way of thinking familiar in advance, even though the primitivist formation radically reverses earlier evaluations.

These evaluative dimensions of Korowai orientations to tourist wealth also involve a further broad cultural sensibility that has shaped Korowai performances of themselves as primitive, namely an ethic of valuing self-deprecation in exchange. When I ask Korowai why tourists come visit, they sometimes say it is because tourists have heard that Korowai live without money and articles, and so out of love and pity the tourists come to divide out these things to them. As one man put it, 'We [Korowai] live here empty handed, and so they say "You people are without articles", and they come divide out to us.' This representation is half accurate: it is true that tourists come because Korowai lack articles, but it is not part of tourists' self-understanding that they therefore visit Korowai in order to give them the articles they lack. In Korowai kinship, though, it is a prototypic act for one person to be lacking in articles and another to be moved by pity and love to give something to him or her. This is the model Korowai project onto tourists when they imagine the foreigners come for the express purpose of giving articles. On this understanding, there is a relation-making value to emphasising one's baseness. Under an egalitarian ethos, to put oneself down can be to ask for a relation. Claiming inferiority means *not* claiming to stand out as better than other people, but instead putting those people in a position of being moved by one's own deprivation to share wealth and create equality.

Performing the primitive toward government officials

This ethic of self-lowering, along with the focus on material objects and on meeting others on their terms, are amply apparent also in Korowai self-primitivising performances toward state actors. Missionaries were more important to Korowai than government personnel in the 1980s, and tourists were the biggest foreign presence across the 1990s. But engagement with state actors has recently intensified, and the primitivist formation that Korowai first developed in tourism contexts has migrated to relations with the state. While Darmono's helicopter visit to Danuwage airstrip was novel in both the elite level of officeholder it involved and in his actual travel to the Korowai area, the encounter followed a script that has circulated widely among Korowai since about 2005, albeit more as an idea than a directly enacted reality. As Korowai anticipate them, these encounters focus on the figure of a 'Big Head' or 'Big Boss' (*xabian-tale*), a new term for all government officials.[5] Or the encounters focus specifically on the figure of a Bupati or 'Regent', who in the Indonesian hierarchy is the head of a Kabupaten or 'regency', between the higher level of 'province' and the lower one of 'subdistrict' (kecamatan, distrik).

For example, in 2007 a woman told me about work of grass-cutting undertaken by residents of a village who had heard that the Bupati was going to come visit. She explained, 'The Bupati will come and everyone will dance celebratorily. These women [the speaker's friends] will take off their clothes. They are doing the work because the Bupati will see it.' I asked her what a 'Bupati' is, to which she replied:

> We haven't seen. We don't know. But we take hold of this work, and he'll come, and divide out money, and we'll get clothes. They [Korowai] dance in formation and they [government officials] regularly pay them. The Bupati is going to pay for the work and the *xasam* [genre of martial dance]. He will see that these people live without money and he'll divide it out. He'll say, 'What money will they buy clothes with? It's rather like forest, it's rather like it's not even a village. They don't know razor blades and fishing line, shorts and shirts, rice and noodles, steel machetes and axes. I'll give them money, and they'll make the village big.'

Another person quoted a visiting Bupati's expected self-account by referencing the split rattan loops that are metonymic of male traditional dress: 'I came for waistbands,' the visitor would explain.

No local village has ever actually been visited by a Bupati from any of the four regencies with jurisdiction over different parts of the Korowai lands (following subdivision of Merauke into smaller units around 2003). But the model these speakers articulated is widely held among Korowai, and underpins their frequent state of expectation toward the prospect of official visits.[6] At its centre is an

---

5 The Korowai word *xabian* 'head' was not formerly used to designate roles of leadership and authority, which did not exist in their society. But it has come to mean 'boss' across the period that Korowai have become familiar with power structures characteristic of state and commerce. In this usage, the Korowai word is being used as a loan translation of Indonesian kepala 'head', as in the government-underwritten office of kepala desa 'village head' (see Stasch 2014c:85–90).

6 Another example of this state of expectation unfolded when I was in the Korowai area in August 2011, staying at a feast site with some German tourists. As the feast's peak grew near, a problem arose with one of the large performance troupes expected to travel to the feast site. The village of Yaniruma lay about ten miles from the feast site, and a rumor circulated that the Vice Regent was going to come to that village by airplane just one day before the feast. Everyone in that direction gave up their plans to travel to the feast, and instead went to Yaniruma. The Vice Regent in reality visited a day earlier than rumored, and stayed for only an hour. Most of the people who travelled to Yaniruma to welcome him thus arrived after he had left. They were not ready to travel back the way they had come to attend the feast, and so the feast performance troupe from that part of the landscape never materialised, to the embarrassment of those who had planned it. For an example from

idea that performing primitivity and deprivation toward a wealthy foreigner will emotionally move him to want to give them objects they lack. The model also involves dense interconnections between nakedness, the aesthetics of coordinated celebratory and martial dancing, lack of commodities, the contrast between 'forest' and 'village', and the telos of a village becoming 'big' (a Korowai idiom for what outsiders would call 'development', and a condition Korowai see as the opposite of naked primitivity). This model also underpinned Korowai performances toward Darmono at Danuwage.

Korowai expectations about this type of encounter have been influenced by earlier experiences with tourists, and by even older practices of spectacular encounter among Korowai themselves at feasts. But their expectations have also been fueled by knowledge of rituals of state-society articulation at distant administrative centres. Around 2005, for example, 20 Korowai and Kombai men performed dance formations in traditional dress for a visiting Bupati at the village of Boma about 30 miles south of the Korowai area. The Bupati was a Wanggom man originating from the next river system east of Korowai. He briefly danced in the midst of the Korowai and Kombai performers, and he gave them 5 million rupiah (more than US$500). In another common kind of event, in 2001 two old men and a younger relative travelled 200 miles to Merauke to seek an audience with the Regent then presiding over their area, in the expectation that the older pair's primitivity would elicit chainsaws and outboards. They told the Regent that their village is small and the Regent needs to tell his functionaries to come make it big. This Regent was again a southern lowlands Papuan, and he shed tears at the old men's resemblance to his own parents, before giving them gifts of cash and equipment. As one person narrated, '[The old men] went to Merauke in just leaf penis foreskin wrappers, and [the Bupati] was wracked by longing/sympathy and gave them two outboards.'

These encounters involve the intersection of different models of transaction across hierarchy respectively held by Korowai and by government officials. Such intersections are occurring with much greater frequency amidst the already-noted shifts in governance now unfolding across Papua. The Bupati for whom Korowai danced in Boma was the head of the newly created Boven Digoel regency, seated far closer to Korowai than the previous capital of Merauke.[7] This man, Yusak Yaluwo, was said to be related to Korowai on his mother's side. As one Korowai

---

another part of Indonesia of the external figure of the Bupati being placed at the centre of local community life, see Allerton (2003). I have elsewhere discussed the circulation of the exogenous figure of the 'police' as a verbal representation with a life of its own among Korowai (Stasch 2001). The figure of 'tourists' (*tulis* or *sulisi*, from Indonesian turis) also has a vigorous discursive life as an ethnic type even among Korowai who have not encountered any of them directly. Korowai orientation to 'heads' or the Bupati figure specifically is another variation on this pattern.

7   The new regency is named after the notorious Dutch camp for anti-colonial political prisoners that had been sited at this location in the 1920s and 1930s. The camp history is a major early wellspring of discourses of isolation and primitivity attached to this specific region of New Guinea.

person narrated Yaluwo's sentiments upon seeing them perform, 'Korowai are my people,' he said. 'They are rather asli people with rattan waistbands, they are naked' (*Kolufo-fe nəyanop dəbo. ango* <u>asli</u> *lenoptabulmananop, aifoyum yanop*). The text and photos of a political biography produced for Yaluwo's 2010 re-election campaign repeatedly portray scenes of him visiting outlying settlements of constituents, where he is greeted by traditional dance performances (Wahyudi 2010: 8, 17, 23, 28, 32, 122). The book also refers to him in passing as 'this best son of Papua who still has the hereditary blood of treehouse descendants' (p. 42), and the cover features the motto 'I come, see, listen, cry, and decree', referring again to a transactional script of a powerful outsider being moved by his constituents' primitive baseness to confer wealth on them.[8] In the event, Yaluwo was indeed re-elected by a strong majority to a second term, but only while being held in jail in Jakarta on charges of misappropriating the equivalent of US$7 million.[9] His example is extreme, but throughout rural Papua today electoral popularity among the rural poor and clientelistic disbursement of money are two sides of a coin. There is an accidental synergy between the clientelistic logics of this state form, trans-ethnic Papuan sensibilities about giving and kinship that flourish and mutate in the new government contexts, and the Korowai sensibilities about relating to wealthy foreigners we have already seen structuring performances toward tourists.

These Korowai sensibilities are what I am most interested in. Performances toward government officials (like the giving of artifacts to Darmono) again reflect a focus on material objects as sites of the truth of social relations and personal being, and reflect a conviction that the way to deal with radical others is to transact with them. We additionally see in these performances something I did not emphasise before that is also present in relations with tourists, namely great ambiguity in the power dynamics of encounters, even when the transactions involve apparent self-lowering. To the extent Korowai *do* understand themselves as manipulating appearances to meet tourist desires and get money or other articles, this involves a sense of occupying not only a position of inferiority but also one of winning in transactions, akin to the understanding of 'raiding the land of the foreigners' described by Rutherford (2003). Such ambiguity is even clearer in performances toward government officials. Martial dancing in elaborate festive decorations, with bodies bare of imported cloth, is an enactment at once of primitive baseness and of the power to compel emotional responses of fear, awe or longing.

---

8   The quoted expressions are '<u>putra terbaik Papua yang masih memiliki darah titisan keturunan rumah tinggi ini</u>', and '<u>Saya Datang, Melihat, Mendengar, Menangis, dan Memutuskan</u>'.

9   See for example 'Graft suspect wins reelection in Papua', *The Jakarta Post*, 8 September 2010 www. thejakartapost.com/news/2010/09/08/graft-suspect-wins-reelection-papua.html, and 'Regent gets 4.5 years in prison for corruption', *The Jakarta Post*, www.thejakartapost.com/news/2010/11/03/regent-gets-45-years-prison-corruption.html (both accessed 3 November 2013).

But it is the pattern of self-lowering that is clearest of all in meetings with government officials. Here as in tourism, new Korowai practices of interethnic relating toward wealthy foreigners follow a prior sensibility that portraying oneself as deprived is a way to create valued relations of care, thanks to the compassion it elicits in others. Recall that the emblematic objects that Korowai gave to Darmono were meant to make him 'join in experiencing our people's hardships'. From these objects he was supposed to know in his own emotions how impoverished Korowai are in their material lives, by comparison to his wealthy life of ease. The scale of economic inequalities between Korowai and the new foreigners is unprecedented. Also new is the primitivist framework the outsiders bring to the encounters, that Korowai quickly learn. But inequality as such is not new. Hamming up their primitivity and deprivation toward state officials, Korowai adapt an earlier mode of engaging with inequalities in kinship life to the greater inequalities of the new economic order and the new hierarchy of primitive and civilised.

Variations on the sensibilities about equality, emotion and exchange that have shaped Korowai uptake of a concept of the primitive are widely encountered elsewhere as well. A perception of institutional abandonment is said to be felt all across peripheral areas of Indonesian Papua (e.g. Anderson 2012, 2013b). The pattern is also common in independent Papua New Guinea. Hoenigman (2012: 291) reports of Awiakay villagers on a Sepik tributary:

> People often say in the lingua franca Tok Pisin, mipela las ples bilong bus, 'we're the last place in the bush'. Awiakay often complain that they are 'inferior' and 'forgotten', not only in comparison with the white man (TP waitman) or PNG town dwellers, but also in comparison with neighbouring groups. This is a common feeling among those Papua New Guineans who are far from roads, shops, health centres, and governmental offices. [footnotes omitted]

This sense of having been passed over by economic prosperity prompts feelings of inferiority or what some authors have termed 'humiliation', and intense desires for change (e.g. Leavitt 2005; and other studies in Robbins and Wardlow 2005). Several ethnographers of PNG societies have described primitivist pageants and slapstick parodies of old time practices performed for mining company representatives or government officials (e.g. Robbins 2006, 2009; Knauft 2002, 2007). These pageants and other representations of humiliation cannot entirely be explained as introjection of hierarchical superiors' actual disdain for rural New Guineans, on the model of Fanon's analysis of black consciousness under white colonisation (2008 [1952]). There is additionally at work a cultural concept of the efficacy of expressions of deprivation in eliciting relational engagement from the powerful. Knauft (2002) writes of a paradoxical pattern of 'recessive agency', according to which Gebusi seek to bring about desired sociocultural transformations by occupying positions of passivity relative to others (a pattern also carefully elucidated in a different context by Wardlow 2006, under the label 'negative agency'). Korowai attraction to the idea of an abstract external figure of power and generosity such as a <u>Bupati</u> or 'Tourist', their expressions of dismay about administrators failing to deliver quickly on promises of making local villages 'big', and their strategies of self-lowering as a way to elicit relations are thus cultural patterns with deep regional resonance.

But allied patterns are apparent in many other communities worldwide, in which people struggle with experiences of deprivation. Writing about southern Africa, for example, Ferguson (2013) has noted that while active seeking of relations of dependent subordination is disturbing to emancipatory liberalism, such relations of social inequality may involve more security, freedom and well-being than the alternative of what Ferguson calls 'asocial inequality'. Conversion of 'asocial inequality' into '*social* inequality' is a reasonable gloss for what Korowai are seeking in their performance of primitivist imagery toward government officials.

Bootstrapping out of the primitive by sending boys to school

The final ethnographic topic I will examine is Korowai boys travelling to faraway towns to go to school, often at the urging of their kin back home. This pattern still involves self-lowering in the terms of a new primitivist hierarchy, but also a stance of assertive effort to reposition oneself from an inferior pole to a superior one.

Before turning to this actual practice, though, I should pause to flesh out the domestic Indonesian primitivist structures within which Korowai now live, so that we can more fully appreciate the pressures to which schooling migration is most directly a response. So far I have emphasised continuities between primitivist frameworks structuring Korowai interactions with government officials and with tourists. But while these formations are historically connected and continue to intersect and overlap, there are three tendencies in the domestic formation that might importantly set it apart from the international one.

First, in the domestic formation the evaluative stance toward the primitive tends to be more pejorative than in contemporary international primitivism. It is a nearly universal feature of primitivist models that they are evaluatively volatile, and that positive and negative stances intermingle in them. Still, as a matter of proportions, contemporary international media and tourist interest in Korowai is at least on its surface dominantly positive and Romantic in tenor, where Indonesian primitivist evaluation of Papuans is dominantly critical. This is amply reflected, for instance, in the basic terminology of state development policy from the recent past. It is well-known that in the 1980s and 1990s, people at the fringes of the Indonesian state's reach were officially categorised in baldly pejorative primitivist terms as 'estranged/wild tribes' (suku terasing), who were 'backward' (terbelakang) and needed state agents to 'make them human' (memanusiakan) through a civilising process of state integration, sometimes only slightly subtler than the army-led campaign of 'Operation Penis Gourd' (Operasi Koteka) imposed on Baliem Valley Dani in the early 1970s and formally inaugurated by First Lady Tien Suharto. Traces of this heritage of emblematising people like Korowai as the polar opposite of a positively evaluated national ideal of socioeconomic development persist to the present (as is evident from Darmono's earlier-quoted statements), even as the official primitivist language has been softened from 'Wild Tribes' to 'Geographically Isolated Customary Law Communities' (Komunitas Adat Terpencil) (see Duncan 2004, 2007).

In popular consciousness, particularly among the more than half of Indonesians living on Java, there have long been strong currents of prejudicial racialisation of Papuans as fearful subhuman inferiors (e.g. Anggraeni 2011: 73). Many Papuans are highly attuned to this prejudice and its primitivist garb, as in the following statement of a Papuan man studying in Java to become a civil servant, supported by Special Autonomy funding: 'To separatist Papuans, I am a traitor. To most of our Javanese teachers, I am a monkey they are trying to lure down from the trees. I just want to feed my family' (quoted in Célérier 2010; see also Hastings 1982: 159; Rakhmani 2012; and Munro, this volume). Illustrations of a contrary evaluative stance are also easy to find, of course. For example, the branch of the Indonesian state that officially defines categories like 'Geographically Isolated Customary Law Community' and is charged with provisioning of special services to them is the Department of Social Affairs. This agency's first brief initiative in the Korowai area in 1986 unfolded in coordination with the activities of Dea Sudarman, a New York-raised Javanese documentary filmmaker and art collector, who had already taken a strong positive interest in Asmat art and culture and who has continued to make her experiences in Papua integral to her cultural projects in Jakarta (see e.g. Sudarman et al. 1986). With the dramatic expansion of Indonesian middle class consumer culture in the 2000s, media primitivism within Indonesia has now partially re-converged with international trends, as reflected in a recent spate of domestically produced television travel show episodes with titles such as 'Hidden treasures of the Korowai'.[10] Still, the resolutely pejorative character of popular primitivist imagining of Papua is better exemplified by the mainstream

---

10   See for example the two episodes of Trans7's travel show Adventurer's Footsteps (Jejak Petualang) available at us.m.mytrans.com/video/2013/01/04/49/17/27/7632/rumah-pohon-suku-korowai and us.mytrans. com/video/2012/06/27/49/17/27/5294/harta-tersembunyi-korowai and the two similar episodes of the same

2011 Indonesian-language feature film distributed under the English title *Lost in Papua*. The 'Korowai' tribe appear centrally in this film, as noble savages among whom the female Javanese heroine has an idyllic sojourn. But later this positive primitivism is heavily overshadowed by the same heroine's lengthy sexual imprisonment by a neighbouring all-female tribe of cannibals, who communicate only by grunts and hoots, and from whom she is finally rescued by a virtuous Korowai warrior.[11]

A second major difference between domestic and international primitivism is also apparent from materials I have already outlined, namely that domestically the primitivist model is also a trajectory of desired historical transformation. The primitive is the opposite not just of civilisation but also of development. Giving up treehouses, forming villages, ending cannibalism and converting to Christianity are one and the same with state and market participation, and with entry into a teleology of advancement and progress. In international media and tourist primitivism, primitive purity is centrally under threat of loss, but this is conceived as extraneous to the idea of the primitive itself. In the regional geopolitical world primitivity is instead a *reason* for transformation.

Third, in the domestic and regional formation, primitivist ideas are lived materially in the geopolitical and institutional order of the landscape, as much as verbally in abstract discursive models or via visual media like photography and television. For example, primitivist ideology is lived in physical movement between a population centre where there is vast monetary wealth and an outlying hinterland where there is not, or in the presence in a village of ministers and schoolteachers. This physicality of the primitive is intertwined with my point about transformation. Across much of the southern lowlands of Papua, in the talk of Dutch, Indonesian or Papuan outsiders, and very quickly that of local populations, 'coming down' from treehouses and aggregating together in permanent villages has been understood as a watershed historical transition (Wamafma 2008; Schoorl 1993), and the transition is strongly aligned

---

channel's My Indonesia (Indonesiaku) available at us.mytrans.com/video/2012/07/03/50/52/154/5333/menembus-rimba-papua-menuju-suku-pedalaman, and us.mytrans.com/video/2012/07/04/50/52/154/5349/mengenal-lebih-dekat-suku-korowai-di-pedalaman-papua-.

11 See www.youtube.com/watch?v=NC2jEIqyebc (accessed 15 March 2013). The filmmakers took inspiration from an urban legend that widely circulates in Papua about a society of women who reproduce by having sex with men who stumble into their midst, before killing them and any male progeny. Many accounts locate this society in the Mamberamo River basin, but it has also been previously tied to Korowai (*The Jakarta Post* 1991). The idea of a society of women who kill their male young has been reported from other parts of Indonesia since at least the early 1500s (Reid 1994: 271). In the film crew's production process, the closest they came to the Korowai lands was Boven Digoel 50 miles to the southeast. It was Papuans from this administrative centre (including the head of the local Bureau of Culture and Tourism) who performed the 'Korowai' roles. Korowai who heard of this arrangement when the film later circulated in Papua on VCD expressed anger toward those who had impersonated them, arguing that they alone are the ones whose place it would be to perform such actions. The film was never distributed theatrically in Papua, having drawn critical anti-primitivist Papuan commentary in newspapers following its very successful release in Java.

also with other iconic contrasts between practices coded as archaic and ones coded as contemporary: between nudity, piercings and scarification versus clothedness and lack of facial ornaments; between cannibalism versus living together peaceably; and so forth. All of these material signs are also central to the primitivism of international tourists and Korowai adaption to it, as we have seen. But as a matter of proportion, I would suggest that on domestic scales the primitivist framework is lived even more at semi-discursive levels of the total physical organisation of life, by comparison to the relatively more verbalised and performatively set apart character of primitivist moments in tourism.

A further important correlative of this 'total' character of the domestic primitivist formation is that it is not a thoroughly state-associated framework of evaluation, nor a framework aligned in a simple way with Indonesian immigrants' political and economic domination of Papuans. In the Indonesian and Dutch colonial eras alike, church workers, government functionaries, schoolteachers and other outsiders who introduce primitivist ideas to local populations have been themselves Papuan. Even more consequential are ways that primitivist frameworks of categorisation circulate and grow *horizontally*, among local Papuan landowners.

As Korowai move through the contemporary political geography of primitivism and learn regionally circulating ideas of an overarching hierarchy of places and human conditions, they have more contexts of life in which they think of themselves as occupying an inferior social position to other people. There are many specific actions they take in response. But perhaps the area of activity where the primitivist framework stands out most starkly is seeking of social advancement through children's education.

Elementary schools have operated sporadically in two southwestern Korowai villages. But most students who attend any school, and all who go beyond six grades, do so by living in towns or large villages anywhere from 20 to 200 miles distant from the Korowai lands. It is almost exclusively boys who migrate for schooling, due to parents' fear that girls would be a focus of marital and sexual advances by strangers, and adults' possessiveness toward their young female relatives' marital prospects and sexuality.[12] There are now at least 50 Korowai youths living in a dozen different towns to attend elementary school, middle

---

12   The only exceptions are two girls from Mbasman village who in 2009 began attending elementary school in Sentani, 200 miles from home, at about age 10. The conditions enabling this included that government staff from the Department of Social Affairs acted as mediators, and it was known that they would live in a female-supervised 'orphanage' for rural girls (originally established by an expatriated Belgian Catholic nun). One of the Korowai girls, though, was brought back to the Korowai area by her father in early 2014, when news circulated that she was no longer living in the dormitory. While men have been more mobile than women in the new era of regular Korowai travel far from their own lands, a colourful counterpoint was expressed by one woman who was telling me about the many different Korowai clan territories to which women from her natal patriclan had moved upon marriage: 'They live all over the place, like foreigners!' (*xofǝxa bau wofǝxa bau,*

or high school, or university. What is striking is the single-mindedness with which these boys and their relatives see schooling as a goal, to the point of enduring severe emotional and financial hardships to make it possible. Boys themselves are often hungry in town, and may stay out of school for long periods due to lack of money for fees or uniforms. Their relatives send them the little money they ever scrape together through income opportunities arising back home. Persons on all sides suffer painful separations, including during crises of illness or death. This extreme parental enthusiasm and self-sacrificial striving in relation to children's education is common throughout rural Papua (see Munro 2013: 26). It is a frequent way that peripheral rural populations worldwide engage with national or global political geography (e.g. Killick 2008).

The most basic Korowai idea motivating this migration is that schooling is how a child can gain any foothold in the system of salaried occupations. Kin want boys to go to school so that they will come back as a Regent, schoolteacher, pastor, soldier, health nurse, policeman or civil servant, a pattern of aspiration again widely attested worldwide (e.g. Pigg 1992: 511). These salaried jobs are roles Korowai routinely lump together under the general term 'head' or 'big head' (*xabian*, *xabiantale*, see note 5). In a typical statement, one man told me that the purpose of boys' schooling is 'So they will become big heads' (*xabiantaleleloxate*).[13] People also routinely express this goal of gaining a civil servant position or other salaried employment using the Korowai-language expression 'become human' (*yanoptelo*). This usage is a loan translation of the Indonesian-language phrase <u>menjadi manusia</u> that also means 'become human', widely used by other Papuans in the region to talk about securing salaried jobs.[14] While the core force of this new Korowai idiom is better translated by the English expression 'become somebody', there is a basic implication that people who lack salaried employment are less than human. The Indonesian and Korowai expressions 'become human' used in this way thus chillingly echo a history of Indonesians with military, political, or commercial power over Papuans deprecating them as not 'human' (<u>manusia</u>). The Korowai expression also echoes and inverts the earlier Korowai ethnonymic pattern of using their vernacular term *yanop* 'human' as an ethnic self-designation, and the term *laleo* 'dead non-

---

laleo-alin ülop). When I asked what she meant by this, she explained that part of the work arrangements for schoolteachers is that they are assigned to job postings in villages far away from their home ethnic territory. She was likening women's experiences of virilocal marriage to this pattern.

13 Desire for schooling and civil servant positions played a central role in the Naomi Robson affair of September 2006, though this was completely hidden to the foreigners involved and their media audiences. In this affair, an Australian tabloid television personality set out unsuccessfully to 'rescue' a small boy named Wawa who was purportedly a Korowai orphan in danger of being killed and eaten as a witch. Her failed mission became the focus of an extended national media firestorm in Australia. What Korowai and Kombai all understood, though, was not that Wawa was a witch but that his relatives wanted to get him out to school.

14 In Indonesian there is an alternative term <u>orang</u> 'person' that does not focalise the human/subhuman boundary in the same way as <u>manusia</u> 'human, humanity'. But among Korowai and people of neighbouring ethnicities in the southern lowlands, it is <u>menjadi manusia</u> that I have heard, in talk about civil servant posts.

human demon' as an ethnic designation for nonlocal foreigners. People also sometimes narrate the purpose of boys' schooling using expressions such as 'So he will become a foreigner' (*laleoimbanteloxai*, literally 'become a member of the demonic dead ethnicity') or 'For our people to become like Whites' (*noxumayox xalxeyoanopüloptelongalxe*) using a new phenotype-focused phrase referring to whites as light-skinned. These expressions are loosely synonymous with saying the boys will 'become human' or 'become a big head' (compare Rutherford 2003; Bashkow 2006).

What all these expressions centre on is the utopian vision of an alternative economic regime that Korowai identify with city-dwelling whites, Indonesians and Papuans, and that we have already encountered in the idea that tourists live from food and money that is 'just there'. From travel to administrative centres outside their lands, Korowai have added to the imagery of tourists eating from endlessly self-replenishing stocks the further observation that civil servants sit in their offices all day, are paid money, and live from consumer goods they buy with that money. The main reason Korowai want access to the system of salaried occupations is this lifestyle of what one man described to me as 'getting articles nicely' (*folulto misafi fongalxe*).

In contexts of interethnic encounter, Korowai further experience themselves as occupying an inferior position in a hierarchy of human worth around a diverse array of bodily practices, beyond the core focus on salaries and food. A recent book by an Indonesian anthropologist recounts one Korowai man's discourse:

> Marthen Hanai … told of his experiences when he went to the town of Kepi. He saw people like civil servants wearing official uniforms, health workers who wore white clothes, and school-aged children going to school. He became sad because there is no possibility for him and the people in Basman village to have such opportunities, because schooling does not operate there the way it should, because they cannot read, and because they cannot count well. [He said:] Despite that there are still many of us who are now naked and there are still those who live up in high trees, we also wish that one day our children could live making use of clothes that are fine, clean, and neat. We also wish that our children could later bathe using sweet-smelling soap, and brush our teeth like city people (Lekitoo 2012: 105–106).

This pattern of experience is common all across Korowai society today.

Concerning how school attendance is actually supposed to lead to salaried employment, one Korowai focus is fluency in Indonesian, and especially the ability to read and write. Korowai also say that it is by being in school away from their home places that children's 'thinking' becomes 'brilliant, clear' (*dialun*), such that they can operate successfully in social contexts of commerce, government and Indonesian speech. Korowai reason that adults who have been fully socialised in their home location are beyond the ability to acquire these skills, and instead need educated children to come home as 'big heads' and tell them how to reorganise their lives. In this way, Korowai articulate an explicit model of the inculcation of new forms of consciousness as a result of living amidst specific institutions. Characteristically, they intertwine that model with ideas of reproduction, or the connection and disparity between relatives of different generations. Faced with their own position of perceived inferiority in a new economic system, Korowai turn to what they are good at, kinship, to crack the problem of what they do not have, the new urban wealth and access to state and market institutions from which this wealth flows.

This turn to the traffic in children as a resource for dealing with history is also apparent in the most common of all ideas that relatives bring up when asked about schooling migration. In a very recognisable New Guinean pattern, relatives of a boy in school frequently say that their intention is to benefit from the 'yield' or 'produce' of the boy after he has attended school and gotten work, as reciprocation for the care they have earlier put into him. For example, when I asked one woman whose son was away at school how she felt about their separation, she said she did not mind, because she occasionally takes sago and pandanus to the boy at his place of schooling, and after he becomes literate he will get money from his own 'head' or 'boss' and give her rice, noodles and clothing, which she currently lacks. Or as one woman narrated the general idea of sending boys to school, 'Let's eat the produce of their hands!' (*yexenep melxalüx ləfen*). The idiom 'yield of hand' or 'produce of hand' (*mel-xalüx*) is here adapted from its earlier use to talk about a basic moral norm of intergenerational care, according to which people who give children food when young will receive the game meats, sago starch or other bounty the child procures upon becoming an adult.[15]

---

15 For both the older institution of parents enjoying the produce of mature children they have earlier fed, and the new one of hoped-for return from boys' schooling, bilingual Korowai translate *xalüx* by the Indonesian term hasil 'produce, effect, profit' (see Munro 2013: 33). I have also heard people refer wryly to children's traditional obligation to give game or vegetal produce to their elders as tugas, Indonesian for 'duty', strongly associated with salaried occupations. The term 'yield' (*xalüx*) has further collocations besides *mel-xalüx* 'yield of hand' designating other transactional forms of kinship debt and recompense across time, such as *lal-xalüx* 'girl yield, bridewealth'. An example of bridewealth issues themselves intersecting with the schooling model was the decision of one bereaved widower in 2005 to take his two sons to Boma 30 miles south of the Korowai area and install them in school there (living with foster-parents from another Papuan ethnic group). He was prompted in part by his reasoning that his wife's death had left him not only emotionally bereft but materially impoverished, due to having given all his possessions away to his wife's relatives as bridewealth. Thus later he would eat the 'yield, produce' secured by his sons borne of the deceased women, after they went to school. Across the years of his sons' residence in Boma, he has regularly travelled there with forest produce and with money earned from tourism, to contribute to the boys' maintenance.

This use of moralities of parent-child debt to try to gain a place in an alien geopolitical system is a first major way that schooling migration aligns with my claim that Korowai live out the new primitivist ideological formation in forms given by their egalitarianism. They live the hierarchical relation between the new and old economic systems in terms of kinship, and specifically in terms of an egalitarian norm of transforming asymmetries in people's capacity to care for themselves and others at different stages of life into an overall symmetric reciprocity of care across time.

After 20 years of educational migration, there is only one clear example of a Korowai man with a salaried government job, and nobody has been posted back to the Korowai area with such a position. Many boys have completed some schooling and then remained in town locations with tenuous economic prospects, or they now bounce between their home region and a town where they have formed ties of patronage, manual labor or courtship. The cohorts of boys who today continue to work their way up through different educational levels may be cannily pressing toward outcomes that will only be clear in another generation, or they may be facing a future of permanently fruitless sacrifices and frustrated hopes (Munro 2013; Sykes n.d.). But whatever the eventual outcomes, another significant pattern in people's reasoning is that they regularly explain their commitment to invest in schooling by citing cases of success from *other* Papuan ethnic groups. Korowai are highly aware of specific speakers of Kombai, Citak, or other neighbouring languages who work as teachers, civil servants and soldiers. Often Korowai describe themselves as feeling inferior to the neighbouring people who have achieved this, or they report being mocked by persons of neighbouring ethnicities who say things like 'You Korowai have stayed eating humans. You won't quickly have a subdistrict or get paid work. You should just stay there doing what you do with the tourists.' One man told me he sent his younger relative to school out of fatigue at Indonesian immigrants telling him that Korowai are illiterate. Awareness of neighbouring groups' success in gaining salaried positions can also take more affirmative forms, as in the extreme case of ex-Regent Yaluwo who is recognised as a relative who made it big from origins similar to Korowai people's current circumstances (though Korowai are not widely aware of his legal troubles). Often the ability to place boys in school at all depends on wider patterns of interethnic patronage and foster-kinship, whether across different Papuan identities, or across the divide of Papuan versus immigrant. The Korowai boys are taken in by members of other groups who have land, food, church or commercial resources at the schooling sites, or the boys live in dormitories on food bought with occasional funds provided by Papuan political patrons.

This embedding of schooling migration in issues of interethnic equality and care is a second and final broad way this area of Korowai activity follows the larger pattern of Korowai taking on primitivist ideology through their egalitarian values. The most direct spur to the schooling venture has been Korowai comparison of themselves to recognisable, proximate consociates. It is through a focus on relations of equality or deprivation in relation to ethnic neighbours that they pass into a larger formation of inequality and striving. Commitment to equality means that for Korowai to see other people living by a new economic system provokes intense desire to do the same. The experience of humiliation and desire in relation to ethnic neighbours' successes in the new system is a first form in which they take on the hierarchy of civilised versus primitive, lived in the terms of characteristically New Guinean concerns with equality and relational standing (Robbins 1994).

Conclusion: Indigenous egalitarianism and exogenous domination

Dean MacCannell, reviewing the film *Cannibal Tours*, puts eloquently a common turn of academic thought about primitivist interactions around the world today:

> The film makes it painfully evident, the choice of the Sepik region drives the point home with precision, that this primitive 'Other' [of tourist-sending societies' popular imagination] no longer exists. What remains of the primitive world are ex-primitives, recently acculturated peoples lost in the industrial world, and another kind of ex-primitive, still going under the label 'primitive', a kind of performative 'primitive'. (MacCannell 1990:14)

And in fact, the notion of a 'performative "primitive"' does point toward the issue I have made my subject in this essay, the uptake of primitive stereotypy by those who are so stereotyped. Yet it would be a shame if the interpretive effect of this notion (or other widely encountered variations on it, in different language) were to end ethnographic inquiry, rather than serve as its beginning. I have shown here that the primitive is a kind of equivocal 'homonym' (Viveiros de Castro 2004) in an overall structure of working misunderstanding. Different parties to the encounter coordinate with each other intensely through this category, even as their understanding of the category's content and implications are systematically *uncoordinated*. The process of close social involvement between these different actors might flourish not just *despite* but *because* of the mutual misapprehension. And the concept of primitiveness that comes to be so central to Korowai actions toward foreigners is a sedimentation of closely intermingled endogenous and exogenous forces (compare Rumsey 2006). Primitivist ideologies enter into Korowai self-consciousness or are reinvented there under pressures of uneven access to wealth that replicate hierarchies of power and worth characteristic of a wider history of colonisations worldwide, within which the primitivist ideologies were originally forged. But the primitivism migrates and is reinvented also in the channels of culturally distinctive Korowai sensibilities about what social inequality is and how to respond to it or live with it. The ways primitivist ideologies enter Korowai self-consciousness or are newly elaborated there have been shaped by Korowai sensibilities about the importance of material objects as direct indexes of human worth and relational truth; their sensibilities about the urgency of getting into transactions with people who are alien and wealthy; their sensibilities about self-lowering as a good way of eliciting care and relatedness from others; their sensibilities about the ambiguity of power and worth in relations where one party appears to occupy the position of inferior; their sensibilities about the foundational character of kinship and generational succession as a resource for bootstrapping one's community into something different than it is; and their sensibilities about equality itself as a prime imperative of social existence. Many foreigners do not have those sensibilities as part of their primitivist ideas, or as part of their understanding of the ends of state order. Korowai gestures of what I have termed 'self-lowering' are being performed toward exchange partners who do not have the same kinds of answerability, empathy, shame and memory that animate the flow of goods among Korowai themselves. Yet the ways Korowai embrace and elaborate primitivism in their own terms seem very basic to the actual efficacy of primitivism as an ideology, in structuring social relations across differences of power and understanding.

The Korowai uptake of ideas of primitivist hierarchy is also tantamount to entry into relations of domination, and so my arguments in this essay also speak to the complexity of state power. Rutherford (2013: 7) asks in passing, 'What would it mean to tell the story of Indonesian colonialism as a tale of weakness, not strength?' The case examined here highlights ways that a society based on kinship, exchange, and an anti-hierarchical political ethos can be exceptionally vulnerable to entanglement with state power, and to certain forms of active participation in extending that power. The very levels of social life that state actors are oblivious of or indifferent to can be foundational to the strength a state holds in people's lives. The case I have examined is a paradoxical one of 'anarchist' egalitarians who are attracted to state power, and state institutions whose efficacy and amplification are partly dependent on non-state sociality.

The three ethnographic areas discussed across this chapter to make these general points have been quite varied, in keeping with a historical situation in which diverse institutional processes are unfolding and no single pattern can stand for the whole field. But the three areas compositely give an overview of Korowai people's condition of lived primitivism today. As a coda, I would like finally to sketch another recent sequence of events, in which all three of the ethnographic areas I have discussed happen to intersect. These events are centred not on Korowai but on a network of young men from the upper Digul River east of the Korowai area, who currently attend high school or university in towns near Papua's capital of Jayapura, or who have returned to the southern lowlands area after graduation. These young men are the kinds of neighbours whose educational and employment attainments spur Korowai people's own aspirations for advancement. Yet in the 2000s, these non-Korowai youths increasingly started referring to themselves by the new Indonesian-language ethnonymic expression 'Eastern Korowai' (Korowai Timur). By 2010, the young men began forming a cultural organisation for advancing their ethnic groups' political interests, and for mediating outsiders' access to their region. Before long, leaders described their organisation as having 130 members, from 43 subgroupings under the 'Korowai grouping in the broad sense' (suku Korowai besar). These leaders were identified in press reports as 'Korowai' persons, although they are at best speakers of neighbouring languages, from the same family as Korowai proper. By early 2012, the network's agenda was focused on creation of a 'Korowai' government regency, to replace the situation in which the territories of their ethnolinguistic groups are governed by five different regencies seated in faraway administrative centres. This lobbying goal was reflected in one of the group's names, 'Team for the Independent Aspiration to Create by Subdivision a Greater Korowai Regency' (Tim Aspirasi Independen Pemekaran Kabupaten Korowai Raya).[16] The most important current leader of the network plans to write his MA thesis in anthropology on creation of such a regency.

This organisational initiative is an overdetermined reconvergence of this chapter's three subjects of tourism, 'big heads' in a time of redistricting, and migration for school. Adoption of the ethnonym 'Korowai' by this network of students was motivated by Korowai primitivist fame: Korowai people's neighbours have sometimes looked on with dismay at being cut out from international tourism, much as Korowai look on with dismay at being cut out from civil servant jobs. Additionally, the youths' initiative has unfolded in the context of their shared positions in the system of educational migration. The actual political project the youths have come to articulate reflects their situation of tenuous mobility toward civil servant and government posts. Creation of a governmental administrative unit defined by the geography and political interests of their ethno-cultural

---

16   I have also heard the name 'Eastern Korowai Youth Group' (Pemuda Korowai Timur). Some participants also use the terminology of Lembaga Masyarakat Adat, or ethno-cultural NGO, an organisational form that came to wide prominence in Indonesia after 1998. See for example tabloidjubi.com/2013/02/07/warga-korowai-minta-pemekaran/, tabloidjubi.com/2013/02/07/sebagian-wilayah-korowai-masuk-lima-kabupaten/, and 'Masyarakat Korowai Belum Deberdayakan' at www.cenderawasihpos.com/index.php?mib=berita. detail&id=549 (all accessed March 30, 2013). I have not met the main leaders of this network, but have spoken with certain of them by phone, and some of my Korowai acquaintances have also been on the network's periphery.

confederation is seen as a route to securing those positions, as well as improving the lives of their relatives generally. The youths are seeking a transactional unification of the polarity of primitive 'Korowai' and civilised, prosperous 'big head' or 'Regent', on a different level than the transactional unification brought about by naked performance of martial dances before a visiting official at a village, and yet bearing analogies to such an encounter.

Given the youths' positions as impoverished and politically unconnected students, their advocacy activities may not bear very direct fruit. Yet their example vividly exemplifies broader current patterns of popular consciousness in a regional world deeply organised by logics of the primitive and the civilised, logics that have been molded in new directions in the course of becoming the currency of formal political administration, Indonesian-Papuan domination, market expansion and Papuan interethnic sociability.

References

Albert, Bruce, and Alcida Ramos (eds) 2000. *Pacificando o Branco: Cosmologias do Contato no Norte-Amazônico*. São Paolo: Editora USP.

Allerton, Catherine 2003. 'Authentic Housing, Authentic Culture? Transforming a Village into a "Tourist Site" in Manggarai, Eastern Indonesia'. *Indonesia and the Malay World* 31: 119-128.

Anderson, Bobby 2012. 'Living Without a State: People in Rural Papua are More Interested in Basic Services than Grand Political Struggles'. *Inside Indonesia* 110: Oct-Dec 2012.

Anderson, Bobby 2013a. 'Land of Ghosts: Papua's Rural Lowlands are Being Transformed by an Encroaching Global Economy, but What Happens to the People There is an Open Question'. *Inside Indonesia* 112: Apr–Jun 2013.

Anderson, Bobby 2013b. 'The Middle of Nowhere: Highland Communities in Papua are Demanding Access to Services, But There is a Limit to What can be Offered in the Most Remote Settlements'. *Inside Indonesia* 111: Jan–Mar 2013.

Anggraeni, Dewi 2011. 'Another East: Representation of Papua in Popular Media'. PROSIDING ICSSIS 2011 4th International Conference on Indonesian Studies, FIPB – Universitas Indonesia: http://icssis.wordpress.com/prosiding/prosiding-icssis-2011/.

Aspinall, Edward 2013. 'A Nation in Fragments: Patronage and Neoliberalism in Contemporary Indonesia'. *Critical Asian Studies* 45(1): 27–54.

Backshall, Stephen, Leffman, David, Reader, Lesley and Stedman, Henry 1999. *Indonesia: The Rough Guide*. London: Rough Guides, 1st Edition.

Bashkow, Ira 2006. *The Meaning of Whitemen: Race and Modernity in the Orokaiva Cultural World*. Chicago: University of Chicago Press.

BBC/Discovery Channel 2005. 'Tribe'. Bruce Parry, presenter. Season 1, Episode 3: Kombai. Broadcast in US by Discovery Channel under title 'Going Tribal', episode 3 titled 'Living with Cannibals'. Seasons 1–3 published on DVD 2008, season 1 episode 3 titled 'The Kombai, hunter gatherers of the West Papua jungle'. London: BBC Worldwide.

Berkmoes, Ryan Ver, Brash, Celeste Cohen, Muhammad, Elliott, Mark, Holden, Trent, Mitra, Guyan, Noble, John, Skolnick, Adam, Stewart, Iain and Waters, Steve 2010. *Indonesia*. Melbourne: Lonely Planet, 9th Edition.

Booth, Anne 2011. 'Splitting, Splitting and Splitting Again: A Brief History of the Development of Regional Government in Indonesia Since Independence'. *Bijdragen tot de Taal-, Land- en Volkenkunde* 167(1): 31–59.

Cahill, Tim 1992. 'No Cannibal Jokes, Please: Upriver into the Swamps of Irian Jaya, and Back in Time'. *Outside* 17(10): 70–77, 186–196.

Causey, Andrew 2003. *Hard Bargaining in Sumatra: Western Travelers and Toba Bataks in the Marketplace of Souvenirs*. Honolulu: University of Hawaii Press.

Célérier, Philippe Pataud 2010. '"Indonesian Democracy Stops in Papua": Autonomy Isn't Independence'. *Le Monde Diplomatique,* English edition, June http://mondediplo.com/2010/06/14indonesia.

Cicada Productions/Travel Channel 2007. 'Living with the Kombai Tribe: The Adventures of Mark and Olly'. 6 episodes. Chatsworth (CA): Image Entertainment.

Clastres, Pierre 1977. *Society Against the State*. New York: Urizen Books.

Dalton, Bill 1991. *Indonesia Handbook*. Chico (CA): Moon Publications 5th Edition.

Douglas, Bronwen 1999. 'Science and the Art of Representing "Savages": Reading "Race" in Text and Image in South Seas Voyage Literature'. *History and Anthropology* 11(2–3):157–201.

Douglas, Bronwen 2011. 'Geography, Raciology, and the Naming of Oceania: Journal of the Australian Map Circle'. *The Globe* 69:1–28.

Douglas, Bronwen, and Ballard, Chris (eds) 2008. *Foreign Bodies: Oceania and the Science of Race 1750-1940*. Canberra: ANU E Press.

Duncan, Christopher 2004. 'From Development to Empowerment: Changing Indonesian Government Policies Toward Indigenous Minorities'. In Duncan, Christopher (ed.), *Civilizing the Margins: Southeast Asian Government Policies for the Development of Minorities*. Ithaca: Cornell University Press, 86–115.

Duncan, Christopher 2007. 'Mixed Outcomes: The Impact of Regional Autonomy and Decentralization on Indigenous Ethnic Minorities in Indonesia'. *Development and Change* 38(4): 711–733.

Fanon, Frantz 2008 [1952]. *Black Skins, White Masks*. London: Pluto Press.

Ferguson, James 2013. 'Declarations of Dependence: Labour, Personhood, and Welfare in Southern Africa'. *Journal of the Royal Anthropological Institute* 19(2): 223–242.

Gow, Peter 1993. 'Gringos and Wild Indians: Images of History in Western Amazonian Cultures'. *L'Homme* 33(126): 327–347.

Hallet, Judith 1994. *Treehouse People: Cannibal Justice* (Also distributed as *Lords of the Garden*). New York: Arts and Entertainment Television Networks.

Hastings, Peter 1982. 'Double Dutch and Indons'. In May, R.J. and Nelson, Hank (eds), *Melanesia: Beyond Diversity*. Canberra: Research School of Pacific Studies, The Australian National University, 157–161.

Hoenigman, Darja 2012. 'A Battle of Languages: Spirit Possession and Changing Linguistic Ideologies in a Sepik Society, Papua New Guinea'. *The Australian Journal of Anthropology* 23(3): 290–317.

Hoesterey, James B. 2012. 'The Adventures of Mark and Olly: The Pleasures and Horrors of Anthropology on TV'. In Whitehead, Neil and Wesch, Michael (eds), *Human No More: Digital Subjectivities, Un-Human Subjects and the End of Anthropology*. Boulder: University of Colorado Press, 245–277.

Institute for Policy Analysis of Conflict 2013. 'Carving Up Papua: More Districts, More Trouble'. *IPAC Report No. 3*.

International Crisis Group 2007. 'Indonesian Papua: A Local Perspective on the Conflict'. *Asia Briefing* 66. Jakarta/Brussels: International Crisis Group.

International Crisis Group 2012. 'Indonesia: Dynamics of Violence in Papua'. *Asia Report* 232. Jakarta/Brussels: International Crisis Group.

Ipenburg, At 2008. 'Christianity in Papua'. In Aritonang, Jan Sihar and Steenbrink, Karel (eds), *A History of Christianity in Indonesia*. Leiden: Brill, 345–381.

Jakarta Post 1991. 'Korowai Tribe in Irian Jaya not all Female'. *Jakarta Post*, 1991/03/20, p. 3.

Killick, Evan 2008. 'Creating Community: Land Titling, Education, and Settlement Formation Among the Ashéninka of Peruvian Amazonia'. *Journal of Latin American and Caribbean Anthropology* 13(1): 22–47.

Knauft, Bruce 2002. *Exchanging the Past: A Rainforest World of Before and After*. Chicago: University of Chicago Press.

Knauft, Bruce 2007. 'From Self-decoration to Self-fashioning: Orientalism as Backward Progress among the Gebusi of Papua New Guinea'. In Ewart, Elizabeth and O'Hanlon, Michael (eds), *Body Arts and Modernity*. Wantage, Oxfordshire: Sean Kingston, 88–107.

Leavitt, Stephen 2005. '"We Are Not Straight": Bumbita Arapesh Strategies for Self-Reflection in the Face of Images of Western Superiority'. In Robbins, Joel and Wardlow, Holly (eds), *The Making of Global and Local Modernities in Melanesia: Humiliation, Transformation, and the Nature of Cultural Change*. Aldershot: Ashgate, 73–84.

Lekitoo, Hanro Yonathan 2012. *Potret Manusia Pohon: Komunitas Adat Terpencil Suku Korowai di Daerah Selatan Papua dan Tantangannya Memasuki Peradaban Baru* [Portrait of the Tree People: The Isolated Customary Law Community of the Korowai Tribe in the Southern Region of Papua and Its Challenges for Entering a New Civilization]. Jakarta: Penerbit Balai Pustaka.

MacCannell, Dean 1990. 'Cannibal Tours'. *Visual Anthropology Review* 6(2):14–24.

McWilliam, Andrew 2011. 'Marginal Governance in the Time of Pemekaran: Case Studies from Sulawesi and West Papua'. *Asian Journal of Social Science* 39:150–170.

Muller, Kal 1990. *New Guinea: Journey into the Stone Age*. Lincolnwood (IL): Passport Books.

Munro, Jenny 2013. 'The Violence of Inflated Possibilities: Education, Transformation, and Diminishment in Wamena, Papua'. *Indonesia* 95:25–46.

Nelson, Jimmy 2013. *Before They Pass Away*. Kempen, Germany: teNeues.

Pagawak, Rony 2007. *Sejarah Masuk dan Lahirnya Gereja Injili di Indonesia.* Wamena: Lembaga P3 GIDI Wilayah BOGO.

Pandian, Anand 2009. *Crooked Stalks: Cultivating Virtue in South India.* Cambridge: Cambridge University Press.

Pigg, Stacy Leigh 1992. 'Inventing Social Categories Through Place: Social Representations and Development in Nepal'. *Comparative Studies in Society and History* 34(3): 491–513.

Rakhmani, Inaya 2012. 'A Note on Jayapura'. *Review of Indonesian and Malaysian Affairs* 46(1): 151–157.

Reid, Anthony 1994. 'Early Southeast Asian Categorizations of Europeans'. In Schwartz, Stuart B. (ed.), *Implicit Understandings: Observing, Reporting, and Reflecting on the Encounters between Europeans and Other Peoples in the Early Modern Era.* Cambridge: Cambridge University Press, 268–294.

Robbins, Joel 1994. 'Equality as a Value: Ideology in Dumont, Melanesia, and the West'. *Social Analysis* 36: 21–70.

Robbins, Joel 2006. 'On Giving Ground: Globalization, Religion, and Territorial Detachment in a Papua New Guinea Society'. In Kahler, Miles and Walter, Barbara F. (eds), *Territoriality and Conflict in an Era of Globalization.* Cambridge: Cambridge University Press, 62–84.

Robbins, Joel 2009. 'Rethinking Gifts and Commodities: Reciprocity, Recognition, and the Morality of Exchange'. In Browne, Katherine E. and Milgram, B. Lynne (eds), *Economics and Morality: Anthropological Approaches.* Lanham (MD): Altamira, 43–58.

Robbins, Joel and Wardlow, Holly (eds) 2005. *The Making of Global and Local Modernities in Melanesia: Humiliation, Transformation, and the Nature of Cultural Change.* Burlington (VT): Ashgate.

Rumsey, Alan 2006. 'The Articulation of Indigenous and Exogenous Orders in Highland New Guinea and Beyond'. *The Australian Journal Of Anthropology* 17(1): 47–69.

Rutherford, Danilyn 2003. *Raiding the Land of the Foreigners: The Limits of the Nation on an Indonesian Frontier.* Princeton: Princeton University Press.

Rutherford, Danilyn 2013. 'Living, as it Were, in the Stone Age'. *Indonesia* 95:1–7.

Salgado, Sebastião 2013. *Genesis.* Cologne: Taschen.

Schoorl, J. W. 1993. *Culture and Change among the Muyu.* Leiden: KITLV.

Scott, James C. 2009. *The Art of Not Being Governed: An Anarchist History of Upland Southeast Asia*. New Haven: Yale University Press.

Smith, Bernard 1985. *European Vision and the South Pacific*. New Haven: Yale University Press.

Smith, Bernard 1992. *Imagining the Pacific: In the Wake of the Cook Voyages*. New Haven: Yale University Press.

Stasch, Rupert 2001. 'Giving Up Homicide: Korowai Experience of Witches and Police (West Papua)'. *Oceania* 72(1): 33–55.

Stasch, Rupert 2003. 'The Semiotics of World-making in Korowai Feast Longhouses'. *Language and Communication* 23(3/4): 359–383.

Stasch, Rupert 2007. 'Demon Language: The Otherness of Indonesian in a Papuan Community'. In Makihara, Miki and Schieffelin, Bambi (eds), *Consequences of Contact: Language Ideologies and Sociocultural Transformations in Pacific Societies*. Oxford: Oxford University Press, 96–124.

Stasch, Rupert 2011a. 'Korowai Treehouses and the Everyday Representation of Time, Belonging, and Death'. *The Asia Pacific Journal of Anthropology* 12(4): 327–347.

Stasch, Rupert 2011b. 'Textual Iconicity and the Primitivist Cosmos: Chronotopes of Desire in Travel Writing about Korowai of West Papua'. *Journal of Linguistic Anthropology* 21(1): 1–21.

Stasch, Rupert 2013. 'The Poetics of Village Space When Villages are New: Settlement Form as History-Making in West Papua'. *American Ethnologist* 40(3): 555–570.

Stasch, Rupert 2014a. 'Primitivist Tourism and Romantic Individualism: On the Values in Exotic Stereotypy about Cultural Others'. *Anthropological Theory* 14(3): 191–214.

Stasch, Rupert 2014b. 'Toward Symmetric Treatment of Imaginaries: Nudity and Payment in Tourism to Papua's "Treehouse People"'. In Salazar, Noel B. and Graburn, Nelson (eds), *Tourism Imaginaries: Anthropological Approaches*. Oxford: Berghahn, 31–56.

Stasch, Rupert 2014c. 'Powers of Incomprehension: Linguistic Otherness, Translators, and Political Structure in New Guinea Tourism Encounters.' *Hau: Journal of Ethnographic Theory* 4(2):73–94.

Steinmetz, George 1996. 'Irian Jaya's People of the Trees'. *National Geographic* 189(2): 34–43.

Sudarman, Dea, Blanchard, Claude and Ushiyama, Junichi 1986. *Dans les Villages des Arbres*. Paris: Adavision. 24m.

Sykes, Karen n.d. *The Worth of an Education in Papua New Guinea: Making the Generation Gap*. Department of Anthropology, Manchester University, unpublished.

Timmer, Jaap 2007. 'Erring Decentralization and Elite Politics in Papua'. In Nordholdt, Henk Schulte and van Klinken, Gerry (eds), *Renegotiating Boundaries: Local Politics in Post-Suharto Indonesia*. Leiden: KITLV, 459–482.

Trilling, Lionel 1972. *Sincerity and Authenticity*. Cambridge (MA): Harvard University Press.

Wamafma, Alex 2008. 'Bertemu Orang Pohon' [Meeting the Tree People]. In Visser, Leontine and Marey, Amapon Jos (eds), *Bakti Pamong Praja Papua di Era Transisi Kekuasaan Belanda ke Indonesia*. Jakarta: Kompas, 149–174.

Wardlow, Holly 2006. *Wayward Women: Sexuality and Agency in a New Guinea Society*. Berkeley: University of California Press.

Wahyudi 2010. *Membangun Negeri Perbatasan: Kiat Membangun Kampung di Perbatasan Papua*. Jakarta: Wadi Press and Pamong Institute.

Widjojo, Muridan 2014. 'Melanesia in Review: Issues and Events, 2013: Papua'. *Contemporary Pacific* 26(2): 506–516.

4. Papua Coming of Age: The Cycle of Man's Civilisation and Two Other Papuan Histories

Jaap Timmer

In Maurice Halbwachs's *Les cadres sociaux de la mémoire* (1952) and *La topographie légendaire des évangiles en terre sainte: Etude de mémoire collective* (1941) (published together in English as *On Collective Memory* in 1992) we learn that it is through membership of a social group that people are able to acquire, to localise and to recall memories. Halbwachs's theory of the social construction of memory demonstrates that 'society tends to erase from its memory everything which could separate individuals' (1992: 182–183). It is in the interaction between the individual and society that individual memories are reshaped and reconstructed. Along these lines, Michael Jackson points out that it is in the process of personal memories becoming collectivised and historicised that 'they cease to be properties of individual minds and enter into intersubjectivity. As such the line between immediate and interpreted experience effectively disappears' (1998: 140). Or, as Paul Connerton, in his reflection on Halbwachs' theory, explains:

> What binds together recent memories is not the fact that they are contiguous in time but rather the fact that they form part of a whole ensemble of thoughts common to a group, to the groups with which we are in a relationship at present or have been in some connection in the recent past. When we wish to evoke such memories it is enough if we direct our attention to the prevailing interest of the group and follow the course of reflection customary to it. Exactly the same applies when we want to recall more distant memories. To evoke such memories, it is enough, once again, to direct our attention to the recollections which occupy a primary place in the thoughts of the group (1989: 36–37).

Histories, then, are narratives possessed of authority for which claims are made not only to the status of truth, 'but what is more, to the status of *paradigmatic* truth' (Lincoln 1989: 24). Bruce Lincoln (1989) presents compelling reasons 'to classify narratives not by their content but by the claims that are made by their narrators and the way in which those claims are received by their audience(s)' (p. 24). In his classification of narratives that includes fables (having no truth-claims at all), legends (making truth-claims but lacking credibility), history (enjoying credibility amid its audience), and, the most crucial one is myth (both credible and having authority). On the authority of myth, Lincoln, following Malinowski and Geertz, argues that it lies in the status of the myth's claim to paradigmatic truth:

> In this sense the authority of myth is somewhat akin of that of charters, models, templates, and blueprints, but one can go beyond this formulation and recognize that it is also (and perhaps more important) akin to that of revolutionary slogans and ancestral invocations, in that through the recitation of myth one may effectively mobilize a social grouping. Thus, myth is not just a coding device in which important information is conveyed, on the basis of which of which actors *can then* construct society. It is also a discursive act through which actors evoke the sentiments out of which society is actively constructed (ibid.: 24–25).

Following Lincoln's view on myth (see White 1987), I will illuminate the paradigmatic truths and related moral components in three historical narratives authored by Papuans about the past, to show how they, in different but overlapping ways, construct the idea that Papua is coming of age in what they claim to be a genuinely historical account. They are vernacular logics of reality and they are performative historicities – much of the meaning that they give to the past is made in the act of their communication to specific audiences (Dening 1991, see Rutherford 2012). This means that they have to be understood in the context in which they are produced. Consequently the analysis below gives prominence to the question whose historicity and whose criteria for truth? (see Ballard 2014: 101).

The phrase 'coming of age' was used by many Papuans with whom I spoke during my visits to Papua since the mid-1990s. Perhaps most explicitly, Albert, in a narrative I cite below, used it to describe Papua as maturing (*'menjadi dewasa'*), as moving up the ladder of civilisation, and becoming an independent nation. With respect to the latter he would say *'menjadi Papua'*. With the phrase coming of age, then, I try to capture both the conditions under which the historicities are produced and what they convey about people's understanding of oneself and Papua as an identity and a nation. In broad terms, I will conclude that the three historicities suggest that Papua is seen as being on the verge of establishing itself as a sovereign nation but that there are obstacles along the way. The essence, the paradigmatic truth, for getting to sovereignty is in place and is exempt from the law of change. The historical narratives bring to the fore that essential elements of Papua's sovereignty are given by virtue of genealogical connection, largely independent of the situational contexts of human activity and human relationships. This illustrates the extent to which Western genealogical models have shaped Papuan historicity, foremost through particular ways of reading the Bible but also through familiarity with Indonesian national history production and modern state genealogy.

It is important to realise that the three Papuan histories do not surface in a democratic environment that provides sufficient public space for debate. There are contests over natural resources and economic and political power struggles, and frictions between different ethnicities, religion, and immigrants and locals (Timmer 2007a). Alternative histories emerging from Papua are seen as controversial and subversive by Jakarta. The banning of books like Benny Giay's (2006) account of the abduction and murder of Theys Eluay in 2001 is just one example to illustrate that history writing in Papua can be a dangerous business and this has been the case since the Indonesian government began to rule the territory in the early 1960s. In such conditions, as Talal Asad points out for the concept of orthodox Islam,

> the process of determining orthodoxy in conditions of change and contest includes attempts at achieving discursive coherence, at representing the present within an authoritative narrative that includes positive evaluations of past events and persons (1993: 210).

The first narrative is entitled the *Cycle of Man's Civilisation* (*Siklus Peradaban Manusia*), which sketches the development of civilisation moving cyclically, not with a teleological goal but propelled by man's inclination to seek completion, because of man's inescapable need for 'the perfect' (*yang sempurna*). According to this history the people of Papua are authentic, pure, indigenous and not to be classified as 'backward' (*terbalakang*) and 'primitive' (*primitip*) by the Indonesian state. The second story traces a genealogical connection between Papua and Java, linking Papua's past to Javanese Kingdoms that are key to Indonesian nationalism. It suggests that original cultural traits from that past are transmitted across generations and provide status to the Onim people of the Southwest Bird's Head of Papua. The third narrative is *Basic Guidelines*, Don Flassy's (1999) *Constitution for West Papua* that through finding the essence of Papuan souls in terms of one soul, one nation – mimicking Indonesian national narrative – seeks to unite Papuans in one nation (see Timmer 2013).

The regional focus of this paper is the Bird's Head (*Kepala Burung*) Peninsula that is well known as the borderland between New Guinea and the Moluccas, where the influences of the sultanates of the North Moluccas have left countless marks and where the first missionaries, C.W. Ottow and J.G. Geissler landed in 1855 (on Mansinam Island).[1] From a cartographic and local millenarian perspective, the

---

1 Generally not cited by Papuans, Thomas Forrest of the British East India Company established friendly relationships with people in the Dorei Bay in 1755, and about two decades later Lieutenant John Hayes built Fort Coronation there and renamed the bay Restoration Bay but the British settlement failed after one year. Also more prominent in European historiography than in local histories is John McCluer who, while surveying the coastline for the British East India Company, found all the survivors in Fort Coronation ill. In the mid-19th century, the British naturalist Alfred Wallace spent nearly six months at Dorei Bay in 1858. A few decades later, Count von Rosenberg visited the village of Andai (in 1869) and the Italian naturalists Luigi d'Albertis and Odoardo Beccari did research in the area in 1873 (Gash and Whittaker 1975: 20–23).

local Reverend Leonardus Jenbise (who is currently a lecturer in a Theological College in Jayapura) portrays the Bird's Head as the upper part that may pull the whole island towards becoming fully established as an independent nation. In the preface to the proceedings of the 1997 Irian Jaya Studies conference in Leiden, Rev. Jenbise is quoted as commenting on the importance of the Bird's Head Peninsula as follows: 'the head must be raised before the bird can fly' (Miedema et al. 1998: xi). Similarly suggesting that Papua is coming of age but with biblical allusions, Flassy writes in *Basic Guidelines* that 'after chucking The Head of the Bird's Like Island, then the whole body on to the tail shined by the Love of Jesus Christ, from Sorong to Samarai' (Flassy 1999: 7).[2]

Redistributing the cards

My reading of the three narratives shows that what these particular views of the past or histories do to people's understanding of current events is a kind of stilling of the tumult of different understandings and motives during past events. In a reflection on this European experience of history, James Scott observes that

> what 'history' does to our understanding of events is akin to what a television broadcast does to our understanding of a basketball or ice hockey game. The camera is placed above and outside the plane of action, rather like a helicopter hovering above the action. The effect of this bird's-eye view is to distance the viewer from the play and apparently slow it down. Even then, lest the viewer miss a crucial shot or pass, actual slow motion is used to further slow the action and allow the viewer to see it in detail again and again. Combined, the bird's-eye-perspective and slow motion make the player's moves seem deceptively easy to viewers, who might fantasize mastering such moves themselves. Alas, no actual player ever experiences the actual game from a helicopter or in slow motion. And when, rarely, the camera is placed at floor level and close to the action in real time, one finally appreciates the blinding speed and complexity of the game as the players experience it; the brief fantasy is instantly dispelled (2012: 136).

---

2   Samarai is a small island offshore the easternmost tip of Papua New Guinea. Because of easy access by boats it was one of the first places where European traders settled. The bird-like shape of the island as evoked by modern cartography has of course a longer history among Europeans. For example, in *The Human Aviary* (Holton and Read 1971), Kenneth E. Read writes that New Guinea is 'like a prehistoric mother bird marshaling and fledgling flock that spreads behind it to the boundary of Polynesia. Its great head points toward its Asian homeland, and in the early morning, as it stirs beneath the covers of its clouds, the air seems to be filled with its rumination on the themes of man and time. It existed long before man found protection under its rainbow plumage' (p. 7).

Indeed, all histories are flat as they erase contingency or rather simplify certain contingencies to highlight events and connections that are of contemporary importance to those who construct the narratives. What it does to their understanding is akin to what Scott describes. Scott's thesis is that the condensation of history is the result of 'our desire for clean narratives, and the need for elites and organizations to project an image of control and purpose' (2012: 141). Papuan desire for narratives about the past is also about control and purpose, and the causations apparent in the three historiographies are meaningful as sinews of divine design that instead of conspiring to convey a false image are part of a quest for authenticity to reveal the true character and spirit of the Papuan people and their nation.

This is what makes them different from histories written by foreign observers. For example, the recent histories produced by Dirk Vlasblom (2004) and Pieter Drooglever (2005) are impressive studies of key events in Papua. Vlasblom's history of Papua is a thoroughly studied account of social, cultural and political development in Papua (see Timmer 2005). Drooglever focuses on the issue of decolonisation and the 1969 plebiscite known as the Act of Free Choice (*Penentuan Pendapat Rakyat*, PEPERA), during which a carefully selected and limited number of Papuans, allegedly representing the voice of local groups, voted in favour of relinquishing sovereignty in favour of Indonesian citizenship (Timmer 2007b: 1102).

Both Vlasblom and Drooglever undertook these studies in response to the Second Congress held in Papua in May–June 2000. This congress followed a first congress, organised by the so-called Independent Committee in October 1961 when the region was still a Dutch overseas territory and the administration in Hollandia (now Jayapura) was frenziedly preparing Papuans for self-determination to comply with demands of the United Nations. The First Congress made four national declarations. They declared the Morning Star flag to be the national symbol, declared the national anthem to be *Hai Tanahku Papua* ('Papua My Country'), declared the name 'West Papua' for the independent state and declared the name 'Papuans' for its people. Two months later, on 1 December 1961, the Morning Star flag was raised alongside the flag of the Kingdom of the Netherlands and *Hai Tanahku Papua* was sung after the Dutch Wilhelmus anthem in front of the building of the New Guinea Council that was inaugurated by Governor P.J. Platteel earlier that year. The official recognition of these names and symbols for a Papuan state by the Netherlands government has since been explained by many as the initiation of the Papuan nation.

During the Second Congress many Papuans expressed the need to *meluruskan sejarah* ('straighten history') or an intervention in Indonesian history writing. Papuans see that Indonesia's representation of Papua limits their history to a nation-building narrative that fails to account for the facts of such events as the Act of Free Choice, which for many features prominently as the epitome of the denial of sovereignty to Papuans (Saltford 2002; Drooglever 2005). Partly trying to answer Papuan demands, the Netherlands government commissioned Drooglever to study the events surrounding the transfer of Netherlands New Guinea to Indonesia. Vlasblom was present during the Second Congress and began to speak with a great number of sources and set himself the task of writing a history of Papua that would answer to Papuan concerns, or at least help them to consider and reconsider certain events in their past. While Vlasblom's study attempts to probe under the skin of Papuans, Drooglever's has limited consideration about what it means to be a Papuan. The study by Drooglever is a factual representation of the past; it is 'intentionally researched and composed according to rational principles' (Hirsch and Stewart 2005: 263).

In contrast, the Papuan quest for history invocates different kind of histories with a past that is seen from a local perspective of Christianisation and familiarity with the idea of nation. These histories typically begin before contact with the European world but the pre-European past is condensed into a kind of limbo between Genesis and the arrival of the missionaries, as if Papuans have since God's creation been waiting for God's Word to reach them. Papuans, have, as Epeli Hau'ofa notes for the Pacific in general, 'no history before imperialism' (2000: 456). They live, in terms of the Dutch journalist Anthony van Kampen, in a land that God forgot (*Het Land dat God Vergat*, 1967). Locally this perception is reflected in histories that suggest a strong attachment to an ancestral homeland that is often, in Christian terms, conceived as a blessed, holy land. Or, as Benny Giay writes in his study of Zakheus Pakage, the religious leader of the *Wege* communities among the Me in the Wissel Lakes region of the Western Central Highlands of West Papua:

> Religion is … part of the collective memory of the society's past which shapes its view of itself and its identity and the aspirations of the society to preserve such an aspiration … The rise of Zakheus's communities and indigenous theological awareness can be seen as a new consciousness to preserve the history of their communities and identity in the midst of change and opposition (1995: 10).

In all three narratives discussed in this paper land features as ancestral homeland. Clearly, the quest for authenticity brings along an attachment to an ancestral homeland that is different from the kind of attachment to the land described by Melanesian anthropologists in terms of identity-through-place. Chris Ballard points out that for the Huli of the Southern Highlands of Papua New Guinea, this sense of connection to the land

> finds expression in the common statement that water from the streams of one's own land is the sweetest – all other streams taste different and

this taste is one of the markers of difference that establishes identity. If you were to take the Huli out of [the] Haeapuga [Basin], as one group, they would no doubt thrive – as Huli do in all the metropolitan centres of Papua New Guinea. But without access and reference to their land, they would cease to be Huli. Urban Huli remain Huli largely through reference to other Huli, and particularly through those who remain 'in place'. Conceptions of what it is to be a social being are grounded in a specific territory (Ballard 1997: 50).

In his study of Reite at the Rai Coast of Papua New Guinea, James Leach similarly shows that 'the incorporation of land and place into a history of social relations is where life exists' (2003: 29).

The three historical narratives do appeal to the idea of descent from an ancestral population that has been living on this land for ages, but they follow a genealogical model that is not traditional Melanesian but that belongs to the discourse of the state.

The genealogical model is deeply implicated in the discourse of the state: indeed it is the principal source of legitimation for the state's sovereign entitlement to defend and administer its territory in the name of the nation. For the state, the land belongs to the national heritage, and is held in trust by each generation of citizens on behalf of their descendants (Ingold 2000: 151).

The Indonesian state suggests that the current generation of Indonesians can trace their ancestry to ancient kingdoms whose mandalas stretched territorially all the way to Papua (and Sabang at the western end). Moreover, these kingdoms embody the virtues of the Indonesian nation. According to nation-builders like President Sukarno and President Suharto, the land of Papua is an integral part of this heritage. The inclusion of the land of Papua in their nation-building narratives not only meant the completion of the (post-colonial) nation; it was also an act that is legitimised on the basis of the state descending from kingdoms that are said to have territorially included Papua. But the limit of this nationalist model is illustrated by the three cases here. What they show is a tendency that James Scott, in the *Art of Not Being Governed* (2009: 307), describes as the mobilisation of people against the state around the idiom of state formation, with appeal to the same kind of genealogy, either with roots in Papua and its near or distant foreign lands or with roots in Indonesia's mythological past. Radical opposition then 'is a question of redistributing the cards in an existing card game, not a question of whether to sit at a table at all or, for that matter, to throw the table over' (Scott 2009: 303).

The cycle of man's civilisation

During the first few months of my first fieldwork in the south-western Bird's Head of what back then, in the early 1990s, was still called Irian Jaya, I was often accompanied by Albert.[3] Albert had just returned home from Jayapura where he had obtained a LL.M (*Sarjana Hukum*) from Universitas Cenderawasih, and while busy trying to secure a job in the district or regional government, he was interested to learn about what I was doing. Although my fluency in Indonesian was still limited, our conversations often revolved around challenging existential questions such as the identity, status, and future of Papua and the Europeans. Albert's thoughts on these matters showed signs of his exposure to a university environment. He described to me an atmosphere of confusion. Most students often voiced anti-Indonesian sentiments and employed texts and theories to underpin a sense of being different as Papuans, often accompanied by reflection on histories of ancient migration to New Guinea, trade connections with Moluccan sultans, Christianisation, Dutch colonisation and Indonesian annexation. At the same time, he noticed that people's noses were oriented towards Indonesia and its government structure that offered tenured jobs and prospects of promotion to head of district or even governor.

'Why is no one looking at Melanesia if that is the region where we tend to affiliate ourselves with when it comes to roots, race and culture?' Albert asked me once. Just a few weeks earlier I was in Jakarta arranging my research permit and affiliation with the Indonesian Institute of Sciences (LIPI). Reflecting on Jakarta's modernity, I told Albert that I could understand why such urban environments as well as the grandness and power of the Indonesian state and nation arouse the interest of Papuans living in the margins. Albert agreed and continued by telling me about the experiences of his brother Yopi, who was doing his studies in medicine at a prominent university on Java.[4] Every time Yopi came home to Teminabuan he brought a lot of electronic gadgets for all his siblings and friends and last year he even brought a stereo set and VCD player and a wide screen TV for his parents. Besides gadgets Yopi also brought home experiences of being discriminated against on Java. People had been calling him a filthy black (*hitam kotor*), a Papuan pig (*babi Papua*) and an ape (*monyet*). These are among the more common kind of verbal harassments that many Papuan students in urban environments throughout Indonesia have to endure (see Munro in this volume). 'You know, this is just one element of all the things that "Indonesia" does to stop us Papuans from reconnecting with the Netherlands.' I was intrigued by this observation and asked Albert to elaborate, which he did by drawing the following figure.

---

3   Albert is a pseudonym.
4   Yopi is a pseudonym.

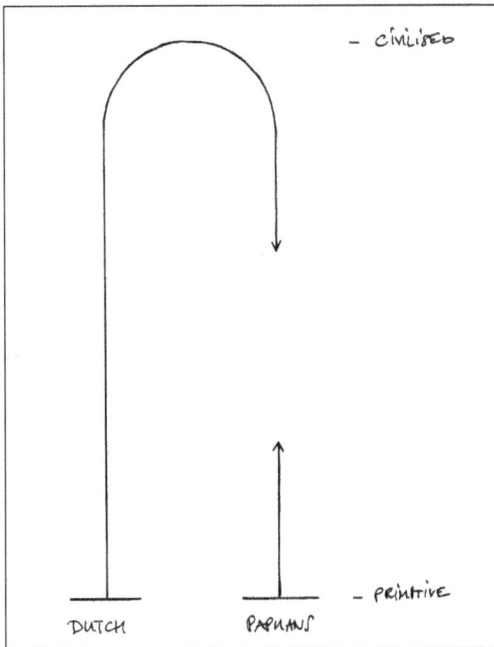

Figure 4.1. Albert's 'Cycle of Man's Civilisation', drawn on the basis of the original rough sketch.

Source: J Timmer.

Albert explains:

> This curve is the cycle of man's civilisation. Man is complex. He has thoughts, concerns, wishes, feelings and so on. And man has a life trajectory, a path, of his own. At whatever stage he is at along this path, he needs a lot of other people to survive while at the same time he feels that he can handle everything by himself. When man is young he needs others to feed him and assist him in learning things, but once he is grown-up he feels that he can do everything by himself. Then, when he has grown old, he will realize that he needs others to help him. He will need help to cut a walking stick, he needs glasses made by someone, and so on. This is the journey or path of life. This path affects his thoughts, his wishes, his concerns, his feelings. There will be moments during which he thinks he is still strong and fit while in fact he already needs a stick for walking. He must return!

> The small child who needs supervision is like *peradaban primitip* ('primitive civilisation'). Because he is still primitive, he will highly value the person who comes and helps him. He will think that the other has better thoughts than him and he will begin to consider himself to

be *bodoh* ('stupid'). An example: *Orang Irian* ('the Irianese') were still primitive according to the Dutch when they first arrived here. They brought him Christianity, education, clothes, and so on. The people here thought 'yes, that is all good' and they began to follow the ways of the white man. In those days the people of Irian knew all kinds of things including secret knowledge like the tradition of *wuon*.[5] But when the Dutch said, 'do A', they did A, and when they said, 'do B', they did B. But after the Dutch left and went back, the Irianese *menjadi dewasa* ('came of age'). 'Coming of age' (*menjadi dewasa*) he developed many different thoughts and began to want a lot of things, and his feelings began to evolve and he started to think that he does not have everything. He became individualistic and forgot about the community. In abstract terms, he has come of age only halfway primitive and *moderen* ('modern') [see the diagram]. His identity shattered.

Grown-ups and their ideas about what is modern affect the Irianese, but to get to the modern stage he needs those grown-ups. This is where we are at. While the Dutch in the past said that our culture is primitive the Indonesians who arrived in Irian Jaya later on say that it is *kuno* ('obsolete', 'bygone') while suggesting that the latest, the modern is to be found in Jakarta. The Dutch said that they would help us to get there and did put effort into that. The Indonesians simply say that they have it and that our ways are hopelessly out-dated. The Indonesians have already reached the modern and when they took over Irian Jaya they realised that some are not yet modern. This is a *lingkaran setan* ('vicious cycle') in which the difference in development between Papua and Indonesia aggravate each other, unstoppable. You see, it will worsen the situation.

At present all the policies of the Government of Indonesia are *pusing* ('confused'). Indonesia wants to become modern without recognising the value of the original. Indonesia is a strange state. Other countries like the Netherlands want to return to *yang sempurna* ('the perfect') because they like that. At the same time, here in Irian no one wants to return to the *adat* ('customs') of the past. Who wants to learn those things that belong to the past? The Dutch and the Indonesian government have forbidden them. They now suggest that tourists may be interested and they may bring a lot of money. *Kacau!* ('Chaos!') According to me this is not good. It is nonsense.

---

5 *Wuon* is the shorthand way of referring to a complex of rituals focused around male initiation. The *wuon* cult was active throughout the region until the Dutch missionaries forbade it in the 1950s. The rituals were lead by *na wuon*, ritual leaders who would conduct the initiation and also use their powers to ensure fertility of gardens, guarantee successful hunting and fishing, heal the ills and battle evil powers such as witchcraft (*lait*).

Albert adopts an evolutionist model to establish a paradigmatic truth about Papua. For Europe, James Ferguson points out that the effect of evolutionist models of history 'was to transform a *spatialized* global hierarchy into a *temporalized* (putative) historical sequence' (2006: 178). This evolutionary scheme was applied to the newly emerging nations in the regions that were decolonised following the Second World War and became the way in which development and state-building in the post-colonies is understood. Like the West used to map history against hierarchy and development time against political status (Ferguson 2006: 177), Albert, among many others in West Papua, map the backwardness of Papuans against an evolutionary hierarchy with Western countries and Indonesia at the top, and Papua at the bottom.

Albert mythologises this bottom to 'the perfect' (*yang sempurna*) in terms of universal and inescapable evolution from being to becoming, from the temporal to the primordial, relating to an original, authentic and timeless truth about Papua. The main issues around inauthenticity or departure from the perfect is, according to Albert, that people in the West are individualistic, that they do not appreciate the importance of relationships and they have lost their connections with the land. He sees that 'Indonesia' is bringing a similar kind of development to Papua and this conflicts with being Papuan.

Genesis and time

Albert's narrative illustrates how many in the Teminabuan region of the Bird's Head understand Genesis in terms of their own past. The primordial perfect state of being called Toror in the Teminabuan region features as the biblical Garden of Eden in most contemporary accounts of local stories surrounding the alleged parallels between the *wuon* initiation cult and Christianity (see Flassy 1985 and 2002). During my research in the early 1990s the few still living *na wuon* (ritual leaders) suggested that they knew the details about Toror but shrouded them in mystery. This mystery, in particular in the present situation in which living *na wuon* are exceptional individuals who retain the meaningful tradition of a once-dominant elite, leads to a multitude of conclusions about Toror.

Toror pictures completeness and unity before the present world came into being. According to Flassy (1985: xii–xiv), this period is called *qolm mqsya* in Tehit, meaning 'the carrying spirit or the guardian spirit'. What Flassy means to say is that people believe that in Toror there was only one spirit. Some informants explained to me that I should understand this *ni mres* ('one spirit') as *kahan* ('the truth, the core secret, the first and most powerful'). This primary state of being is seen as a world where one can get to only when all power and lost knowledge is returned to Imyan.

As said, many compare Toror with the Garden of Eden, but it is not just that Genesis provides an account of the origins of reality – which it does – but that the kinds of meaning that people give to Genesis is related to their ideas about Toror and that ideas about Toror influence the way they read Genesis. The prevailing interpretation of Genesis has a particular temporal dimension not unfamiliar to Western Christians: it is typical of an apocalyptical interpretation that suggests a return of man as mortal creatures to the Garden of Eden at the End of Days (Hendel 2013: 9). This is reflected in Albert's narrative above, in which the suggestion is made that the present imperfect state will come to an end with the return to the perfect era (*yang sempurna*), a paradise.

The other stream in Albert's 'Cycle of Man's Civilisation' revolves around the idea of knowledge in the way it envisions a world that has superior knowledge and is already developed. This is also a dominant concept in Jewish and Christian religious thought (Hendel 2013: 9) that has been brought to Papua through missionisation and colonisation. A story that Seppy Kemesrar (37, Haha village, Teminabuan district) told me further illustrates this and highlights some of the variety of ideas held about Toror:

> The old *na wuon* suggest that at first there was Toror. We do not know about Toror because it is their secret. But from the Bible we know that God created man. Maybe he did create man but not all human beings. From there, the soul [*thalye*] went to other people. Adam was created directly by God. I indeed believe that Allah did this. He created Adam in His own image. Adam was similar to God. But I don't believe that after that, God created all other human beings. He did not give *thalye* to every single person.

> What we see in the world today or what we hear from the many stories that are doing the rounds here, is that there are people who originate from a certain place and others from another place. This means that God created humans as animals, some appear here, and others appear there. Maybe God gave the breath, but where humans would appear was not restricted to the Garden of Eden. For example, the Kefi people [a clan living north of Haha] came out of a hole in a tree. There are also people who came out of the ground, like the Mejefat Lumna [Kemesrar's main ancestor]. How can this be?

> These people may not be children of God. They are animals who might have got their *thalye* by God but they were not created in His image. He brought these beings into being but he did not create them. There is difference between bringing into being and creating. God created Adam but he brought humankind into being. All our genealogies go back to Adam. I therefore question the story that people here tell about their

ancestors coming from a hole in the earth. Like Sagisolo, what is the truth about their origin story? The Sagisolo people come from the Kefi tree. Flassy people came out of the ground. There also the Saflembolo people who came out of the ground at an anthill.

Perhaps the reason behind this is that there were not enough people to inhabit the earth. When God realised this he found other ways to bring people into being. He did that to fill this earth with human beings. God has already promised to the people of Israel in the Old Testament that there should be many people. As many people on earth as there are stars in the sky.

Seppy Kemesrar, Haha village, May 1995.

Kemesrar's discussion should be viewed from the fact that, as I explain in detail in Timmer (2000), among the four groups in the village of Haha, the Kemesrar people most closely relate to Toror and that by extension, others are perhaps animals and may not be God's children. This Christian twist to origin stories marks the importance attached to closeness to God and Toror and the general concern with the cosmic unity in the world. The Toror that Kemesrar describes is the state of being of his Kemesrar ancestors when they still resided at Baimla. Baimla was an 'entrenchment' (*mla*) situated on an island in the estuary of the Segun River, some 40 kilometres east of Cape Sele on the westernmost point of the Kepala Burung Peninsula.

Baimla was important to the rajas associated with the Sultanate of Tidore as a place where forest products and manpower could be gained. Baimla might have been one of the nine *negorijen* or native villages mentioned by De Clerq in 1858 (in Kamma 1947/48: 540).[6] Although the inhabitants of Baimla enjoyed a good life, one major problem concerned them. The story that recounts the migration of the Kemesrar people tells how the inhabitants of Baimla feared the death of newborns because of the suffering endured by expectant mothers. As prevention, they had to cut open her belly to save the child at the expense of its mother's life.[7] All children in Baimla were thus raised as motherless children and fed with water instead of breast milk. The people of Baimla cut children from their mother's womb until there came a woman from the Krimadi people who was exchanged for cloths by the Kondjol people at the Kaibus River.

---

6   People from Biak founded these villages as colonies or trading posts on the mainland of the Bird's Head Peninsula. In this part of West New Guinea, it was mostly Biak people who had long distance trade relations and spread the Biak language as a trade language throughout the western and northern coast of the Bird's Head, the Raja Ampat Islands and Eastern Maluku. The origin story of *wuon* in which Bauk brings a metal axe into the interior of the Teminabuan area relates to this trade history (see Kamma and Kooijman 1973: 25-26).
7   The idea that formerly birth could be given to a child by means of a 'Caesarean' only is also reported to exist among Inanwatan people (Lotgering 1940: 19). After having seen a dog bearing puppies, the women realised that they should do it in a similar way.

After living with the people at Baimla for some time, the Krimadi visitor taught her hosts the proper way to give birth to a child. When the people saw that the new techniques worked, they began to admire their guest for her knowledge. For that reason, the people of Baimla moved to the birthplace of the Krimadi woman, in the direction of where the sun rises. They readied their canoes, sewed sails and prepared provisions for the long journey. In another version of this story, the people of Baimla left unprepared. Because of a conflict surrounding the adulterous act of a Kondororit person, the Kemesrar people had to flee. Others stressed that the story is a Christian story that tells that people had to move away from Baimla because water was overflowing the island. It suggests that Baimla is in fact the biblical Babel and that Noah saved all living creatures from Baimla, the actual origin place of all people.

These stories reveal that people do not read the Bible as a disparate set of texts but instead as a cohesive whole that reveals the nature of local history, the unfolding of time and the purpose of history. The moment Papua's past becomes part of Christianity's eternal truths they become remote in relation to other histories such as migrations, wars, the advent of missionaries, the establishment of the government and so on. Becoming part of religious representation that gives privileged status to Genesis the collective memory about this period, in terms of Halbwachs,

> subsists in a state of isolation and is all the more separated from other social remembrances to the degree that the epoch in which they were formed is more remote, so that there is a more marked contrast between the type of life and social thought that they reproduce and the ideas and modes of human action of today (1992: 91).

Both Toror and the ancient Papua *sempurna* in Albert's cycle are fixed ones and oblige people to mirror their current ways of doing against it. We will keep perception of time in mind until we begin to analyse the Constitution for West Papua which builds on similar ideas and gives an even more compelling sense of how people in this part of Papua bring to light an idealised past and thereby providing biblical underpinning, relationship and dignity to the idea of a Papuan nation.

Journeys between Java and Papua

Also not agreeing with the Western telos of modernity but showing identification with Indonesia's nation-building mythology, in particular its use of a genealogical model of history, is Reverend Jusuf Onim's (1998) brief history of the village of Wersar (also in the Teminabuan region) that recounts the evolution of Onin culture in relation to regional cultural dynamics and its rootedness in the

Kingdom of Sriwijaya and the Kingdom of Majapahit. According to Rev. Onim, the people of the Onin Peninsula are mentioned in the *Nagarakrtagama*, a 14th-century Javanese eulogy to the monarch of the Majapahit Empire, and their roots can be found there. The *Nagarakrtagama* contains detailed descriptions of the Majapahit Empire during its greatest extent and indeed includes a reference to Onin in Papua. Indonesian nationalists evoked these two kingdoms as an illustration of precolonial national unity (Reid 1979). Reid points out that in the eventual assessment of a synchronic history and national destiny,

> it was seen appropriate to concentrate on the grandeur of these pre-colonial kingdoms in a one-dimensional fashion, rather than to inquire further into their diverse social structures, belief systems, and economies. The question of national identity had in essence been resolved, as arising from common oppression by the Netherlands (Reid 1979: 290).

In this national history, as President Sukarno would point out later, Indonesia lost its magnificence with the arrival of the Dutch heralding hundreds of years of humiliation. In particular, during the New Order period, policymakers focused much on reviving the glory of the nation through highly centralised nation-building projects that were always metaphorically rooted in the national but largely Javanese past. Students learned virtually nothing of the political life in the archipelago after 1600, let alone the existence of different histories and cultural dynamics in the outer regions. Papua only became firmly embedded in the national narrative during the Trikora struggle against the Dutch, who were still holding on to the territory after Indonesia had proclaimed independence in 1945, and who finally had to accept Indonesian sovereignty in 1949.

In their struggle against Indonesia, people in Papua are similarly concerned with forging national histories to underpin ideas of unity. But in the absence of a past that shows similarities to glamorous old kingdoms, people tend to emphasise the moral greatness of past cultural traits that were destroyed with the advent of Indonesian colonialism but find support in Christianity, another major element in (most) Papuan cultures that sets them apart from Indonesia. It is therefore quite surprising to find a local historiography that includes references to the *Nagarakrtagama* and the two kingdoms central to Indonesian nationalism.

According to Rev. Onim, the Onin people and people in Papua as a whole enjoyed a special and respectful relationship with the Kingdom of Sriwijaya and the Kingdom of Majapahit, and they provided Papua with an authentic name and identity.

> The book Negara Kertagama, was written by the Mpu Prapanca in 1364/65. The verses 13, 14 and 15 contains place names from Irian. Mohammad Yamin [1903–1962, a well-known nationalist, historian,

poet, playwright, and politician who has written about Indonesia's struggle for independence, the history of Majapahit and who is believed to be the author of the Pancasila, the five pillars of the Indonesian nation], on the basis of a study of verse 14, is of the opinion that the term Wwanin or Onim is identical with region VIII of the area controlled by Majapahit. The verse is as follows:

Butun baggawai kuni ggaliyao mwang I(ng) salaya sumba solot muar muwah tigang i wandan ambwan athawa maloko in timur ewanin ri sran ning angeka nusatutur (Koentjaraningrat [and Bachtiar], *1953* [sic. *1963*]: *47–56)*

Apparently, these places, mentioned in verses 13, 14 and 15 were within the sphere of influence of Majapahit which at that time had its capital at Triloyo, Mojokerto, East Java. The term Wwanin (Onin) is still used in the village of Wersar in poems (songs). One such local song is as follows:

Wndindi wdo wska wana Wanin woro are wdo whriak nai ma afaaf vein eeehhh (An Onim Song).

This expression translates as: '*May the thunder bring changes, so that the weather of Wanin (Onin) will be fine, so that we can sail across to Wanin (Onin)*'. The term Wanin (Onin) is only used in the communal poems and songs of the village of Wersar, Teminabuan. The poem (song) describes life on the sea along the entire coast of the Onin Peninsula and the Bird's Head. The term Wanin is the oldest name to identify the island of Irian. Other names such as Nieuw Guinea, Papua Barat, Irian Barat and Irian Jaya, are names that have been given by foreigners. Only the name Wanin (Onin) and the name Janggi or Tungki, as used by the Chinese sailor Chau Ju Kua in the 13th century (8th century) after the Kingdom of Sriwijaya, and during the Kingdom of Majapahit are original (1998: 1–2).

In the conclusion of the paper, Rev. Onim states that

> the name Wanin … [does] not have a political or racially pejorative connotations as is the case with the name Papua. The connection with Sriwijaya and Majapahit may not have been permanent. Irian was not an area governed by either, but trade relations existed between the two areas (1998: 10).

In his history of Papua, Rev. Onim simulates the idea of sovereignty as enjoyed by ancient Javanese Kingdoms that featured as a motivating rhetoric during the Indonesian independence struggle and still underpins the nationalistic sovereignty of the current nation-state of Indonesia. If Indonesian state sovereignty can be founded on the basis of the history of ancient kingdoms then, in Rev. Onim's view, the current government should logically recognise Papua as sovereign because it featured as an acknowledged sovereign region in the past.

Rev. Onim's claims about the connections between Onim and Indonesian state mythology as underpinning the sovereignty of Papua and the hegemonic character of Onin culture in the South-western Bird's Head region has made him appear to many in the Teminabuan region as a hero. Not only is he the first from the village Wersar to become a reverend and teacher in the Theological College of the Evangelical Christian Church 'I.S. Kijne' (*Sekolah Tinggi Theologia Gereja Kristen Injili* 'I.S. Kijne'), he has also established himself as a historian who not only knows local legends but can meaningfully connect them to the world of myths underpinning the Indonesian nation. It is therefore no surprise that I came across many of his followers, one of them whose narrative I recount here. This narrative is inspired by Rev. Onim's history of the region and was prepared for a large meeting (*sidang akbar*) scheduled to be held in 1996. The purpose of the *sidang* was to resolve, 'once and for all', the ownership of lands in and around the town of Teminabuan: the villages of Kohoin, Wermit, Wersar, Aibobor, Seribau and Kohoin; and among the following descent groups: Thesya, Salambauw, Momot, Wamblesa, Kamesok, Safledrar, Kondororit, Flassy and Kondjol.

While the most important detail in other Tehit groups' histories is their claim of precedence, which is backed up by early contacts with the Wamblesa people, the Kondjol people of the village of Wersar suggest that they arrived even earlier. Many Kondjol people are changing their surnames to Onim or Onin to stress their origins and ethnic identity as their migration histories relate to the Onin Peninsula, where they lived together with the Anggiluly people. Among the Onim or Kondjol people, many claim that almost every important and heroic historical event in the Teminabuan area was due to the powers and influence of their ancestors. Rev. Onim (1988: 26) claims that it was due to the efforts of the Onim ancestor, 'Raja Angguok', that missionisation in Teminabuan, Ayamaru, Aitinyo and Ayfat got off the ground smoothly.[8] Presently, there is a strong Onim/Kondjol political lobby to claim the status of first comers and thus ownership of Teminabuan town and the Kaibus River. Their heroic history also

---

8 See Kondjol (1996: 4). Spelled as Anggok, this raja is mentioned by the government official Dumas in his 1911 *Memorandum for the Afdeeling West Nieuw-Guinea* (1992[1911]: 12) as the only person among the people living in the Kaibus River area on whom the Dutch traders and government officials could count. In current local histories of Kondjol people, Angg(u)ok plays a heroic role. Part of these histories is a song about his courageous travels in the area between the Kaibus River and the Seremuk River. Apparently, he was very successful in capturing people whom he sold to *rajas* at Onin and occasionally to *rajas* at Salawati (see Wanane 1991: 55). He is often portrayed as a mighty man who ruled over the coastal area stretching from Inanwatan all the way to Cape Sele.

wants recognition that the Onim/Kondjol people have contributed to the advent of Christianity. As evidence, they often refer to the important relations that the Onim/Kondjol people had with rajas and the sultan of Tidore.

Some go even further to suggest that the Onim/Kondjol history is still more authentic and more deeply grounded in larger spheres of power. Mince Kondjol[9] recounted in detail a history claiming that they descend from the Javanese. Their having possession of a Javanese wavy double-bladed dagger (*keris*) and a small Buddha statue afford further proof of this. The story told to me by Kondjol goes as follows:

> We originate from the island of Java, at Tanjung Priok, the present-day port of Jakarta. In the tenth century, there was a war between Islam and Buddhism. This was a religious war. Buddhism lost and was dispelled to Bali. Our ancestors kept a *kris* and the [Buddha] statue of a sitting woman. Because of this war, our ancestors, named Onain, fled to the island of Ternate. They sailed to Ternate with a sailboat [*perahu layar*]. They arrived at Ternate in the afternoon at around 4 p.m. and encountered the Anggiluly people.
>
> During the first night, the Anggiluly people accommodated the Onain people and the next day our ancestors built a house for themselves. In the early nineteenth, a religious war broke out. The Onain and Anggiluly people wanted to leave the island because they were afraid of Islam that was laying siege over the whole of Eastern Indonesia. Where could they take refuge? Each group loaded its possessions on a sailboat and headed to Irian. They already knew where Irian was because they had been there to get birds of paradise.
>
> At 8 a.m., they left from the beach of the island of Ternate, met the sultan, and steered towards Irian. In the middle of the night, it was so dark that they lost track of each other. The Anggiluly people went to the island of Ega. In the morning they saw an island shaped in the form of the letter O. They called it Onin. The Onain people travelled to Kowiai and saw that its shape was similar to a *songkok* (a fez-like cap). They named the island after the Ternate word for this cap: Kowiai.
>
> Mince Kondjol, Wersar village, November 1995.

The story continues to describe how the Onim people settled in the Teminabuan region and how later arrivals established relationships with these first comers. This historical narrative illustrates that in situations of conflict, in this case over land, groups may opt to enlarge their genealogy to include connections

---

9   Mince is a pseudonym.

with Java. Such historiography follows a framing that is heavily influenced by the structure of the scripture reminiscent of the ancient-world formations that Benedict Anderson in his *Imagined Communities* calls 'the sacral cultures' (1983: 20). In Anderson's account, sacral cultures such as the Ummah Islam, Christendom and the Buddhist world imagined themselves through the medium of a sacred language and written script.

This is what makes the stories about Onim so fascinating: they can be read as a story about Onim people's registering their relationship with ancient Javanese kingdoms and including Papua firmly in the phenomenon of Indonesian nationalism, of which only phantoms feature in Papuan minds. In recognition of the power of the Indonesian national narrative, they produce a story about Onim culture imbued with a quality of being everywhere but nowhere in particular. It is historiography that accounts for timeless and non-generational connection that instead builds on the idea of paths and journeys between Java and Papua. Another strategy for establishing a paradigmatic truth for underpinning a Papuan identity and a Papuan nation would be to invoke a shared genealogy to a common past and/or common culture, as the following case will illustrate. In both processes, the past is invoked based on present circumstances as a way for previously distinct social groups to redefine themselves and their relationship to one another. Applying the genealogical framework that is central to the authenticating myth of the Indonesian nation does this.

Papua's Constitution

The previous narratives date back to the last decade of the New Order regime. Following the regime's demise with the fall of President Suharto in 1998, Papuans became more outspoken about the status of their land and their interpretations of national history. The period immediately following the resignation of Suharto has been described as the Papuan Spring and in the more socio-political accounts it is seen as marked by demonstrations, flag raisings and heightened expectations about radical changes in inequality and marginalisation amid a flurry of messianic dreams (Van den Broek and Szalay 2001; Chauvel 2005; Kirksey 2012).

During this period Papuans became increasingly vocal towards local and distant audiences communicating historical, racial and national arguments as part of their pursuit of freedom. Most publications so far produced tend to discuss human rights violations and the injustices surrounding the transfer of Papua to Indonesia (for example: Alua 2002; Giay 2000; Karoba et al. 2002; Maniagasi 2001; Pigay 2000; and Raweyai 2002). Only a few, pace Giay (2000), imagine how a new state or nation might be constituted. Standing out is *Basic Guidelines*,

State of West Papua: Papua-Melanesia Threefold Logic, Basic Ideology, General Governance, Constitution of West Papua (Flassy 1999), the founding document for an awaited sovereign state of West Papua. The document was edited by Don A.L. Flassy, one of the most prolific Papuan writers, whose work reflects broad interests, ranging from linguistics and anthropology to natural science and governance.[10] *Basic Guidelines* demonstrates Flassy's erudition and creativity, and, like the two previous narratives, it is a potent blend of biblical, customary and modern discourses. Being a constitution and not an outline of the evolution of mankind or a local historical narrative, the text revolves even more intensely around the ideas of sovereignty and morality.

According to *Basic Guidelines*, the principles behind the constitution are that Papuans are: 'by full glory and warship [sic.], admitting that, The Nation and Country of Papua, is under the authority and truth magnificence of God The Lord – Yahweh, Jesus Christ ...' Next, in capitals, the text continues:

AS COSMOPOLITANS

WE, THE PEOPLE OF THE PAPUAN NATION

DECLARE

Based on the experience we have been undergoing, that colonialism of any kind and name being exercised by any nation is not suitable at all with humanity and justice, and contradict with principles of freedom and human rights. Therefore colonialism must be continuously combated and disappear from the world's surface. For this reason one must be involved in bearing real responsibility for the sake of freedom and human rights. ...

AND FOR IT'S REALIZATION

Endeavors are required in full responsibility to The Papua-Melanesian Triplefold Logic, that is The Papuan Principle of Triple Luster of mercy, allegiance and honesty with full respect to The Triple Spirit of Melanesian Brotherhood principles of one nation, one soul and one solidarity (Flassy 1999: 21–22).

We see here a creative combination of Christian principles, the popular OPM or 'Free Papua Movement' slogan 'one people, one soul' (see Ondawame 2009), international human rights principles, anti-colonial discourse and a fascination with numerical correspondence. Remarkably, 'one nation, one soul and one

---

10   Basic Guidelines is so far the most developed constitution for Papua amid a wide variety of tribal constitutions that are written mostly in response to (threats of) marginalisation, resource exploitation, deterioration of morals and questions of leadership.

solidarity' resonates with catchphrases in the five Irian Barat (the then name for the territory) speeches by President Sukarno. Sukarno's speeches regarding Irian Barat are mainly anti-colonial and speak of Indonesia's right to re-establish the unity of the nation, as it allegedly existed during the struggle against the colonial powers.[11] This unity includes Irian Barat and therefore the Dutch had to leave West New Guinea. Indonesian National Party (PNI) ideologue and then Minister of Information, Roeslan Abdulgani further developed this premise in *Dari Sabang Sampai Merauke: Satu Nusa, Satu Bangsa!* ('From Sabang to Merauke: One Country, One People!') (1964), a guideline for the Indonesian nation (now including Irian Barat). Around the same time in the Bird's Head region, the OPM was shaped in terms of a struggle for a separate nation. Indonesian propaganda inspired their attempt at nation building: *Satu Bangsa, Satu Djiwa* ('One People, One Soul').[12] Paradoxically, in spite of the anti-Indonesian bent of Flassy's initiative, his rhetoric resonates with the rhetoric of Indonesia's liberation of Netherlands New Guinea in the late 1950s and early 1960s. For all the racial and ethnic tension between Indonesians and Papuans, for all of its anti-colonial rhetoric, *Basic Guidelines* also emulates Indonesian state ideologies from the preceding decades.

By emulating the Indonesian state, Flassy powerfully unmasks the Indonesian state and presents an alternative state, or a state within a state, a sovereignty within a sovereignty, to be built on the remnants of a lost Edenic order in which, as I will illustrate, Christian principles converge with customary rules (*adat*). *Adat* and mission Christianity mutually assent to each other, and together they are tantamount to justice, dignity and sovereignty – or 'one people, one soul, one solidarity'. As indicated above, Christianity is a pervasive force in the formation of culture and local, national and transnational identities and its scripture is a likely source of inspiration for constructing a state. Papua is overwhelmingly Christian in the sense that the majority of the population grow up with a basic acquaintance with the Bible, Christian hymns and Christian doctrine. For many Papuans from all walks of life the Bible provides some key discursive and expressive resources. As a result, biblical vocabulary and narratives colour people's life-worlds significantly. 'Chosen people' in relation to Flassy's statebuilding project is prominent and this is illustrated most clearly in the constitution's Welcome Speech (Flassy 1999: ii–iii) that is signed by Theys H. Eluay, the charismatic and colourful leader of the independence movement almost immediately after the fall of Suharto.[13]

---

11   See http://www.papuaweb.org/goi/pidato/index.html for Sukarno's speeches on Irian Barat.

12   The history of the OPM is not documented in any great detail yet (but see Vlasblom 2004: 469, 486–636, Ondawame 2009, and Djopari 1993) but the mimicking of Indonesian nationalist slogans as well as its command structure and dress style resembling the Indonesian military, certainly form interesting aspects for explaining its powers and paradoxes.

13   Through his old connections with the Golkar Party and ongoing business friendship with people in the military, Eluay was seen by many as paving the way to independence. He was brutally assassinated by officers in the Special Forces (Kopassus) of the Indonesian military on 10 November 2001 (Giay 2006).

The Welcome Speech includes a long list of key elements that together underpin the idea that the Papuan Nation is unqualified, natural and divine. A closer look at these suggest a precedent for Flassy's constitution. The first two elements are the shared suffering of Papuans under the New Order government and the popular idea that God chose Papua as a holy land with the first arrival of white missionaries in 1855. God's plan for Papua and the arrival of Christianity needed, as Eluay writes, a longer journey in which God 'allowed' the colonisation of West Papua:

> [He] allowed the Papuan people to undergo colonization under the nation and government of infidel people, namely Indonesia, for 36 years, starting from 1962. Under these conditions, the Papuan Nation grew and discovered itself as no longer being tribal groups surrounded by darkness, but seeing clearly God's brilliance in blessing our nation and land (Eluay in Flassy 1999: ii).

The Papuan nation is the fruit of God's desire. In his words, it is 'absoluteness desired by the absolute truth, namely God, the Creator of sky and earth'.

> The horrifying deeds have been successful in uniting the Papuan people out of their isolation, darkness and hostility. They ware [sic.] earning the Bright of the Gospel of Christ which had formed these huge of tribe to be a Nation on a by God Lottery [sic., Eluay means the lot of land as allocated by God to the tribes of Israel] Land since 5th December 1855. Which His Wisdom and Mercy being then on The 1st December 1961 as bestowed declared its own as a Nation and State of West Papua (Eluay in Flassy 1999: ii).

Inverting as it were the familiar modern European history production which suggests that development moves from barbarism to civilisation through secularisation (see Ferguson 2006: 177–182), Papua's coming of age is in God's hands, and the constitution, Eluay hopes, 'will fulfill our common desire and God's mission for this land Papua' (Flassy 1999: iii). Law here is the culmination of God's mission to Papua and it has a sacred origin.

Throughout Melanesia, the domains of the state and religion, as well as custom, are in most contexts hard to conceptually separate (Timmer 2000). Also, the kind of statebuilding that Flassy is engaged in shows that there are no complex or problematic relations between state and religion. On the contrary, the Papuan nation is seen as part of God's plan for humankind and its people a chosen people destined to play a role in the fulfilment of the book. Through reading the scripture, many in Papua develop a particular notion of nation that is not in anyway antagonistic to a secular variety. Such a secular variety is not part of the equation, if ever pondered. The Papuan notion of nation thus also differs from that documented for nation building in Europe by Benedict Anderson in *Imagined Communities* (1983) which, as noted by Smith 'turn[s] its back on religion and the sacred, in favour of print and vernacular language' (2003: 20). *Basic Guidelines* shows that people believe that they are not moving from a religious world to a secular world, nor do they think that they replace Christian notions of the origin of the community, morality and membership with those of the nation.

As mentioned above, the Bird's Head features in collective memory as the region that God chose for the dissemination of His word to the inhabitants of Papua. This particular nationalist narrative recounts the arrival of the German missionaries of Lutheran conviction Carl W. Ottow and Johann G. Geissler on the island of Mansinam off the coast of Manokwari in Cenderawasih Bay (Kamma 1976: 73). For Papuans, the arrival of the Gospel stands out when narrating the history of their nation (see Young 1997). Throughout Papua but in particular in Protestant and Evangelical circles, the arrival of Ottow and Geissler is exceedingly celebrated with overtones of Papuan nationalism in the shape of flag raising, hymns such as 'Onward Christian Soldiers', and prayers for independence. At a regional level, Manokwari is now known as the Gospel City (*Kota Injil*) and has seen a proposal for government regulations based on the Old Testament. For now it is important to note that in the constitution the sacred character of Mansinam and Manokwari buttresses the first principle of the Triple Principle of Papua Luster: Mercy:

> The emergence of the West Papua Nation had only come true by the willingness of The Mercy or Love of Jesus Christ. In the name of The Lord, Ottow and Geissler, two disciples from Germany had crossed the sea and stepped feet on the island of Mansinam at Dorei Bay, Manokwari. This is The Lottery Land of God (Psalm 125: 3), as stated for its baptism. (1999: 6–7)

Im Namen Gottes betreten wir dieses Land ('In the Name of God we enter this Country') is the alleged first phrase uttered by the missionaries upon arrival at Mansinam. It is often reiterated, in particular by people in the Bird's Head and along the north shores of the territory. This is the region that is most significantly influenced by Protestant and Evangelical missions and movements. Flassy relates it to the meaning of Psalm 125 (1999: 7) which says that 'As the mountains are round about Jerusalem, so the Lord is round about his people from henceforth even for ever', relating to the common understanding of Papua coming of age as a Holy Land with the arrival of God's Word.

Such statements are not rhetorical ploys to persuade those who would otherwise not be convinced of the foundational value of this attempt at West Papuan state building. Instead they show that the scripture plays an integral part in the emergence of concepts of state and nation in West Papua. In significant ways, the constitution for West Papua is part of the fulfilment of the book by Papuans as a covenanted people and thus illustrates the momentum gained by cultural experimentation with the scripture for political invention and state-building.

Conclusion

To the extent that the three narratives discussed in this paper can be generalised, they highlight a tendency in Papua to borrow historical form from the modernist and Christian conceptions of history, generating ideas about paradigmatic truths found in definite beginnings, in Genesis and in primitiveness. The evolving collective memories portray these paradigmatic truths in relation to widespread nationalist narratives about the arrival of the Gospel, the advent of Dutch colonialism and the transfer of the territory to Indonesia. Many in the region are fascinated by these events and their personal recollections of them enter into intersubjectivity, the collective memory that in turn becomes a fertile ground for the kind of historiographies that I discussed above. By including components of metaphysical principle and paradigmatic truth that are related to Christianity and myths of states and nation, the narratives no longer focus on individual or group histories but on larger regional history and even world history.

It was also necessary to analyse the intellectual effort and creativity involved in these undertakings (see Fisher and Timmer 2013, and Timmer 2013). This not only illuminates the different streams of knowledge that influenced the thinking behind these dissecting and overlapping histories, it also acknowledges the extent to which such histories are the product of competing segments of society that each tries to appropriate them and turn them to their own interests (Lincoln 1989: 38–50). What Lincoln (1989: 38) calls the socio-political instrumentality of mythic discourse is most apparent in the narrative about the Onim people as the historical heroes of the region. This narrative builds on the Javanese cultural heritage that has underpinned Indonesia's nation-building project and attempts to associate the Onim people with Java. This association has significance in local land struggles, and also undermines Indonesia's claim to a nationhood that includes Papua on the basis of memories about ancient Javanese kingdoms.

The Cycle of Man's Civilisation broadens this perspective with a temporal perspective that both encompasses Western development terms and the Christian scripture. In terms of Genesis it suggests that Papua, as the Garden of Eden, lies at the origin of humankind and the history of civilisation. In the course of time, the Dutch climbed up the ladder of civilisation while Papua remained at the perfect paradisiacal stage. Then the Dutch came to Papua and brought God's Word, followed by the Indonesians who made the Papuans lose social connections and made them individualistic. Nevertheless, Papua's character as the root of everything, the perfect, survived the tooth of time through the idiom of descent (see Ingold 2000: 135). The Cycle of Man's Civilisation portrays a sense of Papuans being the original inhabitants, being both indigenous and aboriginal, reproducing as it were a 'thoroughly Eurocentric image of the precolonial world as a mosaic of cultures and territories that was already in perpetuity before history began' (Ingold 2000: 132). Ingold argues that this kind of thinking about indigeneity and originality stimulates awareness of historical continuity in terms of descent. Genealogical connection limited to one specific region then suggests that original cultural traits can be transmitted across generations, along chains of ancestors all the way down to the present generation. The Cycle of Man's Culture does not seek to redefine all distinct Papuan groups under one umbrella-notion of cultural and developmental similarity, yet it evokes the idea that all Papuans share a wonderful past that is meaningful and may awaken and produce feelings of affinity for one another.

The Constitution for Papua is an attempt to unite Papuans through the evocation of 'one soul, one people' for the purpose of state-building. It redefines Papua and its history through the invocation of shared unified Melanesian cultural principles that were still uncontaminated before Europeans and Indonesians arrived on the scene. Yet at the same time, the present conflict with Indonesia stimulates the collective memory that evokes newfound affinities. The Constitution explicitly tackles tensions between groups in Papua by showing unity in terms of one soul. It is, like the other two histories, also an example of historical narrative building on the idea that there is a primordial substance. Foul outside forces have affected Papuan souls (see Suryawan 2012), creating imbalances that threaten the reunification that existed in the period of 'isolation and heathen power' (Flassy 1999: 9). The means of reunification proposed by the Constitution is the return to 'God's miracle' – Papuans as chosen people – that would demand from Papuans dedication to their land's role in blessing the world.

Finally, all three narratives demonstrate that the producers of Papuan histories are a diverse crowd, including intellectuals, philosophers, bureaucrats, church ministers and local leaders. All the authors discussed above recognise that historiography is useful for current imaginations of sovereignty, development and identity, and can move people to action. Because of the concern and purpose of their narratives, they do not include doubt, hesitation or modesty but rather conviction about the paradigmatic truths they establish. The narratives confirm the kind of nationalism that seeks to identify pure forms of some putative national culture and flatten the erratic temporality of history. They turn the unpredictable succession of events into retroactive proof of a glorious predestination, and the coming of age of a perfect Papua that has a past that is so holy and remote that it seems exempt from the law of change.

References

Abdulgani, Roeslan 1964. *Dari Sabang Sampai Merauke: Satu Nusa, Satu Bangsa!* [From Sabang to Merauke: One Country, One People]. Djakarta: Departemen Penerangan R.I.

Alua, Agus A. 2002. 'Peringatan 41 Tahun. Tragedi kejahatan terhadap kemanusiaan di Tanah Papua dan Kemerdekaan Papua Barat'. *Seri Pendidikan Politik Papua* 6. Jayapura: Sekretariat Presidium Dewan Papua (PDP) dan Biro Penelitian STFT Fajar Timur.

Anderson, Benedict 1983. *Imagined Communities: Reflections on the Origin and Spread of Nationalism.* London: Verso Editions.

Asad, Talal 1993. *Genealogies of Religion: Discipline and Reasons of Power in Christianity and Islam.* Baltimore and London: The Johns Hopkins University Press.

Ballard, Chris 1997. 'It's the Land Stupid! The Moral Economy of Resource Ownership in Papua New Guinea'. In Larmour, Peter (ed.), *The Governance of Common Property in the Pacific Region.* Canberra: National Centre for Development Studies, 47–65.

Ballard, Chris 2014. 'Oceanic Historicities'. *The Contemporary Pacific* 26(1): 96-124.

Chauvel, Richard 2005. *Constructing Papuan Nationalism: History, Ethnicity, and Adaptation.* Policy Studies 14. Washington, D.C.: East-West Center Washington.

Connerton, Paul 1989. *How Societies Remember.* Cambridge: Cambridge University Press.

Dening, Greg 1991. 'A Poetic for Histories: Transformations that Present the Past'. In Biersack, Aletta (ed.), *Clio in Oceania: Towards a Historical Anthropology.* Washington DC: Smithsonian Institution Press, 347–380.

Djopari, John R.G. 1993. *Pemberontakan Organisasi Papua Merdeka.* Second Edition. Jakarta: Penerbit PT Grasindo Gramedia Widiasarana.

Drooglever, Pieter 2005. *Een Daad van Vrije Keuze: De Papoea's van Westelijk Nieuw-Guinea en de Grenzen van het Zelfbeschikkingsrecht*. Amsterdam: Boom.

Ferguson, James 2006. *Global Shadows: Africa in the Neoliberal World*. Durham: Duke University Press.

Fisher, Daniel and Timmer, Jaap 2013. 'Becoming Like The State: Ethnographic Perspectives On The State And Indigenous Sovereignty In Oceania'. *Oceania* 83(3): 153–157.

Flassy, Don A.L. 1985. *Brendie Ceritra Rakyat (folktales), Toror, Doberai (Bird's Head), Irian Jaya*. Penulisan, Seri, Jaya, Irian and Mansoben, J.R. (eds). Sorong: Studigrup Etnografi Irian Jaya, Dewan Kesenian Irian Jaya.

Flassy, Don A.L. 1999. *Basic Guidelines, State of West Papua: Papua-Melanesia Threefold Logic, Basic Ideology, General Governance, Constitution of West Papua*. Port Numbay (Jayapura): Fajar Melanesia.

Flassy, Don A.L. 2002. *Toror: A Name Beyond Language and Culture Fusion*. Jakarta: Balai Pustaka.

Gash, Noel and Whittaker, June 1975. *A Pictorial History of New Guinea*. Brisbane and Bathurst: Robert Brown and Associates.

Giay, Benny 1995. *Zakheus Pakage and His Communities: Indigenous Religious Discourse, Socio-political Resistance, and Ethnohistory of the Me of Irian Jaya*. PhD Thesis, Vrije Universiteit, Amsterdam. Amsterdam: VU University Press.

Giay, Benny 2000. *Menuju Papua Baru: Beberapa pokok pikiran sekitar Emansipasi Orang Papua*. Jayapura: Deiyai and Els-ham Papua.

Giay, Benny 2006. *Peristiwa Penculikan dan Pembunuhan Theys H Eluay 10 November 2001*. Jayapura: Deijay/Els-ham Papua.

Halbwachs, Maurice 1992 [1941/1952]. *On Collective Memory*. Edited and translated from the French by Lewis A. Coser. Chicago and London: The University Chicago Press.

Hau'ofa, Epeli 2000. 'Epilogue: Pasts to Remember'. In Borofsky, Robert (ed.), *Remembrance of Pacific Pasts: An Invitation to Remake History*. Honolulu: University of Hawai'i Press, 453–471.

Hendel, Ronald 2013. *The Book of Genesis: A Biography*. Princeton: Princeton University Press.

Hirsch, Eric and Stewart, Charles 2005. 'Introduction: Ethnographies of Historicity'. *History and Anthropology* 16(3): 261–274.

Holton, George and Read, Kenneth H. 1971. *The Human Aviary: A Pictorial Discovery of New Guinea*. New York: Charles Scribner's Sons.

Ingold, Tim 2000. 'Ancestry, Generation, Substance, Memory, Land'. In Tim Ingold, *The Perception of the Environment: Essays on Livelihood, Dwelling and Skill*. Oxon and New York: Routledge, 132–151.

Jackson, Michael 1998. *Minima Ethnographica: Intersubjectivity and the Anthropological Project*. Chicago and London: The University of Chicago Press.

Kamma, Freerk C. 1947/48. 'De Verhouding tussen Tidore en de Papoese Eilanden in Legende en Historie, II'. *Indonesië* 1: 536–559.

Kamma, Freerk C. 1976. *Dit Wonderlijke werk: Het Probleem van de Communicatie tussen Oost en West Gebaseerd op de Ervarigen in het Zendingswerk op Nieuw-Guinea (Irian Jaya) 1855-1972, Een Socio-missiologische Benadering*. Oegstgeest: Raad voor de Zending der Ned. Hervormde Kerk.

Kamma, Freerk C., and Kooijman, Simon 1973. *Romawa Forja, Child of the Fire: Iron Working and the Role of Iron in West New Guinea (West Irian)*. Leiden: E.J. Brill.

Kondjol, Zakarias L. 1996. *Riwayat Kedatangnya Suku Onim Anggiluly Kondjol*. Typescript, held in the collection of the author.

Karoba, Sem, Hans L. Gebze dkk. 2002. *Papua Menggugat (11 November 2001, Hari Wafatnya Ondofolo Dortheys Hiyo Eluay)*. Yogyakarta: The West Papuan Community, Alliance of Papuan Students, The Koteka Tribal Assembly and Ndugu Ndugu Research and Publications.

Kirksey, Eben 2012. *Freedom in Entangled Worlds: West Papua and the Architecture of Global Power*. Durham and London: Duke University Press.

Koentjaraningrat and Bachtiar, Harsja W. 1963. *Penduduk Irian Barat*. Proyek Penelitian Universitas Indonesia 102. Jakarta: PT Penerbitan Universitas.

Leach, James 2003. *Creative Land: Place and Procreation on the Rai Coast of Papua New Guinea*. New York and Oxford: Berghahn.

Lincoln, Bruce 1989. *Discourse and the Construction of Society: Comparative Studies of Myth, Ritual, and Classification*. New York and Oxford: Oxford University Press.

Lotgering, F.K. 1940. *Memorie van Overgave van de Onderafdeling Inanwatan over de periode 13 juni 1938 to 23 juli 1940*. Typescript held in the Colonial Archives in The Hague (MMK 478).

Maniagasi, Frans 2001. *Masa Depan Papua: Merdeka, Otonomi Khusus dan Dialog*. Jakarta: Millennium Publisher.

Miedema, Jelle, Odé, Cecilia, Dam, Rien A. C. and Baak, Connie (eds) 1998. *Perspectives on the Bird's Head of Irian Jaya, Indonesia: Proceedings of the Conference, Leiden, 13-17 October 1997*. Amsterdam: Editions Rodopi.

Ondawame, Otto 2009. *One People, One Soul: West Papuan Nationalism and the Organisasi Papua Merdeka*. Belair, SA: Crawford House.

Onim, Jusuf 1988. *Soteriologi Agama Suku Tehit: Suatu Upaya Pemahaman terhadap Konsepsi Pemikiran Agamani tentang Tuhan dan Soteriologi menurut Agama Suku Tehit dalam Perjumpaannya dengan Agama Kristen di daerah Teminabuan, Kabupaten Sorong*. Unpublished MA thesis, Sekolah Tinggi Theologia, Jakarta.

Onim, Jusuf 1998. A Regional History of Desa Wersar (in the Sub-district of Teminabuan) on the South Coast of the Bird's Head in Irian Jaya Indonesia. Unpublished Manuscript.

Pigay, Decki Natalis 2000. *Evolusi nasionalisme dan sejarah konflik politik di Papua (Sebelum, Saat dan Sesudah Integrasi)*. Jakarta: Pustaka Sinar Harapan.

Raweyai, Yorrys Th. 2002. *Mengapa Papua Ingin Merdeka*. Jayapura: Presidium Dewan Papua.

Reid, Anthony 1979. 'The National Quest for an Indonesian Past'. In Reid, Anthony and Marr, David (eds), *Perceptions of the Past in Southeast Asia*. Southeast Asia Publication Series 4. Singapore: Heinemann Educational Books (Asia), 281–298.

Rutherford, Danilyn 2012. *Laughing at Leviathan: Sovereignty and Audience in West Papua*. Chicago and London: The University of Chicago Press.

Saltford, John 2002. *Anatomy of a Betrayal: The United Nations and the Indonesian Takeover of West Papua, 1962-1969*. London: Routledge Curzon.

Scott, James 2009. *The Art of Not Being Governed: An Anarchist History of Upland Southeast Asia*. New Haven and London: Yale University Press.

Scott, James 2012. *Two Cheers for Anarchism: Six Pieces on Autonomy, Dignity, and Meaningful Work and Play*. Princeton and Oxford: Princeton University Press.

Smith, Anthony D. 2003. *Chosen Peoples: Sacred Sources of National Identity*. Oxford: Oxford University Press.

Suryawan, I Ngurah 2012. *Jiwa yang Patah [Broken Soul]*. Manokwari and Yogyakarta: Pusbadaya Universitas Negeri Papua and Kepel Press.

Timmer, Jaap 2000. *Living with Intricate Futures: Order and Confusion in Imyan Worlds, Irian Jaya, Indonesia*. Nijmegen: Centre for Pacific and Asian Studies, University of Nijmegen.

Timmer, Jaap 2005. 'Review of Dirk Vlasblom, *Papoea: Een Geschiedenis* (2004)'. *Journal of Pacific History* 40(1): 117–119.

Timmer, Jaap 2007a. 'Erring Decentralisation and Elite Politics in Papua'. In Nordholt, Henk Schulte and van Klinken, Gerry (eds), *Renegotiating Boundaries: Local Politics in Post-Suharto Indonesia*. Leiden: KITLV Press, 459–482.

Timmer, Jaap 2007b. 'A Brief Social and Political History of Papua, 1962–2004'. In Marshall, A.J. and Beehler, B.M. (eds), *The Ecology of Papua*. The Ecology of Indonesia Series Volume VI. Singapore: Periplus Editions, 1098–1123.

Timmer, Jaap 2013. 'The Threefold Logic of Papua-Melanesia: Constitution-writing in the Margins of the Indonesian Nation-State'. *Oceania* 83(3): 158–174.

van den Broek, Theo and Szalay, Alexandra 2001. 'Raising the Morning Star: Six Months in the Developing Independence Movement in West Papua'. *Journal of Pacific History* 36(1): 77–91.

van Kampen, Anthony 1967. *Het Land dat God Vergat*. Hilversum: C. de Boer jr.

Vlasblom, Dirk 2004. *Papoea: Een Geschiedenis*. Amsterdam: Mets and Schilt.

Wanane, Teddy K.E. 1991. *Makna Kain Timur dalam Kehidupan Masyarakat Tehit di Daerah Kepala Burung*. MA Thesis, Fakultas Ilmu Sosial dan Ilmu Politik, Universitas Cenderawasih, Jayapura.

White, Hayden 1987. *The Content of the Form: Narrative Discourse and Historical Representation*. Baltimore: The Johns Hopkins University Press.

Young, Michael W. 1997. 'Commemorating Missionary Heroes: Local Christianity and Narratives of Nationalism'. In Otto, Ton and Thomas, Nicholas (eds), *Narratives of Nation in the South Pacific*. Amsterdam: Harwood Academic Publishers, 91–132.

5. Under Two Flags: Encounters with Israel, *Merdeka* and the Promised Land in *Tanah Papua*[1]

Henri Myrttinen

On 19 October 2011, the Third Papuan Congress, held in the outskirts of the Papuan provincial capital Jayapura, ended in chaos and bloodshed. During the three-day congress, several thousand participants had discussed the current situation in *Tanah Papua*, how to improve the lives of the indigenous 'sons of the soil' as well as their fears of social, cultural, religious and economic marginalisation.[2] The answer was not a new one: not for the first time, the Land of Papua proclaimed its independence from Indonesia, a new government was declared and, amongst other measures, the Dutch New Guinea Guilder was introduced as the national currency (GKI 2011).[3] The Indonesian security forces reacted to this act of secession by storming the meeting, arresting and physically abusing several hundred participants. According to the national commission of human rights, at least three, possibly six Papuan civilians were killed in the process under unclear circumstances.

I argue that symbols – often with a heavily religious/mythological overtone – play a central role in Papuan nationalist politics. In order to gain a better understanding of Papuan aspirations and dreams of a better future one needs not to merely look at socio-economic statistics but also to investigate symbolic offerings. The Declaration of Independence itself was a heavily symbolic act, but it was buttressed by other symbols seen as being imbued with power and meaning. Why was the congress opened with not just the waving of the

---

1   The chapter is an adaptation of a paper presented at the 'Becoming Like The State' panel at the Annual Meeting of the American Anthropological Association, 16–20 November, 2011, Montréal. The author would like to thank Jaap Timmer and Daniel Fisher who organised the panel and the Nordic Institute of Asian Studies in Copenhagen who hosted him at the time of writing. The title is a nod to Benedict Anderson's Under Three Flags (2005), an excellent study of anti-colonial imaginaries and struggles for national independence.
2   There is a certain amount of potential confusion surrounding the names used to refer to the western part of the island of New Guinea. The area is divided into the two Indonesian provinces of Papua and West Papua, which were previously the province of Irian Jaya, later renamed Papua. Somewhat confusingly, both in Papuan society and outside, both provinces are often lumped together either as 'Papua' or 'West Papua' (Papua Barat). In an effort to avoid confusion, I will use the terms West Papua and Papua to refer to the respective provinces and the adjective 'Papuan' as pertaining to social, political, economic, cultural, etc. dynamics within the indigenous community in both provinces. I will use the term Tanah Papua (Land of Papua) to refer to the area covered by the two provinces jointly.
3   As discussed in the final section of the chapter, Israeli national symbols are not the only ones seen as having a certain potency; also old Dutch symbols are often utilised. As Jaap Timmer (2000: 36) points out, an exaggerated value is often ascribed to the old Dutch New Guinea Guilder in Papua/West Papua. As Chauvel (2006: 181) notes, 'Papuan memories of the Netherlands' administration have become rosier with the passage of time, in part as a mirror of their experience of Indonesian governance since 1963'.

outlawed Papuan Morning Star flag (*Bintang Kejora*) but also the Israeli national flag?[4] Why were Indonesian citizens of Melanesian descent expressing their discontent with their current political status through the national symbols of a state over 10,000 kilometres away?

Though I had been to the Indonesian provinces of Papua and West Papua several times previously, it was only during a visit in early 2009 that the issue of 'Israel' in Papuan society and political discourse piqued my interest. It was both the time of Israel's attack on the Gaza Strip ('Operation Cast Lead') and an increased sense of fear of 'Islamisation' in Papuan society.[5] During this visit, I noticed the emergence of Star of David graffiti in the streets of the provincial capital Jayapura, of indigenous Papuans sporting pro-Israel t-shirts, of functionaries of the Christian congregations using Israeli and Jewish symbols as wallpaper on their laptops and smart phones. I started paying more attention to references to the Middle East both in the local political discourse and in everyday life.

Over the next few years during which I visited the two provinces, I started noticing references more frequently – Israeli flags painted on shop fronts, as stickers on cars and mopeds, on displays at football matches of the local team Persipura; increased pilgrimages by Christian Papuans to the Holy Land;[6] as well as comparisons between *Tanah Papua* and the Holy Land made at different levels of societal discourse. Nor was this phenomenon restricted to Papua and West Papua – a similar 'Israel boom' also became visible in predominantly Protestant North Sulawesi and in Catholic Timor-Leste, though under somewhat different circumstances and very different readings.[7]

Almost as if to mirror this, the Middle East theme has also been used by Indonesian Muslims in their attention to *Tanah Papua*. Indonesian Islamist websites such as *Suara Islam* and *Sabili* argue that Papua (or *Nuu War*) was Muslim before it was Christian. The websites show pictures of Islamic proselytisers in Papua clad in Palestinian *khaffiyahs*. The very last mosque on the Indonesian side

---

4   A video of Sampari ('Morning Star') dancers at the opening ceremony of the Third Papuan Congress is accessible at http://www.youtube.com/watch?v=wUQWulFz2nM and the Israeli national flag is visible several times at 0:24, 1:56 and 2:20, respectively.

5   Indigenous Papuans are, for the most part, Protestants and Catholics, while a majority (though not all) migrants from other parts of Indonesia tend to be Muslim. The issue is a very sensitive one and reliable figures are difficult to come by. In many of the urban centres of the two provinces, migrants quite possibly are in the majority and play a dominant role in the economy.

6   Given the political sensitivities around the issue, I would like to clarify that in using the term Israel I refer to the State of Israel and in using the term 'The Holy Land' to the somewhat vaguely defined geographical area commonly seen as being sacred in the Christian tradition and which is currently for the most part administered by the State of Israel and the Palestinian Authority.

7   Regarding Timor-Leste, see for example Kammen (2009: 400–401, 404) and Myrttinen (2010: 263), while for North Sulawesi, see for example Swazey 2010. Israel/Holy Land-related political imaginaries are, however, neither restricted geographically to the Indonesian archipelago nor temporally to the present day, but can be found in a wide variety of contexts, from radical German Anabaptists in the 1500s (Kirchhoff 1973) over Ronald Reagan (1984) to present-day Solomon Island villagers (Timmer 2008).

before the Papua New Guinea (PNG) border on the road between Jayapura and Vanimo is called the al-Aqsha Mosque, in reference to the eponymous mosque in Jerusalem, which is the third holiest site in Islam.[8]

Figure 5.1. Al-Aqsha Mosque, Keerom Regency, Papua.

Source: Henri Myrttinen.

Though Israel seems to be increasingly prominent in Papuan discourses, it needs to be stated to avoid any misconceptions that the State of Israel has not actually been showing any interest in the issues of Papua/West Papua.[9] Indonesia and Israel do not maintain diplomatic relations and there is no official presence in the country. Israeli civil society groups have also not been at the forefront of demands to place Papuan issues onto the agenda. The 'special relationship', therefore, seems to me to be a decidedly one-way affair.

This chapter aims to chart some of the ways in which 'Israel' has been and is being used in Papuan discourses. After sketching some of the conditions that contribute to Papuan political discourses I will look at three different ways in which the relationship of *Tanah Papua* and Israel/The Holy Land manifests itself in these discourses:

1. Israel as a perceived ally, and as a projection surface of hopes and aspirations,

---

8   More generally, the Israeli–Palestinian conflict, Jewish history (especially with regard to the Holocaust) as well as often elaborate conspiracy theories of all shades linked to radical Islam, Judaism and Nazism seem to hold a special sway over Indonesian readers, at least judging by what is on offer at bookstores. Though not representative, in a quick browse through the rather limited political and social science section of the main book store in Jayapura, the capital of Papua province, on a visit in 2011, I found books on Hitler's alleged secret post-World War II life in Indonesia, on Jewish World Conspiracies, on purported ties between Nazis and al-Qaeda, on why Malaysia is supposedly a Jewish state and on why Barack Obama allegedly is the 'Black Hitler'.
9   A possible exception was the reception of an OPM representative by Israel in the 1970s, though the source, the late John Otto Ondawame, himself an OPM representative, casts a degree of doubt on to the question whether the meeting actually ever took place (Ondawame 2010).

2. Spiritual links between Israel/the Holy Land and Papua, and

3. Israel/the Holy Land as (metaphor for) *Tanah Papua*.

In the first discourse, the State of Israel is mainly perceived as a political ally of the Papuans, with both deemed as sharing a common cause, such as a struggle against more powerful (Muslim) neighbours. The second discourse focuses more on spiritual links established through Christianity and readings of Biblical texts in which the Holy Land itself, along with Judeo-Christian symbols, takes a central place. The third discourse goes further, with Israel/the Holy Land becoming a metaphor of the Land of Papua – or even merging with it. It should be noted that in the interviews and discussions I conducted, there was not always a clear distinction made between the different approaches and they often flowed into one another.

This chapter is based on interviews carried out with Papuan political actors (these were mostly from outside Indonesian state structures), church representatives (both Papuan and international), civil society actors (both Papuan and international) and researchers. While the bulk of the interviews were carried out in Papua and West Papua provinces, others were carried out in other parts of Indonesia, Australia, Papua New Guinea, Vanuatu and various European countries over the course of 2009–2011. Rather than being the result of a fully fledged research project, this is more a sketch based on notes and observations made over the years, and should be seen as such. This has in one part been due to personal limitations, but also to a great part due to the restrictions placed by the Indonesian central government on foreigners working or researching in the two provinces of Papua and West Papua. Given the sensitivity of the issues discussed here, all interviewees have been anonymised.

In this chapter I sketch undercurrents in contemporary Papuan thought and discourse, but these trajectories are not wholly representative of Papuan ideological orientations. A number of potential respondents reacted with what I felt was a certain degree of impatience and irritation to my questions on 'Israel', either declaring it more or less irrelevant or on occasion muttering darkly about 'cargoism' but refusing to elaborate. Both the English term and the Indonesian term, '*kargoisme*' can have pejorative undertones of racial and evolutionist stereotypes of Papuans (and other Melanesians) as being 'backward' (*tertinggal*) or 'still stupid' (*masih bodoh*), or of hanging on to pre-Christian beliefs.[10] The background of my interviewees often shaped responses, with more politically minded people using political analogies, those with more religious backgrounds

---

10   As Holger Jebens (2004: 4) points out '[...] the negative connotations of primitivism and irrationality derived from the term "cargo cult" first being coined by planters, colonial administrators, and missionaries in order to denote and dismiss whatever they saw as obstacles to their respective intentions. These negative connotations are also characteristic of indigenous discourses in that they can be detected when Melanesians talk about cargo cults themselves.'

more likely to use Biblical metaphors and so on. Many of the more mainstream Christians (e.g. from church organisations) did not take a kind view of more 'cargoist' interpretations (see KPKC 2009).

Identification with Israel and the Holy Land is clearly evident in Papuan discourse, as is the even more ubiquitous discussion of *merdeka*, but as the chapter demonstrates, there are multiple ways in which these links are understood and configured. Also, not all associations with Israel or even *merdeka* are necessarily political in the conventional sense of the word, but are more of a spiritual nature or refer to freedom from want and fear in a more material sense.

Political discourses of discontent

Since its controversial integration into the Indonesian state over the years 1962–69, what now constitutes the provinces of Papua and West Papua has been engulfed in a political and military struggle over the status of the territory. While Indonesia considers the territory to be an inalienable part of the republic, significant voices of Papuans inside the territory and in exile demand a revisiting of the controversial 1969 'Act of Free Choice', which sealed the integration into the Indonesian state. In addition to voices demanding self-determination, the low-level insurgency of the *Organisasi Papua Merdeka* (OPM) has since 1964 sought to militarily challenge the *status quo*. In addition to the over-arching issue of the political status of the territory, Papuan debates often focus on issues of both real and perceived social, economic and political exclusion; fears of 'Islamisation' linked to the influx of migrants from other parts of Indonesia; exploitation of the national resources of the two provinces by outsiders and acts of discrimination and oppression at the hands of members of the Indonesian security forces (see Hernawan in this volume).[11] There is a pervasive sense that the Papuan nation as a whole is under threat and references to 'genocide' are not uncommon.

I found pro-Israel references in Papuan discourse to be closely linked to discontent over the political status of the territory and Muslim migration to the area. Many of the websites and Facebook pages linking Papua and Israel, for example, include calls for Papuan self-determination (see also Figure 2 and Figure 3). This discontent stems from the history of the incorporation of what was then Dutch West New Guinea into Indonesia in 1961–69 and subsequent military repression (see for

---

11   The use of the term 'real and perceived' is in no way meant to question, diminish or in any other way downplay the very real and serious issues of socio-economic marginalisation, lack of access to basic services, serious environmental degradation, land grabbing, security fears and the like faced by the inhabitants of Tanah Papua, be they indigenous or migrants, on a daily basis. Rather, what I want to point out is that these are augmented by perceived fears and threats emanating from a socio-political discourse both in Papua and in Indonesia more generally in which rumour, conspiracies and innuendo play a central role (see for example Bubandt, 2008).

example Drooglever 2005 and Saltford 2003 for a history of the transfer). Since the mid-1960s, the *Organisasi Papua Merdeka* (OPM – Free Papua Organisation) has waged a small-scale war of independence. While the Indonesian term '*merdeka*' is usually translated as 'independence' in English, I found the term to be used much more ambiguously in my interviews (see also Golden 2003 and Kirksey 2012: 16–18 for a discussion of the term). The vast majority of my respondents were highly critical of the current socio-economic, political and cultural predicament of both the indigenous Papuan nation/people (*Bangsa Papua*) and 'The Land of Papua' (*Tanah Papua* – which covers both provinces), placing much of the blame squarely with the Indonesian central government. Nonetheless, *merdeka* was understood in a number of ways, including freedom from want, spiritual freedom, liberation in the religious sense, self-determination and various forms of autonomy, confederation or full independence.

Figure 5.2. Banner of a Papuan website with an outline of *Tanah Papua* in Israeli colours, Birds of Paradise and 'Israel' in Hebrew.

Source: http://papua-israel.blogspot.com (accessed 16.01.15).

My interviews were carried out mostly in a time of heightened political activity in the two provinces, which have enjoyed close to a decade of special autonomy (*Otonomi Khusus* – Otsus). Although Otsus has, in theory, brought the two provinces unprecedented financial largesse and political power, the vast majority of Papuans I have interviewed over the years in both provinces, regardless of their social and political backgrounds, viewed the autonomy package as a failure.[12] In 2010, a coalition of civil society organisations symbolically returned Otsus to the central government, demanding a review of the package, a call echoed in 2011 by a high-level coalition of local churches. In parallel, my interviewees often conveyed an increasing sense of anxiety over the possibility of communal conflict not just between Papuans and migrants but also between Papuans themselves, for example highland migrants and the local lowland population in urban centres. Since 2009, there have been numerous unresolved cases of

---

12   The implementation of Otsus is a highly contentious issue and most of my Papuan interlocutors considered it a failure and/or a plot hatched in Jakarta to dissuade Papuans from seeking *merdeka*. When I raised the point that vast amounts of money visibly has been disbursed in the two provinces and that, unlike in most other provinces, there are legal safeguards ensuring that only 'sons (and more seldom, daughters) of the soil' can run for local government offices such as governor, vice-governor, or district head, this was often brushed aside. My interlocutors tended to downplay the power of Papuan officials, portraying them as puppets of more powerful masters in Jakarta or in the security forces. The 'special autonomy elite', as Richard Chauvel calls them (2011: 107), have on the one hand been one of the main beneficiaries of Otsus funds but are also caught between pressures both from Jakarta and their local constituencies.

violence, mostly in Papua province, including a multi-year series of shootings around the Freeport gold and copper mine in Timika, unresolved killings around Jayapura and ongoing attacks in Puncak Jaya. While a civil-society coalition together with a team from the Indonesian Institute of Sciences LIPI has been successful in bringing about some initial steps for a peaceful dialogue between representatives of Papuan society and the central government, most Papuans I interviewed put little faith into promises by the government, be it at the local, provincial or at the national level.[13] It is in this atmosphere of mistrust, anxiety and suspicion but also hope of a resolution that my interviews were carried out.

Israel as a perceived ally, and as a projection of hopes and aspirations

Though by far not all references to Israel in my interviews had a political undercurrent, many interviewees likened their sense of the Papuan political struggle and sense of being under threat to the situation of the Jewish State. In these discourses, which are also prevalent among certain Christian groups in the West as well as in other parts of Indonesia, Judaism and Christianity are seen as being essentially 'on the same side'.[14] Thus Israel and Papua find themselves as allies as well, especially with regard to the 'significant Other': Islam. Papuan informants described Israel as a righteous, plucky 'underdog', a 'small nation fighting against overwhelming odds'.[15]

Figure 5.3. Banner of the website Papua-Israel News (http://papua-israel. blogspot.com), combining the Morning Star flag and Israeli flag with an outline of *Tanah Papua*.[16]

Source: http://papua-israel.blogspot.com (accessed 16.01.15).

---

13   For summaries of the dialogue process and Papua Road Map, see Tebay 2009 and Widjojo et al. 2008.
14   The simplistic dichotomy of Jewish Israel vs Muslim Palestine, and by extension Judeo-Christian West against Muslim Arabs, which is not uncommon in Western representations of the Israel-Palestine conflict, not only reduces a complex conflict to a clash of religions but also completely overlooks the fact that neither is the whole of the Palestinian population Muslim nor the Israeli population wholly Jewish.
15   Interviews, Jayapura and Manokwari.
16   Last accessed on 31.07.2013.

The idea of fighting against the odds resonated with Papuans who said they were fearful of an Islamisation of their society, especially as Palestine is a *cause célèbre* among politically active Muslims in Indonesia. A direct comparison was made between how 'most of the lands described in the Bible had once been Christian (sic) and had now become Muslim', a portent for what was happening in Papua.[17] Israel thus was seen as a substitute 'defender' of Jewish and Christian rights against perceived Muslim encroachment.[18] Papua was described to me in one interview as being a 'lone Christian island surrounded by Muslims', and the thought of a powerful ally seemed to bring solace.[19] Sometimes the view of the Jewish state as a 'natural ally' of Christian *Tanah Papua* manifested itself in rumours of Israeli assistance to the Papuan struggle. For example, some informants asserted that the Israeli secret service Mossad is purportedly helping the OPM.[20]

Some Papuans liken Israel's lack of recognition in the international community to West Papua's lack of recognition by the Indonesian state. As the website 'Papua-Israel News' (http://papua-israel.blogspot.com/), which advocates for a referendum, puts it:

> West Papua and Israel share a common fate in the eyes of heathen (kafir) nations of the world, including Indonesia, because Indonesia and some other nations have not yet recognised the independence of the State of Israel on 14 May, 1948 and the independence of the State of West Papua on 1 December, 1961, hence our friendship and our struggle for the respect and self-regard of the two nations.[21]

Similar sentiments were also raised by Andrianus Merdhi in the short documentary film '*Der Schwarze Messias*' ('The Black Messiah', 2010) which examines Papuans' identification with Israel.[22] This imagined common fate of the States of Israel and West Papua, however, overlooks fundamental differences

---

17 Interview, Jayapura.

18 Interviews, Jakarta and Jayapura.

19 Interview, Jakarta.

20 Interviews, Brisbane (Australia), Jayapura and Sorong. The bitter irony is that if there is indeed any form of Mossad involvement, it is more likely not to be on the side of the Papuan nationalists but on the side of the Indonesian armed forces. Though there are no official links between the world's largest Muslim-majority nation and Israel, there are indications that unofficial links have existed between the Israeli secret service and Indonesian special forces Kopassus (Aditjondro 2000).

21 Original text: 'West Papua dan Israel punya nasib yang sama di mata negara-negara kafir di dunia termasuk indonesia, karena indonesia dan ada beberapa negara belum akui Negara Israel merdeka 14 mei 1948 dan Negara West Papua merdeka 1 Desember 1961, persabatan kami demi berjuang untuk kehormatan dan harga diri ke dua bangsa' (author's translation, last accessed 31.07.2013). There is a certain (unintended?) irony in the blogger's use of the Indonesian term 'kafir,'or unbeliever, to refer to those countries which have not recognised the State of Israel, as with the exception of North Korea these are Muslim-majority nations and the term kafir derived from the Arabic term كافر kāfir, and usually is used in Islamic theology to refer to unbelievers in the sense of non-Muslims.

22 As interviewee Khaled puts it in the documentary, 'Israel and Papua face the same struggle for self-determination'.

between the two with respect to international law. The Israeli government is *de facto* and *de jure* in control of its national territory. While several Papuan politicians claim to represent a government of a Free West Papua in exile, none of these can claim to control territory of significance. One hundred and fifty-seven states have full diplomatic relations with Israel and only 20 do not recognise Israel as a state; in contrast, only Vanuatu seems to support the West Papuan quest for self-determination. And although West Papuan independence has been declared several times, the raising of the Morning Star flag in front of the *Nieuw Guinea Raad* on 1 December 1961 was not one of these occasions.[23]

While the vast majority of my interviewees took a positive view of Israel, it is important to stress that amongst politically active Papuans this is not an uncontested view. As a student activist in Manokwari stated after he had listened in on my discussion with an older, pro-Israel Papuan leader:

> I really don't understand this whole Israel thing. I mean, look at it: it's the Israelis that are taking away Palestinian land and the Israeli army is acting just like the TNI [*Tentara Nasional Indonesia* – Indonesian Armed Forces] is acting here, breaking human rights, shooting people … If we're to identify with someone's struggle, then it's the Palestinians.

His fellow activist agreed and opined, unfortunately without wanting to elaborate any further:

> I don't get it either … but you know, I think it's mostly the older people who do it [display Israeli flags], and I guess the Baptists. It's like they expect some power from it. They're always going on about Israel, Israel, Israel … but I don't really get it. I don't really know much about it.

Victor Yeimo, influential speaker of the *Komite Nasional Papua Barat* (KNPB – National Committee of West Papua), also drew parallels to the Israeli occupation when comparing the Indonesian government's support of Palestinian statehood with its policies in Papua and West Papua (KNPB 2011). This is an interesting contrast with the West Papua National Authority (WPNA)[24] statement below, given the generally close political ties between the two.

---

23 The Nieuw-Guinea Raad was a consultative body of indigenous Papuans established by the Dutch colonial government in the final stages of Dutch control over West New Guinea. On 1 December 1961, the national symbols of the territory were displayed publicly for the first time. These included the Morning Star flag, the anthem Hai Tanahku Papua and the Crowned Victoria Pigeon with an emblazoned Morning Star as a national coat of arms, which were to be used in conjunction with Dutch national symbols. In spite of the display of these national symbols, independence was only envisioned for the time after a 10–15 year period of transition (Saltford 2003: 9–12). Nonetheless, the date 1 December 1961 has entered Papuan political imagination as the date of the declaration of independence.

24 The WPNA is one of several umbrella organisations (such as the West Papua National Coalition for Liberation, WPNCL) which claim to be the legitimate representatives of the Papuan nationalist movement.

Spiritual links between Israel/the Holy Land and Papua

A more spiritual reading of the relationship between *Tanah Papua* and Israel is based on views that the two areas are bound by a divine link. This is not always separable from a more political reading of the relationship. The 'God of Israel' and Jewish symbols such as the Star of David and the *menorah* are routinely used in conjunction with Christian and Papuan symbols, for example in signs denoting customary (*adat*) land or banners of the *Dewan Adat Papua* (DAP – Customary Council of Papua), as visible in Figures 5.4 and 5.5.

Figure 5.4. Office of the *Dewan Adat Papua*, Manokwari, West Papua.[25]

Source: Henri Myrttinen.

A further example of Papuans' invocation of Israel in the context of the nationalist struggle is illustrated in a recent speech by Reverend Terrianus Yoku, the President of the National Congress of the WPNA. Reverend Yoku who has taken to signing his proclamations as Reverend *Israel* Terrianus Yoku (my emphasis):

> [...] Firstly – we must all give thanks to God in the name of Jesus Christ, the God of Israel, God of the Glorious Papuan Morning Star, the hero of the liberation of Papuans. [...] (WPNA, 2011)

The special link between Papuans and the Holy Land also manifests itself through pilgrimages to the Holy Land which informants said are becoming increasingly popular as Special Autonomy funds flow into the two provinces.[26] In part, these have been organised by local politicians hoping to increase their standing with the electorate.[27] The pilgrimages usually involve not only visits to the holy sites

---

25   The text on the banner reads 'Thy Kingdom come, thy Will be done, in Manokwari the City of the Gospel and across the Land of Papua as it is in Heaven'.
26   Unfortunately, I was not able to come by reliable figures and some of the figures given by interviewees seemed inflated.
27   Interviews, Manokwari and Wuppertal (Germany).

but also a baptism in the River Jordan.[28] One pilgrimage in particular seems to have captured the public imagination, when a delegation of 34 Papuans donated a kilogramme of gold from Papua and an undisclosed sum of money for the reconstruction of the Third Temple on the Temple Mount in Jerusalem (HaLevi 2007).[29] The story of Papuans bringing gold to the Holy Land was related to me by several interviewees, though they described the donation as supporting the building of 'a golden bridge' from Papua to the Holy Land in anticipation of the Second Coming of Jesus Christ, rather than the reconstruction of the Temple.[30]

Figure 5.5. Office of the *Dewan Adat Papua*, Manokwari, West Papua.[31]

Source: Henri Myrttinen.

Many of the links between *Tanah Papua* and the Holy Land can be traced back to local readings and interpretations of the Scriptures. Glazebrook (2008: 146–147) traces one of these sources to a Dutch pastor whose sermon was influential in the West Papuan refugee camps in Papua New Guinea:

> A schoolteacher at East Awin explained Leenhout's revelation to me. In 1948, the pastor apparently received divine revelations relating to Romans 9 and 11, and Ephesians 2:11–22 in the New Testament. The revelation occurred at the time of two significant events, both involving Israel. First, at the formation of the World Council of Churches its membership included churches that did not recognise Jesus as Messiah. Second, Israel's constitution as a political state denied its non-secular nature as Promised Land. Leenhout preached that Israel was a window through which God viewed the world but while Israel remained a political state, peace would elude the world. God had intentionally hardened the heart of Jews so that Christ's teachings would be spread to

---

28 Interviews, Jayapura and Manokwari, as well as Merdhi (2010).
29 According to the Israeli news article on the event (HaLevi, 2007), the Papuans were inspired by the Biblical verse Zechariah (6:15), 'And the distant ones will come and build the Temple of God'. The gold and funds for the controversial project were given to the Temple Institute.
30 Interviews, Jayapura and Sorong.
31 The text on the banner reads 'Hail the Land which is protected by the God of Israel'.

other nations. The salvation of black colonised nations, including West Papua, was said to be wrapped up in the fate of Israel, and it was the responsibility of the peoples of these nations to evangelise Israel.

In fact, Leenhout's sermon made scant reference to West Papua. So we might deduce that the West Papuan translator, himself a pastor, as well as congregation leaders and followers at East Awin, have interpreted Leenhout in light of their own theological and political standpoints.

The (re-)reading of Leenhout's sermon described here by Glazebrook with its implicit obligation for Papuans to go to Israel and evangelise is similar to the views which I encountered in some interviews that the Star of David is actually the Morning Star which was taken by Israel from Papua and needs to be 'returned'.[32] There are definite echoes here of Rutherford's (2003) 'Raiding the Land of the Foreigners' as well as Kirksey (2012: 29–33) and the links they draw to the millenarian Koreri cycle, though one needs to be cautious with transposing a Biak-Numfor area myth directly into other Papuan cultural contexts.[33] The Morning Star, prominently displayed on the Papuan flag, plays a central role in the Koreri cycle of myths which, above caveats in mind, has been a source of inspiration for Papuan nationalist movements (Kamma 1972; Rutherford 2003 and 2012; see also below for a more detailed discussion of the Koreri movement).[34]

The notion that powerful symbols have been misappropriated from *Tanah Papua* by outsiders is also raised by Glazebrook (2008), Kirksey (2012) and Timmer (2000), e.g. with respect to the Indonesian state symbols such as the Garuda.

The spiritual linking of *Tanah Papua* with Israel is thus strongly intertwined with Christianity or, more precisely, Papuan readings of Christianity in which the belief systems introduced by outside missionaries are reinterpreted locally, be it through myths (e.g. reading Biblical stories and the role of Israel/The Holy Land through the Koreri lens, as it were) or through more confrontational approaches where outsiders, including Israel, are accused of having misappropriated powerful Papuan symbols. In the next section, I shall examine a further understanding of the Papuan-Israeli relationship, one in which the distinction between the two becomes more blurred.

---

32 Interviews, Manokwari.

33 The Koreri cycle, in brief, tells the story of the mythical hero Manarmakeri who, having been banished by his fellow villagers, travels the world bringing knowledge and riches to foreign lands, and whose return home is to usher in a new era of plenty. For far more in-depth, nuanced and complex explorations of Koreri than can be presented here, see Kamma (1972) and Rutherford (2003 and 2012: 91–124). Both Kirksey (2012: 31 and 243–244) and Rutherford (2012: 103) point to Biak readings of Manarmakeri being equated with the Father of, and/or with Jesus Christ.

34 Not all Papuan political leaders whom I interviewed, however, saw the Morning Star as a symbol of Papuan aspirations for merdeka. One leader who associates himself with the Pan-Melanesian 14 Star Movement regarded the Morning Star as a 'symbol of Lucifer'. Interview, Melbourne.

Figure 5.6. Motorbike decal in Jayapura, Papua.

Source: Henri Myrttinen.

Israel/the Holy Land as (metaphor for) *Tanah Papua*

The third kind of discourse around Israel/*Tanah Papua* focuses on the metaphorical level. This covers a spectrum of understandings, starting with the use of Biblical references in everyday speech to more literal readings of Biblical events as having happened, happening or going to happen in the Land of Papua. It was not always possible in all my interviews to draw a distinct line between where events in Papua were merely compared to those occurring in the Bible and narratives in which Biblical events were actually considered to have happened *in* Papua.[35] For the most part, though, Biblical events were 'left' in the Holy Land but used as a point of comparison for the situation in Papua and West Papua (on the use of Biblical language, see also Timmer 2000: 233). Given widespread Papuan sentiments of marginalisation and oppression, a common theme was that of exile and captivity, be it the Biblical story of exile in Egypt or in Babylon, a thematic undercurrent also visible for example in Afro-American and Afro-Caribbean Christianity.[36] These stories were invoked in part when discussing the overall situation of the *Bangsa Papua* or personal captivity.[37]

---

35   The distinction between the two may be one that only seems pertinent from my Western perspective.

36   Interviews, Jayapura and Wuppertal. Timmer (2000: 297–300) also discusses Imyan conceptualisations of the Tower of Babel having been built in Baimla.

37   Interviews, Port Moresby (Papua New Guinea), Port Vila (Vanuatu) and Jayapura.

Figure 5.7. Star of David graffiti, Jayapura, Papua.

Source: Henri Myrttinen.

As Diana Glazebrook (2008: 146) relates in her study of West Papuan refugees planning to return to Indonesia from refugee camps in PNG, the theme of Moses and return from exile can go beyond the strictly metaphorical to a more personalised and localised reading, though with a globalised twist. In this case, the Moses trope was projected onto the persona of a refugee evangelical pastor, Jeronimus, who had established the West Papua Indigenous Peoples' Association (WPIA) after receiving mail from a transnational forum of indigenous people based in Geneva:

> Jeronimus was hailed as a Moses figure by his WPIA constituency: In the story of Exodus, through the prophet Moses, God performed ten miracles of plagues and still Pharoah was hard hearted, refusing to let the Israelis out of Egypt. The Israelis were slaves. Suharto was like Pharaoh. Jeronimus is a prophet and deliverer like Moses. As we have seen from the history of Israel, Moses led them home. West Papuan people can similarly be saved.

> [...] In a 1998 Christmas sermon posted to East Awin, the translated sermon mentioned the government of Israel's plea for members of the Jewish diaspora to return to Israel to help develop their nation. WPIA leaders interpreted this sermon analogously as a call for West Papuans to return to Irian Jaya to assist develop the nation-state,[38] rather than return in its wake. The idea of connection between Irian Jaya and Israel may

---

38 Based on Glazebrook's text, there seemed to be differing readings among the West Papuan refugee community as to whether this referred to returning to help re-build an Indonesian-controlled Irian Jaya, as advocated by Jeronimus, or an independent West Papua as argued by his detractors.

have been influenced by a publication titled 'From Jerusalem to Irian Jaya' which had been advertised and reviewed in the Catholic weekly *Tifa Irian*, a newspaper that occasionally circulated at East Awin. While I knew of no copies of the book at East Awin and knew of no-one who had read the book, many people referred to its title.

As outlined by Jaap Timmer (2000: 285, 297–300) in his study of the Imyan in West Papua, Biblical stories and Biblical locations can also be taken beyond the merely comparative and be redefined as having actually taken place in *Tanah Papua*. In 2008 and 2009, a religious movement in the Mamberamo area was also based on reinterpreting Biblical events in the context of Papuan political struggles. Inspired by the visions of an elderly lady from Biak, Nela Yanseren, a group of armed civilians who identified with the OPM occupied an airfield in Kapeso in expectation of the Second Coming of Christ and Papuan independence. In *Ibu* (Mrs or Mother) Nela's visions, the Mamberamo River was recast as the River Jordan, the nearby Lake Rombebay was the Sea of Galilee and the OPM military commander Richard Yoweni was cast as Moses who has led his people through the Wilderness for 40 years but could not cross into the Promised Land. Instead, it would be up to the armed men led by Decky Imberi, now cast as Joshua and calling his men the Army of Joshua, to lead the people out of slavery. The struggle against the Indonesian state was stated by Ibu Nela as being a precondition for the Second Coming of Christ (KMSKP 2009 and KPKC 2009).

The Kapeso airfield occupation is not the first case of a millenarian movement in the Mamberamo area.[39] Freerk Kamma (1972: 294–298) documents a movement in the region in 1956–62 but the more obvious parallels are with the Koreri movement in the Biak-Numfor area in 1938–44. As outlined in Kamma (1972: 157–213) and also Rutherford (2003: 24–28, 2012: 157–161), the movement combined religious elements from Christianity with local mythology, in which a local culture hero Manarmakeri is to return to Papua with the promise of material wealth and eternal life, secrets which the Morning Star had bestowed upon him. Though similar movements were far from uncommon (Kamma alone lists several dozen cases), the Koreri movement was not only marked by longevity but also by an explicitly political agenda of an independent New Guinea under the leadership of Angganitha Manufaur, who also bore the title *Bin Damai ro Judea* (Woman of Peace from Judea) and *Ratu Mas ro Judea* (Golden Queen of Judea). Like Ibu Nela, she had a following of an army of sorts and, as in the case of the Kapeso airfield occupation, sites from the Holy Land were 'relocated' to Papua: Judea was the island of Insumbabi and Bethlehem the island of Aiburanbondi, both off the coast of Biak. In an effort to appease Manseren, who was to return to

---

39   Kirksey (2012: 46–50) and Rutherford (2003: 13–19 and 2012: 91–124) have also pointed to millenarian elements in the events which preceded the 'Bloody Biak' massacre of 1998, although Rutherford stresses that the central figure in the flag-raising, Filep Karma, did not himself draw any links to the Koreri movement.

Insumbabi/Judea, amongst other things the consumption of pork was forbidden (Kamma 1972: 159–160). Rutherford (2012: 157–164) furthermore stresses the 'power of the foreign' that the Koreri movement sought to harness, linked here directly with the Biblical Holy Land. Both the Kapeso airfield occupation and the Koreri movement ended at the hands of security forces without reaching their goals of a millenarian solution to the political status of Papua.

Discussion

I have thus far sketched some of the ways in Papuans link Israel and the Holy Land to *Tanah Papua* and to Papuan aspirations for *merdeka*, whichever form this freedom might be imagined to manifest itself in. Papuan re-readings of Israel, the Holy Land and events of the Bible are complex, overlapping and in part contradictory. For example, the stories of Moses, the Exodus and entering the Promised Land are reflected in Papuan stories of returning refugees (Glazebrook 2008) and occupying Kapeso airfield, but they came to opposite conclusions. Returning refugees saw the Biblical narrative as an exhortation to return to the Indonesian state, while the Kapeso airfield occupants interpreted the story as an instruction to struggle against it. Both groups, however, interpreted Papua as the Promised Land of Biblical stories.

In Papuan discursive engagements with Israel, either as a beleaguered Jewish/ Christian nation-state, or as the Holy Land, we may see what seem like elusive symbolic interpretations, contradictions and leaps of faith. However, Papuan understandings of Israel/the Holy Land should be interpreted in terms of local logic and experience. Israel and the Holy Land are seen in these re-readings from a very Papuan perspective which is informed by Christianity and local mythology such as Koreri, a history of oppression and marginalisation of the indigenous population, fears of the loss of Papuan identity through an influx of Muslim migrants, and limited possibilities of having open, critical and informed political discussions on issues feeding Papuan discontent.

When Papuans emphasise the special relationship of Papua to a perceived centre of power, we may read this as an attempt to escape marginality and regain agency (Timmer 2000). Drawing on the potency of perceived allies who (often without knowing it) are seen to share a special relationship, the mostly forgotten Papuan political struggles start taking centre stage, at least from the Papuan perspective.

It is not only Israel which is seen as possessing power that, possibly, was once in the hands of Papuans and was misappropriated by outsiders, a theme also encountered in the Koreri myths. Papuans also invoke Dutch, Indonesian and American, and United Nations symbols of sovereignty. As Glazebrook (2008: 145) discusses,

> Other WPIA members attributed a kind of supernatural agency to UN paraphernalia like logos—as though they were enspirited … Like the UN logo, national flags were considered to have a sort of human agency, or witnessing capacity.

The potency of Dutch, American, Indonesian and UN symbols can be seen in the context of Papuan history: it was these powers that played key roles in the events, perceived by many of my interviewees as 'traumatic', through which Dutch West New Guinea became the Indonesian province of Irian Jaya, and these powers should now undo the damage done. Though Israel has played no role in the historical events of the past 50 years that have shaped *Tanah Papua*, it is perceived as an ally. The most obvious link from the Papuan perspective is religion: Judaism and Christianity are seen as being on the same side of a struggle against creeping Islamisation. Doctrinal differences between Judaism and Christianity are glossed over as are differences in terms of the *de facto* and *de jure* political status of the State of Israel and *Tanah Papua*. Israel (rather than, for example, Palestine) is seen as a righteous underdog in this struggle, but nonetheless as a powerful underdog. Non-recognition of Israel and of West Papuan ambitions for *merdeka* by the Indonesian state are at times conflated. Israel thus becomes an inadvertent ally for some (i.e. those not seeing more of a parallel with Palestine), its national symbols signifying opposition to perceived Islamisation and, in some cases, the policies of the Indonesian government (Merdhi 2010).

Other understandings of the special relationship are more bound to Christian practice, such as making a pilgrimage to the Holy Land and an adult baptism in the River Jordan. Biblical stories and metaphors, which are often the most accessible texts especially in villages, are used to make sense of a social, political and economic situation that seems inherently skewed against Papuan aspirations. References to Jewish captivity in Egypt and Babylon have a special resonance among my Papuan informants.

In some cases, as with Papuans' donation to the construction of the Third Temple and the (possibly apocryphal) notion of building a golden bridge for the Second Coming, there is a clear break with mainstream Christian orthodoxy. Even more complex understandings of the special relationship are found in millenarian movements such as Koreri and in what happened more recently in Kapeso. Here Christian eschatology became mixed with local mythology and Papuan political aspirations, taking place in a *Tanah Papua* which has become, at least in part, the Promised Land.

In all their complexity and richness, the multiple Papuan narratives linking *Tanah Papua* with Israel and the Holy Land are about aspirations of Papuans towards *merdeka* – whatever form this *merdeka* is expected to take. Israel, without knowing it, is at times seen as a potent ally, a source of spiritual power and solace, and at times Papua becomes the Holy Land and the Holy Land becomes Papua. Based purely on my own observations in Papua, but also in other parts of eastern Indonesia, the centrality of Israel in Christian discourses and also visually, especially in urban areas, seems to be increasing. In part, this may be part due to a heightened religious polarisation in the country, but also due to increased use of internet-based media and organised pilgrimages to the Holy Land. As I hope to have sketched here, however, these discourses are not straightforward or uncontested among Papuans. Rather, Papuan narratives linking *Tanah Papua* with Israel and the Holy Land involve numerous different voices, bringing together local mythology, understandings of Christianity, political aspirations and readings of global politics.

References

Aditjondro, George 2000. 'Ninjas, Nanggalas, Monuments and Mossad Manuals – An Anthropology of Indonesian State Terror in East Timor'. In Sluka, Jeffrey (ed.), *Death Squad: The Anthropology of State Terror*. Philadelphia: University of Pennsylvania Press, 158–188.

Anderson, Benedict 2005. *Under Three Flags: Anarchism and the Anti-Colonial Imagination*. London: Verso.

Bubandt, Nils 2008. 'Rumors, Pamphlets, and the Politics of Paranoia in Indonesia'. *The Journal of Asian Studies* 67(3): 789–817.

Chauvel, Richard 2006. 'Violence and Governance in West Papua'. In Coppel, Charles (ed.), *Violent Conflicts in Indonesia: Analysis, Representation, Resolution*. London: Routledge, 180–191.

Chauvel, Richard 2011. 'Policy Failure and Political Impasse: Papua and Jakarta a decade after the "Papuan Spring"'. In King, Peter, Elmslie, Jim and Webb-Gannon, Camellia (eds), *Comprehending West Papua*. Sydney: University of Sydney, 105–115.

Drooglever, Pieter 2005. *Een Daad van Vrije Keuze: De Papoea's van Westelijk Nieuw-Guinea en de Grenzen van het Zelfbeschikkingsrecht*. Amsterdam:Uitgeverij Boom.

GKI 2011. 'The Third Papuan Congress and The Declaration of Independence.' Report by KPKC, Synod of GKI, Jayapura, 21 October, 2011.

Glazebrook, Diana 2008. *Permissive Residents: West Papuan Refugees Living in Papua New Guinea*. Canberra: ANU Press.

HaLevi, Ezra 2007. 'West Papua Delegation Donates Gold For Holy Temple'. Arutz Sheva. http://www.israelnationalnews.com/News/News.aspx/123837 (accessed 10 July 2007).

Jebens, Holger 2004. 'Introduction'. In Jebens, Holger (ed.), *Cargo, Cult, and Culture Critique*. Honolulu: University of Hawai'i Press, 1–13.

Kamma, Freerk 1972. *Koreri – Messianic Movements in the Biak-Numfor Culture Area*. Den Haag: Martinus Nijhoff.

Kammen, Douglas 2009. 'Fragments of Utopia: Popular Yearnings in East Timor'. *Journal of Southeast Asian Studies* 40(2): 385–408.

Kirchhoff, Karl-Heinz 1973. *Die Täufer in Münster 1534/35: Untersuchungen zum Umfang und zur Sozialstruktur der Bewegung*. Münster: Aschendorff.

Kirksey, Eben 2012. *Freedom in Entangled Worlds: West Papua and the Architecture of Global Power*. Durham: Duke University Press.

KMSKP 2009. 'Gerakan Kargoisme Yang Dibelokan Oleh Gerakan Atas Nama OPM di Kapeso'. Jayapura: Koalisi Masyarakat Sipil Untuk Keadilan dan Perdamaian di Tanah Papua.

KNPB 2011. 'Indonesia backs Palestine at UN, what about West Papua?' Press Release: West Papua Media Alerts, 21 September 2011.

KPKC 2009. 'Bentrok di Kapeso, 4 Warga Papua Tewas'. Jayapura: KPKC Sinode GKI di Tanah Papua.

Merdhi, Andrianus 2010. *Der Schwarze Messias*. Documentary film accessed at http://vimeo.com/25197078.

Myrttinen, Henri 2010. *Histories Of Violence, States Of Denial – Militias, Martial Arts And Masculinities In Timor-Leste*. Ph.D. Thesis, Durban: University of KwaZulu-Natal.

Ondawame, John Otto 2010. *One People, One Soul – West Papuan Nationalism and the OPM*. Adelaide: Crawford House Publishing.

Reagan, Ronald 1984. 'Remarks Accepting the Presidential Nomination at the Republican National Convention in Dallas, Texas, August 23, 1984'. Transcript accessed at http://www.reagan.utexas.edu/archives/speeches/1984/82384f. htm.

Rutherford, Danilyn 2003. *Raiding the Land of the Foreigners: The Limits of the Nation on an Indonesian Frontier*. Princeton: Princeton University Press.

Rutherford, Danilyn 2012. *Laughing at Leviathan: Sovereignty and Audience in West Papua*. Chicago: Chicago University Press.

Saltford, John 2002. *The United Nations and the Indonesian Takeover of West Papua, 1962–1969: Anatomy of a Betrayal*. London: Routledge.

Swazey, Kelli 2010. 'Circulating Israel in Indonesia: Publics of Pilgrimage and National Christian Subjecthood in North Sulawesi'. Paper presented at the American Anthropological Association Annual Meeting, New Orleans, 17 November, 2010.

Tebay, Neles 2009. *Dialog Jakarta-Papua: Sebuah Perspektif Papua*. Jayapura: SKP.

Timmer, Jaap 2000. *Living With Intricate Futures – Order and Confusion in Imyan Worlds, Irian Jaya, Indonesia*. Nijmegen: University of Nijmegen.

Timmer, Jaap 2008. 'Kastom and Theocracy: A Reflection on Governance from the Uttermost Part of the World'. In Dinnen, Sinclair and Firth, Stewart (eds), *Politics and State Building in Solomon Islands*. Canberra: ANU Press, 194–212.

Widjojo, Muridan S., Elisabeth, Adriana, Amiruddin, Pamungkas, Cahyo and Dewi, Rosita 2008. *Papua Road Map: Negotiating the Past, Improving the Present and Securing the Future*. Jakarta: Indonesian Institute of Sciences, Jakarta.

WPNA 2011. 'WPNA Rejects LIPI-Peace Network Conference Because West Papua Is An International Issue Requiring International Third Party Mediation.' Press Release, Yapen Waropen Mamberamo, 6 July 2011.

6. Hip Hop in Manokwari: Pleasures, Contestations and the Changing Face of Papuanness

Sarah Richards

Hamburgers and evangelical Christianity are highly successful American exports and so too hip hop has proven to be 'the cultural form most widely appropriated into new contexts around the world' (Bucholtz 2002: 543). In Manokwari, the capital city of the province of West Papua, young people have passionately embraced the music and music videos of American hip hop at a time when cable television and online networks have displaced national control and censorship over print and visual media. Locally referred to as '*lagu rap*' (rap songs), '*r 'n' b*' (R and B) or '*lagu karpet dans*' (carpet dance songs), commercial hits manufactured by the hip hop industry are popular amongst men and women in their teens and twenties. Since it became a capital in 2003,[1] new digital platforms, more reliable electricity and increased access to money in Manokwari have facilitated the consumption of American hip hop. The music is watched on MTV and the internet, and downloaded onto laptops, android-platform cell phones and other music file-holding devices. This African-American cultural form, characterised by four elements (rap music, DJ-ing, break dancing and graffiti art), emerged in the 1970s as a resistant expression to white American hegemony and urban hardships (Chang 2006). In the last two decades hip hop has become a globalised genre appropriated and recontextualised within diverse cultural settings at the same time as becoming a corporate complex that inscribes image and lifestyle through commodities, verbal and body language, and attitude (Kitwani 2004). Hip hop as a marker of lifestyle and identity is apparent amongst Papuan youth who dress in the iconic styles of this genre, wear t-shirts with images of their favourite artists, perform breakdance in the streets and sketch graffiti art on urban walls.

The aims of this chapter are twofold. One, I examine the engagement of Papuan youth with American hip hop as well as the opinions of parents about these engagements. Two, I ask what interests in and opinions of hip hop can tell us about the changing shape of beliefs that Papuans are a good and worthy collective, what I call the Papuan pride movement. Taking as my starting point the notion that meaning is not passively received but created through negotiations between cultural context, media content and the priorities of audiences, I explore local

---

1 In January 2003, a presidential decree (Inpres 1/2003) was issued to divide the province of Papua into three. To date only two have transpired: Papua to the east and the western division now called West Papua (*Papua Barat*).

reception to American hip hop in Papua as a way of inquiring into political and moral concerns in Manokwari today. As we shall see, Papuans read hip hop in either a positive or negative light depending on their relationship to complex historical intersections constituted by racist histories, political and social change and emergent religious tensions and moral anxieties in their city. For younger enthusiasts, hip hop presents as a global black aesthetic (Stemmer 2013; Ellis 1989) which, in the context of racial histories and landscapes, is being appropriated to configure an esteemed vision of Papuans as attractive, stylish, talented and potentially wealthy. The decreasing and more outspoken cohort who oppose hip hop do so on the grounds that it is 'un-Papuan', undermining of a Christian-traditional way of life and also threatening of school success and even economic prosperity for Papua.

That hip hop incites both claims to Papuanness and provides aesthetic resources for uplifting ethnic esteem amongst young Papuans suggests that Papuan identity and nationalism is moral and emotional as well as symbolic and political. To date these dimensions have been unexplored in contrast to understandings of Papuan national identities based on a shared phenotype (black skin, frizzy hair), religion (Christianity) and histories of suffering (Farhadian 2005; Chauvel 2005). Papuanness is a sentiment of pan-tribal identification that is generated through histories of perceived cultural and racial oppression and relies on stereotypes to position Papuans as a collective that is distinct from Islamic Indonesians. In recent years, Papuanness has become articulated via new digital technologies and social media and is configured through idioms of Christianity, tradition and love of land (which informs the popular expression, *Tanah Papua,* or Land of Papua). In the literature Papuanness is associated with politics, an identity that is intimately entwined with nationalist aspirations for *merdeka,* a word that translates as freedom but has semantic associations beyond national secession (Kirksey 2012). Scholars tended to have located the nexus of Papuan/*merdeka* in overt symbols of independence, religious scripture (Farhadian 2005; Rutherford 2003) and traditional expressions, especially song (Rutherford 2003; Glazebrook 2004; Smythe 2013).

This paper expands the frontiers of our understanding of Papuanness by exploring its lesser known and emergent properties: how it is also a realm of moral proscription (behaviours and expectations attached to being Papuan) and a zestful energy of ethnic pride that may or may not be attached to political aims of *merdeka*. Understanding Papuanness in the latter sense, as a collective energy that animates pride, allows us to identify how, at the heart of contested meanings, lies a pathos of missed meaning between those who are pro and those who are anti-hip hop. Whether mediating the hip hop imaginary in ways that promote Papuan beauty, talent and goodness or opposing this imaginary by recourse to an 'authentic' culture and Christian morality, parents and youth share a common impulse – to invigorate a pan-Papuan identity with virtue, dignity and pride.

This paper is based on 27 months of fieldwork with 'coastal people' (*orang pantai*) in Manokwari between 2003–2005 and 2011. This diachronic perspective provided a vantage to view practices and attitudes to hip hop and the broader cultural field as dynamic and evolving. 'Coastal people' is an emically derived term to designate Papuans who originate from islands in and around nearby Cenderawasih Bay or mainland regions who consider themselves different to both mountain Papuans and western Indonesian migrants. My informants were mostly born and raised in Manokwari with the vast majority identifying as from Biak and Numfor islands[2] and were neither the richest nor poorest members of society. They spoke Indonesian as their first language, valued education and employment with the civil service, and most were government employed or supported by someone who was. They were committed to a variety of churches but mostly Protestant denominations.[3] Though Papua and West Papua provinces have pluralistic religious and ethnic landscapes, my informants are part of the indigenous majority who are of Christian faith and hold their Papuan Christian status as a marker of opposition to the 88 per cent national Islamic majority (Perwita 2007: 1; Farhadian 2005). In the following I provide some cultural and political context for reading hip hop in Manokwari and describe current understandings of pan-Papuan identity and cultural pride. I then present some meanings of hip hop for older and younger Papuans respectively, followed by a discussion of these meanings, their point of convergence and their relevance for understanding configurations of Papuanness in Manokwari.

Hip hop culture: Local uptake of a global form

As I watch television with a group of teenagers one afternoon, Bacchanalian scenes of MTV Asia flicker across the screen. It is hip hop hour and as hypnotic beats fill the room our gaze is turned on toned black and golden skin. In the first clip, young women dance in red sequined bras and matching shorts that reveal their leg line. The young men in the clip, paired with the girls, have hairless and glistening chests, they wear sunglasses, tight low-cut denim shorts and puffy, expensive sneakers. I miss the name of this artist but take note that the next clip is by Jay Z and Kanye West, who maintain a cool masculinity while modifying a car and racing it. In the next clip, Rihanna sings in mesmerised union with a man. Sexual longing is fetishised with camera shots of her long,

---

2   Biak-Numfor are adjoining islands in the Cenderawasih Bay with large and historically migratory communities.

3   Most informants identified as *orang GKI* (*Gereja Kristen Indonesia*; Christian Church of Indonesia), the biggest church in town, but many were also *orang GPdI* (*Gereja Pentekosta di Indonesia*; Pentecostal Church); GBI (*Gereja Bethel Indonesia*; Bethany Success Family); GPKAI (*Gereja Persekutuan Kristen Alkitab Indonesia*; Christian Bible Church of Indonesia); *Gereja Katholik* (Catholic Church); GSJA (*Gereja Sidang Jemaat Allah*; Assemblies of God); and GKII (*Gereja Kemah Injil Indonesia*; KINGMI).

orange-nailed hands entwined with his fingers, their faces often poised to kiss, her long legs ending in stilettos and entwined around him. This clip, racy by public Papuan standards, is tame relative to the next, by Nicki Minaj. With a doll-like face plastered in makeup and pulling contorted expressions, the singer moves her body in hyper-sexualised moves. At the beginning, she dances with half a dozen lookalikes in denim shorts and singlet tops revealing their bra and midriff. At the end of the clip the lookalikes are in white leotards, glowing under ultraviolet light, performing writhing lap dances on buff men sitting on chairs. The audience is expressionless as all eyes are fixed on the show. When my friend's mother arrives home with her younger sibling, the channel is switched to a less confronting Javanese soap (*sinetron*).

American hip hop is one of multiple 'mediascapes' (Appadurai 1990) constitutive of new social imaginaries in Papua. In the mid-2000s Papuans listened to it through pirated CDs sold cheap at the market, which were often copied and shared between peers. Mobile phones are now the prime technology where hip hop is downloaded, stored shared and, for the growing number with android platforms, watched as video files. Hip hop is a genre that jostles with others emitted from CD shops, karaoke bars and public buses including *lagu India* (screen hits from Bollywood), songs associated with specific regions (i.e., *lagu Jawa*, *lagu Ambon*, *lagu Manado*) and other kinds of *lagu barat* ('western song') that include singers such as Mariah Carey and Englebert Humperdinck.

In general, Papuans in Manokwari classify music into three spheres: *lagu gereja* (church music), *lagu daerah* (traditional songs from a particular region) and *lagu dunia* (world/secular music). Within this scheme, hip hop falls within the latter category. In contrast to traditional and church songs that are considered 'good' because they connect Papuans to their history and to God, *lagu dunia* is described as a fickle pleasure at best, morally eroding at worst.

During my first fieldwork period hip hop was referred to as *musik karpet dans* (carpet dance music) after the squares of mat that boys, and less often girls, used to cushion dancing bodies. Building on older embodiments where youth used their bodies as a tool of expressive play, the vigorous gymnastics of hip hop dance found a ready audience in Papua. Public dancing took two forms. There were groups of dancers who put their carpet mats and a boom box on the ground close to shops in the evening and danced often until about 9pm or until the *adat* (customary, traditional) police or an irate trader moved them on. A more formal platform manifested as competition dance, where same-sex groups of up to a dozen dancers competed in a government-built hall. Whenever I was a member of the audience at these events, one of a hundred or so who sit in a stiff chair in a hot and stuffy hall, I was always amazed by the athleticism and panache of the dancers. Dance groups went to great effort designing and sewing 'uniforms', using shiny and bold-coloured materials worked into body-covering trousers and shirts. Faces and synthetic clothes quickly became wet during the performance as troupes engaged in high-energy, tightly choreographed dances that appeared as if straight from a music video clip, save for a significant exception. Just as their costumes were more sport than sex, so too their dancing lacked the grinding, twerking and other sexually provocative moves characteristic of American hip hop (Munoz-Laboy et al. 2007).

From dance to style: Development and moral anxieties in the Gospel City

The commercialisation of hip hop (see Chang 2006) has dovetailed with the radical growth of Manokwari and concomitant fears about the moral impact of social change on the town's youth. In 2005, all young women save for those said to be *nakal* (naughty, sexually immoral), *sombong* (arrogant) or *yang tidak tahu malu*[4] (do not know shame) wore loose-fitting and well-concealing jeans (or skirts well below the knee) and t-shirts (or button-up shirts). Makeup was for church, jewellery was limited to little more than a necklace with a small crucifix and hair was short or tied and slicked back to look neat and straight. Fast forward to 2011. Most young women still dress like this, in what people call 'Papuan style' (*gaya Papua*) but there are many who no longer conform to this dress code. Especially in the late afternoons, evenings and Saturday night, times when youth like to dress up and *jalan jalan* (travel about without clear purpose), it is increasingly common to see girls wearing makeup, skinny jeans, short skirts and singlet tops that reveal shoulders. Though not limited to hip hop style, mimesis of hip hop celebrities is apparent in the popularity of 'bling' (bold metal jewellery), flamboyant hair styles and, for young men, baggy trousers that reveal the top of their undershorts as well as heavy chain jewellery, sunglasses, sneakers and baseball caps worn backwards.

The greater appearance of fashions that girls would, only a few years earlier, have been too afraid to wear lest they be gossiped about is related to the rapid growth and development of the town since it became a capital city of a new province. Facebook friends had warned me prior to my return five years after my first period of fieldwork that 'Manokwari has changed a lot' (*Manokwari merubah sekali*). These warnings could not prepare me for the scale of change I witnessed. The town had become bigger, louder and, to my senses, uglier and smellier. Tentacle-like, it wound further around Dorey and Wosi Bays, it crept into the green rainforest-covered hills beyond, there were now a great deal more shops, and grand new

---

4   *Malu* is a Malay/Indonesian word that pertains to both a state of feeling shame or shyness and ideal feminine embodiment. It is commonly described by Papuans (Munro 2009, this volume) in reference to specific affective configurations to do with loss of prestige as much as an internalised sense of shame. In Papuan contexts, *malu* is a category and experience shaped by local structures, cultures and biographies but, in contrast to other parts of Indonesia, within Papua, shame is more closely related to social standing.

government offices lined new roads. Manokwari had a number of firsts, including a gated community; a two-storey mall; a five-star hotel; and a children's birthday party venue. In 2005, the town had one traffic light that was turned off at ten o'clock to save electricity. Now there were six that operated day and night.

If the growth of hip hop in Manokwari is linked to an expanding social and urban scale, attitudes to this genre are related to complex interpretations and experiences of development. People spoke of change in epochal terms, as Manokwari having 'already developed' (*sudah dibangun*). They attributed this to funds sent from Jakarta to build the infrastructure and the personnel required for expanded governance. They also understood development as the result of enterprising in-migrants and the political processes of *otonomi khusus* (special autonomy) and *pemekaran* (administrative subdivisions).[5] Papuan civil servants, believed to be operating within a KKN (*Kolusi, Korupsi, Nepotisme* – Collusion, Corruption and Nepotism) economy, were said to have become wealthier in recent years. The rising standard of living amongst some contrasted with the majority who, and perhaps with greater bitterness given their hopes for change, continue to struggle to find money in the day to day. While a growing divide between Papuan have and have nots is a new trend, the competitive advantage of migrants in a racially structured economy is a continuation of economic patterns in Papua (Upton 2009). Patterns of migration are indeed diverse and include newcomers from within as well as outside Papua, but when accounting for demographic and economic change, migrant-owned shops and houses that have sprung up, squeezed between older buildings, figure strongly in Papuan explanatory frames. In the post-Suharto landscape, Papuan disgruntlements with economic exclusion are increasingly vocalised and amongst the more conservative, increasingly through the axis of religion. The changing ratio of church spires to minarets has provoked concern that the Gospel City (*Kota Injil*), as Manokwari is famously known due to being the site of the first mission in Papua,[6] is becoming Islamicised and losing its Christian character.

Within this broad context of economic and political concern, hip hop is implicated in discourses of 'sex panic' (Herdt 2009), an analytic offshoot of moral panics theory (Cohen 1980). Though hip hop music, fashion and dance are not a strong target of public concern, it is fuelling a generalised anxiety that youth cultures are sexualising as they are changing. Youth interest in edgy and sexy appearances are, for the morally concerned and as is common in scenarios of moral panic (Cohen 1980), a sign of poor foreign influence and a 'slippery

---

5 The Special Autonomy (*Otonomi Khusus*, Otsus) Bill was approved for Papua in 2001. It was intended to address Papuan grievances to centralised governance by granting greater power over local administrations and budgets. In practice it has been a contentious and fraught legislation that has benefitted few. *Pemekaran*, the process of proliferating administrative divisions in the scramble for power and resources, has been an unanticipated consequence of the Otsus bill.

6 German Lutherans from the Utrecht Mission set up camp on nearby Mansinam Island in 1854.

slope' to social decay and ruin. Even though new fashions are modelled on an American cultural form, local histories and nationalist concerns configure 'the foreign' as 'Indonesian' in discourses of panic. To be clear, pre-marital sex is not the only target of panic,[7] yet the flush of cash through bureaucratic veins combined with the felt need or desire for money and commodities are triggering fear that more young women are exchanging sexual services for money (especially to buy mobile phone credit) or gifts of jewellery, clothes and mobile phones. Within the frame of Christian sensibilities, daily gossip, speeches of *adat* leaders, sermons and media editorials are preoccupied with the behaviour of youth who are said to be having more sex, with the possibility of more children being born out of wedlock, and with schoolgirls said to seduce married men and so 'destroy families'. From an anthropological perspective, seismic shifts in pop culture, fashion and sexual culture are the result of complex intersections at local, national and global levels and cannot be reduced to the influence of 'pop culture' or even 'hip hop'. Yet the salience of hip hop music and dance in the lives of many young people gives substance to parental concerns that youth are acting un-Papuan by following a foreign and sexually dubious cultural form.

Papuanness: The wider context

Papuanness is a 'revitalisation movement' in Wallace's (1956: 256) classic sense of 'a deliberate, organized, conscious effort by members of a society to construct a more satisfying culture'. Revitalisation is a promising analytic because it can account for Papuan identity as political-symbolic but also provides analytic space to capture the moral and emotional dimensions of behaving and feeling Papuan. Before I ask questions and comment on these dimensions, I provide a brief history of Papuanness. The term 'Papuan' to designate an overarching ethnic identity that runs in parallel to localised identifications is not new, and is found in the colonial (Chauvel 2005) and even the pre-colonial era (Rizzo 2004). As a dynamic axis of identity, Papuanness has evolved in recent years from being unspeakable, a term associated with 'anti-government, anti-Indonesian and anti-military' (Farhadian 2005: 156) to being the subject of a discursive explosion.

Vocal expressions of symbols and imaginings of Papuans as a unified *ras* (race) were made possible by cracks in state machinery and political reforms at national and provincial levels following the fall of Suharto in May 1998.[8] In the

---

7 Pre-marital sex is not the only target of moral panic for Manokwarians are also excessively concerned with *orang mabuk* (drunk men), opportunistic theft and greed-induced corruption.

8 Scholarship by Farhadian (2005) highlights the role of Christianity in fortifying the sense of Papuanness by pointing to the power of faith and religion in political opposition. The renewed interest in being 'Papuan', he argues, can be traced to GKI and Catholic reports published in Indonesian in the mid-1990s that detailed human rights abuses across the province (Farhadian 2005: 155).

new climate of *reformasi* (reform) characterised by new freedoms of speech and government accountability, 'civilian political expression in Papua flourished' (Ballard 2002: 468). Democratic reforms were limited, and many Morning Star (Papuan Independence) flag raisings ended with military fire in the second year after Suharto's resignation, but a Pandora's Box of disgruntlement and desire had been opened and Papuans were less fearful. An iconic moment in this respect was the Great Consultation (*Musyawarah Besar*, MUBES) of 2000 when Papuan leaders from across the province arrived in Jayapura to enter a dialogue forum on the future of Papua dressed in striking traditional finery (ICG 2001; Chauvel 2005; Ballard 2002). The symbolism of this gesture, in light of New Order histories that have denigrated Papuan culture, spoke volumes about a willingness to push Papuan heritage and identity onto centre stage.

Expressions of Papuan pride, though by different actors and with different effects, have circulated through a variety of realms in the service of the 'greater good', however defined. For instance, the importance of pan-Papuan sympathy for the goal of *merdeka* (freedom) is the subtext of the Morning Star flag and the Star of David, which have both become more ubiquitous in visual culture (Farhadian 2005; Myrttinen this volume). Papuanness is a concept mobilised by HIV prevention campaigns, it is manipulated by politicians to secure votes in the new system of direct elections, and it is a key underpinning of new *adat* organisations such as *Lembaga Masyarakat Adat* (Traditional Community Institution, LMA) and the *Dewan Adat* (Traditional Council). Visions of Papuanness are found in new local media, in songs that praise Papuan land and customs, and in an emergent genre of books that define 'the Papua problem' and recommend spiritual, behavioural and educational solutions to help lift Papua from relative economic disadvantage (Giay 2001; Flassy 1999; Poli et al. 2008). These diverse examples attest to the emergence of Papuanness as a highly elaborated cultural trope in contemporary Papua.

Papuanness resembles other discourses of sub-national difference found throughout post-Suharto Indonesia that draw on *adat* and religion to construct unique identities (Purdey 2004; Davidson and Henley 2007). Notwithstanding regional parallels, the content and intensity of contemporary Papuanness is shaped through histories of largely reluctant engagement with nation. Relationships to Indonesian governance, as this volume highlights, are highly diverse and characterised by deep entanglements (Kirksey 2012). A study of Papuanness, however, requires that we read history through the lens of negative experiences and opposition to institutions and agents of the state. It would take me too far afield to document how New Order dynamics have dialectically charged a passion for Papuanness but, as it is critical to understanding the resistant potential of hip hop, some words on histories of cultural and racial denigration are necessary. Building on colonial categories of civilisation/

primitive, state interventions to meet the aims of economic progress and national stability were justified by discourses of Papuans as a backwards, savage and undeveloped people (Kirksey 2012). This racialised gaze has taken many forms such as Java-centric programs and policies[9] and repressive controls over cultural expression.[10] It has stripped Papuans of rights in the case of land and resource alienation at the hands of non-Papuan migrants and foreign-owned companies and dehumanised them to a violent military apparatus (Hernawan this volume; Chauvel 2005; Kirksey 2012; Braithwaite et al. 2010). This is not the whole story, and for every Papuan I knew who had felt discriminated against by migrant teachers, employers or neighbours, there was another who had migrant friends from school, work or church. Within spaces of intimacy, there is both the potential for racism to be acutely experienced and potentially subverted through relations of dissidence.[11]

Such histories have become etched into consciousness through what Munro (2013, this volume) calls, after Robbins (2005), 'discourses of diminishment'. The idea that racial constructions can produce 'humiliation and a sense of inferiority' (Munro 2013: 27) can be traced to the theories of Marshall Sahlins (1992) and before him, Franz Fanon's (1986) evocative idea of the colonial mirror and need to decolonise the mind. In the context of Papua, emergent discourses of Papuanness can be understood as fulfilling the psychological need to assert a collective sense of dignity by reinscribing the mindset imposed on them through the racial national imaginary. In sum, Papuanness is an evolving and dynamic construct of grassroots communities, Papuan intellectuals, politicians and community leaders, and scholars have provided valuable insight into the macro-determinants of political identity and vision. Important questions remain regarding other facets of meaning, meanings that may or may not be tethered to realpolitik. By investigating attitudes to hip hop, I ask how does Papuanness manifest morally and emotionally to raise the esteem and dignity of a people?

---

9 Even trans- and spontaneous migration has been justified by, as one of many reasons, the modelling of Javanese morality, culture and industry.

10 The New Order state held a tight rein on *adat* (culture, custom, local history), only permitting its expression in the service of economic growth and nation building. Building on Dutch efforts to classify the customs of the 'East Indies', the New Order domesticated culture by officialising regional songs, dances and dress (Hellman 2003). Transforming culture into 'spectacle' (Acciaioli 1985) boosted the tourist economy and visually represented the national motto 'Unity in Diversity' in times of parade and other events of national celebration. In regions with desires for secession, objectifying culture had the additional benefit of keeping track of customary expressions that may be veiled political statements. Surreptitious enactments of 'culture' could be interpreted as a sign of potential treason and so be punished by the armed forces.

11 Due to its historical proximity to eastern Indonesia, it would be possible to write a history of love between Papuans and migrants in the Bird's Head region.

Hip hop: Un-Papuan versus inevitable

The athletic style of restrained hip hop dance in Papua suggests that as it has gained traction, hip hop has been reconfigured through Papuan codes of sexual and gendered ethics. This is not how many parents understand the situation and since its appearance on the social landscape, hip hop has been perceived as morally suspect. During my first period of fieldwork I found little nuance in opinions. All parents, many heartfelt while others seemingly in a knee-jerk reaction, expressed the belief that *karpet dans* was a negative influence. Reasons for this were intuitively straightforward – the music was '*tidak baik*' (no good) because it was '*bukan asli Papua*' (not authentically Papuan). In this statement we can see that as a decidedly 'foreign' cultural form, hip hop is more than incommensurate with the 'local', it is corrosive of Papuan moral character. Narratives of culture as something that can be lost to modern ways have been documented elsewhere in the Pacific and, as in these cases, what comes to be considered 'local' and 'foreign' are not geographically anchored but morally negotiated outcomes (Knauft 2002).

By the early 2010s, attitudes to hip hop were as diverse as attitudes to development, which hinged on personal politics and biographies and could be plural, ambivalent and contradictory. The formulaic interpretation of hip hop as bad and un-Papuan was still in circulation, yet this opinion had shifted to a conservative fringe; parents that were described by others as 'strict' (*berdisiplin*) or, in ways suggestive of their ethical decision-making framework, as '*adat* people' (*orang adat*) or 'fanatical Christian' (*Kristen fanatik*). This latter term was new, no doubt borrowed from global religious landscapes, and spoke to a growth in (or at least classification of) what Cohen (1980: 1) has referred to as 'right thinking people'. At the same time, increasing numbers of parents have come to condone, accept and even enjoy the hip hop music and dance of the young. They represent a growing middle class that may be dissatisfied with aspects of social change but, overall, accept development. 'This is how it is now in Papua', one friend told me when I asked why so many parents had changed their minds about hip hop. As if an afterthought she added, 'Manokwari has already developed.'

Ani, an unusually outspoken and mature 13-year-old, told me while her parents nodded in agreement: 'Kids are the same everywhere ... they all like this music'. This idea, that hip hop was inevitable because urban growth and technological change had catapulted Papuan youth into the time-space dimensions of peers in large global cities was common. A 57-year-old Serui-Biak fisherman, who was melancholic about the growing size of the city, looked to the horizon as he explained the new dance craze: 'We have entered *zaman globalisi* (era of globalisation). Our kids are like kids in other big cities, they want to listen to modern music and follow *selebriti* (celebrity).' Others, such as grey-haired mama

Aroy, a Biak woman with 28 grandchildren, were positively enthusiastic: 'I love to watch the children,' she grinned with betel-stained teeth, 'They are very clever at dancing.'

The polarisation of opinion can be understood in relation to a broad fracturing of Papuan society into those considered highly moralistic and the majority who, at my prompting, described themselves as a *'orang biasa'* (usual people, normal people). As a heuristic, we can visualise this as a spectrum where all Papuan parents value Christianity, tradition and disciplined childrearing to varying degrees but some enact these moral templates with greater vigour. A 52-year-old neighbour, a civil servant and lay pastor with the Pentecostal Church, held opinions typical of conservative views: 'This kind of dance is not good for Papuan children. When they follow this style, they follow foreign ways and forget *adat Papua* (Papuan customs).' As a Pentecost, readers versed in Melanesian literature might find my neighbour's coupling of morality and culture surprising. Given that fundamentalist denominations are well known for demanding followers sever from old ways of life to bring about a new kind of spiritual individual (Robbins 2004), his seamless reference to tradition alludes to how, in Manokwari at least, these twin spheres may be fused in the service of a moral identity.

To be sure, there are people known as *'adat* people' (*orang adat*) and as 'church people' (*orang gereja*); *adat* is selected and modified through Christian frames but not vice-versa. Frictions are not entirely absent between the two spheres. Yet from the GKI Reverend who incited Papua's future when urging youth to follow Christian ways of life in a Gospel City Day speech, to the pastor who requested I look in my anthropology book to re-learn how to build traditional houses, to the traditional costumes the majority wear in an increasingly popular annual parade that celebrates the arrival of the Gospel, to the priest who danced wildly at a bridewealth party, Christianity and tradition are largely entwined constructs that are drawn upon in discourses of what makes Papuans unique and special. For more conservative Papuans, they are also schema for drawing clear bounds between good and bad behaviours.

To understand claims that equate hip hop with Papuan inauthenticity, we need to ask what an authentic Papuanness might be? Such a question highlights that Papuanness is more than a matter of culture (*budaya*), land (*tanah*), customs (*adat*) and history (*sejarah*) that are distinct from other regions and peoples in Indonesia. Papuanness implies a special character too. The notion that 'Dani', 'Asmat', 'Biakis' and 'highlanders' (*orang gunung*), for example, have certain attributes is common knowledge amongst Papuans though what these attributes are differ depending on if one is or is not a member of the group. So too is Papuanness, precisely because of its grassroots legitimacy as symbol of unity, becoming a discourse of *being Papuan*, of possessing a moral character that is based on respect for religion and tradition.

In the context of social change and moral anxieties, being Papuan means to have a different moral character to Indonesians, a character people were keen to share. For instance, Papuans were said to be emotionally expressive and open. 'We are not like Javanese who are always calm and smile ... then knife you in the back when you are not looking,' explained a 33-year-old Biak woman, 'If we Papuans are angry, you will know. Our character is honest (*sifatnya jujur*).' Papuans, due to both customary living and Christian ethics, are thought to be inherently caring, willing to share the abundance with which God has blessed them.[12] 'Papuans don't *merantau* (leave Papua in search of economic opportunities),' a 22-year-old Biak man told me, 'because we have plenty. God gave Papuans oceans full of fish and good soil to grow vegetables.' A common expression that many recited was 'Papuans cannot be poor because they are rich in family'. An old, angular man spoke to me one rainy night, saying: 'We are a Christian people but it is also our tradition to care for other people. In Java people can die of hunger and no one knows. They find the body months later. That would never happen in Papua. No one goes hungry because we share, and God has blessed Papua with fertile soils and many fish.'

Given greater entanglements with national and global cultural flows, there is a certain irony in drawing rigid boundaries to create ethnic essentialisms. Giay and Ballard (2003) point to problems in creating a Papuan identity based on allegedly pure forms. Such constructions may be read as a response to contemporary entanglements, a desire to locate laudable moral qualities in order to simplify a complex situation and bestow dignity upon the collective. That my informants say that Papuans have a certain character does not, it is worth mentioning, preclude other kinds of social identifications nor is it to deny that Papuan cultures and identities are a mediated product of geographic and technological border-crossings.[13] I concur that Papuanness is accomplished through perceptions and interactions with 'audiences' (Rutherford 2012); that Papuans express affiliation with a tribe, a village *and* the ethno-nation; that they often identify with other Melanesians and share community with globalised Christian fellowships. The point is, as anthropologists have found in other world areas where indigeneity is a space of purity and goodness (Brison 2008; Gagné and Salaun 2012), Papuanness presents as a sacred certainty that Papuans are special people with rich customs and distinct virtues.

---

12 What Wardlow (2006: 35) calls 'auto-orientalism' is a common phenomenon whereby barbs and shadows are contained within dominant constructions. I have heard Papuans, in a candid moment, blame their lack of progress on a general laziness and tendency to gossip, which are seen as a dark side of their otherwise good sociality.

13 Intersectional spaces, for instance, include transnational fellowships (Farhadian 2005); relationships with international activists (Kirksey this volume); the (impossible) domestication of foreign goods and technologies (Rutherford 2003); colonial representations of Papua (Cookson 2008).

Hip hop and worries about sexual moral decline

Sexual morality is an example of a cultural realm where the contours of Papuanness are becoming fixed as a set of standards used by some to judge the actions of others. Premarital chastity is considered a quintessential Papuan value upheld by interpretations of the custom of bridewealth and Christian imperatives. Sex before marriage is said to be a 'sin' (*dosa*) and can be avoided through obedience and respect for parents, daily discipline and a personal relationship to God though prayer and a demure comportment and modest dress, the kind noted earlier as a 'Papuan style'. In these moral interstices, hip hop is perceived as an indiscriminate element in a cluster of developments feared to be weakening Papuans' moral fibre. Tom, a Serui man and a senior official in the Department of Education, spoke of hip hop indirectly when expressing concerns with a decline in the sexual morality of youth:

> This music the children dance to, it is not polite. You see them at the market on Saturday night, the music loud, boys and girls mingling, girls in rude clothes like *tali satu* (one string, singlet tops). This is not Papuan behaviour. It is bad for Papua's future. These kids listen to music, they dance, they drink, are delirious and have sexual relations. Girls get pregnant, leave school, there are so many children now who do not know their father.

Hip hop, for the conservative, indexed moral decline in an increasingly cosmopolitan city, the changing nature of which had facilitated mobility, anonymity and relaxed moral surveillance. It was associated with a set of immoral practices, revealing clothes, hetero-social mingling and drinking alcohol, that were clustered with illicit sex and personal and political ruin. If Tom speaks the language of moral panic by invoking the slippery slope, his specific concern with children born without fathers and Papua's future alerts us to how the 'political moment' (Weeks 2012) of Manokwari is configuring sex panics in which music and dance figure prominently. Economic disappointment is heightening fears that young women, especially with the rise of 'sugar daddy' civil servants, are more willing to sell sexual services. Growing numbers of migrants and the marginalisation of Christianity in the Gospel Town is raising the stakes of what kinds of behaviours are essential for helping Papuans travel the path to economic prosperity. This taps a meta-discourse raging in Papua about what factors are preventing the realisation of wealth that God, by virtue of bequeathing them great natural resources, had obviously meant for Papuans.

For 'regular people', hip hop was said to be a medium for expressing modern individualism. Even with the liberalisation of attitudes to foreign pop and culture, evaluations of broad shifts in the bounds of modesty in fashion could never be dislodged from the hegemony of a Christian sexual morality. Riasa, whose 16-year-old daughter wore the shortest skirts in the neighbourhood, looked me in the eye as she explained, 'It is just fashion. They are still good kids.' This argument was typical of parents who defended sexy looks by drawing a distinction between surface aesthetics and inner goodness. This comment highlights how the parameters of shame, as ideal feminine embodiment, are being renegotiated within a shifting social terrain. At the same time, that more flesh and flash looks are being defended belies the normative power of Christian standards of sexual goodness.

The foreign can be a source of potency and value in this Bird's Head region (Rutherford 2003) but hip hop alerts us to how the foreign is also a source of threat (see also Butt this volume). The young know hip hop as American in origin, but within reactionary discourses hip hop becomes a generic element of 'outside influences' (*pengaruh dari luar*) where 'outside', in the context of immediate concerns about migration, Indonesian media saturation and Islamicisation, stands for Indonesia or Java. Papuan friends were sure that the looks, aspirations and behaviours of the young had changed in recent years because they were 'following outside' (*berikut di luar*), which is to say they were 'following Indonesia' (*berikut Indonesia*). Fitting the continuum of moral orientation, some did not see this as necessarily displacing the moral compass of youth while others were sure that to adopt the behaviours of migrant peers and glitzy Javanese actors and models on television was to lose Papuan-Christian values. If we switch signifiers, from 'westernisation' to 'Indonesianisation', Papuan moral panics resemble moral panics occurring across Indonesia where Islamic and pro-family organisations are demonstrating 'moral outrage' against 'free sex lifestyles' as promoted by 'the West' (Schaefer 2013). Continuities with Islamic and other conservative groups in Indonesia notwithstanding, attitudes to popular cultural forms like hip hop are mediated through histories of social dissatisfaction with development and the nation.

Other problems with hip hop

Some parents believed hip hop to be a problem because it interfered with academic performance. Educational success is a factor widely believed to be a key to lifting Papuans from alleged ignorance and conditions of poverty (Stasch this volume; Munro 2009, 2013), yet links between hip hop and schooling prioritise the personal and practical over the abstract. Marta, a mother of two teenage daughters, explained this problem on a wooden bench under the shade of a mango tree one humid evening:

Papuan kids are crazy for this kind of music but I don't let my daughters follow. The problem with this kind of thing is that when kids stay up late practicing and dancing they are tired the next day. They cannot catch the learning. All their concentration, all their effort has been directed into learning the dance steps. So they are drowsy and not thinking of their schoolwork.

Marta, who was an exemplar of a *berdisiplin* (strict) parent, believed *karpet dans* to be so physically strenuous that it detracted from a child's ability to concentrate on school. School is highly regarded as a means to obtain the diploma needed to apply for waged employment and so, given familial investment to pay for school fees, uniforms and schoolbooks, hip hop can threaten to derail future economic stability. Reference to hip hop as redirecting effort from school is also based on 'local biologies' (Lock 2001), understandings of bodily capacities as finite and needing to be regulated by balance in day-to-day routines. Spending the evenings dancing runs counter to ideas of health as built from moderate and consistent regimes of work, sleep, study and prayer.

The last oppositional discourse I mention complicates the generational and moral lines I have drawn in pro- versus anti-hip hop stances. There are young men who problematise the sexy and edgy looks of young men and women but without a sexual moralism. This position can be illustrated by Teus, a 25-year-old economics graduate with dreadlocks, who does not so much attack hip hop as the kinds of lifestyles it is promoting:

> You see them everywhere, kids with long hair, lipstick, and tight jeans. Stylish, stylish, following *selebriti*. The problem with this is that they are forced from the outside to be like this. This is not original (*asli*) Papua, this is Jakarta style. These kids are not prepared for modernisation, they appear like they are already developed. They spend their time not learning about Papuan history, or working to progress Papua … They just wake up, think about their appearance, do their hair, then go about (*jalan jalan*), stylish modern. What do they have at the end of the day? Nothing. When they go home there is no dinner, no lighting, a dirt floor. A sparkling mobile phone and no food. This is not progress, this is a lie.

I do not know if Teus had read Marx, whose writings are illegal in Indonesia, but his argument had clear echoes of the late German. Here, fashion is a kind of 'opiate of the masses' productive of a kind of 'false consciousness' since the slavish adherence of youth to new fashions and styles was anathema to economic wellbeing. While parents who describe youth as 'following outside' (*ikut dari luar*) deny them agency, Teus' reference to Papuan kids being 'forced from outside' situates them as victims, a space with greater potential for moral redemption. Teus' expresses his vision of how the younger generation can reclaim autonomy by learning the 'truth' of history and confronting the reality of their economic impoverishment. Only by acknowledging this truth, Teus maintains, can the young be motivated to the kinds of learning and behaviour required to usher in a better future.

Hip hop: Meanings of Papuan youth

Papuans primarily enjoy hip hop because of its melody and beat, which is said to inspire dance. 'Rap music makes Papuan kids spirited,' (*musik rap bikin anak Papua semangat*) said one friend. Hendry told me: 'If we hear these songs, our bodies start to move' (*Kalau dengar lagu lagu ini, kami punya badan langsung mulai dans*). Sixteen-year-old Ruis alluded to its therapeutic value: 'When we hear this music we forget our worries' (*kalau dengar musik ini kami lupa pikiran*). As Indonesian speakers, being receptive to the music over the lyrics arguably enhances this visceral pleasure. This is not to say, however, that immediate sensory pleasures are disconnected from cognition for it is precisely the emotional charge of hip hop that creates an avenue for political meanings.

Women especially stressed the value of hip hop in terms of the beauty of its singers. Naomi, a 16-year-old student from the Wandamen region, explained why she and other Papuan kids like hip hop:

> You can see Rihanna and Beyonce are very pretty. They have black skin and frizzy hair like us. They show us how to wear makeup, stylish clothes and style their hair so we can look good too. Before, when I was young we saw some artists on the music video but we could not follow them. Kids now have entered the modern era, we like to follow them.

Naomi's words reveal how American hip hop artists have held appeal to young Papuans for many years but it is only since the rapid expansion of Manokwari that new freedoms have enabled celebrity emulation. They are worth emulating, she suggests, because of the similarity between Papuans and Afro-American phenotypes. The subversive potential of this identification can only be appreciated through recognising the role of Jakarta-based media and advertising industries in discourses of diminishment. While there are more diverse representations of Papua in national media and individuals are known to be celebrated for their prowess as athletes, singers and dancers, hierarchies of racial worth circulate through visual and print media as well as advertising. In moral hegemonies of beauty, pale-skinned and straight-haired people sit at the apex while darkness stands for that which is ugly, backwardness, inferiority and so bad (Prasetyaningsih 2007). While any reader who has seen Rihanna or Beyonce may question the extent to which they do in fact resemble a classic Melanesian look, from a local vantage they are more Papuan than they are Javanese and so provide scripts for Papuans to rework beauty within their physical parameters, effectively disrupting the reproduction of racial hegemonies in Papua.

Naomi's exegesis is supported by the relatively flamboyant hairstyles that some Papuans are adopting, clearly inspired by Afro-textured trends. Girls often like to dye their hair blonde or other bright colours and wear their hair out or straightened, crimped or extended. Teenage boys too, who only a few years earlier lacked elaborate grooming or body adornment, have come to dye their hair, often just a patch of colour, and as with hip hop artists, shave zigzags and other patterns into their locks. Hair, given histories of Indonesian denigration of and also forced cutting of Papuan hair (Cordell 2013), can be read as more than just an affordable site of hip hop expression. In ways that deserve greater attention, hair is becoming a key site of 'racial malleability' where Papuans are engaging the 'sensory modalities' (Roth-Gordon 2013: 298) of hip hop to transform experiences of their bodies in relation to a global blackness that presents as an alternative sphere of value. The resistant politics of hair was implicit in Sali's answer to my question of why she had taken the whole day to glue hair extensions on her friend. 'I don't know, something to do,' Sali replied, then after a pause, added with a wry smile, 'our crown is our glory.' According to her Biak heritage, a large, round, well-groomed frizz was a sign of moral and physical health and so a symbol of the strength of a community.

That men enjoy hip hop styles suggests these insights are applicable across the gendered divide. Men framed their interest in hip hop according to a different set of concerns. Perhaps because of the gendered double standards where men enjoy greater mobility and less scrutiny of reputation, hip hop was all about the dance for men. The music compelled dance and affirmed feelings of physical strength and talent for dance as well as provided a means for emotional release. For the more politically motivated, these sensations connected young men to Papuan history and culture. Twenty-one-year-old Solomon, a political activist and a member of a hip hop dance group, explained:

> The first artists I heard were Snoop Dog and 50 cent. I was surprised when my friend played me this music. I had not heard this kind before. When I was small, there was only *lagu pop* (pop songs), *lagu gereja* (church songs), *dangdut* (a popular form of Javanese music). That's all I knew. This sound arrived. It had strong drum, like in Papua. This beat makes us drunk with dance. Like drum beat for our ancestors. It is very different to traditional music but still, when I dance to hip hop, I feel respect for my ancestors.

Solomon articulated an instant connection with hip hop, based on a sense that it was distinct from any other kind of music he had heard. The hip hop beat, even though electronically produced, was felt to have elemental affinities with the drumbeat of traditional forms of music. This connection allowed hip hop to be experienced as what Smythe (2013: 74) calls a 'living symbol' or 'participative practice that invites the physical engagement' of the body across space and time. That Solomon selected drum beat in his explanation was not coincidental. Once a sign of primitiveness, a sound pertaining to cannibal feasts and war victories that struck fear into missionary hearts (Ottow and Geissler 1857), the *tifa* (a tapered traditional drum) has become emblematic of a shared Papuanness. The Papuan drum, found in various regions, is played at ritual and public events, is a key motif in Batik Papua, and is considered an iconically Papuan ethno-musical item.

What we might call a discourse of black affluence is another instance of how youth reinvest hip hop with notions of Papuan worth. Both men and women expressed delight at the sight of *'orang hitam'* (black people) displaying the trappings of wealth and luxury in hip hop music videos. Valeri, a self-assured 19-year-old, shared her position:

> When Papuan kids watch the film clips, we are happy to see black artists (*artis yang hitam*) in Lamborghini, or covered in diamonds, very stylish (*bergaya gaya*) … It feel surprising and good because this is not usual to see. When we turn the channel, only see white people and Javanese people, or Chinese people are rich. Why are black people not shown? There are rich black people. But when we see black people they are poor. They are hungry. They are sick.

Valeri's narrative highlights how enjoyment of what Watts (1997) calls the 'spectacular consumption' in 'gangsta rap', serves as a refreshing counterpoint to depictions of black people as universally poor or ill. In this respect she may be referring to the ongoing stereotypes of Papuans as undeveloped that can emerge in surprising guises in the post-Suharto landscape. In a recent Nutrisari commercial for instance, Papuans are depicted along with other colourful *suku suku banggsa* (ethnic groups) in traditional costumes in order to market the orange drink powder (Swarati 2012). Though tradition has been reconfigured as a national treasure, such representations perpetuate primitivising codes that position Papuans as backwards and living in the past. Valeri's opinion may also be shaped by the oft-shown news reports and images of Papua's HIV/AIDS toll, the highest in the nation, as well as other images of Papuan suffering, such as reports of Papuans as the latest victims of violent clashes around the province. She may even have world news reports in mind, such as from Africa where black bodies are often depicted as in trouble and turmoil. At the level of social imaginaries, when we take into account Papuans' economic disadvantages (Chauvel 2005), hip hop can generate a sense of ethnic worth through the utopian vision of black people as economically privileged.

Conclusions: Contested meanings, similar concerns

Young Papuans in Manokwari attach distinctive and pluralistic affective meanings to the music and video aesthetics of American hip hop. Some derive pleasure and satisfaction from the glittering sight of attractive, stylish and wealthy Afro-American singers, while others are attracted to the rhythmic seduction of dance and its mood-lifting capacity. Beliefs in personal and Papuan talent for dance generate pride. For others still, hip hop can be an avenue for connecting youth to Papuan history and traditions by rendering salient the primacy of its drum beat. Parental understandings of hip hop are equally pluralistic, with some holding neutral or positive attitudes and others identifying it as a foreign influence that, as with other immoralities, is indexing and perpetuating social problems in urban life. In ways that suggest that Papuanness is more than an identity of opposition, it is an ethnic reification becoming an ethical template in a battle of moral control, hip hop lifestyles are said to be un-Papuan. Through the idiom of an ethnic essence, in other words, hip hop poses specific moral issues related to sexual purity, educational diligence and obedience to parents.

In light of research into youth cultures, there is nothing surprising about hip hop's tendency to polarise eager youth and morally suspicious parents. Though intergenerational conflict is not peculiar to modern life (Herdt and Leavitt 1998), since youth have become the target for consumptive practices that are defined in opposition to past generations (Bucholtz 2002) taste can become grounds for such conflict. Yet if we suspend the analytic of 'spirit' from the 'content' of Papuan pride, we can locate a common emotional energy and a common aim to raise the esteem of Papuans between those differentially positioned attitudes to hip hop. Whether using hip hop as a resource for subverting negative depictions of *orang hitam* (black people), raising esteem through creative movement or connecting with the past, or to draw attention to cultural elements blocking the reproduction of authentic Papuan selves, both hip hop enthusiasts and its detractors aim to elevate Papuans as a worthy and good people. Though one discourse is sensory and indirect and the other uses the proscriptive voice of tradition and Christian ethics, both those who express enthusiasm and opposition relate to hip hop through concerns with pride in Papua.

The pride in being Papuan through the joy of hip hop points to a significant dimension of an evolving ethno-nationalism. That is, while the political cannot be separated from the psychological, Papuanness has an affective core that exists above and beyond political discourse. In recent years, a palpable spirit, for want of a better word, is breathing life into feelings of respect for Papuans and all things Papuan. This could be unique to Manokwari, an outcome of the majority Biak population who have long prized themselves in defining the terms and symbols of Papuan nationalism (Rutherford 2012) or, it could be a resistant product of rapid change in light of feeling threats to the religious character of the Gospel City. I suspect this spirit transcends place as gauged by the ubiquity of the 'I love Papua' t-shirts, the rise and rise of Batik Papua (Cookson 2008), contemporary songs that extol Papua's majestic beauty, and in the words of praise I have heard in sermons in other cities for God blessing Papua with bounty. *Bahasa Papua* (the Papuan dialect of Indonesian) has become ever more elaborated in mediating a pan-regional identity and friends were eager to explain how Papuans say things, their words, tone and inflection, as opposed to people from Ambon, Makassar and Java. Sentiments that underpinned pride resemble the recently classified emotion of 'elevation' (Haidt 2000), a feeling of moral beauty and uplift closely related to awe and gratitude. Exploring Papuanness in relation to feelings of elevation is particularly promising since, as a moral emotion, evidence points to its power in building cohesion through commitment to a subjectively identified community.

Finally, let me briefly raise the issue of how local embracements and rejections of hip hop might inspire future research into Papuan identity and nationalism. For one, it demands we inquire into how Papuanness is being operationalised as a series of supposed facts about moral attributes and character. What is it to 'be Papuan', who has the authority to claim Papuanness, and how are its emergent qualities becoming moral proscriptions to judge, shape and even enforce behaviour in new social worlds? It would be useful to compare and contrast the moral contours of ethnic identities in daily conversations and practices as well as in the varied discourse of elites. How are pastors invoking Papuan futures to argue for certain moral outcomes? What moral arguments are implicit or explicit in new literatures that speak to the economic and political challenges facing Papua? How are notions of an indigenous essence being manipulated in discourses of moral panics? Exploring the construction of moral character will lead us to consider how Papuanness is much more than a symbol of unification, it is a trope deployed in contests about proper being in the world at a time of growing moral and religious anxiety.

When Papuan pride is conceptualised in terms of a vitalising emotional core generative of novel cultural content, we are encouraged to look beyond the expected for expressions of ethnic identity. As well as the symbolic realms of Christianity and tradition, Papuanness is being communicated, with or without the political aim of *merdeka*, through emergent and unexpected domains like pop culture and language. If Papuanness can be known consciously through alternative discourse and politics, how is it generationally inflected, or, for that matter, does it have a gender, a class, or another social axis? As Papuan societies become fractured along new lines of economy and power and as the region moves into an era of complex and digitised global processes, it is timely that we strive to access marginal, incipient and heterogeneous manifestations of Papuan pride and nationalism.

References

Acciaioli, Greg 1985. 'Culture as Art: From Practice to Spectacle in Indonesia'. *Canberra Anthropology* 8(1–2): 148–174.

Appadurai, Arjun 1990. 'Disjuncture and Difference in the Global Cultural Economy'. *Public Culture* 2(2): 1–24.

Ballard, Chris 2002. 'West Papua'. *Contemporary Pacific* 14: 467–476.

Braithwaite, John, Braithwaite, Valerie, Cookson, Mike and Dunn, Leah 2010. *Anomie and Violence: Non-truth and Reconciliation in Indonesian Peace-building*. Canberra: ANU E Press.

Brison, Karen 2008. *Our Wealth is Loving Each Other*. Plymouth: Lexington Books.

Bucholtz, Mary 2002. 'Youth and Cultural Practice'. *Annual Review of Anthropology* 31: 525–152.

Chang, Jeff 2006. *Can't Stop Won't Stop: A History of the Hip-Hop Generation*. New York: St Martin's Press.

Chauvel, Richard 2005. *Constructing Papuan Nationalism: History, Ethnicity, and Adaptation*. Policy Studies 14. Washington D.C.: East-West Center Washington.

Cohen, Stanley 1980. *Folk Devils and Moral Panics: The Creation of the Mods and Rockers*. Oxford: Martin Robertson.

Cookson, Mike 2008. *Batik Irian: Imprints of Indonesian Papua*. PhD thesis, The Australian National University.

Cordell, Marni 2013. 'Indonesian Police Open Fire on Civilians in West Papua'. *The Guardian*, 25 September 2013. Accessed on 10 February 2014.

Davidson, Jamie and Henley, David (eds) 2007. *The Revival of Tradition in Indonesian Politics: The Deployment of* Adat *from Colonialism to Indigenism*. Oxon, New York: Routledge.

Ellis, Trey 1989. 'The New Black Aesthetic'. *Callaloo* 38: 233–243.

Fanon, Franz 1986. *Black Skin, White Masks*. London: Pluto Press.

Farhadian, Charles 2005. *Christianity, Islam and Nationalism in Indonesia*. New York and London: Routledge.

Flassy, Don A.L. 1999. *Basic Guidelines, State of West Papua: Papua-Melanesia Threefold Logic, Basic Ideology, General Governance, Constitution of West Papua*. Port Numbay (Jayapura): Fajar Melanesia.

Gagné, Natacha and Salaun, Marie 2012. 'Appeals to Indigeneity: Insights from Oceania'. *Social Identities* 18(4): 381–398.

Giay, Benny 2000. *Menuju Papua Baru: Beberapa Pokok Pikiran sekitar Emansipasi Orang Papua*. Jayapura: Deiyai and Elsham Papua.

Giay, Benny and Ballard, Chris 2003. 'Becoming Papuans: Notes Towards a History of Racism in Tanah Papua.' Paper presented at the annual meeting of the American Anthropological Association, Chicago.

Glazebrook, Diana 2004. 'Teaching Performance Art is Like Sharpening the Blade of a Knife'. *The Asia Pacific Journal of Anthropology* 5(1): 1–14.

Haidt, Jonathon 2000. 'The Positive Emotion of Elevation'. *Prevention & Treatment* 3(1): 1–5.

Hellman, Jorgen 2003. *Performing the Nation: Cultural Politics in New Order Indonesia*. Nordic Institute of Asian Studies. Copenhagen: NIAS Press.

Herdt, Gilbert (ed.) 2009. *Moral Panics, Sex Panics: Fear and the Fight over Sexual Rights*. New York: New York University Press.

Herdt, Gilbert and Leavitt, Stephen (eds) 1998. *Adolescence in Pacific Island Societies*. Pittsburgh: University of Pittsburgh Press.

International Crisis Group (ICG) 2001. 'Indonesia: Ending Repression in Irian Jaya'. ICG Asia Report No 23. Jakarta/Brussels.

Kirksey, Eben 2102. *Freedom in Entangled Worlds: West Papua and the Architecture of Global Power*. Durham: Duke University Press.

Knauft, Bruce 2002. *Critically Modern: Alternatives, Alterities, Anthropologies*. Bloomington: Indiana University Press.

Lock, Margaret 2001. 'The Tempering of Medical Anthropology: Troubling Natural Categories'. *Medical Anthropology Quarterly* 15: 478–492.

Munoz-Laboy, Miguel, Weinstein, H. and Parker, Richard 2007. 'The Hip-Hop Club Scene: Gender, Grinding and Sex'. *Culture, Health & Sexuality* 9(6): 615–628.

Munro, Jenny 2009. *Dreams Made Small: Humiliation and Education in a Dani Modernity*. PhD thesis, The Australian National University. Available at: www.papuaweb.org.

Munro, Jenny 2013. 'The Violence of Inflated Possibilities: Education, Transformation and Diminishment in Wamena, Papua'. *Indonesia* 95: 25–46.

Ottow, Carl Wilhelm and Geissler, Johann Gottlob 1857. *Geelvink Bay:A Brief Survey of the Land and People on the Northeast Coast of New* Guinea (Mansinam, 29 January 1857). Introduced and Translated by Jan A. Godschalk. Nationaal Archief, Den Haag, Ministerie van Kolonie n, 1850-1900, access number 2.10.02, inventory number 889.

Perwita, A.A.B. 2007. *Indonesia and the Muslim World: Islam and Secularism in the Foreign Policy of Soeharto and Beyond*. Nordic Institute of Asian Studies. NIAS Reports No. 50. Copenhagen: NIAS Press.

Poli, W.I.M., Salle, Agustinus, Purnomo, Bazergan, Etty, Manda, Martin L., Abubakar, M.D. 2008. *Habel Melkias Suwai: The Empowering Inner Voice: The Concept of Community Empowerment in the Regency of Jayapura* (English Abridged Version). Makassar: Hasanuddin University Identitas.

Prasetyaningsih, Luh Ayu S. 2007. *The Maze of Gaze: The Color of Beauty in Transnational Indonesia*. PhD thesis, University of Maryland.

Purdey, Jemma 2004. 'Unity in Diversity: Ethnicity and the Nation.' *Inside Indonesia* 78: Apr–Jun.

Rizzo, Susanna 2004. *From Paradise Lost to Promised Land: Christianity and the Rise of West Papuan Nationalism*. PhD thesis, University of Wollongong.

Robbins, Joel 2004. *Becoming Sinners: Christianity and Moral Torment in a Papua New Guinea Society*. Berkeley: University of California Press.

Robbins, Joel 2005. 'Humiliation and Transformation: Marshall Sahlins and the Study of Cultural Change in Melanesia'. In Robbins, Joel and Wardlow, Holly (eds), *The Making of Global and Local Modernities in Melanesia: Humiliation, Transformation, and the Nature of Cultural Change*. Aldershot, Burlington: Ashgate, 3–21.

Roth-Gordon, Jennifer 2013. 'Racial Malleability and the Sensory Regime of Politically Conscious Brazilian Hip Hop'. *The Journal of Latin American and Caribbean Anthropology* 18(2): 294–313.

Rutherford, Danilyn 2003. *Raiding the Land of the Foreigners: The Limits of the Nation on an Indonesian Frontier.* New Jersey: Princeton University Press.

Rutherford, Danilyn 2012. *Laughing at Leviathan: Sovereignty and Audience in West Papua.* Chicago: University of Chicago Press.

Sahlins, Marshall 1992. 'The Economics of Develop-Man in the Pacific'. *Res* 21, 12–25.

Schaefer, S. 2013. 'What Gives Rise to Moral Outrage?' *Inside Indonesia* 111: Jan–March.

Smythe, Julian 2013. 'The Living Symbol of Song in West Papua: A Soul Force to be Reckoned With'. *Indonesia* 13(95): 73–91.

Stemmler, Susanne 2013. 'The Global Cipha: The Transcultural Dynamics of a Black Aesthetics in James G. Spady's Rap Oeuvre'. *Western Journal of Black Studies* 37(2): 112–125.

Swarati, Stefani Haning 2012. 'Selling Nationalism'. *Inside Indonesia* 110: Oct–Dec.

Upton, Stuart 2009. *The Impact of Migration on the People of Papua, Indonesia: A Historical Demographic Analysis.* PhD thesis, University of New South Wales.

Wallace, Anthony 1956. 'Revitalization Movements'. *American Anthropologist* 58(2): 264–281.

Wardlow, Holly 2006. *Wayward Women: Sexuality and Agency in a New Guinea Society.* Berkeley, Los Angeles and London: The University of California Press.

Watts, E. 1997. 'An Exploration of Spectacular Consumption: Gangsta Rap as Cultural Commodity'. *Communication Studies* 48(1): 42–58.

Weeks, Jeffery 2012. *Sex, Politics and Society: The Regulation of Sexuality Since 1800.* London: Pearson Education.

7. 'Now we know shame': *Malu* and Stigma among Highlanders in the Papuan Diaspora

Jenny Munro

When Penggu,[1] a 30-year-old university student from the highlands of Papua proclaimed that, 'Our elders used to wear just the penis sheath [*koteka*] and did not feel ashamed, but now, now we know the feeling of shame [*malu*]', he articulated a central problematic I had encountered during my fieldwork. Prior to colonialism and Christianity, Dani societies clearly knew shame in their own ways (Alua 2006; Heider 1979). Penggu's comment can be partially understood in relation to Indonesian state interventions aimed at eliminating highlander men's practice of wearing the *koteka* in the name of modernisation, and missionaries' concerns about the moral implications of near-nudity.[2] Yet among young people with whom I lived in North Sulawesi and Papua, assertions that Dani people now experience themselves as *malu*, the Indonesian term for embarrassed, humiliated, ashamed, or shy, in a host of novel contexts and encounters held sway even as it contrasted sharply with their private behaviour and usual confidence among Papuan highlanders.

Malu is described as 'a highly productive concept that has effects in a wide array of personal and social realms' (Collins and Bahar 2000: 35). *Malu* connotes appropriate deference and/or shyness, and is traditionally significant in Indonesian culture in maintaining social and political hierarchies (Keeler 1983; Goddard 1996; Collins and Bahar 2000). It is commonly said that to know shame is a positive character attribute if it means that an individual is successfully submitting to gendered and status-oriented expectations of behaviour (Boellstorff and Lindquist 2004: 441).

Recent analyses of *malu* depict ways that individuals may experience *malu* in relation to living up to national values and expectations, or in relation to threats to perceived national values. Lindquist (2004: 503) found that young urban migrants were ashamed of their lack of economic success. Because economic success is linked to national ideals of modernity and development, '[i]n this context *malu* appears as an emotion that describes the failures to live up to

---

1   All names are pseudonyms, most chosen by the participants.

2   The earliest Indonesian state development program in the central highlands' Baliem Valley, called the Koteka Operation, was supposed to provide a variety of educational activities for indigenous inhabitants. In practice, these initiatives were overwhelmed by one facet of the operation: the effort to force highlander men to stop wearing penis-sheaths (*koteka*) and wear Western clothes instead. See Naylor (1974).

the ideals of the nation'. Similarly, in Boellstorff's (2004) analysis of violence against *gay* men in Indonesia, those who perpetrate public forms of violence are said to be lashing out as a result of feeling *malu*. *Malu* in this case arises because a particular kind of nationalised masculinity is at stake, and the nation is perceived to be in imminent danger of being represented by non-normative men (Boellstorff 2004: 469).

What is less apparent in current explications of *malu* as an affective tradition is how it informs relationships grounded in cultural, ethnic and/or racialised difference. In Indonesia, large numbers of so-called tribal populations are deemed 'different and deficient' (Li 1999: 3), and ethnicity or tribal origins (*suku*) are popularly seen as predictive of cultural and personal characteristics. I am interested in how the study of *malu* may shed light on cultural, racialised and ethnic hierarchies that are being challenged by current patterns of education and mobility among those minority groups who have long been treated as estranged (*terasing*) and backward (*terbelakang*).

The experiences of youth from the Papuan highlands present an opportunity to examine what *malu* reveals about ethnic and racial politics and struggles over stigma for an indigenous minority. This paper is based on interviews and extensive participant observation over the course of 16 months of ethnographic fieldwork in North Sulawesi and Papua in 2005–2006.[3] The context of North Sulawesi is significant because Indonesian-Dani relationships take place outside Papua, where some hazards may be minimised, and there are potential bonds around Christianity. But North Sulawesi is also home to a highly educated local population with significant levels of prosperity and concomitant cultural confidence. Despite past conflicts with the central government, today North Sulawesi is well-integrated with national perspectives and ideals (Harvey 1977; Buchholt and Mai 1994), including, I demonstrate, racial-cultural hierarchies that rank Papuans at or near the bottom of Indonesian civilisation.

Malu, I argue, as it is expressed by Dani university students, describes both the feeling of awareness, including a dimension of struggle, of being persistently viewed as primitive and uncouth, as well as the feeling that erupts when conflicts over the right to respectful recognition are aired in public. This struggle constructs scenarios that problematise practices of remaking and revision through which Papuans may position themselves anew, as this volume explores.

After situating Dani experiences in terms of cultural constructions of shame and the effects of stigma among migrant youth, I document the struggles that

---

3   This research was supported by the Department of Anthropology, Research School of Pacific and Asian Studies, The Australian National University and sponsored locally by Sam Ratulangi University in Manado, North Sulawesi. Supplementary materials were gathered during research in Papua in 2009, 2011 and 2012. Writing was supported by a postdoctoral fellowship at the University of Calgary.

students engage in to define how they are seen, and treated, by others, showing how persistent stigmas of primitiveness and racial-cultural inferiority clash with students' perception of their capabilities and accomplishments. By asking to be seen as university students (*mahasiswa*) – educated, up and coming, successful and politically engaged – who in many ways reflect national ideals concerning youth development, I argue that Dani youth ask to be recognised in ways that challenge racial stigma and concomitant cultural and evolutionist hierarchies. Then, case studies hone in on Dani-Indonesian encounters in which experiences of *malu* relate to public conflict over expectations of submission and deference in the face of disrespectful treatment by Indonesians.

Stigma and shame in migration

What Dani students describe as *malu* arises at the intersection of Melanesian constructs of shame, stigma and local cultural and racialised hierarchies they encounter in the context of school migration. In Melanesian cultural contexts, Strathern (1975: 35) describes shame as 'a notion of a loss of prestige or inadequacy caused by a confrontation with the power of the community'. Epstein (1984: 32) proposes, 'Shame tends to be elicited when one's shortcomings are exposed to the concentrated gaze of others.' Dani highlanders have their own culturally defined understandings of shame (*nekali* and *nayuk*) that emphasise concern over appearances, reputation and privacy. Shame is said to arise if private behaviours or personal weaknesses are exposed, or if someone fails to live up to exchange obligations, such as not having pigs to give at a funeral or marriage celebration. Traditionally, how one is seen by others comes into play for men who wish to publicly show capabilities and hide shortcomings as they jostle for authority and status in the group, while women might be said to be concerned to show their capacities for garden work and child-rearing, or to appear demure and submissive in the context of traditional marriage arrangements (Alua 2006). Today, what counts as shameful is increasingly shaped by new cultural and political forces that lessen the potency of traditional norms and engender novel expectations and judgments (Butt and Munro 2007).

The opportunities of migration, especially for schooling, are potentially vast, and certainly form part of the attraction for Papuan youth leaving home. Leaving familiar cultural worlds where one is consistently placed by others in terms of family lineage, village and language, may open up new questions and concerns about how one will be perceived by others in a new place, questions of identity that are highly important for youth (Jenkins 1996). Colonising curricula, racism and the disciplinary efforts of the state and missionaries are well documented in the school experiences of Melanesian youth (Fife 1994; LiPuma 2000; Robbins and Wardlow 2005). Cultural and social disruption is captured by terms like 'disconnection' and 'deterritorialisation' (Amit-Talai and Wulff 1995; Sykes 1999). Young people from communities stigmatised as primitive and underdeveloped may be forced to confront stereotypes and scrutiny (Howarth 2002).

In their interactions with Indonesians, Papuan youth may confront stereotypes that are derived from racial and evolutionist thinking that positions them as *orang Papua* (Papuan), an essentialising construction of ethnic and cultural difference. McCallum (2005: 100) writes, '[R]acialization takes place when differences between human beings are simplified and transformed into Difference, overvaluing particular bodily differences by imbuing them with lasting meaning of social, political, cultural, economic, even psychological significance.'

The idea of 'the Papuan' as primitive and racially inferior to 'the Malay' predates Indonesian control of Papua (Ballard 2008; Pouwer 1999; Rutherford 2012). While initial presumptions and definitions of *orang Papua* varied in name and content, by the 19th century a pervasive, if inconsistent, 'colonial racial logic' had developed (Ballard 2008; Giay and Ballard 2003). This racial thought was initially influenced by a science of race in which key external diacritics came to stand for morality, intelligence and abilities, based on observations that position indigenous populations 'within a gradient or hierarchy of value' (Giay and Ballard 2003). Perhaps the most significant legacy of these early ideas is the emphasis on the racial difference of Papuans and Malays.

'The notion that racial differences are materially true and determine the physical, intellectual, moral, or social qualities of identifiable groups' (Douglas 2008: 3) is highly acceptable and widely popular in contemporary Indonesia. Papuans are treated as primitive and inferior to Indonesians in their alleged capacity to conform to national development agendas, and these representations serve political ends of governance (Kirksey 2002; Timmer 2000). Racial thinking creates antagonism between Papuans and Indonesians in a variety of settings including health care (Butt 2012, 2013). Contemporary stigma also positions *orang Papua* as poor quality human resources, a reference to level of education and skill development that is supposedly lacking among Papuans and hampered by culture, lifestyles, ways of thinking and innate psychological difference (Munro 2013).

Recent anthropological arguments draw attention to how stigma inhibits moral status, particularly when moral status depends on being able to meet social obligations and norms (Yang et al. 2007; Kleinman and Hall-Clifford 2009). Yet these arguments, developed around disease- and disability-related stigma, remain largely untested in relation to racial and evolutionist stigmas such as primitiveness. To the extent that shame relates to the 'value of a person in her own eyes, but also in the eyes of her society' (Wikan 1984: 649; Pitt-Rivers 1965), racial thinking about Papuans shapes the experiences of young migrants who see themselves differently than the Indonesian majority.

Human resources

Dani youth see themselves as pursuing dreams of education that will translate into political and cultural power in highlands contexts (Munro 2013). The significance of education and skill development for indigenous youth has taken on epic proportions in the Papuan highlands. Politically, indigenous men and women view education as critical to overcoming Indonesian oppression and restoring indigenous control over lands and social life. A Dani informant explained the significance of human resource development for achieving independence (*merdeka*) in Papua:

> We want to become the human resources for Papua. We want independence but right now there are not enough human resources. It's like this: if we have an exam, we have to prepare first, right? So if we want independence we have to prepare first. If people's *SDM* [*sumber daya manusia,* human resources] improves they will be more prepared. (Jally)

Nation-building pressures from the Indonesian state also motivate education, albeit frequently in denigrating ways that point to alleged cultural primitiveness and racial thinking regarding Papuan capacities (Munro 2013). In Papua, shame may follow on from entrenched practices of diminishment, colonial discourses that criticise indigenous capacities for economic and cultural development (Robbins 2005: 11; Munro 2013), and derive from thoughts about how one is seen by others (Reddy 1997: 397).

The rhetoric of human resource development is entrenched in national and local discourses of progress: to contribute to, rather than inhibit, modernisation in the highlands, Papua young men and women must remake themselves to fit the criteria of skilled, worldly and pious (Munro 2004, 2009). Economically, highlanders are competing with ever increasing numbers of Indonesian and Papuan migrants for limited urban jobs. Culturally, the ability to do good things for others, a classic understanding of the big man style of political authority (Zimmer-Tamakoshi 1997), is now increasingly dependent on bureaucratic know-how, networks that include Indonesians, and educational qualifications that confer status. Confidence, competitiveness and charisma, once defining features of Dani leadership, are now often described by young people as something they lack and must learn through formal education and related accomplishments (Munro 2009).

University students (*mahasiswa*)

One way that Dani youth seek educational qualifications and new experiences that may lead to prestige back home is by migrating for education and living away from home. North Sulawesi is a popular choice. Dani and other highlanders have been travelling to this province, on the island of Sulawesi, since the late 1980s. It attracts more Papuan highlanders to its higher education institutes than any other province. Students say North Sulawesi offers an affordable educational experience in a Christian, modern and safe atmosphere.[4]

North Sulawesi province is home to approximately two million people, of whom over 600,000 claim Minahasa cultural origins. Duncan (2005: 28) describes a long history of regional movement among the peoples of North Sulawesi, Gorontalo, the Sangir archipelago and the Maluku Islands. Yet claims of diversity and multiculturalism are undermined by the dominance of Christianity and the Minahasa cultural majority (Jacobsen 2002).

Papuan students who call themselves *orang Wamena* (Wamena people) originate from one of three dominant cultural groups in the Papuan central highlands – Dani, Lani and Yali. Exact numbers of Papuan students in North Sulawesi are difficult to assess, but they number several thousand. The majority of Dani people in Manado, the provincial capital, and Tondano, a small town in the mountains south of Manado, are students; a handful of Dani men have married local women and remained in the area. Male students far outnumber female students (approximately 4:1), though this also varies by origins within the highlands.

Dani men and women overwhelmingly wished to embrace, indeed, embody, the identity of 'university student' (*mahasiswa*).The word itself was popular among my informants, and evoked pride and status that differentiated them from others. John, for example, said, 'We are *mahasiswa* now, we have to act accordingly and not get into trouble with alcohol or otherwise.' Other noteworthy deployments of the term came when my friend Minke regularly challenged her male relatives who requested that she wash their dirty laundry, cook for them or wash dishes by shouting, 'We are all university students here!' Lavinia defended a premarital pregnancy by asserting with confidence, 'I say we are not in high school anymore. We are university students' (Munro 2012: 1022).

Students living in the rural area around the National University of Manado were affronted by how they were sometimes treated by locals who were primarily rice

---

4 North Sulawesi is approximately 70 per cent Christian, though Minahasa regency that surrounds the capital city of Manado (population 434,000) is estimated to be 90 per cent Christian.

farmers and kiosk operators. Gigi, for example, said, 'People around here are difficult. They never went to school but they act like they know everything (*bikin tahu-tahu*) and they talk to us impolitely.'

Political and social activism is a long-standing tradition for Indonesian university students (Douglas 1970; Aspinall 1993, 1999), a tradition that Papuan students embrace. In Papua, student activism is widespread but typically repressed by the state. In North Sulawesi, in contrast, there are opportunities for activism or demonstrations, and these are practices around which Papuans may build relationships with like-minded Indonesian students. Papuan students participated in many forms of activism in North Sulawesi, such as International Workers' Day, a march I attended alongside a group of Dani students. However, they also felt increased scrutiny from authorities and faced tactics to dissuade them from taking part, even in activities that had nothing to do with Papuan independence.[5]

Besides activism and intellectual development, broadening one's horizons and social networks was an important ambition among students. There was a strong commitment to new relationships with Indonesians in North Sulawesi that were perceived to be nearly impossible in a politicised context like Wamena. The concept of *keterbukaan* (openness) prevailed in students' descriptions of their attitude towards the educational journey abroad, where it was hoped that politics would not interfere with relationships and academic experiences. For many students, North Sulawesi represented a place of peace, modernity and stability with a Christian atmosphere. Despite the intensity of violence, colonialism and prior trauma in highlands Papua, statements like, 'We want new experiences here', (Laurence) suggest they wanted different experiences from their time in North Sulawesi.[6] They desired relationships in which they learned from locals, exchanged assistance with locals, and were invited to become part of the community.

---

5   In recent years there have been reports of growing concern among authorities in North Sulawesi that Papuan students are voicing separatist aspirations locally that they would be unable to express in Papua because of much tighter restrictions on speech and the presentation of emblems such as the Morning Star flag in Papua. For example: http://beritamanado.com/manado-basis-gerakan-perjuangan-mahasiswa-papua-merdeka/.

6   The time during which the Dani students I describe in this paper were abroad in North Sulawesi was perhaps a particularly difficult time in which to form bonds with Indonesians, to learn from others and to feel safe amongst non-Dani. Most of the students were in the latter stages of high school or had just left the highlands for university between 1999 and 2001 after the end of the 33-year Suharto dictatorship and at the height of the *reformasi* period – which in Papua was characterised by critiques of Indonesian governance, expressions of independence desires and talking about suffering. Students spoke of military violence and extreme inequalities with Indonesian migrants as evidence of the 'trauma' they and others were suffering at home. While these experiences could hamper new relationships with Indonesians, students were also quick to draw distinctions between circumstances in Papua and North Sulawesi, where they expressed hope for relationships with Christian Indonesians in a peaceful, developed province known for high quality education.

Bringing home results

Besides the attraction of being *mahasiswa*, and thus, in some understandings, worthy of respectful engagement, students had significant hopes for personal achievement in North Sulawesi. Minke, born in 1983, came to North Sulawesi through the support of her eldest sister and her sister's husband. Minke recalled,

> They said, the courses are good and you will get away from this environment in Papua, where people are drunk and quitting school. At Unima [National University of Manado] there is much spirituality (*rohani*), there is worship every day, and discussions and organizations where you can stand up in front of people and improve your confidence. When you return you will be respected and have the authority to tell people what to do ...

There was a desire to deliver tangible results to communities back home by publicly demonstrating skills, including leadership, communication and organising.[7] Upon graduation, a student named Kodar gave a speech to the crowd of highlander students, saying, 'Development means making Papuans prosperous, safe and healthy. It means turning on the electricity and teaching old people to read. This is what we want to do. I hope I will become Regent some day and bring modernity to Yahukimo.' Speeches generally expressed the need to develop Papua and the important role for graduates. Etinus, for instance, posed the question, 'If we do not do it, who will?'

Most graduates return to Papua, many to the central highlands, as they are drawn back to the potent cultural fold of family and friends, and the attractive emotional space of Wamena, where belonging is less of a struggle. As I have described elsewhere (Munro 2009, 2013), the results that educated Dani women and men are able to achieve in the central highlands are severely limited by political conditions that continue to favour Indonesian settlers and migrants. For example, in the central highlands, local governments continue to hire more Indonesian than Papuan employees in the public service. Without increased prosperity, university graduates have a difficult time demonstrating tangible results to those who financed their studies or dealt with their absence from clan and community activities. While a few elite graduates have maintained the local clout needed to work themselves into leadership roles in village governance or church structures, for many returnees, social and personal outcomes of education, such as enhanced prestige or status, are minimal.

---

7   Diana Glazebrook (2008) also comments on the cultural potency of the notion of bringing home *hasil* (results) among Dani highlander refugees living in Papua New Guinea.

In North Sulawesi, the opportunities that are ostensibly offered by mobility among educated Papuans are challenged by conditions where intimidation and anxiety prevail, and racial/evolutionist constructions emphasise Papuan primitiveness.

Racial and cultural 'primitives'

Racial thinking is prevalent in North Sulawesi, both in terms of how locals view themselves, and how they view Papuans. Local people regularly expressed that Dutch colonialism had contributed to the Minahasa ethnic constitution through intermarriage and education, providing locals with superior intelligence and light skin. Black or dark skin was denigrated while pale or white skin was sought after, and could determine marital choices. Mrs Dessy, a housewife with two children whom I lived with when I first arrived in Manado, explained, 'When we want our children to get married we look at the status of the person, their heritage, their economic status, but look at me, I married someone who is black because he is a good man with a strong career as a professor and a businessman.' Dessy and the children regularly teased their father for being dark-skinned (*hitam*, or black).

Men and women encountered racial stigma similarly, on the grounds that they are equally *orang Papua* and similarly 'black', and differently, in relation to gendered expectations. Women experience more judgments on their sexuality, which is seen as promiscuous because a few Papuan students have children while ostensibly unmarried (Munro 2012). Dani and other Papuan men were subjected to name-calling by children in the streets who would yell, 'Black person!' or 'Monkey!' (*monyet*) as they ran away. *Ale* and *sobat* are names that some Indonesians call Papuan men. The words literally mean 'friend', or 'buddy', but when locals call out to Papuans on the street using these terms they are often used in a provocative, aggressive way.

During a graduation ceremony Dani students held at their dormitory in Tondano, the local Minahasan government representative gave a speech. 'I am happy to see so many Papuan kids graduate. Papuans are good-hearted. Minahasa people like to think of themselves as being white but I think Papuan students are black-skinned but with white hearts…' There were a few laughs in the audience of students, but most looked at their neighbours, perhaps wondering, as I was, if the official was trying to be critical or friendly? Was he paying them a compliment or trafficking in racialised stereotypes? Were *orang Papua* to feel good about being black with white hearts, or did he mean that Minahasans think too highly of themselves, when Papuans are just as good-hearted? It seemed like he was saying that *orang Papua* are black, but they are still good (to his surprise). Perhaps above all, the speech seemed to reveal what is normally not openly stated in interactions between Papuans and Indonesians but is readily identified by those on the receiving end of stigma. There is a racial construction of *orang Papua*, there is some judgment by local people on the character of *orang Papua*, and black skin colour, as a racial marker of difference, is ranked in local hierarchies. These normally unvoiced assumptions were publicly revealed and acknowledged because perhaps the government official thought he was paying students a compliment.

North Sulawesi is not the Indonesian nation writ small. Minahasans and other local people consider themselves different from Indonesians living in South Sulawesi, Sumatra or Java, yet they criticise Papuans in ways that parallel mainstream views, focusing on alleged primitiveness, inferior intellect and dangerous tendencies. When I arrived in North Sulawesi, I initially lived with a local Minahasan family and spent time with their neighbours, friends and university acquaintances in Manado and Tondano. I had many conversations with these informants about my project with Papuan students. I heard stereotypical and stigmatising perspectives that prevailed among even those who emphasised their good relationships with Papuans. I was repeatedly warned not to live in dormitories with Papuan students. Typical comments were, 'They are drunks, you'll never have any peace', or 'You'll get raped'. Papuans were also likened to Islamic terrorists who might attack state institutions at any time. Papuan intellect was also challenged, for example,

> The students are really quiet, very shy, they are slow-thinkers, like you know James and David – they have been here for ten years already but they are still students! Their minds are not yet, not yet … good. (Mrs Christo, professor's wife)

Stigma existed in everyday contexts, on campus and in other institutional settings, and was overtly and subtly expressed (Munro 2012). Herbert, a 29-year-old Dani student, described an incident that shows the extent of stigmas of primitiveness embedded in racial stereotypes, and specifically speaks to the importance of male cultural symbols like the *koteka* as an emblem around which Indonesian and Dani perceptions may clash. Herbert recalled, 'Once a student brought a *koteka* to campus and laughed at us. They asked us if we eat humans and all this sort of stuff …' Herbert went on to describe how he and some other Dani students 'beat that guy up and he moved to a different university' (Munro 2012: 1016).

Good labourers

Not all racial thinking about Papuans was overtly negative. The most common way that students, especially males, related to locals was by providing labour. Students were often in need of money for basic daily expenses, and locals invited them to work, perceiving that Papuan men are good for yard labour, and to a lesser extent, household chores.

> The Papuan students are very poor, but good, polite, hardworking. If they come asking for work we usually give them some grass-cutting or laundry to do. (Mrs L, wife of Pentecostal minister)

It was possible for significant relationships to develop out of the ongoing provision of assistance by Dani students to locals. A number of students who said that they had good relations with certain families had built those relationships based on construction and yard labour. Sometimes students were paid outright for their work, but often as the relationship developed there was more expectation that the student would do labour as requested and be paid whenever the 'boss' or, more commonly, the 'uncle' (*Om*) decided the time was right. I met one of my first informants, Jally, when he came to perform household chores, such as taking out the garbage and cleaning up after his uncle's children, at the Indonesian-owned house where I was staying at the time. There, I was surprised to see Jally doing housework typically performed by women, such as cooking and serving food, but came to find that this was not unusual for Jally or other Dani students in similar relationships. Since Jally often came to me to ask for small amounts of money, usually enough for bus fare or to purchase cooking supplies, I once asked him if he did not receive money from his uncle, to which he responded, 'Sometimes he pays, sometimes he doesn't, but he promised when I want to go home to Papua for a visit he will give me the money for the ticket,' and, smiling, 'He invited me to spend Christmas with them.'

Relationships based on labour raise questions about the conditions under which Dani and locals get along. Penggu described how students have become better at establishing relationships with local people over the past 10 years: 'We had to learn how to talk to them, and show them that we can be honest and trustworthy.' Penggu considered members of his church, a small congregation of about 20 members, to be people with whom he had a good relationship. He and the other Papuans always sat near the back of the church, or, during a hymn, stood at the back of the group, and never went to the front of the church to sing or speak. Penggu and the other Papuans usually in attendance were always extremely deferential and helpful, consistently taking on chores such as cleaning duties, collecting offerings and stacking and unstacking chairs. Although in their absence the Indonesian church members described Papuans as 'stupid' or 'dumb' (*bodoh*), they always invited Papuans to be part of a work party when there was church maintenance or yard labour to be done. Penggu considered this a successful relationship between Papuans and Indonesians, but it also suggests that success may hinge on the actions of Papuan men who are helpful and deferential, and who do not place themselves in positions of prominence or authority in front of Indonesians.

Relationships based on Dani labour are not necessarily problematic for students, in that some men find it rewarding to be perceived as strong, hardworking and reliable. They also appreciate the potential avenue that it opens up for them to develop relationships based on reciprocity, however uneven, so that they might call upon these resources in times of need. Experience suggests that these relationships are not, in fact, very reliable in times of need,[8] and a sense of being exploited made some students reluctant to embrace this path to belonging. Doing good (labour) for others is a culturally valued masculine practice, but one that could also reinforce stigmas of primitiveness and intellectual inferiority. Moreover, a capacity for yard work and household chores is not the kind of skill recognition that Dani students are seeking in North Sulawesi.

Dangerous to society

In addition to being perceived as culturally primitive, but good for labour, Dani students were stigmatised as threats to local security. Again, men are seen as more dangerous than women. The notion of local security was highly significant for Indonesians in the area who regularly described their sense of pride and vigilance at defending peace and stability. In a region surrounded by communal violence since the Maluku riots of 1999, locals such as Sonny, a car salesman, argued, 'We let those refugees come here, but we said to them, you will not disturb our security and order.' As a result of this stigma, students described a constant state of concern and anxiety regarding relations with their neighbours, especially in tightly packed urban settlements (*kampung*), where they were often blamed for conflict or disagreements that took place as neighbourhood government officials (*pala*) treated students as troublemakers (Munro 2009). Certain Dani student activists reported receiving threatening phone calls and text messages and being followed around the area. Others said that Intel agents approached them on the street and questioned them about their identities and activities. Students advised each other not to travel alone, particularly after dark, because they feared being confronted by government intelligence agents

---

8 When the local village headman raided Jally's dorm (discussed later in this chapter), the fact that Jally was arguably friends with some of the men and had gone out of his way to be friendly and helpful to the village headman did not improve the treatment received by Jally and other students.

or by disgruntled locals.[9] So far, students in North Sulawesi have managed to escape physical violence and punishment from the police, but the fate of fellow student activists tortured and murdered in detention in Papua is never far from their minds (see Asian Human Rights Commission 2011; Conoras 2009).[10]

Studying shame 'throws into relief complex struggles over meaning, manners, personal values, social allegiance and cultural survival' (Kwok 2012: 28). Struggles over perceptions come to light most critically when expectations of deference and submissiveness are at stake. The following two cases show that *malu* amongst Dani students relates to Indonesian attempts to enforce deference and polite acceptance of treatment that students find unfair. Specifically, students' attempts to exercise independent action based on educational know-how or 'common sense' are cut short. Both cases highlight that it is men who more often come into open conflict with Indonesians over expectations of deference in the face of disrespect.

Case 1: Lex and the village headman

Lex Elosak, a 25-year-old student in his ninth semester at the National University of Manado, argued that it is important for Papuans to get out of Papua and see how things are done elsewhere: 'Even though the Papuan kids have to be careful with the locals, here we can meet with and talk with *orang Indonesia* [Indonesians]. Here we can also join organisations and mix with other students.' 'We students feel that the locals [*orang sini*] are quite impolite, and we advise new students to be careful [...] not to get into fights with them. We have to be extremely polite to them,' Lex said, clasping his hands together and bowing his head a little.

In January 2006, a local *Lurah* (Village Headman) and several of his friends (whom students refer to as *anak buah*, or protégé, but who are not actually government employees) raided the Yepmum dorm where I lived with Dani

---

9   The tensions between students and local people, and the degree of students' vulnerability to violence, were powerfully revealed in October 2014 as this chapter went to press: according to media reports, on 19 October 2014, Petius Tabuni, a student from the highlands, was beaten to death by locals after he emerged in a drunken state from a graduation party in Tata Aran and caused some commotion at a kiosk. When five of his friends arrived they got into a fight with locals. Subsequently, Papuan students were unable to leave their dormitories or homestays for several days because of fears of being attacked. Government officials refused to permit students in Tondano to travel to Manado for the funeral of the deceased student. http://www.nabire.net/mahasiswa-unima-asal-papua-tewas-dibacok-orang-di-minahasa-sulawesi-utara/.

10   Students were sometimes targeted in retaliation for violent incidents that occurred in Papua and elsewhere in the region. In January 2006, Papuan asylum seekers arrived in Australia by boat seeking protection from Indonesian state violence, action that stirred emotional reactions across Indonesia. Shortly thereafter a rumour spread through Manado that Papuan students were planning to seek political asylum in the Philippines by travelling via Manado, and several students reported that police picked them up off the street and put them into a jail cell. They were interrogated and released unharmed.

students around midnight. Students who answered the door reported that the men said they had come to search for weapons. Jally, John and Ally discussed the matter and tried to convince them to come back another time. Some students in their bedrooms upstairs heard the voices as I did and came out to peer down the stairway at the men. After a few minutes, two men came upstairs, banged on doors and made everyone open their bedroom doors so they could look for weapons. The dorm's inhabitants were alarmed and shaken at the events, and phoned their friends at the other Dani, Lani and Yali dorms in the area to warn them.

A few days later, Lex was told to appear at the office of the *Lurah*. Coincidentally, I was also called to appear before the *Lurah* that day. Jally and I heard the entire conversation while we sat in the waiting area outside his office door.

In the office, surrounded by the same men who had raided the dorm, Lex was berated because, according to the men, Dani students had been telling their friends and the locals in the area that the men who came to the dorm were intoxicated. The *Lurah* argued that Lex had no proof and that this was slanderous. One of the men asked Lex if he was stupid. At one point, one of them announced that he was 'very upset (*ganas sekali*) about this' and ought to 'punch Lex in the head'. Lex tried to argue that the dormitory was under the protection of a former Wamena regent (*bupati*) who lives in Manado and cannot be forcibly entered as it was that night. He also asserted an argument I heard among students after the incident, namely that the *Lurah* should have brought a letter of explanation signed by higher authorities or the police to legitimate the late-night search. Lex also argued that the men should not have come in the middle of the night, frightening students and disturbing them from their sleep. Jally and I could hear the emotion in his voice. The heated conversation continued, with the *Lurah* and his men repeating their accusations and threats until Lex conceded that he agreed that it had been wrong for students to say the men were drunk and that the *Lurah* was within his rights to raid the dorm. The emotion in his voice suggested tears. At this point the *Lurah* further asserted that raiding the dorm was necessary for local security and was therefore in the students' best interest. 'We know there have been a lot of problems of separatism in Papua,' he stated. He also referred to previous conflict between Manadonese youth and Dani students that resulted in injuries on both sides. Lex mumbled in agreement.

Lex emerged from the office and averted his eyes, suggesting to Jally and I that he was ashamed of the whole encounter. As we left, the *Lurah* demanded to know when the students were going to come and help with the construction of his office. Jally promised to get some students organised to assist with the labour. Jally tried to make light of the situation on the walk home. He said it was better not to speak at all or just to agree with everything because otherwise 'they just go on and on'. Lex did not laugh. When another student joined us in the street and asked how things had gone Lex just said, 'These people are difficult [*susah*], and I am sick and tired of talking to them.'

For the rest of the day, Lex stayed in his room. Jally and others argued that Lex was feeling ashamed (*malu*). He was supposed to be the leader of the dorm and speak on their behalf but instead he had been forced to agree with the *Lurah*. Lex was in fact normally a strong leader, articulate, organised and authoritative. Before the encounter with the *Lurah*, Lex expressed that he wished for new experiences abroad and advocated politeness and submissiveness as the best way to get along with locals, though he disagreed with allowing wrongdoers get away with their actions.

This case is not just about *malu*, which is only one part of Lex's experience. It is also about the way that Dani students are singled out for treatment as 'security threats' by local officials, and the way they are made to feel that they have no rights or status. Students talked about the incident for many weeks, astonished that even when drunk men come crashing into their bedrooms in the middle of the night, they are still wrong to criticise or challenge this treatment, and should act submissively. They should not assume that the logical arguments of educated individuals who are aware of certain legal protections should hold up when they face off with Indonesian authorities. They should, as the Lurah's actions demonstrated, accept responsibility for making other men feel shame for losing face but may claim no loss of reputation themselves, nor expect others to have regard for the feelings of *malu* that the sleeping dorm residents felt at the invasion of privacy. While students' claims on the respect and status that is typically afforded university students or educated people is overruled, the Lurah asserts the ostensibly legitimate positioning of Papuan students in the local environment by insisting that they come and help build his office.

Case 2: The Dani dancers

The Lorenzo Guest House (*Wisma Lorenzo*) is a Catholic meeting place in Lotta, a beautiful semi-rural area on the outskirts of Manado. The large property, next to a church, contains various meeting halls and dormitory-style accommodation for guests. A Dutch priest who has spent most of his life in Indonesia operates the guesthouse. *Pastor* Van Paassen has taken a special interest in helping highlanders survive in North Sulawesi and succeed in their studies. He donates rice to their dorms each month, lends money to individual students, and often provides funding for their Christmas and Easter events. He also oversees the funding of two dormitories for Catholic students.

Figure 7.1. Students in costume waiting to dance at the priest's birthday party, Lotta.

Source: Jenny Munro.

Pastor, as students call him, is 88 years old. His secretary, a Minahasan woman called Mrs Anita, is in charge of daily matters at the *wisma* and organises the assistance the Pastor provides to Dani students. On the priest's birthday in May 2006, Mrs Anita helped organise a grand celebration attended by many clergy from the region, most of the members of the priest's congregation and Dani students, some of whom are also regular members of the congregation. Students organised a dance for the priest in which they wore Papuan costumes which, as they explained laughing, they thought reflected something coastal Papuans would wear (Figure 7.1). They did not wear the *koteka* (penis gourd) traditional to the highlands, perhaps in consideration of how they might be regarded by the conservative religious and predominantly Indonesian crowd. They had been preparing for the dance for about a week and were extremely nervous beforehand; a few described needing to drink alcohol to get over their nerves and shyness. After mass, in front of a crowd of approximately 50 Indonesian members of the congregation, students danced outside the church and while accompanying the priest during his five-minute walk down the street to his compound where the celebration was set to begin (Figure 7.2).

Figure 7.2. Student leader accompanying priest during the dance, Lotta.

Source: Jenny Munro.

Figure 7.3. Nuns and other attendees eating lunch at the priest's birthday, Lotta.

Source: Jenny Munro.

Guests were to sit themselves at one of the many long tables lined with banana palm leaves and then send representatives to the kitchen to pick up grilled fish and bowls of rice and vegetables to share (Figure 7.3). By the time the Dani dancers had changed out of their costumes, there were no empty tables left. There were a few seats at other tables, but no place for the Dani students to sit together. They hung back, and sat around on benches outside the main eating area. Some commented that they were hungry and asked other Dani how they thought they should proceed without a table. Eventually a few of the younger students went to the kitchen, grabbed some plates and started serving themselves. Mrs Anita saw them doing this and came over and yelled at them. She grabbed a plate out of one of the men's hands. Without asking for an explanation, she sent the group out of the kitchen. After a minute, she came out and criticised loudly, asking them why they could not eat off leaves like everyone else was doing, and commenting that, 'Wamena people are special eh?' One of the Dani men, Markus, dumped his food in the bush, tossed his plate on the ground and stormed off.

All of this took place approximately five metres from the main table reserved for the priest, who had not taken his place yet, and the main eating area, where approximately 100 Indonesian guests had gathered. The guests were now watching the scene near the kitchen. Mrs Anita yelled at Markus for throwing his rice and said, 'Wait until Pastor hears about this.' Dani students gathered nearby, some wanting to know what had happened. Markus said he could not believe how rude Mrs Anita was. He said that she had humiliated him in front of others. He was sorry about throwing food, but felt ashamed and angry about being yelled at by Mrs Anita.

The students decided they would not eat, in protest. They left the party area, some to buy snacks out on the street. They expressed that they were upset that they wanted to celebrate the priest's birthday. The event had only just begun, and they had gone to the trouble of dancing for everyone, and they were hungry and now they felt unwelcome. One of the older students who said he had a good relationship with Mrs Anita went to apologise for the thrown food and to smooth things over. She still looked angry and she loudly stated that it was terrible to throw rice away, but after a few minutes, the priest emerged and took his place at his table. The few remaining Dani students found a space at the end of one of the long tables near the back and ate from their banana leaves.

This case highlights how public shaming may result if Dani students question the authority of Indonesians. A clash of perceptions is also evident. The students expressed a strong bond with the priest, and wanted to demonstrate their appreciation of this relationship and the material gifts they had received from him (such as rice and money) by performing at his party. They saw themselves as contributing to the event. Mrs Anita suggests that Dani students should accept the situation without complaint or action, and in other words not expect to have their considerations or needs attended to. This may be read as an assertion that in fact students are not equals to the other guests at the party, and their feelings are less important than others'. They were allowed to participate, as cultural performers, not cultural equals, because of their special relationship with the priest, a relationship that Mrs Anita openly and regularly rejected with some hostility. Whether or not they felt valued or even welcome was not of importance; this may be seen as an assertion that Dani students should take what they are given with gratitude and obedience.

The feeling of *malu*, in this incident, also serves to 'electrify the racial divide' (Kwok 2012: 39). Students' behaviour suggests that they were already uncomfortable with the situation and feeling *malu* about splitting up into groups of two or three and joining Indonesians already seated at tables with banana leaves. Many had decided to delay eating rather than do this. The result of this incident was that students were more convinced that they should stay away from events involving Indonesians in order to avoid the risk of being made *malu*.

In the foregoing cases, feelings of *malu* are linked to situations in which students, especially men, are expected to show deference, acceptance and submissiveness in the face of potentially unfair or rude treatment. Having others, especially Indonesians, bear witness to this treatment adds to the offence.[11] Dani understandings of shame are shown to be significant, in that students are particularly concerned with having their supposed shortcomings publicly exposed to others. What is critically different from other shaming scenarios is that Dani students do not see themselves as possessing shortcomings or inadequacies in these situations. The shortcomings at stake are present in the views of Indonesians, a reflection of stigma and a refusal to accept *orang Papua* as equals. Students see themselves as trying to act respectfully and participate in local activities, thus they argue they are treated unfairly. Moreover, conflict arises due to Indonesian expectations of Papuan deference and acceptance in the face of disrespectful or offensive treatment.

Although it is more often men who take a public stand, and may suffer as a result, both men and women are struggling with the perceptions of Indonesians, and particularly views that position them as primitive, troublesome and inferior.

---

11 On the whole, students do not appear to suffer from shyness in front of other highlanders or Papuans, even those they do not know well. For example, at the Christmas party for the Papuan Students Network (Imipa) held in December 2005, a group of Dani students presented themselves in front of the crowd and sang songs. On another occasion, Wamena students organised a celebration that was attended by a number of Papuans; they led the events confidently and some students even participated spontaneously, giving advice to the group on successful study habits.

Views like these directly oppose their sense of being university students and members of a young generation that is embracing, if not epitomising, development, capabilities, mobility and success.

Struggles with the perceptions of others were similarly revealed during a conversation that took place in a dormitory on Unima (National University of Manado) campus that I recorded in my field notes. Penggu, Minke, Leo and I were watching television. A domestic travel program advertised that the next show would be on location in the interior of Papua. As always, students were excited that something about the highlands was on national television. Some footage of Yali people wearing penis gourds (*koteka*) followed. There were shouts of, 'Oh no!' and 'Oh my God!' when the pictures of the men in *koteka* appeared. Leo, a Yali student, said, 'Oh no, everyone will see our parents wearing *koteka*. This is really embarrassing. But it is our culture and we cannot escape it.' Penggu laughed, 'The government tried to give them pants but they refused to wear them!'

Although students are well aware of the dominant perception of the *koteka*, they still speak respectfully of those who wear it. Elders who wear the *koteka* are said to find it to be comfortable, appropriate and a statement of cultural identity.

> Clothes are from the government and the missionaries. Some of our people were happy about clothes. We like wearing clothes. But some people prefer the *koteka*, no matter what others think or say. (Penggu)

Many male students claim to have worn a *koteka* for battle re-enactments (*perang-perangan*) or for dance competitions, or even at political demonstrations. It is said to be incredibly exciting to wear because it takes great courage to overcome the shame and embarrassment of being almost entirely nude. While students understand the primitive connotations associated with not wearing clothes or still wearing *koteka*, this is not the whole story for them. Wearing the *koteka* can be a preference. Wearing the *koteka* also demonstrates, for students and others, courage, tenacity and commitment. Understandings of the *koteka* reflect broader tensions that Papuans face: the everyday challenge to confront stigmatising views held by many Indonesians and to evaluate themselves according to their own, often different, perspectives and standards. When Dani and other central highlanders are allowed to see themselves according to their own perspectives and standards, they are tenacious and courageous. What worries them is having to see themselves through others' gaze.

Conclusion

Feelings of *malu* can be linked to locals' refusal to acknowledge any of the achievements of the young Papuans in their midst, and, rather, an insistence on seeing and treating them as primitive, labour-ready and potentially dangerous. Strained relationships attest to the existence of powerful racial-cultural hierarchies. Unwavering hierarchies cause concern for Dani students who are seeing themselves in the negative light of Indonesian terms, not in West Papua, but in a different environment with its own intricacies. A powerful sense of local hierarchies, and students' positioning near the bottom, contributes to awkwardness and silences amongst normally critical and confident young people. These findings affirm the need to consider *malu* at the intersection of racial politics: 'Interactions with whites are more potently minimised by defining or experiencing the relationship itself as one attended by shame and hence by avoidance and/or other restrictions on behaviour' (Kwok 2012: 39). In other words, Dani assertions of *malu* should also be considered a way to justify avoiding these types of situations in the future, and by extension, public interactions with Indonesians (see Munro 2009).

Submissiveness is a key understanding of *malu* described by Keeler (1983), and public gestures of submissiveness by Dani students seem essential for maintaining relationships of tolerance with Indonesians, particularly those who hold stigmatising views of Papuans. In contrast, assertiveness by students can create open conflict. It is clear that it is more often male students who defy these expectations and may react with both shame and anger. Considering the gendered forms of propriety that *malu* usually entails (Collins and Bahar 2000; Lindquist 2004; Boellstorff 2004; Slama 2010), the public shaming of Dani men raises questions about emasculation and its role in sustaining racial hierarchies.

These experiences, and the politics of submissiveness that they evoke, should give us pause when considering mobility as a trajectory primarily characterised by opportunity rather than vulnerability. New opportunities to interact with Indonesians may become new ways to experience conflict and inadequacy when judgments and stigma are widespread, and linked to prevailing national cultural hierarchies. The confidence that allows Lex, for example, to take action when he feels that local authorities have treated Dani students unfairly, is based on a sense of being educated and living in a place where it is more possible to express discontent. On a more positive note, for every student like Penggu, who is more tolerant and satisfied with the terms on which he relates to local Indonesians, there are other students like Lex, Markus and their supporters, who seem to expect more respectful recognition. How they are seen by others fuels anger and ambition, not just shyness or shame.

Penggu's comment, 'Now we know shame', can be read as a new awareness of dominant perceptions and expectations associated with new relationships and cultural contexts in which Papuan youth participate. Awareness is grounded in encounters 'where racial ideas and representations were enacted, reworked, or forged' (Douglas 2008: 14). Considering that Dani students approach their time in North Sulawesi with a certain amount of humility and openness, acknowledging that they are not 'masters of the house' (*tuan rumah*), the relationships they achieve and the submissiveness they are expected to show exemplifies the 'confrontation with the power of the community' described by Strathern (1975). That new relationships, cultural understandings and the networking with Indonesians cannot take place even amongst those who call themselves 'kin' (*saudara*) united by Christianity in a region characterised by peaceful stability raises questions about whether Papuans may achieve a sense of belonging anywhere beyond their homeland.

Lindquist (2004: 498) suggests that young urban migrants feel *malu* because they find themselves outside national propriety, and amiss of personal expectations, when they apparently fail to live up to ideals of progress (*kemajuan*). Dani university students' experiences illustrate a different possibility, in which a stigmatised cultural and ethnic minority begins to achieve national ideals and expectations, at least in terms of education, skill development and mobility. In doing so, they pose a critical challenge to powerful national precepts concerning development potentials and inherent cultural and ethnic traits. By their educational successes, Papuan youth may offer convincing proof that cultural minorities deemed backward in the Indonesian national imaginary are not, and maybe never were, held back by their ethnic and/or racial constitution. These challenges do not, and will not, go unnoticed. When so-called primitive tribals get educated, get mobile and get vocal, they pose as much of a threat to the normative nation as Boellstorff's (2004) *gay* men.

References

Alua, Agus A. 2006. *Nilai-Nilai Hidup Masyarakat Hubula di Lembah Balim Papua*. [Life Values of the Hubula People in the Baliem Valley Papua] Abepura: Sekolah Tinggi Teologi Fajar Timur.

Amit-Talai, Vered and Wulff, Helena 1995 (eds). *Youth Cultures: A Cross-Cultural Perspective*. New York: Routledge.

Asian Human Rights Commission 2011. 'Human Rights in Papua 2010–2011'. http://tapol.gn.apc.org/press/files/Human-Rights-in-Papua_Report-2010 -2011.pdf (accessed 24 August 2012).

Aspinall, Edward 1993. *Student Dissent in Indonesia in the 1980s*. Melbourne: Monash Asia Institute.

Aspinall, Edward 1999. 'The Indonesian Student Uprising of 1998'. In Budiman, Arief, Hatley, Barbara, and Kingsbury, Damien (eds), *Reformasi: Crisis and Change in Indonesia*. Melbourne: Monash University Asia Institute, 212–229.

Ballard, Chris 2008. '"Oceanic Negroes": British Anthropology of Papuans, 1820–1869'. In Douglas, Bronwen and Ballard, Chris (eds), *Foreign Bodies: Oceania and the Science of Race 1750-1940*. Canberra: ANU E Press, 157–201.

Boellstorff, Tom 2004. 'The Emergence of Political Homophobia in Indonesia: Masculinity and National Belonging'. *Ethnos* 69(4): 465–486.

Boellstorff, Tom and Lindquist, Johan 2004. 'Bodies of Emotion: Rethinking Culture and Emotion through Southeast Asia'. *Ethnos* 69(4): 437–444.

Buchholt, Helmut, and Mai, Ulrich 1994. *Continuity, Change and Aspirations: Social and Cultural life in Minahasa, Indonesia*. Singapore: Institute of Southeast Asian Studies.

Butt, Leslie 2012. 'HIV/AIDS Testing, Treatment and the Sedimentation of Violence in Papua'. Indonesia. *Western Humanities Review* 66(3): 35–57.

Butt, Leslie 2013. 'Local Biologies and HIV/AIDS in Highlands Papua, Indonesia'. *Culture, Medicine, and Psychiatry* 37(1): 1–16.

Butt, Leslie and Munro, Jenny 2007. 'Rebel Girls? Unplanned Pregnancy and Colonialism in Highlands Papua, Indonesia'. *Culture, Health & Sexuality* 9(6): 585–598.

Collins, Elizabeth F., and Bahar, Ernaldi 2000. 'To Know Shame: Malu and its Uses in Malay Society'. *Crossroads: An Interdisciplinary Journal of Southeast Asian Studies* 14(1): 35–69.

Conoras, Yusman 2009. 'Analysis of the Human Rights Situation in Papua, April – July 2009: Papua in a Cycle of Conflict'. http://tapol.gn.apc.org/press/files/hr-report-papua-april-july-2009.pdf (accessed 24 August 2012).

Duncan, Christopher R. 2005. 'Unwelcome Guests: Relations between Internally Displaced Persons and their Hosts in North Sulawesi, Indonesia'. *Journal of Refugee Studies* 18(1): 25–46.

Douglas, Bronwen 2008. 'Foreign Bodies in Oceania'. In Douglas, Bronwen and Ballard, Chris (eds), *Foreign Bodies: Oceania and the Science of Race 1750-1940*. Canberra: ANU E Press, 3–30.

Douglas, Stephen A. 1970. *Political Socialization and Student Activism in Indonesia*. Urbana: University of Illinois Press.

Epstein, Albert 1984. *The Experience of Shame in Melanesia: An Essay in the Anthropology of Affect*. London: Royal Anthropological Institute of Great Britain and Ireland.

Fife, Wayne 1994. 'Education in Papua New Guinea: The Hidden Curriculum of a New Moral Order'. *City and Society Annual Review* 7(1): 139–162.

Giay, Benny and Ballard, Chris 2003. 'Becoming Papuans: Notes Towards a History of Racism in Tanah Papua'. Paper presented at the annual meeting of the American Anthropological Association, 19–23 November, Chicago.

Glazebrook, Diana 2008. *Permissive Residents: West Papuan Refugees Living in Papua New Guinea*. Canberra: ANU E Press.

Goddard, Cliff 1996. 'The "Social Emotions" of Malay (Bahasa Melayu)'. *Ethos* 24(3): 426–464.

Harvey, Barbara S. 1977. *Permesta: Half a Rebellion*. Monograph Series (Publication No. 57). Ithaca, New York: Cornell Modern Indonesia Program.

Heider, Karl 1979. *Grand Valley Dani: Peaceful Warriors*. New York: Holt, Rinehart and Winston.

Howarth, Caroline 2002. '"So You're From Brixton?": The Struggle for Recognition and Esteem in a Stigmatized Community'. *Ethnicities* 2(2): 237–260.

Jacobsen, Michael 2002. 'On the Question of Contemporary Identity in Minahasa, North Sulawesi Province, Indonesia'. *Asian Anthropology* 1(1): 31–58.

Jenkins, Richard 1996. *Social Identity*. New York: Routledge.

Kirksey, S. Eben 2002. *From Cannibal to Terrorist: State Violence, Indigenous Resistance and Representation in West Papua*. M.Phil. Thesis, University of Oxford.

Keeler, Ward 1983. 'Shame and Stage Fright in Java'. *Ethos* 11(3): 15–165.

Kleinman, Arthur and Hall-Clifford, Rachel 2009. 'Stigma: A Social, Cultural and Moral Process'. *Journal of Epidemiology and Community Health* 63(6): 418–419.

Kwok, Natalie 2012. 'Shame and the Embodiment of Boundaries'. *Oceania* 82(1): 28–44.

Li, Tania M. 1999. 'Marginality, Power and Production: Analysing Upland Transformations'. In Li, Tania M. (ed.), *Transforming the Indonesian Uplands: Marginality, Power and Production*. London: Taylor and Francis, 1–44.

Lindquist, Johan 2004. 'Veils and Ecstasy: Negotiating Shame in the Indonesian Borderlands'. *Ethnos* 69(4): 487–508.

LiPuma, Edward 2000. *Encompassing Others: The Magic of Modernity in Melanesia*. Ann Abor: University of Michigan Press.

McCallum, Cecilia 2005. 'Racialized Bodies, Naturalized Classes: Moving through the City of Salvador da Bahia'. *American Ethnologist* 32(1): 100–117.

Munro, Jenny 2004. *Taking on Development: Papuan Youth, HIV/AIDS and State Discourse in Eastern Indonesia*. MA Thesis, University of Victoria, Canada. Ann Arbor: UMI.

Munro, Jenny 2009. *Dreams Made Small: Humiliation and Education in a Dani Modernity*. PhD thesis, The Australia National University.

Munro, Jenny 2012. '"A Diploma and a Descendant!" Premarital Sexuality, Education, and Politics among Dani University Students in North Sulawesi, Indonesia'. *Journal of Youth Studies* 15(8): 1011–1027.

Munro, Jenny 2013. 'The Violence of Inflated Possibilities: Education, Transformation and Diminishment in Wamena, Papua'. *Indonesia* 95: 25–46.

Naylor, Larry L. 1974. *Culture Change and Development in the Balim Valley, Irian Jaya, Indonesia*. PhD thesis, Southern Illinois University at Carbondale.

Pitt-Rivers, Julian 1965. 'Honour and Social Status'. In Peristiany, Jean G. (ed.), *Honour and Shame: The Values of Mediterranean Society*. London: Weidenfeld and Nicolson, 19–77.

Pouwer, Jan 1999. 'The Colonisation, Decolonisation and Recolonisation of West New Guinea'. *The Journal of Pacific History* 34(2): 157–180.

Reddy, William M. 1997. 'Against Constructionism: The Historical Ethnography of Emotions'. *Current Anthropology* 38(3): 327–351.

Robbins, Joel 2005. 'Humiliation and Transformation: Marshall Sahlins and the Study of Cultural Change in Melanesia'. In Robbins, Joel and Wardlow, Holly (eds), *The Making of Global and Local Modernities in Melanesia: Humiliation, Transformation, and the Nature of Cultural Change*. Ashgate: Aldershot and Burlington, 3–21.

Rutherford, Danilyn 2012. *Laughing at Leviathan: Sovereignty and Audience in West Papua*. Chicago: University of Chicago Press.

Slama, Martin 2010. 'The Agency of the Heart: Internet Chatting as Youth Culture in Indonesia'. *Social Anthropology/Anthropologie Sociale* 18(3): 316–330.

Strathern, Andrew 1975. 'Why is Shame on the Skin?' *Ethnology* 14(4): 347–356.

Sykes, Karen 1999. 'After the Raskal Feast: Youth's Alienation in Papua New Guinea'. *Critique of Anthropology* 19(2): 157–175.

Timmer, Jaap 2000. *Living with Intricate Futures: Order and Confusion in Imyan Worlds, Irian Jaya, Indonesia*. Nijmegen: Centre for Pacific and Asian Studies, University of Nijmegen, Department of Anthropology.

Wikan, Unni 1984. 'Shame and Honour: A Contestable Pair'. *Man, New Series* 19(4): 635–652.

Yang, Lawrence H., Kleinman, Arthur, Link, Bruce G., Phelan, Jo C., Lee, Sing and Good, Byron 2007. 'Culture and Stigma: Adding Moral Experience to Stigma Theory'. *Social Science & Medicine* 64(7): 1524–1535.

Zimmer-Tamakoshi, Laura 1997. 'The Last Big Man: Development and Men's Discontents in the Papua New Guinea Highlands'. *Oceania* 68(2): 107–122.

8. Torture as a Mode of Governance: Reflections on the Phenomenon of Torture in Papua, Indonesia

Budi Hernawan

Torture in Papua,[1] Indonesia,[2] gained new attention when graphic footage was leaked to *YouTube* in October 2010. There are two separate incidents captured in the footage. The first part of the footage depicts eight Papuan highlanders stripped naked of their shirts in front of two Indonesian army soldiers. Two of the victims were identified under the names of Kotoran Wonda and Dipes Tabuni. While interrogating these terrified Papuans and calling them '*monyet*', '*anjing*' or '*bajingan*' (monkey, dog, bastard), the soldiers kicked their heads with their army boots, and hit their heads using their helmets. The soldiers demanded they confess to being members of the Papuan separatist movement OPM (*Organisasi Papua Merdeka* or Free Papua Movement). The second footage shows two petrified Papuan highlanders: Telangga Gire had a knife at his throat (see Figure 1) and Tunaliwor Kiwo was being burnt on his genitals by members of the Indonesian army to get the men to confess the location of OPM weaponry near the highland town of Mulia.[3]

The leak prompted a wave of international public reaction putting pressure on the Indonesian government to address this atrocity. Instead of showing its usual resistance to international pressure, the Indonesian government responded fairly quickly. Court martials were established in early 2011 in Jayapura, the provincial capital of Papua, to hear the cases. As a result, seven soldiers[4] were

---

1 This chapter adopts the term 'Papua' which refers to the Western half of New Guinea Island under Indonesia's jurisdiction. It consists of two provinces: the province of Papua and the province of West Papua.
2 This is an advance version of a working paper presented at the Yale Indonesia Forum's workshop on 'New Perspectives on Papua', in New Haven, 15–16 April 2011, and at the 111th Annual Meeting of the American Anthropological Association in San Francisco, 18 November 2012. I thank John Braithwaite, Jeroen van der Heiden, Natasha Tusikov, Robyn Holder and Martin Slama for their critical comments whilst I am solely responsible for any mistakes of this chapter.
3 This footage appeared for the first time on *YouTube* on 17 October 2010 but then was removed on the following day. On its press release dated 17 October 2010 (http://www.humanrights.asia/news/press-releases/AHRC-PRL-021-2010), the Asia Human Rights Commission acknowledged that it received the footage and then published it on its website at the same date (http://video.ahrchk.net/AHRC-VID-012-2010-Indonesia.html). Similarly, the Fairfax News Media independently received the first part of footage and uploaded it on the same website (http://www.youtube.com/watch?v=uEisR8rFLOo&feature=related). By 7 January 2014, the number of viewers reached 143,761.
4 The cases of seven soldiers were filed in five different dossiers. The first dossier No. PUT/ 186-K/PM.III-19/AD/IX/2010 includes Private Sahminan Husein Lubis, Private Dwi Purwanto and Private Joko Sulistiono who were all sentenced to five-month imprisonment. The second dossier No. 187-K/PM.III-19/AD/IX/2010 contains the case of Lieutenant Cosmos, the commandant of the group, who was sentenced to seven-month

found guilty and sentenced to jail for five to ten months. The appeal court later reduced the sentence of three soldiers to only three months.[5] The court did not find them guilty of torture. Rather, they were found guilty of 'not following orders' from their relevant superiors. Similarly, the court found the commandant of the group guilty and sentenced him to seven months not because of torture, but because he 'deliberately provided an opportunity to his subordinates to not follow his orders'. As the verdicts fixed on the matter of 'following orders' the court martial failed to recognise torture as a form of state-sponsored brutality. To make it worse, without any reason the court did not actually try the cases of Kiwo and Gire.[6] Rather, it only dealt with the cases of Dipes Tabuni and Kotoran Wonda in the first part of the video who were tortured because they were accused of being commandants of the OPM.

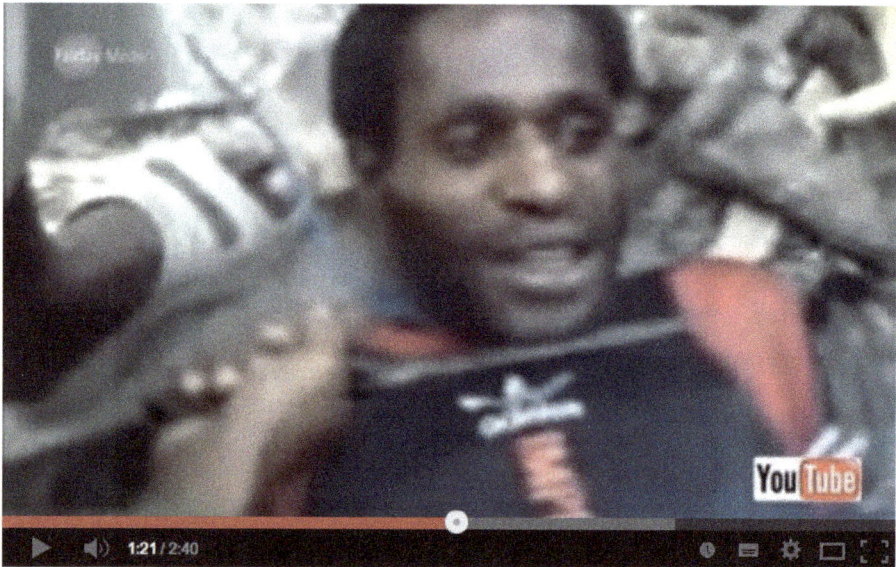

Figure 8.1. Torture video uploaded on YouTube.

Source: http://www.youtube.com/watch?v=uEisR8rFLOo&feature=related (accessed 16/01/15).

imprisonment. The third dossier No. PUT/03-K/PM.III-19/AD/I/2011 contains the case of Private Tamrin Mahangiri who was sentenced to eight-month imprisonment. The fourth dossier No. PUT/04-K/PM.III-19/AD/I/2011 contains the case of Sergeant Irwan Rizkyanto who was sentenced to ten-month imprisonment. Finally, the dossier No. PUT/05-K/PM.III-19/AD/I/2011 contains the case of Private Yakson Agu who was sentenced to nine-month imprisonment.

5   The appeal court decision No. 66-K/PMT.III/BDG/AD/XII/2010 reduced the sentence of Private Sahminan Husein Lubis, Private Dwi Purwanto and Private Joko Sulistiono from five to three months imprisonment. The other soldiers did not appeal.

6   For the discussion of the confusion of these two separate incidents, see Human Rights Watch analysis at http://www.hrw.org/news/2010/11/21/indonesia-stop-stalling-investigating-torture-video-episode-0.

These verdicts go to the essence of this chapter. It opines that torture in Papua constitutes a state-sponsored crime and has become a mode of governance. Torture, however, is not the only coercive method that is frequently employed by the Indonesian security services to intimidate civilians in Papua and across Indonesia. The Indonesian state apparatus has no hesitation to use killing, surveillance, arbitrary arrest and detention, and disappearances to control civilians.

In this chapter, however, I focus on torture, as this, among a number of other crimes, falls under the category of crimes against humanity under international law. Further, in the context of Papua, the empirical evidence reveals a disturbing pattern of public display that is distinct from what we have seen in the Abu Ghraib model of torture. The latter has prompted the resurgence of scholarly interest in torture in relation to the war on terror (Dershowitz 2002; Dratel 2005; Levinson 2004; Post and Panis 2011). In this literature, torture is used by liberal democracies as part of criminal investigations aimed at collecting intelligence from terrorist suspects with an assumption that the suspects will not willingly provide any information unless they are coerced. Since torture in this context is unlawful and thus any torturer might be held accountable and any information might be deemed inadmissible in court, the Abu Ghraib kind of torture is carefully designed to avoid legal consequences and public scrutiny. That is why this type of torture is commonly hidden from the public.

Torture in Papua is the opposite. The identifiable patterns, such as the one on YouTube, suggest torture is not something very secret. It has been done in public space in the front of a public audience, so anyone, including women and children, can witness an actual event of torture. It suggests the interrelationship of sovereignty and audience. Therefore, it raises fundamental questions such as why the Indonesian security services employ torture in such a public way. What would be the purpose of this brutal method? More broadly, what would be the meaning of employing torture for half a century?

This chapter aims to answer these questions drawing on an analysis of 431 codified cases over the period of 1963–2010. The cases are selected from 12 different non-government sources that have been formally submitted to the Indonesian authorities for prosecution and have become public documents. As a complement, I was also granted access to use two private archives of Papuan specialists[7] who have done extensive research on human rights issues in Papua. This archival method is largely coupled with face-to-face interviews with three different types of actors, namely torture survivors, Indonesian state authorities and third parties, in order to reconstruct what happened as well

---

7   I thank Dr Chris Ballard from The Australian National University in Canberra and Reverend Dr Benny Giay from the 'Walter Post' School of Theology in Jayapura who granted permission to use some of their private materials.

as to explore broader narratives by which these three types of actors perceive and give meaning to torture. This investigation is not limited to Papuans living inside Papua but also the Papuan diaspora who have taken asylum in Papua New Guinea, Australia, the Netherlands, the United Kingdom and the United States. As such, this chapter does not intend to provide a comprehensive history of torture in Papua nor a comparative study on the narratives of torture among three different actors. Rather, I focus on the meaning of torture in Papua as it has been constructed over the period of Indonesian administration since 1963.

In exploring this theme, first this chapter briefly examines the historical and political context in the late 1940s, when the question of Papua was raised in conjunction with Indonesia's decolonisation from Dutch rule. Second, it continues with an analysis of the anatomy of torture in Papua to grasp the nature of coercion. Third, it delves into the meaning of torture. Finally, it discusses the implications of coercive practice as a mode of governance.

Historico-political context of torture in Papua

The genealogy of coercive governance in Papua derives from the complex power relations that underpin the question of sovereignty in the context of Indonesia's decolonisation from the Netherlands in the late 1940s. I employ the Foucauldian notion of sovereignty as established in *Discipline and Punish* (1991) and later more developed in *Society Must be Defended* (2003). This argument contains a number of key terms that need clarification, including 'governance', 'coercion' and 'sovereignty'. The term 'governance' denotes a process of 'societal steering and co-ordination of interdependent actors based on institutionalized rule systems' (Treib, Bähr and Falkner 2007: 3). In other words, governance addresses the question of power relations. Governance is characterised by key elements of political steering and co-ordination between networks. In Foucault's language, governance is framed as 'art of government' to encapsulate his argument that power governs—and in turn, produces—a subject, rather than the other way around (Foucault 1982: 778).[8] Coercive governance, however, refers to state coercion in which the state resorts to force to build a society and to construct a structure of political domination that extends into all parts of the country. From this perspective, torture constitutes a form of state coercion.

---

8   In interpreting Foucault's notion of governmentality, Mitchell Dean highlights the core element as 'different rationalities' or different ways of reasoning. Governmentality constitutes an interaction between 'different types of agency and authority and different types of thought' (Dean 2010: 27). Therefore, in Dean's interpretation, the analysis of governmentality centres on the interplay between rationalities (or thought) and technologies (its manifestation in practice).

The term 'sovereignty' adopted in this chapter is different from that used in the legal and political discourse of the formation of nation states. While legal and political discourse conceives the question of sovereignty in relation to state boundaries and mapping a geographical area, Foucault perceives the same question under the notion of the right over death and life. Sovereignty is manifested through the power of awe and only becomes effective in an action of killing and injuring.[9] I argue that both the Indonesian security apparatus and Papua freedom fighters have manifested their sovereignty by claiming their rights to kill or injure since the first arrival of Indonesia's administration to Papua on 1 May 1963.

During the first two decades of the formation of the Indonesian nation-state from the 1940s to the 1960s, Papua seemed to be a 'pebble in the shoe' of the foreign relations between Indonesia and the Netherlands. There were three different clusters of power relations competing over sovereignty: first, the Dutch attempted to recreate new boundaries of sovereignty over the former Dutch East Indies by proposing the union of Indonesia and the Netherlands in the late 1940s. Second, Indonesia, as a new emerging nation, asserted its sovereignty over the former territory of the Dutch East Indies, including the then Dutch New Guinea in the early 1960s (Cholil 1971; Dinas Sedjarah Militer Kodam XVII/ Tjendrawasih 1971; Pusat Sejarah dan Tradisi TNI 2000; Soekarno 1962; Yamin 1956). Third, almost simultaneously in the early 1960s, the embryonic Papuan state asserted its sovereignty over former Dutch New Guinea (Alua 2000; Drooglever 2009). These rivalries over sovereignty have not been resolved, notably the dispute between Indonesia and Papuans over control of Papua (Chauvel 2005; Chauvel and Bhakti 2004).

Vlasblom[10] (2004) documented torture in Papua committed by the Indonesian security forces as early as 1963. This act of injuring was deployed to silence a student protest in Manokwari that was calling for 'one man, one vote'. The protest concerned Article XVIII (d)[11] of the 1962 New York Agreement[12] that stated that Papuan adults, men and women, were entitled to cast a secret

---

9   Further discussions on the relationships between Foucauldian notion of sovereignty and torture can be found in Stephen Morton and Stephen Bygrave (2008).

10   In this chapter, I use an unofficial English translation of the original Dutch version voluntarily provided by a source that wanted its identity to be kept confidential since the translation is solely meant for private and non-commercial use.

11   'The eligibility of all adults, male and female, not foreign nationals to participate in the act of self-determination to be carried out in accordance with international practice, who are resident at the time of the signing of the present Agreement and at the time of the act of self-determination, including those residents after 1945 and who return to the territory to resume residence after the termination of Netherlands administration.'

12   The 1962 New York Agreement provided the legal basis to solve the legal and political disputes between the Netherlands and Indonesia on the issue of the sovereignty over Papua involving the United Nations by holding a plebiscite for Papuans. The plebiscite was considered flawed, however (see Alua 2000; Drooglever 2009; Saltford 2003).

ballot during the plebiscite. The protest was met with harsh measures from the Indonesian military as many people, including university students, were arbitrarily arrested, detained and tortured. The use of these brutal methods to terrorise the whole community increased on the eve of the date of the plebiscite. However, the reported cases from the period of 1962–1969 only constitute a small percentage of the total cases of torture in the last 40 years.

Drawing on notes from an interviewee who was formerly part of an intelligence unit deployed to Papua in 1967, the small figure of recorded cases may indicate the lack of documentation at the time rather than the actual cases that occurred in the 1960s. He explains that he was trained and deployed to carry out intelligence operations for the Indonesian army. 'My role was to identify and arrest OPM members and took them to Kodam. What I did was simply ask them to take a walk with me and they would disappear'.[13] This story suggests that he was part of a bigger system of arresting, kidnapping, torturing and causing alleged suspects to disappear.

Once Indonesia officially gained power over Papua's territory and was met with armed resistance, the use of torture and other brutal techniques intensified. The practice was eventually institutionalised when Papua was declared a Military Operation Zone (*Daerah Operasi Militer/DOM*) in the 1980s. Many torture survivors and a few former army soldiers explained that a number of military installations around Jayapura, including Ifar Gunung, Kloofkamp and Dok V, were designated to detain and torture anybody who was targeted as an OPM member or sympathiser. However, none of the survivors[14] could verify whether these places still existed in the 1990s.

On the Papuan freedom fighters' side, the efforts to assert sovereignty over Papua manifested in their frontal armed resistance from 1967 until 1977 when Indonesian security forces succeeded in defeating them militarily. Since then, the OPM has modified its strategy, focusing on low-level armed guerilla tactics, and occasionally launching deadly attacks on military and police installations. At the same time, the notion of Papuan sovereignty has been transformed into a wider political struggle.

After the incorporation of Papua into Indonesia, the Indonesian state regulated Papua under martial law for almost two decades (1980s–1998). This status allowed the Indonesian army to have full control over the territory, resulting in a militarised Papua. The militarisation was not limited to the domain of politics but also law and society. In this context, Papua became exempt from the general legal and political protection provided by the Indonesian state for its citizens. For instance, special treatment as an autonomous region introduced in 1969 with

---

13   Interview II/E3 in Papua on 4 September 2010.
14   Interviews III/D1 in Papua on 18 July 2010 and III/D7 in Papua on 28 August 2010.

Law 12/1969 was annulled. Further, in relation to torture, the state of emergency may explain why legal protection against torture within the Indonesian legal system is very limited and thus has played little role in prevention.

Following the dramatic political saga at the national level when President Soeharto stepped down in 1998, Indonesia entered a new phase of reconstructing its power relations with Papua in the spirit of democracy and the rule of law. *Reformasi* brought about a fundamental change in the relations between the state and society in Indonesia, particularly on issues of civil-military relations. Together with Aceh and East Timor, Papua was granted special autonomy status by the MPR (People's Consultative Assembly), the highest legislative body within the Indonesian legal system. In the context of torture prevention, Indonesia ratified the UN Convention Against Torture in 1998, which opened doors to international scrutiny to assess the situation of torture in Indonesia.

Whilst *Reformasi* paved the way to demilitarisation of the Indonesian political landscape, some analysts found little change in the nature of the Indonesian military in Papua (Alagappa 2001; Mietzner 2009). A recent study by the Jakarta-based human rights NGO Imparsial (Araf et al. 2011) reveals continuity in the militarisation of Papua by the expansion of the infrastructure and suprastructure of the army and BRIMOB, the police special forces. This ever-growing phenomenon has contributed to the increase of violence and human rights abuses across Papua. This article, however, does not discuss impacts of the militarisation of Papua on a broader spectrum, such as the rule of law, public policy and the daily life of Papuans.

In the past 50 years, Papuan political struggle has been marked by a number of significant occasions on which aspirations for *merdeka* (independence) have been expressed. More recently, these occasions include the Second Papuan Congress in 2000 that elected a collegial leadership under the name of the 'Papuan Presidium Council' and the recent Third Papuan Congress in October 2011, which was met with harsh measures from the Indonesian security apparatus. The cycle of oppression and resistance has left deep marks on the history and polity of Papua. This is the context in which patterns of torture must be understood.

Anatomy of torture

The codified cases reveal ten major patterns of torture. *First*, most of the victims are subsistence farmers, males, civilians and highlanders that live in the rural areas, including the two men in the notorious *YouTube* torture video. Only a few cases involve victims that were actual OPM members or OPM leaders. Most victims, such as Kiwo and Gire, are innocent civilians and have nothing to do with pro-independence movements. They have become 'collateral damage' of a military or police operation ostensibly intended to eradicate the separatist movement.

Another element which features frequently is labeling the torture victims with the notion of animality (monkey, pig, or dog), racial notions (black/ *'hitam'*) or the notion of underdevelopment (primitive, idiot or stone-age/ *'zaman batu'*). In the *YouTube* video, for instance, the soldiers called Wonda and Tabuni *'monyet, anjing, bajingan'* (monkey, dog, bastard). The labels of animality and primitiveness are not uncommon in the daily attitude of Indonesians towards Papuans. Some interviewees, Papuans and non-Papuans alike, suggest ways in which these stereotypes have shaped daily interactions. An Indonesian migrant stated:

> The people here are too demanding, don't follow the rule, come to work but don't work, don't want to be developed, and are jealous with the migrants … we feel sad here of being treated as a second-class citizen by the local government. The government's priority is on the locals whereas the migrants are only in the second … the Dayaks have the same things. They want independence. The difference is they [Dayak] are committed to work, to learn from the migrants so they are developed; whereas here, if you give them a book to read, they don't want to read it. This is a clear indication that they don't want to learn because books are the source of knowledge.[15]

On the other hand, a Papuan interviewee expressed a similar stereotyping approach to non-Papuans:

> I came to Java, got educated in Java until I became smart. I got a job as a public servant in Java, lived in Java, understand Javanese culture and speak Javanese, so that I am able to 'kill' the Javanese … In a negotiation, you need an argument. If you deal with Javanese using the Papuan ways [that rely on physical force], definitely you'll lose [the negotiation] because an argument doesn't match [physical force] … I often hear people call me 'black, monkey, [and say] kill him'. This made us hate each other. This pushed us to fight to death.[16]

The labels have influenced their relationships with a sense of prejudice, distrust, disgust and frequently arrogance and hostility.[17]

---

15   Interview with a civil servant II/C11 on 2 August 2010 in Papua.

16   Interview with a senior state prosecutor II/C20 on 26 August 2010 in Papua.

17   For a critical analysis on the correlations between primitive labeling and justification of militarisation of Papua, see Kirsch (2010).

In the context of torture, however, these stereotypes are woven into the architecture of state brutality so that the impact of violence can be more destructive. These labels inform the mindset of the torturer and might help neutralise his sense of morality that resonates with Kelman's (2005) theory of crimes of obedience discussed below.

Second, the fact that rape features as a preferable method to sexually torture Papuan women is striking. Twenty-eight per cent of female survivors have been raped while 5 per cent experienced other forms of sexual torture without rape. Thirty per cent experienced non-sexual torture. The phenomenon might be related to the strategy of conquest introduced by the Indonesian state when it gained control over Papua in 1962. This correlation between rape and war resonates with a broader pattern of the use of rape as a weapon of war in a combat zone.

The recent joint study project by National Commission on Violence against Women (*Komnas Perempuan*), International Center of Transitional Justice (ICTJ) Indonesia and Papuan People's Council (*Majelis Rakyat Papua/MRP*) sheds new light on this issue (Komnas Perempuan 2010). It covers the period of 1963–2009 and examines 261 files of violence against Papuan women. The study found two major types of violence, state violence in 138 files and domestic violence in 98 files. Fourteen women suffered both forms of violence. Eleven women suffered from communal violence. The study not only confirms the pattern of security sector rape, but shows how Papuan women are vulnerable to multiple abuses even in their own families, which are supposedly protective of their safety and wellbeing.

Third, torturers are mostly members of the Indonesian state security apparatus: TNI (The Indonesian Armed Forces) and the Police. They are 65 per cent military personnel, 34 per cent police officers and only 1 per cent militia. The *YouTube* video exhibits this pattern. This finding is disturbing because it reveals that the Indonesian state apparatus has become a major agent of terror and brutality. Instead of delivering services and protection, the Indonesian state apparatus is willing to resort to terror and brutality as a mode of governance rather than to legal and democratic procedures. Put into the horizon of the history of Papua, this reality is even more disturbing as the practice has been basically unchallenged in the last 50 years.

Fourth, techniques of torture are inexpensive and require no skill. The most frequently used physical torture is 'beating', followed by 'kicking'. This might be related to the fact that, generally, the Indonesian security services are underpaid, provided with poor equipment and minimal facilities to carry out their duties. So the members of the military and the police can only use whatever is accessible such as their own hands and legs, guns or other equipment that is available on the spot (see Rejali 2007). The following testimony during court-martial hearings provided by soldiers illustrates the simple methods.

> ... The indictee became irritated and hit the head of Mr Dipes Tabuni, the commander of the resistance, with his helmet one time, kicked Mr Dipes Tabuni's back with his army boots ...[18]

Torture as a technique is simple and cheap but when the technique is interwoven with a sophisticated architecture of domination, the impact can be devastating.

Fifth, torture in Papua regularly takes place based on unproven and one-sided accusations by the Indonesian security apparatus. These include *accusations* of killing members of security services or company employees (e.g. of the mining company PT. Freeport Indonesia or timber companies), *accusations* of being a member of the OPM and *accusations* of attacking government installations. It is obvious that accusations alone have been considered sufficient for the torturers to commit offences in Papua during the last half century as we learn from Kiwo's testimony below:

> And then they demanded ... 'You have to be honest!' ... 'You have to be honest!' ... But I don't know anything, I'm just a regular person ... over and over again ... but they kept pushing me ... You're lying, you have to tell the truth that you're OPM, right?' ... we were constantly pushed that we were so confused to talk, we were numb and our voice was trembled, we couldn't answer properly because we were nervous ... eventually they kept torturing me ... repeatedly ... back and forth beating me from head to toe while my hands and feet were already in tied position ... I've become powerless ...[19]

Furthermore, accusation or labeling has also become the basis of legal proceedings that have led to the imprisonment of torture survivors. These accusations function as an excuse for the TNI and the police to inflict great pain on the bodies of the suspects. These examples suggest that torture in Papua is mostly politically motivated and is justified by the Indonesian security apparatus as acts against anyone who is perceived as an enemy of the Indonesian state. Therefore, it is predictable that any individuals associated with OPM are likely to be subjected to torture when they confront the TNI or the police. On the other hand, accusation as the basis for torturing Papuans reveals the lack of professionalism of the Indonesian security apparatus. Allegations should be dealt with through professional investigation as part of the rule of

---

18   See the court martial decision No. PUT/ 186-K/PM.III-19/AD/IX/2010 para 9 page 20.
19   For full transcript of Kiwo's testimony see http://www.engagemedia.org/Members/dewanadatpapua/news/kiwotranscript-en (accessed on 28 June 2013).

law. The widespread use of torture not only strengthens the perception of the implementation of the state of abjection in Papua but also undermines the ability of the Indonesian judiciary to uphold the rule of law as part of Indonesia's democratisation.[20]

Sixth, under conditions of lawlessness and political transition, the Indonesian state apparatus has heavily relied on torture as a technique to handle secession movements. Over the period of 50 years, the pattern of torture is as follows: out of 431 codified cases of torture, 42 per cent occurred during *Reformasi*, which is the period between the fall of Soeharto's New Order in May 1998 and the enactment of the Special Autonomy Law for Papua in November 2001. This transition period records the highest frequency of torture. It is followed by the second highest (37 per cent) during the New Order period (1967–1998) and the third highest in the present *Otsus* era which constitutes 19 per cent of the total figure. The lowest figure can be found in the Soekarno period (1963–1967), which only constitutes 2 per cent of the total. However, another explanation of these findings relates to the involvement of local people in reporting torture (a pattern described subsequently) and to the fact that during *Reformasi* Papuan civil society gained momentum to operate with far greater freedom to monitor and document cases of torture across Papua as well as to expose them to the attention of the broader public.

Seventh, drawing on the judgments of the International Criminal Tribunal for Yugoslavia (ICTY) and the International Criminal Tribunal for Rwanda (ICTR), such a long-term and unpunished practice of state-sponsored torture can only be possible if there is a plan or policy (Boot 2002; Hansen 2011; Schabas 2006). The Papuan torture practice has repeatedly targeted Papuans, i.e. mainly farmers, male, civilian and highlanders, in the last 50 years. The practice has only involved members of the Indonesian state security services as perpetrators and their facilities, which implies the involvement of high-level political and/ or military authorities. The torture dataset records 431 cases of torture, suggesting a large scale of unpunished acts of torture.

Eighth, cases of public torture constitute 82 per cent of the total number of cases whereas only four per cent occurred in private (14 per cent in unknown locations). This pattern shows the central element of a spectacle: public display of the injured Papuan body. Location matters here. Drawing on this evidence, it can be argued that the power of spectacle does not lie in the act of inflicting actual pain and suffering but more in the act of communicating such an experience through the display of mutilated bodies (Rothenberg 2003).[21]

---

20   Concerning the concept of abjection see my discussion of Kristeva (1982) below.

21   The interaction of public display of power and its audience is a complex theoretical issue which requires separate discussion to ponder its nature. This problem not only resonates with Rutherford's (2012) analysis of the positive intercorrelations and reciprocity between sovereignty and audience but also with a broader

The eighth pattern becomes very relevant with the distribution of digital video footage, as this constitutes a distinctive phenomenon in Papua that is not found in other torture situations in Indonesia, such as those involving drug dealers (Nowak 2008) or terrorist suspects. Most of the torture files I analysed describe the torture being committed in a public arena, such as on city roads, in the backyards or front yards of Papuans' homes, the marketplace and other open areas that are accessible and visible to anybody, including women and children. For example, the martial court verdict states that according to the confession of the convicted soldiers, the women and children were only 50 metres away from the crime scene and only separated by huts and trees. It was highly likely that they could have heard the screaming of the victims. This pattern has identified the public space as the locus of torture.[22]

In the case of torture committed in military and police compounds, many victims were tortured in open areas inside the compound. Public display of bodies is not unique to Papua. A similar method has been employed by the Indonesian state in various contexts, such as in Aceh (Aspinall 2006; Rahmany 2001), in former East Timor (CAVR 2005: 259–260, 310-11) and to 'combat criminals' in the 1980s in various places, where dead bodies were left in public for display (Soeharto 1989: 389–390). However, in Papua the torturers keep the bodies alive so they can transmit and amplify the terror to Papuans as a community. Yet unlike the Papuan social body, the international audience is clearly not the target of the message from the sovereign power, as the *YouTube* video shows. This audience has been inadvertently exposed to the brutality of the torturers, but did not succumb to the shock and awe produced by the sovereign power of Indonesia. Thanks to communication technology, the international audience amplified the call for justice from the torture survivors and generated strong pressure on the Indonesian authorities which led to the prosecution of the torturers – rather an exception than the rule, as the next characteristic shows.

Ninth, the element of colonisation of public space that has led to almost complete impunity constitutes an important characteristic of Papuan experiences of torture. Seventy-one per cent of the torturers have never been brought to justice and 5 per cent of those who were brought to court were eventually acquitted, whereas 24 per cent of cases have been pending. Despite the TNI reform agenda

---

discussion of the multifaceted ambiguity of witnessing torture (Cohen 2001; Graziano 1992; Taylor 1997). In his study of an abstract audience of torture in Argentina's Dirty War, Frank Graziano (1992: 78) identifies the range of the notion of witnessing from gazing in a literal sense to a symbolic sense and an abstract sense. In a literal sense, witnessing means seeing and even engaging with an actual event. In a symbolic sense, witnessing is watching a representation of a torture event mediated and filtered by the media. In an abstract sense, however, witnessing can only draw on an idea of torture based on knowledge of sites and events of torture although this knowledge is suppressed or surrounded by denials.

22   See the court martial decision No. 187-K/PM.III-19/AD/XI/2010.

sanctioned by law, the territorial command structure[23] remains unchallenged (Reiffel and Pramodhawardhani 2007). In the Papuan context, this fact suggests that the strategy of militarising Papuan space will continue in the near future.

The *tenth* characteristic of torture in Papua is that local actors play a more dominant role in exposing torture than international actors. Churches and local NGOs reported 80 per cent of torture cases, while international NGOs exposed the remaining 20 per cent of cases. This statistic indicates the capability of local actors with regard to confronting torture in Papua.

Making sense of torture

The chief patterns of torture outlined above resonate with the analysis of torture that Foucault uses to explain the public execution of Robert Damiens, a regicide, in 1757 in Paris as an opening of his *Discipline and Punish*. Foucault (1991) argues that under the order of the King, the executors tortured Damiens to death in front of Parisian spectators to signify the unrestrained power of the King. This was a 'power that not only did not hesitate to exert itself on bodies, but was exalted and strengthened by its visible manifestations' (Foucault 1991: 57).

> It was the effect … of a certain mechanism of power: of a power that not only did not hesitate to exert itself directly on bodies, but was exalted and strengthened by its visible manifestations; of a power that asserted itself as an armed power whose functions of maintaining order were not entirely unconnected with the functions of war; of a power that presented rules and obligations as personal bonds, a breach of which constituted an offence and called for vengeance; of a power for which disobedience was an act of hostility, the first sign of rebellion, which is not in principle different from civil war; of a power that had to demonstrate not why it enforced its laws, but who were its enemies, and what unleashing of force threatened them; of a power which, in the absence of continual supervision, sought a renewal of its effect in the spectacle of its individual manifestations; of a power that was recharged in the ritual display of its reality as 'super-power' (Foucault 1991: 57).

In Foucault's view, the ritual of public execution is a manifestation of technologies of power in which visibility is a *conditio sine qua non* (an absolutely necessary condition). The ritual was a public exhibition of graphic atrocity to maximise the visibility effect and to minimise misinterpretation from the

---

23   Despite the 1998 *Reformasi* which paved the way to institute democracy led by a civilian government, the Indonesian military remains preserving its physical infrastructure across the country under the territorial command structure. This structure runs parallel to the civilian government from the sub-district to the national level.

audience. Power is a sacrosanct quality inherently embedded in the personality of the King. Any sign of disobedience constitutes an act of rebellion, which is punishable by agonising pain, leading to disgraceful death as exemplified by Damiens. By commending this sort of public execution, Foucault argues, the sovereign recharges its power. Therefore, the ritual of public execution of Damiens is not only meant to transmit the message of the sovereign power to the Parisian audience but also to reinforce the power of the King.

In a similar fashion, since 1963, the Indonesian security apparatus has employed torture to demonstrate the unrestrained power of a state that is willing to take any necessary measure to assert sovereign power over Papua. Torture has become a manifestation of the right to kill and to injure in a Foucauldian sense. In this context, any sign of opposition is deemed intolerable and will meet harsh measures from the Indonesian state. Papuan resistance is never tolerable as it seeks to compete with the sovereign power of the Indonesian state in asserting its rights over Papua. The Indonesian state apparatus manages to control the entire landscape of the Papuan social body and it has little fear of being held accountable. This power has infused terror into the social body by leaving scars on particular Papuan bodies and on the collective memory of Papuans. Therefore, such power shows little intention to hide what it has committed because it defines the meaning of killing and injuring as a form of power. That is also the reason why such power needs only 'accusation' to justify its brutality. Moreover, graphic punishment has the effect of renewing Indonesian sovereignty.

The Foucauldian analytical framework helps explain the phenomenon of the public display of torture in Papua in that such acts signify the way in which the state apparatus communicates to the broader audience. As torturing Damiens' body is not an end in itself, neither are the tortured Papuan bodies. Rather, torture is a medium that carries the message of the Indonesian state's unrestrained power to the broader audience of Papuan society. This is the real target. The whole society has to feel and to experience the intrusion of the sovereign power of the Indonesia state so that all members will understand that any sign of opposition will not be tolerated.

The fact that Indonesian security forces no longer maintain their 'torture chambers', hidden places within military and police stations designated to torture Papuans around Jayapura, but rather, practices torture in plain view, affirms the symbolic power of torture. The public practice of torture takes place in a context in which security forces are increasingly occupying public space in Papua. The territorial command and the heavy presence of the army from the village level to the provincial government administration level have been effective in transmitting the message of the pervasive influence of the Indonesian state. Even though there is growing public scrutiny from the emerging human rights monitoring regime in Indonesia, the latter has not been able to eradicate torture as a mode of the production of meaning constructed and maintained by the Indonesian state apparatus. The military institution continues to perform its role as a quasi-government *vis-à-vis* the democratically elected civilian government.

What is the impact of the unrestrained power on individuals? Whilst the Foucauldian framework provides a useful means to explain processes at the structural level, it has limits to answer these questions. Therefore, I draw on Kristeva's (1982) notion of the abject that provides a theoretical framework for explaining a process of dehumanisation,[24] such as torture. In her *Powers of Horror*, she coins the term 'abject' as a metaphor to explain the construct of nonperson, an entity between subject and object, which is rejected both by subject and object. The abject equals non-existence (Kristeva 1982: 1). Kristeva underscores the notion of the abject as an opposition to the subject or 'I'. The notion of 'otherness, detached, non-correlative, autonomous' suggests a stark contrast between *I* and the abject but also a total separation. The subject, however, claims and retains the abject at the border between subject and abject in order to form the existence of the abject.

So how does Kristeva's theory of abjection help explain torture in Papua? The unrestrained power of the Indonesian state not only controls Papuan society but also inscribes its power over bodies. Torture constitutes a physically harmful act that aims to destroy the subjectivity and agency of Papuans. By targeting the lowest class, ethnicity, non-combatants, more men than women, torture has turned these individual Papuans into non-existence. It has infused the notion of meaninglessness and formlessness into these people so that they lose control over their own subjectivity.

The loss of subjectivity is reflected in the experience of torture survivors who express loss of trust and disconnection from others. For instance, one interviewee shared her stories on how she lost her ability to talk after being subjected to torture.[25] The survivor was not only subjected to excruciating pain which seriously damaged her body but also, torture crippled her capacity to express her pain to her community. As a result, her story has never been heard. The survivor becomes an invisible and impenetrable being because language, the bridge between the survivor and the world, has been destroyed. Kristeva's analytical approach helps explain one of the most extreme processes of dehumanisation that occurs at the individual level when an individual is subjected to torture.

The practice of torture suggests that the Indonesian state regards Papuans in abject terms as undesirables who are nonetheless useful for marking the boundaries of

---

24 Elaine Scarry's (1985) *The Body in Pain* provides a similar analytical framework for explaining the internal dynamics of torture at the individual and personal level. However, her work is more relevant for hidden torture as part of coercive efforts to gain intelligence information or to obtain confessions.
25 Interview with a torture survivor II/A20 in Papua on 11 August 2010.

the sovereign state. On the one hand, as an abject, Papuans are being excluded to the margins of the Indonesian state but on the other hand, they continue to be claimed and retained tightly as a non-negotiable entity. As part of the abjection process, Papuans have also experienced dehumanising treatment by being labeled as 'monkey' or 'stone-age people'. On the *YouTube* video, we can hear one of the soldiers clearly calling the victims 'monkey'. Although these stereotypes are not the basis of torture, they have informed the mindset of the Indonesian security apparatus to neutralise their moral conscience so that torturers perceive that they only torture non-humans, situated one level below the torturer's self-identity. This process will be further elaborated in the following section of this chapter.

The process of dehumanisation is never entirely complete. As Kristeva argues, the abject inherently contains resistance. This energy enables the abject to confront the subject by attempting to penetrate the boundaries between the abject and the subject. That is why the abject can 'revolt'[26] in Kristeva's terms. This element also explains why Papuans continue their revolt despite the oppression from the Indonesian state. Papuans, as the abject, inherently possess the energy to resist. So while they will not be entirely destroyed, they will continuously pose a threat to the Indonesian state. In contrast to Kristeva's prognosis, however, Papua's experience suggests that the abject is more than capable of crossing boundaries and asserting aspirations for *merdeka*. Papuans are not entirely turned into powerless abjects; they manage to penetrate the boundaries of the Indonesian sovereign power by expressing their claim for sovereignty.

The production of the meaning of torture is not a single event. The meaning of torture is produced dialectically. The exercise of the right of the sovereign to injure generates an incremental process of dehumanisation in the form of the abject. As a response, the abject revolts and exerts its energy to resist, which meets increasing force from the sovereign. This dialectic generates a vicious cycle of violence, which we have seen in the history of Papua. The arrival of the Indonesian administration generated oppression that met revolt from the Papuan freedom fighters. This revolt has been met with greater oppression from the Indonesian state, which reinforces and maintains its rights to kill and to injure.

Torture has become an integral part of governing Papua since the Indonesian state took over the territory. The state apparatus has used torture to steer and to co-ordinate social dynamics in Papua, which are characterised by resistance and low-level armed struggle. These coercive methods lie beyond traditional models of parliamentary governance, but they are sanctioned nonetheless. Because of this, we might conclude that torture has become a mode of governance.

---

26   In Kristeva's *Revolt, She Said*, she defines the term 'revolt' distinct from 'revolution'. She states, 'I work from its etymology, meaning return, returning, discovering, uncovering and renovating. There is a necessary repetition when you cover all that ground, but beyond that, I emphasize its potential for making gaps, rupturing, renewing. Rebellion is a condition necessary for the life of the mind and society' (2002: 85).

Internal dynamics of governance through torture

Torture is a medium that can transmit and amplify the awesomeness of power. The main point is to communicate a message from the sovereign to the whole community through the injured body (Rothenberg 2003). This message must be made very explicit and blunt so as to avoid any misinterpretation. It is important to consider how torturers become enlisted in carrying out the state's message, because this reveals some of the internal dynamics within the state structure that lead to torture. How do state agents become torturers? Why are they willing to engage in heinous acts and show little remorse for such a long period of time? My analysis of the Papua torture files reveals what Herbert Kelman (2005) calls, 'crimes of obedience'. Kelman (2005: 124) argues that an analysis of torture should 'go beyond the characteristics of the individual perpetrators or even of the situation in which torture is practiced, and focus attention on the larger policy context in which the practice of torture is embedded'. Therefore, he defines torture as 'a crime of obedience: a crime that takes place, not in opposition to the authorities, but under explicit instructions from the authorities to engage in acts of torture, or in an environment in which such acts are implicitly sponsored, expected or at least tolerated by the authorities' (Kelman 2005: 125).

Torture is facilitated by doctrines of state legitimisation: maintaining law and order or stability, the rule of 'the people' whom the state claims to embody, or national stability. Agents must believe that they are part of a 'transcendent mission, a task that serves a high purpose that transcends any moral scruples they might bring to the situation' (Kelman 2005: 131). In the case of Papua, the territorial integrity of the Unitary State of Indonesia remains a *sacrosanctum* that justifies any means to be upheld.

In this process, Kelman proposes, the agents of torture are defined as a professional force with a significant role in protecting the state against internal threats to its security. In Papua, the torture case files reveal that torture takes place in the absence of professionalisation because the indoctrination of agents' purpose in protecting the state is so powerful. With the exception of the Indonesian Army Special Forces (*Kopassus*), most units of the Indonesian security services are poorly funded, poorly trained and underpaid. In this context, they might not be trained as torturers *per se* but they have to undergo a rigorous process of indoctrination and socialisation to obey any orders coming from superiors and to embrace the Indonesian state doctrine *'NKRI harga mati'* (the territorial integrity of Indonesia is non-negotiable). The following testimony of an ex-army soldier may exemplify this pattern:

> My job at the time was in charge of combat intelligence unit and had
> to be in disguise. The training I had to take was really really heavy:
> trained to steal documents like a pick pocket without being spotted and
> all sorts of other training. In Papua, my job was to arrest members of
> the OPM and take them to KODAM. So I invited him to take a walk
> with me around here and then disappeared. Another unit took him. This
> applied to the hardliners but for those who were more approachable, we
> provided vocational training on agriculture.[27]

The emphasis on the 'really really heavy' training illustrates the rigorous process
to develop his professional skills. Although he did not specifically mention
torture, his testimony captures a systematic way to target those who were
considered 'hardliners' and those who were 'approachable'. This categorisation
led to serious consequences because the hardliners were 'disappeared' while
the approachable were spared and given agricultural training instead. In other
words, the categorisation is not simply an administrative classification but all
about life and death, which resonates with Foucault's interpretation of the
public execution of Robert Damiens.

Torturers may participate in sanctioned violence because the targets of torture
are defined as enemies of the state who constitute serious threats to the state's
security and survival. When Papuans are positioned as OPM, as inferior, or
as estranged from mainstream ethnicity and culture, they are placed outside
the protection of the state. Papua was under martial law during Soeharto's
New Order regime until 1998. This status suggests that the Indonesian state
identified the Papuan resistance movements as its enemy. However, the first
pattern of the anatomy suggests that the treatment is not limited to the OPM but
applies to any Papuans, particularly those who are most vulnerable: subsistence
farmers, highlanders and women, who are imbued with the notion of animality
and primitiveness. Whilst martial law was lifted in 1998, legacies of treating
Papuans as enemies have changed little, as we can see from the *YouTube* video.

At the level of implementation, Kelman (2005: 131) states, 'The justification of
torture as a means of protecting the State against threats to its security helps to
authorize the practice; the development of a profession of torturers as part of
the State's security apparatus helps to *routinize* the administration of torture;
and the designation of the targets of torture as enemies of the State who are
excluded from the State's protection helps to *dehumanize* the victims.'

These three social processes contribute to weakening the moral restraints
against engaging in torture and other gross human rights violations because
authorisation abolishes any responsibility to make any personal moral choices on

---

27 Interview with a retired Indonesian army officer III/E3 in Papua on 4 September 2010.

the basis of standard moral principles; routinisation enables them to ignore the overall meaning of the task they are undertaking and eliminates opportunity to raise moral questions; dehumanisation excludes victims from the perpetrators' moral community, making it unnecessary to relate them in moral terms. The failure of the court to try Kiwo's and Gire's cases and the similar failure to present any victim witnesses[28] before the court of Wonda's and Tabuni's cases illustrate the exclusion of Papuans from the moral community of the perpetrators.

The following excerpt from a police interviewee might illuminate the element of routinisation that has neutralised any personal moral choices, particularly the sense of guilt:

> Torture is still everywhere but notably in Papua because of the low level of education of the police officers. Hit [a suspect] first, then interview [him/her]. Such a thing still exists in Java too. When I was in the police academy, I saw our senior put a table foot on a suspect foot. The table was made of steel. Of course, the foot was punctured. Or pulling fingernails. But it changed now. It leaves no marks. Slapping or punching doesn't leave any mark. You wash your face and it's gone. So the practice remains but using *'pola manis'* (smooth methods).

> The police academy contaminated my attitude. I used to be a bad boy with violent behaviour but had stopped before joining the police force. When I did my training at the police academy my past behaviour came back because of the atmosphere. I did shoot a criminal so he had to have amputation but that's it. I stopped. I have not hit anybody including my boys since then because if an officer hits somebody, his soldiers will follow his example.[29]

He acknowledges that the rampant practice of torture has a direct connection with the atmosphere of the Indonesian police academy where he had received his training. As a result, his past violent behaviour was revived. He learnt how to deal with criminal suspects by witnessing the ways his seniors used methods of torture to obtain confession from suspects, which in fact were considered a common practice.

In other words, he acknowledges that his formation[30] has laid the ground for justification of a policy of torture. It has a direct causality with the practice

---

28   The decision of the court martial of appeal specifically mentioned the absence of witness testimonies as one of the legal flaws of the first court martials hearings: '… and in fact, since the court hearings adjourned until the verdicts were delivered, civilians, who had become the victims, were never been presented before the court …' See the decision of the court martial of appeal No. 66-K/PMT.III/BDG/AD/XII/2010 page 12.

29   Interview III/C16 with a middle ranked police officer in Papua on 18 August 2010.

30   In his recent doctoral thesis on professionalism of the Indonesian military, Robertus Purwoko Putro (2012), an Indonesian airforce middle-ranking officer, concludes that the problem of impunity is deeply entrenched

of dehumanising suspects, who were not entitled to protection from the state. Further, torture was considered commonly practiced by his seniors who authorised these brutal methods to be used by their subordinates. His seniors lifted any moral constraints and responsibility that might have deterred the use of torture. *Authorisation* and *routinisation* have led to *dehumanisation* of suspects as forms of crimes of obedience (Kelman 2005).

The police officer's story exemplifies how the in-group (Post and Panis 2011; Janis 1972) generates enormous pressure for uniformity in action among members of the police academy and overrides any moral constraints and personal judgments because they perceive the criminals as the enemy.

Another story from a senior army officer suggests a completely different element in ways in interpreting 'the enemy'. He identifies the MRP (Papuan Peoples' Assembly),[31] a state institution in Papua, as a threat to Indonesian power, and the state of mind of being colonised as a challenge to the Indonesian state.

> MRP does not follow its role and has stepped into a political domain by issuing Decree No. 14. An election belongs to the political domain. They intervened and endorsed a regulation that the regent and its deputy have to be indigenous Papuans. *Otsus* itself only applies such a thing for the governor and its deputy. Even so, is it the right time to issue such a decree when the district election is only 3 months away? Is it true that it was MRP who issued the decree? MRP 'handed back' *Otsus* whereas this institution itself comes from *Otsus*. The Chairman [of MRP] explained it happened because of the huge pressure from the people. But they issued a letter on behalf of the 'Papuan nation'. They use the word 'nation' not 'tribe'. This actually reflects their dissatisfaction.

> A real challenge, apart from heavy terrain, is an image of being colonised: how to convince the people that they are not colonised? How to address the stigma of being strangers? How to convince the people that TNI here is not a coloniser? The migrants are not colonisers either. This is the real challenge for us whereas those enemies in the jungle will realise that what they did is wrong.[32]

These excerpts represent a much more sophisticated analysis of how the Indonesian army defines the enemy of the state, precisely by identifying a defiant element and state of mind. He did not refer the OPM as a threat or a challenge. For him, MRP is a real threat because it possesses a state power

---

not only into the structure of the Indonesian army but, more importantly, in its psyche. In combination with the historical legacy of the military domination in Indonesian politics particular during the New Order, the culture of impunity within the Indonesian military has seriously undermined their professionalism.

31   The interviewee specifically referred to the MRP from the period of 2005–2010.

32   Interview with a senior army officer II/C24 in Papua on 2 September 2010.

to formulate legislation that has legal and political bindings. The challenge he describes is also sophisticated. Instead of referring to security or military threats, he points to the Papuan state of mind of being colonised. His comments indicate a higher degree of analysis to legitimise torture, which is not found in previous legitimation for torture.

The officer's comments offer a personal perspective on how the doctrine of territorial integrity of Indonesia is nonnegotiable. The doctrine serves as a mind guard that puts pressure on members of the state apparatus not only to support the doctrine but more importantly, to be the vanguard of the doctrine.

Internal governance dynamics not only shape the practice of torture at the level of the individual practitioner, but the situation of Papua puts strain on Indonesia's democratic emergence. While Kelman (2005) states that torture is endemic in the autocratic state but less likely to take place in democracies even though there is no guarantee for it, Darius Rejali's (2007) work on the correlations between torture and democracy shows that torture not only can occur within a democratic framework but even inevitably co-exist.

Rejali (2007) identifies three reasons why torture coexists with democracies that help elucidate why torture in Papua has increased, not decreased, during Indonesia's new democratic era. In some cases, 'officers practice torture as part of a proactive strategy to combat an enemy in an emergency. Victims may be local or foreigners, but they are always chosen because of their suspected political activities' (Rejali 2007: 49). This also suggests that democratic transitions are often marked by violence and instability, which promotes and enables 'emergency' measures. In other cases, 'torture enters democracies through a legal system that highly values the confession of the accused' (ibid. 50). Torture may also coexist in democratic countries because 'the democratic state is unable or unwilling to provide public security, perhaps because the territory is too great or its resources too limited' (ibid. 57). Torture, Rejali (ibid.) argues, 'generates different disciplinary orders, sharpening differences among human beings'. The bottom line is the differentiation between citizens and non- or quasi-citizens, in which citizens are imagined to possess virtue while non- or quasi-citizens do not. Those who do not possess virtue can be subjected to torture as they are not entitled to state protection. The labelling of Papuans as 'monkey' and 'idiot' encapsulates the notion of Papuans being non-persons who do not possess the same virtue as other Indonesian citizens.

Nonetheless, this research suggests that it might be a long way to go for Indonesian authorities to be able to eradicate the practice of torture in its policies towards Papua and across Indonesia because, borrowing Rejali's terms, the Judicial Model and/or Civil Discipline might replace National Security institutions as the source of torture.

Torture has become a mode of governance as it constitutes a social policy applied to the Papuan community. Torture has been institutionalised through the state bureaucracy, military and police structures, as well as intelligence services. Further research needs to examine the impact of torture as a mode of governance on education, judiciary, health and cultural systems.

Conclusions

The prolonged practice of torture in Papua has generated spectacles of shock and awe. These spectacles derive from the ways in which the Indonesian state exercises its sovereign power over Papua through public displays of torture. The phenomenon of torture is deeply embedded in the policies and practices of the Indonesian state apparatus in dealing with Papuans. The recent distribution of torture videos from Papua on *YouTube* underlines the fact that the practice of torture in these easternmost provinces of Indonesia remains. The justice system continues to fail in addressing the practice.

However, the spectacle of awe is not the ultimate goal of state-sponsored brutality. Rather, it is designed to send a very clear message of the presence of unrestrained power of the state that reaches far beyond the Indonesian security sector. As a network of power we can suspect that it may infuse the Indonesian government bureaucracy, the education system and development policy. Totality of control based on coercive governance is the ultimate goal of torture-as-awe.

Aside from control, the torture also aims to dehumanise Papuans and turn them into the abject. This mechanism is expressed in the notions of animality, primitiveness and racism during events of torture as recorded in the *YouTube* footage. The dehumanisation, however, is not simply an individual and incidental act. Rather, it is informed during the professional development of the Indonesian security apparatus and thus habituated and institutionalised through practices and indoctrination of the Indonesian state ideology. Furthermore, the dehumanisation facilitates the treatment of Papuans as quasi or even non-citizens in that this group of people are not only placed outside the protection of the Indonesian state, but more importantly, are considered incapable of meeting the standards of civility of the Indonesian citizens. Therefore, it is not only that they are treated as non-citizens, but more importantly, torture is considered the only means to discipline them.

Despite the overwhelming influence of the power of torture over Papuans, the recent distribution of the *YouTube* video suggests something else as well. This kind of spectacularity invokes unintended consequences for the sovereign once it is exposed to a different audience. Instead of reproducing and intensifying the existing terror for the Papuan audience, its widespread distribution to the international audience has inadvertently provoked backlash which eventually pressured the Indonesian state to hold the perpetrators accountable.

For over 50 years, this form of governance has produced and reproduced crimes of obedience that, in turn, have reinforced the totality of coercion. Under the emerging Indonesian democracy, this phenomenon has posed a serious question not only to Papua but also to the whole construct of the Indonesian state. The question is whether the Indonesian state will continue to respond with coercive governance in Papua whenever any sign arises and is considered posing a threat to national stability.

Learning from Papua's experience, any reform agenda should go beyond law, politics and the security sector. It should be able to address the cyclical production of meaning that has enabled torture as the mode of governance. It must advance a politics of the alternative, a liberation politics. Understanding torture in Papua is the beginning of acknowledging the reality of suffering among Papuans.

References

Alagappa, Muthiah 2001. 'Investigating and Explaining Change: An Analytical Framework'. In M. Alagappa (ed), *Coercion and Governance: the Declining Political Role of the Military in Asia*. Stanford University Press: Stanford, 29–68.

Alua, Agus A. 2000. *Papua Barat dari Pangkuan ke Pangkuan Suatu Ikhtisar Kronologis*, 2nd edn. Seri Pendidikan Politik Papua, Biro Penelitian STFT Fajar Timur, Jayapura.

Araf, Al, Aliabbas, Anton, Manto, Ardi, Reza, Bhatara Ibnu, Satriya, Cahyadi, Mahruri, Ghufron, Nurhasya, Jaky, Simun, Junaidi, Safa'at, Muchamad Ali and Indarti, Poengky 2011. *Sekuritisasi Papua: Implikasi Pendekatan Keamanan terhadap Kondisi HAM di Papua*. Jakarta: Imparsial.

Aspinall, Edward 2006. 'Violence and Identity Formation in Aceh under Indonesian Rule'. In A. Reid (ed), *Verandah of Violence: The Background to the Aceh Problem*. Singapore and Seattle: National University of Singapore Press and University of Washington Press, 149–176.

Boot, Machteld 2002. *Genocide, Crimes Against Humanity, War Crimes: Nullum Crimen Sine Lege and the Subject Matter Jurisdiction of the International Criminal Court*. Antwerpen, Oxford, New York: Intersentia.

CAVR 2005. *Chega! The Report of the Commission for Reception, Truth, and Reconciliation Timor-Leste*. Dili: The Commission for Reception, Truth, and Reconciliation Timor-Leste (CAVR).

Chauvel, Richard 2005. *Constructing Papuan Nationalism: History, Ethnicity, and Adaptation*, Policy Studies 14. Washington D.C: East-West Center Washington.

Chauvel, Richard and Bhakti, Ikrar Nusa 2004. *The Papua Conflict: Jakarta's Perceptions and Policies*, Policy Studies 5. Washington D.C.: East-West Center Washington.

Cholil, M. 1971. *Sedjarah Operasi2 Pembebasan Irian Barat*. Jakarta: Pusat Sejarah ABRI.

Cohen, Stanley 2001. *States of Denial: Knowing about Atrocities and Suffering*. Cambridge: Polity Press.

Dean, Mitchell 2010. *Governmentality: Power and Rule in Modern Society*, 2nd edn. London: Sage.

Dershowitz, Alan Morton 2002. *Why Terrorism Works: Understanding the Threat, Responding to the Challenge*. New Haven and London: Yale University Press.

Diken, Bülent & Lausten, Carsten Bagge 2005. 'Becoming Abject: Rape as a Weapon of War'. *Body and Society* 11(1): 111–128.

Dinas Sedjarah Militer Kodam XVII/ Tjendrawasih 1971. *Irian Barat dari Masa ke Masa*. Djajapura: Dinas Sedjarah Militer Kodam XVII/ Tjendrawasih.

Drooglever, Pieter 2009. *An Act of Free Choice, Decolonization and the Right to Self-Determination in West Papua*. Oxford: One Word.

Foucault, Michel 1982. 'The Subject and Power'. *Critical Inquiry* 8(4): 777–795.

Foucault, Michel 1991. *Discipline and Punish: The Birth of Prison*. London: Penguin Books.

Foucault, Michel 2003. *'Society Must Be Defended': Lectures at the College de France*. New York: Picador.

Graziano, Frank 1992. *Divine Violence, Spectacle, Psychosexuality, & Radical Christianity in the Argentine 'Dirty War'*. Boulder, San Francisco, Oxford: Westview Press.

Greenberg, Karen J., and Dratel Joshua L. (eds) 2005. *The Torture Papers: The Road to Abu Ghraib*. Cambridge: Cambridge University Press.

Hansen, Thomas Obel 2011. 'The Policy Requirement in Crimes Against Humanity: Lessons from and for the Case of Kenya'. *The George Washington International Law Review* 43(1): 1–41.

Human Security Research Group 2012. *Human Security Report 2012: Sexual Violence, Education, and War Beyond the Mainstream Narrative*. Vancouver: Simon Fraser University.

Kelman, Herbert C. 2005. 'The Policy Context of Torture: A Social-Psychological Analysis'. *International Review of the Red Cross* 87(587): 123–134.

Kirsch, Stuart 2010. 'Ethnographic Representation and the Politics of Violence in West Papua'. *Critique of Anthropology* 30(1): 3–22.

Komnas Perempuan 2010. *Stop Sudah! Kesaksian Perempuan Papua Korban Kekerasan dan Pelanggaran HAM 1963–2009*. Komisi Nasional Anti Kekerasan terhadap Perempuan, Majelis Rakyat Papua. Jakarta: ICTJ.

Kristeva, Julia 1982. *Powers of Horror: An Essay on Abjection*. Trans. Roudiez, Leon. New York: Columbia University Press.

Kristeva, Julia 2002. *Revolt, She Said*. Cambridge, MA and London: MIT Press.

Levinson, Sanford (ed.) 2004. *Torture: a Collection*. Oxford: Oxford University Press.

Mietzner, Marcus 2009. *Military Politics, Islam and the State in Indonesia*. Singapore: ISEAS.

Morton, Stephen and Bygrave, Stephen (eds) 2008. *Foucault in an Age of Terror: Essays on Biopolitics and the Defence of Society*. New York: Palgrave Macmillan.

Nowak, Manfred 2008. *Report of the Special Rapporteur on torture and other cruel, inhuman or degrading treatment or punishment, Addendum, Mission to Indonesia*. New York: United Nations General Assembly.

Post, Jerrold M. and Panis, Lara K. 2011. 'Crimes of Obedience: "Groupthink" at Abu Ghraib'. *International Journal of Group Psychotherapy* 61(1): 49–66.

Pusat Sejarah dan Tradisi TNI 2000. *Sejarah TNI Jilid I* (1945–1949). Jakarta: Markas Besar Tentara Nasional Indonesia Pusat Sejarah dan Tradisi TNI.

Putro, RAP 2012. *The Professionalism of the Indonesian Military*. PhD thesis, University of New South Wales.

Rahmany, Dyah P. 2001. *Matinya Bantaqiah, Menguak Tragedi Beutong Ateuh*. Banda Aceh: Cordova.

Reiffel, Alexis and Pramodhawardhani, Jaleswari 2007. *Out of Business and On Budget: The Challenge of Military Financing in Indonesia*. Washington D.C.: The Brookings Institution.

Rejali, Darius 2007. *Torture and Democracy*. Princeton and Oxford: Princeton University Press.

Rothenberg, Daniel 2003. '"What We have Seen has been Terrible": Public Presentational Torture and the Communicative Logic of State Terror'. *Albany Law Review* 67(2): 465–499.

Rutherford, Danilyn 2012. *Laughing at Leviathan: Sovereignty and Audience in West Papua*. Chicago and London: The University of Chicago Press.

Saltford, John 2003. *The United Nations and the Indonesian Takeover of West Papua, 1962–1969, The Anatomy of Betrayal* 1st edn. London and New York: RoutledgeCurzon.

Scarry, Elaine 1985. *The Body in Pain: The Making and Unmaking of the World*. Oxford: Oxford University Press.

Schabas, William A. 2006. *The UN International Criminal Tribunals: The Former Yugoslavia, Rwanda and Sierra Leone*. Cambridge: Cambridge University Press.

Skjelbæk, Inger 2012. *The Political Psychology of War Rape: Studies from Bosnia and Hersegovina*. London and New York: Routledge.

Soeharto 1989. *Soeharto: Pikiran, Ucapan dan Tindakan Saya: Otobiografi seperti Dipaparkan kepada G. Dwipayana dan Ramadhan K.H.* Jakarta: PT Citra Lamtoro Gung Persada.

Soekarno 1962. *Pembebasan Irian Barat: Kumpulan Pidato dan Keterangan-Keterangan mengenai Perdjuangan Pembebasan Irian Barat dari 17 Agustus 1961 sampai 17 Agustus 1962*, Djakarta: Departemen Penerangan R.I.

Taylor, Diana 1997. *Disappearing Acts: Spectacles of Gender and Nationalism in Argentina's 'Dirty War'*. Durham and London: Duke University Press.

Treib, Oliver, Bähr, Holger and Falkner, Gerda 2007. 'Modes of Governance: Towards a Conceptual Clarification'. *Journal of European Public Policy* 14(1): 1–20.

Vlasblom, Dirk 2004. *Papoea: een Geschiedenis*. Uitgevers: Mets & Schilt.

Yamin, Muhammad. 1956. *Kedaulatan Indonesia atas Irian Barat: Jaitu Uraian tentang Tuntutan Rakjat terhadap Wilajah Indonesia bagian Irian-Barat*. Bukittinggi: Nusantara.

9. 'Living in HIV-land': Mobility and Seropositivity among Highlands Papuan Men

Leslie Butt

Introduction: Men and mobility

The lure of Papua as a discrete, politically distinct space has curtailed the study of Papuan mobility, or the impacts of the mobile technologies, peoples, objects and ideas that flow in and out of the province on the indigenous men and women who live there. The tendency has been to privilege the fixity of culture in place, and the site of the production of cultural knowledge itself, over the fluidity and porosity of cultural boundaries and cultural transformations brought about through mobility. The tried-and-true approach, as I have taken in many of my own academic papers, is to assert that particular indigenous tribes of the central highlands region culturally value personal mobility across space, social flexibility across kin lines, and are affected by migrants who have moved into the region, but to then go on to focus analytic attention only on what takes place within the fixed space of their ancestral lands.

This paper explores the critical role of mobility for a particular group of highlands men – HIV-positive men – whose personal trajectories intersect with the mobile flows of viruses, drugs and technologies. In particular, I focus on the intersection between mobile men, the mobility of HIV, and the imported, idealised and highly technological models of HIV diagnosis, testing and anti-retroviral therapy (ART) that have become the new standard for dealing with HIV since the new millennium.

Male mobility has been the focus of HIV/AIDS behavioral interventions for almost two decades, notably under the rubric of MMM, where special risks of HIV transmission were attributed to Mobile Men with Money (UNDP 2004). Within migration streams in Papua, for example, men who leave their highland homes to find work at the well-paying Freeport-McMoran gold and copper mine, in the town of Timika, are seen as more likely to contract HIV than their less affluent, less mobile stay-at-home relatives. While the structural pressures on men to seek opportunities and to engage in risky sexual behavior are well documented, the experiences of the men themselves have been less closely scrutinised. Gender has been recognised as essential to understanding patterns around HIV infection in Melanesian societies, but women tend to have been more closely scrutinised than men, with men's experiences often left completely unaddressed in interventions (Eves 2010). Men in Melanesia are typically raised in strongly gender-demarcated societies. Communities emphasised warrior training through childhood, and expected aggression, which translates in the present day to engagement with political and personal violence as a way to compensate for insecurities embedded within a Melanesian ethos of masculinity – be it against women, theft or other forms of often brutal violence (Knauft 2011). This masculinity has been described as in crisis, with many rituals designed to affirm male adulthood through recognised rites of passage now destroyed or abandoned (Knauft 1997, 2011). Within Papua, men increasingly leave home and encounter in their journeys alternate models of successful masculine accomplishments, novel displays of wealth or the acquisition of commodities, and the adoption of new forms of marriage, spousal relations and family. In part, men are seeking to counter the emasculating effects of colonialism (Macintyre 2008), as well as their desire to maintain and build a male collectivity (Knauft 2011).

This paper describes what happens to highlands Papuan men after they receive a diagnosis of HIV, how they come to terms with their new status, and their experiences in their home communities when they are seeking treatment. In Indonesia, HIV-positive persons are termed *ODHA (orang dengan HIV/AIDS,* or persons living with HIV/AIDS), and upon being so defined by the event of receiving a positive diagnosis, enter into 'HIV-land', the land where the identity of being an *ODHA* comes to dominate personal world views, decisions and actions.[1] Klitzman and Bayer (2003) coined the term 'living in HIV-land' to describe the universe of languages, treatments and protocol that HIV-positive people enter into when accepting a diagnosis. For many men, being an *ODHA* means returning home for treatment (UNDP 2004), where men must engage anew with past traditions and expectations, and where the insecurities and opportunities of new forms of mobility intersect with local community norms and kin expectations. These conditions shape their view on how to deal with their status, and affect who they tell. A desire for continuities and the resumption of routine often characterises men's response to serious personal crises (Becker 1997). Leaving home disrupts the social influence a man has; upon his return, he is less capable of getting care and compassion, or of being able to negotiate social networks, and these deficits have a significant impact on how HIV-positive men negotiate their social relationships. The effects of their decisions, and the scope of their desires, are magnified by an introduced HIV treatment program which is poorly developed, and offers a highly technological, complicated and limited service that demands adherents remain in fixed locales in order to receive treatment.

---

1   See Boellstorff (2008) for an Indonesian example.

After reviewing the limitations of current anti-retroviral therapy (ART) in highlands Papua, this paper describes the interwoven ways mobile highlands men respond to HIV: by invoking long-standing place-based strategies for dealing with serious illness, including ritual diagnosis, avoidance and isolation; by explaining their condition as a result of their mobility or the mobility of others and the dangers that movement produces; and by engaging with the imported routines and standards of contemporary international HIV treatment protocol despite the frictions and failures of this model when applied in Papua. The particular experiences and strategies of men, distinct in many ways from women's responses, highlight how movement and mobility interweave with longing for closure and acceptance through most aspects of their lives.

Methods

Our research team conducted 32 in-depth interviews with HIV-positive Papuans and 15 interviews with health care workers in urban and peri-urban sites in the central highlands region in 2009 and 2010. I worked with a team of three experienced indigenous researchers from the regional university in Jayapura.[2] The male interviewers were originally from the highlands, and were able to use their indigenous Yali or Mee language for many of the interviews. All respondents were diagnosed as being HIV-positive at least six months prior to their interviews. All had some experience with medications available for *ODHA*, although their commitment to drug regimens varied widely. I have described women's struggles elsewhere (Butt 2012, 2014), focusing on how racialised identities and gender expectations combine to contain women's aspirations and render them highly vulnerable to stigmatising practices by health workers and community members. Here I provide some comparison between men and women, but focus primarily on men's experiences. In particular, this paper draws from in-depth interviews conducted with 15 HIV-positive indigenous men from the highlands region. They are from the Dani, Lani, Mee, Western Dani and Yali tribes, and their ages range from 15 to 52, with an average age of 25. Overall income and education levels were fairly low. Typical of the highlands, men's income level was higher than women, averaging about $100/ month versus approximately $50/month, and men were more likely to have finished high school than women. Several men had travelled outside of Papua to pursue higher education elsewhere in Indonesia. With only one exception, all men were interviewed in locations which were different from where they grew

2   Researchers Jack Morin, Gerdha Numbery, Andreas Goo and Ibrahim Peyon helped define research questions, brought methodological expertise to research activities, and detailed insights to the analysis of research results. I am grateful to them for their spirited collaboration (see Butt et al. 2010). Research was funded by the Social Sciences and Humanities Research Council of Canada.

up, highlighting high levels of personal mobility as a constant theme among this young cohort, as well as the limited access to therapies which forces those who wished to adhere to drugs to relocate to a town, usually the one closest to their natal home, where clinics have been set up.

Current trends in HIV infection and treatment

The province of Papua has one of the fastest growing rates of HIV infection in Asia. Estimated infection rates range between 3 and 7 per cent of the indigenous population, who make up around 75 per cent of HIV cases (Rees and Silove 2007). HIV has reached generalised epidemic status for indigenous Papuans, but not for migrants to the province. Farmer (1997) has argued that HIV follows along the 'fault lines' of society, reinforcing vulnerabilities and hardening inequities along the lines of income, race and gender. In Papua, HIV infects indigenous males and females in equal number, but drawing the provincial fault lines show there are more indigenous 'housewives', (to use the head of the provincial AIDS commission's term) that is, monogamous Papuan subsistence gardeners, who are HIV positive than Indonesian sex workers, and far more Papuans than Indonesian migrants.

The response to infection appears to be fairly consistent across genders, with nearly equal numbers of Papuan men and women going for tests and initiating a course of ART, although descriptive statistics based on testing patterns in the highlands suggest men are more likely than women to be tested for HIV but less likely to begin a course of ART (Butt 2012; Butt et al. 2010). Because records are so poorly kept, and opt-out testing is not standard either at pre-natal services or at the internal diseases ward at the hospital,[3] where many HIV patients end up housed, it is impossible to ascertain whether these numbers reflect actual patterns of HIV infection, testing, or responses to treatment. Most qualified assessors say infection rates are much higher. Health workers employed at the VCT sites set up in the past few years were interviewed about their experiences dealing with *ODHA*. Most stated that *ODHA*, as a rule, do not seek out ART. Several health care workers described the dominant pattern as: 'run back to the village and die'. Health workers estimate that 75 per cent of the men and women they initially speak to about testing respond in this way, and 90 per cent of those who test positive also flee without seeking care. These

---

3   In 2010, a Family Health International consultant visited the internal diseases ward in a highlands town, where four known patients with HIV were housed in a separate room. The consultant requested that all patients within the ward receive HIV tests as standard procedure. In the inaugural test, 20 patients were tested, with seven of them receiving a positive result.

descriptive statistics signal the clear necessity for more accessible testing, and more rigorous documentation of the demographics of those who drop out of treatment regimens.

Some of the reasons for the gaps in documenting who is receiving testing have to do with disjunctures between the increasingly bureaucratised and standardised international models of intervention, and on-the-ground political and geographical realities. Access to testing, medication and care remains extremely limited (Green 2010). Corruption, lack of follow-through, poor training and an erratic drug supply explain in part why ART has only been available reliably in the province since 2007 and in four urban locations in the highlands − Timika, Enarotali, Wamena and Mulia − really only since 2008. Uptake is low. Preventing mother-to-child transmission programs or prenatal screening was still unavailable as of July 2010. At the same time, managing HIV has become a huge project that involves collaboration between the state, the military, business, mission groups and international NGOs. In 2011, for example, highlands providers of testing and treatment included The Global Fund, UNAIDS, AusAID, USAID, The Clinton Foundation, the provincial health department, the national AIDS Commission, international mission groups, Médécins du Monde and World Vision. Systems have improved recently but there is little doubt most Papuans living in rural sites continue to lack access to ARTs, and few Papuan *ODHA* currently take them. Whereas earlier initiatives focused on behavioral modification, now ART dominates. ART travels with 'baggage', protocols and guidelines about who, when and how to provide treatment (Hardon and Dilger 2011: 136; Sullivan 2011) (see Figure 9.1). ART remains hard to access in the highlands because protocol dictates drugs cannot precede labs and training. The protocol makes urban sites a good choice for the highland VCT centres, but it makes the centres inaccessible for anyone more than a 15-minute bus ride away, and challenging for people living even two or three kilometers out of town. Treatment becomes an urban affair, with the elite and educated more likely to get on and stay on regimens. Protocol exacerbates the gap between expectations by these global agencies that an *ODHA* can respond to testing, counselling and treatment in a way that is independent of social context (Eves 2010), and the local, grounded reality, which is that local context strongly shapes behavior, decisions and assessments about quality of treatment (Lepani 2012).

These challenging conditions are compounded by racialised relationships between mostly Indonesian migrant providers and mostly indigenous clients. Associations between contagion and primitivism were redolent in reports and assessments of practices in the new millennium when HIV prevention and treatment initiatives geared up (Munro and Butt 2012). Despite the technocratic nature of new treatment models which would seem to encourage a routinised distribution of medications and testing locations, or perhaps because of it, there is little effort made to integrate political and racial realities into how health employees are trained in Papua. Increasingly, Papuan nurses and peripheral staff are being recruited into VCT work, which is an important step towards providing culturally sensitive treatment, but what they learn at training sessions replicates international ideals, allowing for racialised understandings about infection and treatment to endure, on both sides of the equation.

Figure 9.1. Lab materials.

Source: Andri Tambunan.

Figure 9.2. The clinic doctor leads health workers in morning prayer before the clinic opens. Low ranking staff are dressed in white uniforms. The VCT director is second to right in the front row, wearing a white *jilbab*.

Source: Andri Tambunan.

Feelings of mistrust precede and colour the clinical encounter. Counseling and treatment are mostly run by high-ranking doctors and trained registered nurses who are usually Indonesian migrants (see Figure 9.2). Most admissions staff are newly located to the province.

This creates tension along ethnic lines. Papuans and Indonesians tend to racialise each other. The new migrants typically know little about Papuan culture and values, and often choose not to learn about them, acting instead as the 'medical evangelists' who promote a biomedical model (Robins 2009). Many of these employees are quick to criticise Papuans. A Clinton foundation employee described entrenched judgments among his migrant Indonesian colleagues:

> [Papuans] getting AIDS is just viewed as come-uppance, as in 'what do you expect from a bunch of fornicating half monkeys? Let them die'. And no, that is not too strong. Of course not all think that way but there is definitely an underlying element of 'Uwww, the savages'.

Papuan health workers criticise back, using equally essentialist terms:

> You can't trust [migrants'] feelings. Papuans don't want to go [to their clinics]. Migrants are ignorant. We say when you go there the [migrant] staff use instruments to work on HIV-positive patients and then [migrants] say they have to throw out the tools. Very ignorant. There is bitterness.

When the Papuan health ministry adopts international protocol, the migration of a rigid set of ideas (see Figure 9.3) about treatment legitimates local hierarchies. While services in the province continue to improve as drug distribution becomes more widespread and testing more accessible, there is little doubt that implementing universal access to international drug protocol has resulted in increased inequities around who is infected with HIV and who gains access to treatment (Nguyen 2010), reinforcing the fault lines of society along which HIV in Papua already travels. These conditions make it difficult for *ODHA* to get drugs and to stay on them. In the following section, the experiences of male *ODHA* we interviewed, all of whom at one point attempted to access medications through formal VCT, bring out in subtle ways the disjunctures between what is expected of the *ODHA* with regards to treatment adherence, and the challenges and realities of 'living in HIV-land' for the men who returned home or relocate for treatment.

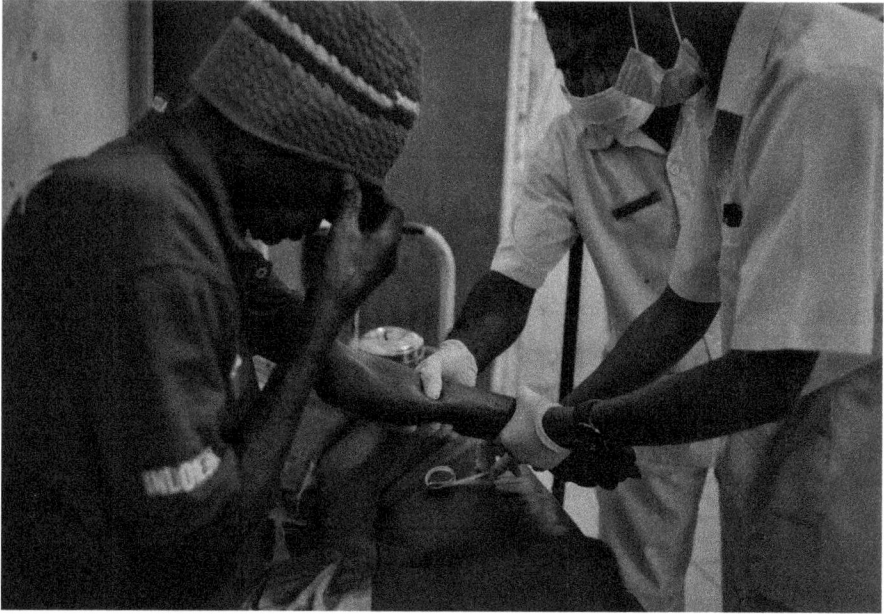

Figure 9.3. The gloves, clothes and masks required for all health workers giving an HIV test are some of the technologies that clients find unpleasant and that strike fear in many.

Source: Andri Tambunan.

Living in HIV-land: The narrative of contagion

For the 15 male *ODHA* who discussed their status in in-depth interviews, ascertaining the moment of HIV infection appears to play a significant place in coping with their everyday realities of being HIV positive. The narrative they repeat for the interviewer was typically presented in highly stylised, fact-laden depictions. Unlike, for example, questions about age, current housing conditions, or monthly income, where men often offered vague responses, questions about how they thought they contracted HIV elicited detailed, stylised contagion narratives where with only one exception respondents with a great deal of certainty identified the person and the place where they believed they had contracted HIV. The explanations highlight the importance of mobility in men's experiences. For example, one young man who was from the Baliem valley explained how he contracted HIV when he travelled outside his community to the western Dani town of Tiom:

> I got this sickness from a woman who already had AIDS. Several friends
> and I drank hard liquor when we were visiting in Tiom and we invited

a woman who was AIDS positive. When we were drunk we had sex with that woman. That was in 2008 and that woman is already dead. She was from the Kogoya clan and shortly after that I felt sick. In February 2009 the worker from the hospice and Mr Jhon asked me to go to the hospital to test our blood. We went, 8 men and 5 women, to get our blood tested. Then the doctor told us 4 men were positive and 4 women were positive also.

This young man links an episode of sex and drinking which took place only months before testing as the source of his infection. As with most respondents, he selects a sexual episode which occurs away from home and where he has sex with a woman who is from a different tribe or province. Contagion narratives often fit with local political realities and validate and reify pre-existing categories of otherness (Eves and Butt 2008; Lindenbaum 2001). Another young man explained how he contracted HIV from a Manadonese woman while he was away studying in another province:

> I contracted this virus while I was studying in Manado at the beginning of 2007. I suspected I was positive because my symptoms were that I was hot, had diarrhea, my body was weak and grew progressively skinnier, and I had prolonged coughing. I got sick because I had sex with a woman from Manado. Right after that I got sick.

In particular, non-Papuan women were seen to be the source of contagion for many. The following explanation by a 52-year-old man to the young male researcher emphasises both how concretely respondents described how they became infected, but also the association for many Papuan men between newcomers to Papua and contagion:

> I started to feel sick in 2008 and in 2009 in July I felt truly sick. I had many symptoms, my head hurt, my body was tired, I had diarrhea and my body was getting thin. So I voiced my complaints and was told to go to the hospital in Wamena. Son, I'm sorry to have to tell you this, but I got sick because I strayed [*jalan salah*]. I didn't think like an elder person and I behaved badly all on my own. I had sex with a straight-haired woman. One of those fallen women who work in the food stalls in town. I had sex in 2006 with that woman. Son, I was just going along on my business, at that time I was the assistant to the pastor at my church. I arrived in Wamena and I felt hungry so I went into one of the food stalls. While I was sitting down and eating, that fallen woman with her straight hair came right up to me and opened up her slacks and showed me her genitals. Well, I was not able to contain my lust.

In another case, the young man left home for a trip and came back with the symptoms of HIV after having sex with an Indonesian migrant.

I knew I was infected August 14, 2007. I had been feeling sick for a few weeks, my body was limp and skinny. My head hurt so I went to the hospital right away and got my blood tested. I had been infected two months before. At that time the head from my village came and invited us to a drinking party and we went and got drunk. While we were drunk, we left home and went to the village of Hom-Hom. Then we went into the Bar near the police station in Hom-Hom. In that Bar there were a lot of Javanese women and we had sex with them.

In sum, men were prone to explaining they contracted HIV by having sex with a woman who was not their wife or girlfriend at the time. In addition, the woman was identified as not of the same tribe as the respondent. The sexual episode which the respondent identified as the source of their HIV typically occurred shortly before the respondent fell sick and was tested. Last, the sexual encounter where HIV was contracted occurred while the respondent was away from home. Thus it is not just the migration in to the province which is associated with contagion, the act of departing from home is also linked to risks associated with HIV.

Living in HIV-land: Community and local cures

For Papuan men, futility, frustration and fear characterise life in HIV-land. In societies where social relations of obligation are dominant, and can be profound, secrecy for HIV-positive persons is a highly compelling strategy. Stigma is powerful: the *ODHA* is afraid of being viewed as 'an affront to the moral order' (Keusch et al. 2006), internalising fears of ostracism and avoiding judgments. This fear of judgment, and possible retribution, makes many men afraid to disclose their status to anyone. Our researchers asked both men and women to list the persons they had disclosed their status to: we found men disclosed on average to only 1.6 persons; women to only 1.1 persons. Both these figures are much lower than global norms, where typically people disclose to parents, spouses and siblings early on, and to increasingly large numbers of people as time passes (Klitzman and Bayer 2003; see Zhou 2007).

Unlike many women respondents, who worry constantly about the need to maintain secrecy in the domestic domain, men appear less troubled by the work of hiding their condition, and do not appear to spend time worrying about keeping up appearances. They appear to remain confident in their sense of social worth and in their ability to maintain their secret. A keyword search of respondent discourse around HIV found men tended to frequently reference bodily conditions and symptoms. Concerns about spouses or the household, or emotional words such as 'anger', for example, were rarely used. For men, in interviews the word most frequently associated with HIV was '*sakit*' (sickness, or sick). For women it was '*takut*' (afraid). As one respondent noted, his work and his social position protected him:

> The people believe in me because I am the village head and the village is working the same as usual. The people always do what I ask them to. Because they chose me to be the village head there is no chance they will abandon me now.

Unlike women, for whom secrecy is almost always associated with maintaining comfortable domestic relations, most men emphasised the reason for keeping a secret is to maintain their public social roles as best they are able. As Yebo notes:

> I kept my disease a secret because this disease I got is a secret disease. If other people find out then they will broadcast it around and the knowledge will be shared, so this is why I still keep it a secret. Because I am also on the church congregation committee ... For as long as I have been sick I have not gone to the church congregation meetings because I have already sinned. I have already stepped down from my committee responsibilities. But I still go to church to pray or to make offerings of pigs. I used to be active in the church but now I have withdrawn from this work because I feel guilty. But as a member of the congregation I am still active, I have just stopped the committee work. Stopping active work supporting the church is a rupture of my personality that I have to endure alone.

This respondent expresses his concern about loss of social relations by referring in particular to his loss of church-based social status. Most respondents, in contrast, did not emphasise religion, God, or Christian ritual in their coping mechanisms. Some male respondents mentioned praying, but only the above respondent and Yohlua (discussed below) specifically mentioned the impact of their HIV status on their religiosity. In contrast, men overwhelmingly honed in on social networks as the key site of concern. This suggests that social relations are what matter the most to persons who have experienced significant disruption in their lives through an HIV diagnosis.

Another feature of male discourse is one that emphasises agency. Men talk so as to emphasise their personal choices to take ART medications, to try locally produced healing tonics, or not to take drugs at all. For example, one respondent described a ready willingness to go to the hospital for testing, using a language of personal choice:

> I knew in my heart I should get checked, and once I found out I made a decision right away to go to the hospital and get medications.

Many men emphasised in the language used in interviews their apparent comfort using health services to get tested, and appear to be willing to listen to health care workers' suggestions on how to adhere to ART:

> I shared my HIV-positive status with the religious assistant so he could help me choose the right path. He urged me to take the medications as directed so I can get better. So I have been following the routine until now, without any problems. For as long as I have been taking the medications at the clinic, I haven't had any problems.

However, some men avoid seeking help from VCT centres. Evading all forms of care is a major concern among health workers and HIV advocates, for both men and women, but in particular, men appear to adhere to a culturally grounded response to epidemic disease which guides them in promoting silence and evasion (Wood and Lambert 2008). All cultural groups included in our interviews hold to a set of values which views AIDS as similar to other epidemic diseases. The person often self-secludes, lives alone in the forest, and if the disease is said to be contagious food is placed at a distance from the hut and the person has no social contact. Both the community and the individual expect the person to remove themselves from social relations. For the Yali, for example, AIDS is associated with leprosy, due to the similarity with large oozing, open sores and disfiguring skin conditions. The patient is isolated as the community fears the sick person harbours an epidemic that will eliminate the population. The person is isolated in the forest, and the only one who can visit is the *dukun* (indigenous healer), who may be able to cure the patient. If the patient dies the forest home must be burned. The *dukun* must conduct rituals to protect the close family of the dead person. As researcher Ibrahim Peyon argues (pers. comm.), there are widespread implications of this concept, as it extends to people who do not feel able to be part of community obligations: 'A person who is seen as not useful, dirty, or who has committed wrongs must be removed from the community or relations with that person must be broken. AIDS fits within this category because through their suffering they get stigmatized by the community.'

For example, one respondent from the Dani tribe noted:

> In the culture of our village, a person who gets sick is a person you don't sit next to, eat with, work with or live with. They have to build a house just for this sick person all by themselves far away from the village. They build a house in the middle of the forest and there the sick person lives.

Another Lani respondent, speaking in terms of personal responsibility, emphasises his choice to avoid the sanctions and isolation of cultural options:

> I haven't told anybody because if I told my father for sure he would get angry. Because my father is a bit harsh in the home so we are all scared.

So, up to now I am the only one who knows. In our [Chrisitan] religion it is not forbidden [to be HIV-positive] but I am the one who is ashamed so I don't want to tell anyone at all, including pastors from my church or anyone. In my culture, someone with AIDS is someone you don't sit with, eat with, work with or live with. We have to make a house for that person far from houses, in the middle of the forest and there the person lives. If they die we have to burn them beside the river and throw their bodies in the river. Because they say this disease can be transmitted… It's like another disease we had before AIDS… it's really similar to AIDS, the person suffers as they get skinny, their body is weak, they have diarrhea and other symptoms. Because of this, in the Lani language we call it *'maluget'*, or 'not good disease'.

Male respondents[4] were also quick to take up indigenous medicines as possible cures for HIV, in particular a popular and expensive fruit tonic made from the pandanus fruit [*buah merah*] in Papua, widely perceived across Indonesia as being able to cure a plethora of illnesses:

When I have money I try and buy some pandanus tonic because I'm starting to feel better. I am certain the tonic can cure me. For example, the symptoms I experienced such as cuts on my genitals are now healed with just one dose. So if I drink the tonic some more then maybe I will be healed, and quickly too.

Before my soul was like a wave, my mood would go up and down, but now that I take that pandanus tonic I am starting to feel better.

In sum, highlands men who are able to obtain care in their home community or who have returned home for care are able to access local treatments that are familiar to them. They are also required to mediate familiar social networks such as church communities or family expectations. On the one hand, the familiar comforts of home offer refuge and succor; on the other hand, familiarity creates new minefields, forcing careful, secretive social relations in order to maintain an active and viable social network. As the following section shows, avoiding stigma is critical but not all are as successful at this task as others. People who have spent time away from their homes find it harder to establish and maintain the successful social relations necessary to shield themselves from stigma and discrimination.

---

4 No female respondents said they had tried indigenous medicines.

Living in HIV-land: Stigma

Secrecy and denial are acts of refusing to give in to the stigma and hopelessness that seems to accompany HIV diagnosis in Papua. Secrecy allows men to maintain their social status, which in turn is linked to accomplishments achieved through success in negotiating social relations. Men did not expect support from extended family or friends. In fact, active stigmatisation happens often among distant kin and neighbours, and is the form of stigmatisation most *ODHA* worry about. Our research shows that widespread disclosure has serious consequences. In the main, people were afraid to disclose because they were afraid of being discriminated against. We had many respondents express fears like this:

> It's hard for me to talk to people about it [my status] because I am scared, scared they won't want to talk to me, or spend time with me anymore, and they will keep away from me. They won't want to eat and drink with me.

Dominant themes were feeling worthwhile as a person by fulfilling their social roles in the family, with regards to food, responsibilities, children, marriage obligations, work and financial contributions. One man put the challenge succinctly:

> I don't feel respected, I have an education but I feel I am not useful anymore because I have got this disease.

While most men were able to integrate religion, culture and social relations into their lives in ways they were comfortable with, the case of Yohlua illustrates the horrific implications of stigma when fully enacted. Yohlua's story stands out not just because of the extent of discrimination, but because it illustrates the consequences of mobility on the ability to retain strong social networks in the home community. When Yohlua returned home with HIV, he could not marshal the social support necessary to protect him from the violence of total exclusion, and he relied exclusively on his parents and his faith in God after experiencing complete community shunning.

Case Study Yohlua: 'I am horribly tormented in my soul'

Yohlua was interviewed at age 23, after he returned from the town of Manado in Sulawesi, where he had gone to do a bachelor's degree. While there he fell sick in his fourth semester.

On July 27 2007 I fell very sick and my friends from the highlands that were also doing a bachelor's degree brought me to the hospital. After the doctor told me I was positive for the AIDS disease, my parents sent me Rp. 1.500.000- (US$150) so I could return to Wamena. Everyone in the villages of Jimugima and Siepketi knew about my status. Their reaction was, they all rejected me and forbid me to live there. After that nobody came to see us in our house, not people from our church and not people from my family. When we moved in, the people who were living there left.

I am horribly tormented in my soul. My parents asked for the people in the church to pray for me but they refused to help us. It was the Catholic church group leader who told everyone in the church that I had AIDS. Then he told all the clan leaders, so everyone who went to church knew. He said 'Yohlua has AIDS so he can't eat, sleep, talk, shake hands with any of us' ... I asked the church group leader to pray for me but they didn't want to. I have already asked them for help three times but they always refuse. So my parents and I say it doesn't matter because God is not blind, God will be the one who will help me.

Yohlua goes on to describe several other episodes of involuntary disclosure, including being barred from the church, being forced to leave another location, and finally finding a refuge away from family and church at the highlands' only hospice. Yohlua's social network is minute, but he perceives the social support he receives from his parents and sister to be very powerful. He also sees God as part of his network of support, drawing out through repeated reference the place of God in replacing the social networks of those who abandoned him.

I ask myself will I die or not. And my parents truly look after me, and they ask the same thing, will Yohlua die or not. My father constantly searches for medications, he conducts diagnosis rituals for ancestor spirits [adat] for me. So, for as long as my parents are praying to God for me, my parents get blessings every day and my father's relatives have given money for my medicines ...

Yohlua's invocation of God's forgiveness stands out because he was the only male respondent to strongly articulate the need to rely heavily on God as a source of succor. Yohlua was also the most discriminated against of our respondents. The only other respondent who spoke of relying mostly on God was a woman who was very ill, and had experienced similar levels of discrimination and ostracism as a consequence of her physical appearance.[5]

---

5   See the case study 'Tina' in Butt (2014).

Yohlua expresses extreme shame. He brings shame not only to himself but to his family, what Davies (2014) calls 'kinships of shame', where feelings of not living up to moral standards extend out to affect the moral evaluation of close kin as well.

> I always ask myself why do people talk like that. Will I die or not. Only God knows, I give myself to God only. Then I think it was because I behaved badly. But then I feel very ashamed because all the people of the villages of Waliloa and Dieplowan know and they have all rejected me. I feel guilty because everyone around here also rejects my father so I feel even more guilty. I feel even more ashamed. My shame is not just about me, it includes my parents and my family who also feel shame. We can't walk free because everyone sees us and avoids us so we constantly feel truly ashamed.

In Yohlua's case, extreme shunning and his failure to get a university education appear to exacerbate his shame and by extension that of his family. Because of the family's total ostracism by religious and cultural communities, they are unable to address the shame and provide closure, an act Davies (n.d.; see also Becker 1997) identifies as critical to negating the regulatory effects of kin-wide shame in other parts of Indonesia. Yohlua is also experiencing what Lindquist (2009: 12) describes as a lack of closure common to Indonesian migrants, where the failure to achieve what family and community expect exacerbates feelings of anxiety and uncertainty. Compounded by a poorly organised HIV care system, Yohlua's needs are not being met because he no longer has the acute understanding of local dynamics so as to be able to protect himself and his family, to prevent church leaders from disclosing his case, or to negotiate safe and quiet places where he might live in peace. The only closure available to Yohlua is through a God that is 'not blind' and that will 'help' when no others will, which, I suggest, is a thin and unsatisfactory compensation for what he really wants, which is community acceptance. For Yohlua, living in HIV-land is not about the drugs and the technologies of treatment taking over, but rather about coping with the consequences of partial, incomplete care for *ODHA* that only offers medications in some contexts, and that does not take social contexts and considerations into account except in the most superficial ways (see also Zhou 2007). For Yohlua, living in HIV-land means that shunning and ostracism is absolute. His story highlights his longing for an unattainable return to normalcy, not just to have medications that work but also to be free to be mobile, to return to the village, to be able to pray to God in church together with his community rather than alone with his parents, and to revel in forgiveness, acceptance and inclusion.

Discussion

This paper has explored the impact of mobile flows of people, technologies and viruses on how highlands Papuan HIV-positive men respond to their diagnosis. The stories of Yohlua and his fellow *ODHA* signal the anxieties and challenges men face as they suffer through the consequences of a diagnosis that, for most Papuans, is still a death sentence. Most men we interviewed strive for belonging through retaining social roles, exploring local healing alternatives and evading stigma through secrecy and silence. Anxieties typically identified with Melanesian men, such as around gender and masculinity, do not surface in these accounts (see Knauft 1997). Instead, *ODHA* stories tell us mobility and migration are sites of anxiety, and mobility affects what these men experience and how they understand their current situation. *ODHA* do not look to former regional enemies from times of tribal warfare to explain the transmission of HIV, as non-infected Papuans regularly do (Butt 2008). Instead, *ODHA* look to the women who embody the threat of immigration into the province, and they attribute the virus to them. The enmity Yohlua experienced was that directed at an outsider, someone whose return to the home community set in motion resentment and retribution perhaps for the wider project of having left, of having sought an education elsewhere, or of implicitly challenging some of the social norms of highlands life. Through *ODHA* accounts of personal suffering we can gauge some of the wider issues exacerbated by migration and mobility.

The narratives also tell us how difficult it is for these men to build a life of continuities, to return somehow to something approaching normal. Instead, living in HIV-land forces on the one hand an identity as an *ODHA* that requires secrecy and deception as an everyday feature of life. On the other hand, most *ODHA* we interviewed (as well as the many who evade all forms of treatment altogether and who we were not able to recruit to this study) are denied regular access to viable medications, and the support necessary to remain on them, which might allow for some semblance of normalcy to develop. The political conditions whereby endemic racism and colonial mentalities make their way into health care regimens exacerbate the challenges of getting on drugs and staying on them. Stigma and its vicious effects clearly are partly to blame. However, many respondents do not rely on ART because they cannot. They are victims of the triage logic of the international AIDS 'juggernaut' (Nguyen 2010) that sets up a difficult and demanding drug regimen in remote locales and then fails to provide the full armature of services required for those drugs to be readily available and effective. The triage which is required in order to get drugs out into remote places like Papua means that some people are left out, while those who wish to belong have to aggressively earn their place by strict conformity, tight network management, the strategic deployment of affluence, and otherwise being savvy about the scope of social networks and opportunities available. Thus the Papuan context supports Fassin's (2007) claim that rather than a normalising, equalising effect, HIV treatments maintain and exacerbate inequalities, and help keep alive the ruptures in the fabric of community.

What these stories ultimately suggest is that fault lines are etched deeply for Papuan men. All the men we interviewed were mobile, travelling within Papua or beyond it, and in their mobility, they have the chance to construct and reconstruct identities and opportunities with a degree of self-consciousness not always available to those who remain put (Williams 2007). But as Lindquist (2009) so carefully documents for other parts of Indonesia, opportunities are not always forthcoming: many mobile aspirants return home empty-handed, the lure of middle-class status unattained. Opportunities are even less readily available for the return Papuan HIV-positive migrant, who adhered to expectations and followed opportunity, and yet who self-consciously returns home requiring care and compassion. Stalwart community networks such as church congregations, and respected public figures such as religious leaders turn out not to be reliable sources of support and forgiveness. The HIV-positive person is compelled to secrecy in these conditions, and for some, HIV also forces a re-envisioning of relations with God. Upon his return the mobile HIV-positive man finds that the mechanisms of discrimination within the nation get replicated in the machinery of HIV health care. Mobility and opportunity have resulted in his relative immobility – he is forced to stay put in order to access care, yet he is unable to strengthen his social relations and expand his networks because, ultimately, the mechanisms of social control within the home community continue to privilege those who have sufficient local cultural knowledge to make it through.

References

Becker, Gay 1997. *Disrupted Lives: How People Create Meaning in a Chaotic World*. Berkeley: University of California Press.

Boellstorff, Tom 2009. 'Nuri's Testimony: HIV/AIDS in Indonesia and Bare Knowledge'. *American Ethnologist* 36(2): 351–363.

Butt, Leslie 2008. 'Silence Speaks Volumes: Elite Men and HIV in Papua, Indonesia'. In Butt, Leslie and Eves, Richard (eds), *Making Sense of AIDS: Culture, Sexuality, and Power in Melanesia*. Honolulu: University of Hawai'i Press, 116–132.

Butt, Leslie 2011. 'Can You Keep a Secret? Pretences of Confidentiality in HIV/ AIDS Counseling and Treatment in Eastern Indonesia'. *Medical Anthropology* 30(3): 319–338.

Butt, Leslie 2012. 'HIV/AIDS Testing, Treatment and the Sedimentation of Violence in Papua, Indonesia'. *Western Humanities Review* 66(3): 35–57.

Butt, Leslie 2014. 'Sexual Tensions: HIV-positive Women in Papua'. In Bennett, Linda Rae and Davies, Sharyn Graham (eds), *Sex and Sexualities in Contemporary Indonesia: Sexual Politics, Health, Diversity and Representations*. Hoboken: Taylor and Francis, 109–120.

Butt, Leslie, Morin, Jack, Numbery, G., Peyon, I., and Goo, A. 2010. *Stigma and HIV/AIDS in Highlands Papua*. Jayapura, Universitas Cenderawasih: Pusat Studi Kependudukan.

Davies, Sharyn Graham 2014. 'Surveilling Sexuality in Indonesia.' In Bennett, Linda Rae and Davies, Sharyn Graham (eds), *Sex and Sexualities in Contemporary Indonesia: Sexual Politics, Health, Diversity and Representations*. Hoboken: Taylor and Francis, 29–50.

Eves, Richard 2010. 'Masculinity Matters: Men, Gender-based Violence and the AIDS Epidemic in Papua New Guinea'. In Luker, Vicki and Dinnen, Sinclair (eds), *Civic Insecurity: Law, Order and HIV in Papua New Guinea*. Canberra: ANU E Press.

Eves, Richard and Butt, Leslie 2008. 'Introduction: Gender, Sexuality and Power in Melanesia'. In Butt, Leslie and Eves, Richard (eds), *Making Sense of AIDS: Culture, Sexuality, and Power in Melanesia*. Honolulu: University of Hawai'i Press, 1–23.

Farmer, Paul 1997. 'Social Inequalities and Emerging Infectious Diseases'. *Emerging Infectious Diseases* 2(4): 259–269.

Fassin, Didier 2007. *When Bodies Remember: Experiences and Politics of AIDS in South Africa*. Berkeley: University of California Press.

Green, Cris W. 2010. 'Care, support and treatment for PLHIV in Indonesia'. http://spiritia.or.id/art/bacaart.php?artno=2018.

Hardon, Anita and Dilger, Hansjörg 2011. 'Global AIDS Medicines in East African Health Institutions'. *Medical Anthropology* 30(2): 136–157.

Keusch, Gerald T., Wilentz, Joan and Kleinman, Arthur 2006. ,Stigma and Global Health: Developing a Research Agenda'. *The Lancet* 367: 525–527.

Klitzman, Robert and Bayer, Ronald 2003. *Mortal Secrets: Truth and Lies in the Age of AIDS*. Baltimore: Johns Hopkins University Press.

Knauft, Bruce 2011. 'Men, Modernity and Melanesia'. In Lipset, David and Roscoe, Paul (eds), *Echoes of the Tambaran: Masculinity, History and the Subject in the work of Donald F. Tuzin*. Canberra: ANU E Press.

Knauft, Bruce 1997. 'Gender Identity, Political Economy, and Modernity in Melanesia and Amazonia'. *Journal of the Royal Anthropological Institute* 3: 233–259.

Koch, Erin 2011. 'Local Microbiologies of Tuberculosis: Insights from the Republic of Georgia'. *Medical Anthropology* 30(1): 81–101.

Lepani, Katherine 2012. *Islands of Love, Islands of Risk: Culture and HIV in the Trobriands*. Nashville: Vanderbilt University Press.

Lindenbaum, Shirley 2001. 'Kuru, Prions and Human Affairs: Thinking about Epidemics'. *Annual Review of Anthropology* 30: 363–385.

Lindquist, Johan A. 2009. *The Anxieties of Mobility: Migration and Tourism in the Indonesian Borderlands*. Honolulu: University of Hawai'i Press.

Macintyre, Martha 2008. 'Policemen and Thieves, Gunmen, and Drunks: Problems with Men and Problems with Society in Melanesia.' *The Australian Journal of Anthropology* 19: 179–193.

Munro, Jenny and Butt, Leslie 2012. 'Compelling Evidence: Research Methods, HIV/AIDS, and Politics in Papua, Indonesia'. *The Asia Pacific Journal of Anthropology* 13(4): 334–351.

Nguyen, Vinh-Kim 2010. *The Republic of Therapy: Triage and Sovereignty in West Africa's Time of AIDS*. Durham, NC: Duke University Press.

Rees, Susan and Silove, Derrick 2007. 'Speaking Out About Human Rights and Health in West Papua'. *The Lancet* 370: 637–639.

Robins, Steven 2009. 'Foot Soldiers of Global Health: Teaching and Preaching AIDS Science and Modern Medicine on the Frontline'. *Medical Anthropology* 28(1): 81–107.

Sullivan, Noelle 2011. 'Mediating Abundance and Scarcity: Implementing an HIV/AIDS-Targeted Project Within a Government Hospital in Tanzania'. *Medical Anthropology* 30(2): 201–221.

UNDP 2004. *Development, Spatial Mobility, and HIV/AIDS: A Workshop on Interelations and Programmatic Responses*. Bangkok: UNDP and CICRED.

Williams, Catharina Purwani 2007. *Maiden Voyages: Eastern Indonesian Women on the Move*. Singapore: Institute of Southeast Asian Studies.

Wood, Kate and Lambert, Helen 2008. 'Coded Talk, Scripted Omissions: The Micropolitics of AIDS Talk in an Affected Community in South Africa'. *Medical Anthropology Quarterly* 22(3): 213–233.

Zhou, Yanqiu Rachel 2007. '"If You Get AIDS...You Have to Endure it Alone": Understanding the Social Constructions of HIV/AIDS in China'. *Social Science & Medicine* 65: 284–295.

10. Papua as an Islamic Frontier: Preaching in 'the Jungle' and the Multiplicity of Spatio-Temporal Hierarchisations

Martin Slama

This contribution attempts to examine accounts of Papua that perceive the territory as a frontier where borders of nation states, civilising missions, predatory capitalism and violent conflicts converge, and to which images of the stone-age, the primitive, the uncivilised, etc. are so persistently attached. The anthropology of Indonesia has generated particularly rich accounts of frontier regions including valuable theorisations of the concept (e.g. Li 1999; Rutherford 2003; Tsing 2005). This chapter engages with these approaches by understanding Papua not only as a frontier in the sense that has been discussed in the literature so far, but also by exploring decentred, non-Western perspectives. Whereas Engseng Ho (2004) in a seminal piece investigated 'empire through diasporic eyes' and revealed fascinating historic parallels between European colonial empires in the Indian Ocean and the current global empire of the United States, this chapter takes a diasporic perspective on the Papuan frontier –the diasporic eyes belonging to Muslims with a particular trans-regional history. Such as in the case described by Ho (2004), the diaspora in question is formed by Muslims of Arab descent originating from the Hadhramaut, a south-eastern territory of today's Republic of Yemen, who have crossed the waters of the Indian Ocean and the Indonesian archipelago since medieval times (Freitag and Clarence-Smith 1997; Jonge and Kaptain 2002; Ho 2006). Boosted by the opening of the Suez Canal and the advent of steam shipping, their migration to Indonesia reached its height from the middle of the nineteenth to the middle of the 20th century. It substantially decreased after Indonesia's independence due to nationalistic policies and economic uncertainties in the early post-colonial period. Today, Hadhramis form distinct communities in Indonesia and are particularly engaged in trade and Islamic proselytising not only in the country's centres but also on its peripheries (Slama 2011), including Papua.

Investigating the manifold entanglements of Islam and capitalism in the peripheries of the Malay world, Joel Kahn (2012: 26) asserts: 'It was/is in these commercially dynamic "frontier" zones that Muslims – merchants, traders, entrepreneurs, artisans and cash croppers on the one hand; holy men, religious teachers, and missionaries on the other – have played very significant, active and constructive roles since the beginning of the modern era.' Hadhramis exemplify the Muslims to which Kahn refers, especially with regard to their roles in eastern Indonesia where they managed to become persistent players in the local power structure from colonial to present times (Clarence-Smith 1998; Slama 2011). In fact, from the beginning of their diasporic engagements, Hadhramis' eyes did not only spot imperial centres of power but also their marginal frontiers – and their perceptions and intentions clearly differed from Western ones. As a result, travelling with Hadhramis to Papua, as this chapter intends to do, indicates the influential force and, at the same time, the limits of Western notions of the frontier, thereby revealing multiple forms of spatio-temporal hierarchisation. The chapter thus explores Papua as an Islamic frontier based on perspectives that differ and, at the same time, borrow from prior conceptualisations.

How Indonesian frontiers have so far been defined, is aptly summarised by Tania Murray Li (2001: 41): 'In Indonesia, it is the interior of the larger islands and the smaller islands of the eastern part of the archipelago that are usually characterised as culturally distinct frontiers incompletely inscribed by civilization, world religions, and the power of governing regimes.' Li (1999: 16), who draws on her research in upland Central Sulawesi, also speaks of 'frontier zones' that are made accessible by logging roads attracting new migrants with the result of increasing state control over people and resources. Li's discussion thus comprises two aspects of the frontier that are salient in the literature at large: as a (neo)colonial project aimed at 'pushing back the frontier of civilization' as well as 'a metaphor for national development in its material and ideological senses' concerned with 'spatial expansion and delimitation' (Fold and Hirsch 2009: 95).

Inspired by her research in Kalimantan, Anna Tsing (2005: 28) theorises the temporal and spatial dimensions of the frontier that can give rise to imaginaries upon which this chapter – and indeed the whole volume – is focused:

> A frontier is an edge of space and time: a zone of not yet – not yet mapped, not yet regulated. It is a zone of unmapping: even in its planning, a frontier is imagined as unplanned. Frontiers aren't just discovered at the edge, they are projects in making geographical and temporal experience. Frontiers make wildness, entangling visions and vines and violence; their wildness is *both* material and imaginative. This wildness reaches backward as well as forward in time, bringing old forms of savagery to life in the contemporary landscape. Frontiers energize old fantasies, even as they embody their impossibilities.

One of these imaginaries, as McCarthy and Cramb (2009: 113–114) note, concerns the alleged 'backwardness' of those who inhabit the frontier being contrasted with modern agricultural techniques in the case of oil palm expansion, of which Papua is a major target area.

Being associated with the stone-age, Papua occupies a special place in these imaginaries by exemplifying the most extreme form of backwardness in evolutionist/developmental discourse as well as in accounts of wilderness in Western travel writing. Rupert Stasch (2011: 7; see also Stasch in this volume) examined the latter discourse that sensationally depicts Papua as 'one of the last great wilderness areas in the world', 'one of the earth's last true frontiers' or as 'the final frontier in an ever-shrinking world'. As examined in the introduction to this volume in more detail, such discourses display a hierarchy of primitivisation and thus a hierarchy of frontiers relegating Papua to the lowest civilizational and spatio-temporal level.

Obviously, such accounts of Papua, which heavily resonate within Indonesia, stand in sharp contrast to how many Papuans appropriate 'civilization' and imagine themselves in the world – and to how Islam constitutes frontiers (as we will see below). Danilyn Rutherford's (2003: 19) study of Biak notions of the foreign recognises 'an ideology that … turned what is foreign into a source of agency and an object of desire'. This is particularly expressed in the myth of Koreri, which Rutherford reads 'as a utopia: an imagined state of pleasure and perfection' (ibid. 25) 'evoking frontiers that are not only spatial but also conceptual' such as between Biak and Indonesia (ibid. 26). The myth climaxes in a millennial return of a messiah-like figure called Manermakeri indicating the advent of a paradisiacal condition 'when the foreign and the local converge' and frontiers collapse (Rutherford 2003: 26). Furthermore, Koreri also inspired reinterpretations of Christian narratives – and Islamic ones (as we will see below): 'Koreri prophets claimed to have discerned the Bible's secret significance: it was a rendering of Biak myth. Jesus Christ was really Manermakeri' (Rutherford 2012: 157–158). By relocating the Bible's central figure to Papua, this belief in a 'Papua Jesus' heavily undermines the evolutionist logic of the stone-age image. It turns Papua into the source of a 'world religion' rather than into a territory of exemplary backwardness. Similarly, among the Yali in the eastern highlands of Papua, Eben Kirksey (2012: 8–10) recorded a narrative about the beginning of time when 'whites' and 'blacks' lived happily together and all goods from electric generators to rice were available in abundance in Papua. But then the whites disappeared into a hole in the earth taking with them all the goods. Being able to seize foreign power, reveal foreign power's Papuan origin, or show that Papua was already part of a modern world (as in the Yali case), these examples attest to rich Papuan discourses that run counter to images of Papua as a wild, deficient, yet-to-be developed stone-age frontier (see also Timmer in this volume).

However, the stone-age is only one notion in the Western repertoire of spatio-temporal hierarchisation. Since this chapter is occupied with Islamic ways of seeing peripheral regions, one should not pass over the fact that the Islamic world itself became subject to Western othering that in some cases is particularly built around imaginaries of a frontier between the 'orient' and the 'occident' (Gingrich 2010). In the course of orientalist perceptions that rest upon dynamics of positive and negative stereotyping (Baumann 2004), Muslim societies are often equated with the Middle Ages and thus also relegated back in time; or they are kept at a 'distance' in spatial terms (Heiss and Feichtinger 2013). Long before the emergence of modern European discourses of temporal and spatial degradation, however, Muslims have developed their own concepts of the frontier. Let me thus refer to notions of the frontier as they can be deduced from the rich sources of Islamic scholarship, after which I will ask to what extent Islamic perspectives challenge imaginaries of the frontier, as discussed so far, and how these perspectives attest to the multiplicity of spatio-temporal hierarchisations that one can find in Indonesia today.

Islamic frontier notions

In the 8th century CE, Abu Hanifa, after whom the Hanafi school of law was named, introduced the term *Dar al-Islam*, 'house of Islam' or 'abode of Islam', for territories that were under Islamic rule. The lands reigned over by Muslim leaders also became known under its synonym *Dar as-Salam* or 'house of peace'. Marking the borders of the Islamic world, *Dar as-Salam* was used to characterise Muslim realms at the peripheries of the Islamic world such as Daressalam in East Africa or Brunei Darussalam and Aceh Darussalam in Southeast Asia (see also Ahmad 1976). The territories bordering *Dar as-Salam* are called *Dar al-Harb* or 'House of War', 'whose leaders are called upon to convert to Islam', as the Oxford Dictionary of Islam explains; and when they 'accept Islam, the territory becomes part of dar al-Islam, where Islamic law prevails'.[1]

Yet apart from this territorial definition of a frontier, another prominent concept in Islamic thought illustrates a notion of frontier defined not by space but by time. Whereas the distinction between *Dar as-Salam* and *Dar al-Harb* was introduced by scholars of jurisprudence in medieval times, the *jahiliyyah* – literally 'ignorance' – is mentioned in the Qur'an, referring to pre-Islamic Arabia as an age of idolatry when ignorance of divine guidance prevailed. In the 20th century the concept was revived by various Muslim thinkers, most notably by the Egyptian Muslim Brotherhood intellectual Sayyid Qutb, who saw a reappearance of *jahiliyyah* in many Muslim countries as a result of the lack of observance of Islamic law. This view entails a considerable reinterpretation of the concept, since 'it means neither a particular period in time, before or after Islam, nor a particular place, race or state or society. It is, rather, a condition of

---

1   The Oxford Dictionary of Islam, see: http://www.oxfordislamicstudies.com/article/opr/t125/e490.

any time and place where Allah is not held to be the highest governmental and legal authority' (Khatab 2006: 3). This extension of the concept to other times and places than pre-Islamic Arabia makes it also relevant for contemporary Islamic discourses in Indonesia, as we will see. However, 20th-century reinterpretations of the concept, as will also become clear below, do not necessarily lead to the dissolution of the temporal hierarchy between an un-Islamic and a fully implemented Islamic order.

Throughout Islamic history one finds influential figures exploring the frontiers of the Islamic world pointing to the 'ever-changing, porous boundaries' that form the social background of a legal concept that, as Travis Zadeh (2011: 87) emphasises, rests upon a clear demarcation between 'two realms, divided between the lands of peace and lands of war, [that] stand as mirror images of each other'. Before Hadhramis became major players in the Indian Ocean it was Ibn Batutta (1304–1386 or 1377) who in some instances crossed these porous boundaries and travelled to places that later also became intersections of Hadhrami networks. Ross Dunn (2005: 6–7) indicates how the frontiers of the Islamic world affected the routes of Muslim travellers like Ibn Batutta and his successors:

> Ibn Batutta … spent most of his travelling career within the cultural boundaries of what Muslims called the Dar al-Islam, or Abode of Islam. This expression embraced the lands where Muslims predominated in the population, or at least where Muslim kings or princes ruled over non-Muslim majorities and where in consequence the *shari'a*, or Sacred Law, of Islam was presumably the foundation of the social order. In that sense Islamic civilization extended from the Atlantic cost of West Africa to Southeast Asia.

Yet Dunn (ibid.) also mentions those Muslims who formed communities outside this continent-spanning zone of Islam: 'Moreover, important minority communities of Muslims inhabited cities and towns in regions such as China, Spain, and tropical West Africa that were beyond the frontiers of the Dar al-Islam.' As indicated above, Ibn Batutta visited some of these Muslim communities outside the *Dar al-Islam* – and he did particularly so in East and Southeast Asia, as the following quote from his *Rihla* (travelogue) confirms: 'I then proceeded for one and twenty days through his [a Muslim ruler's] dominions, after which we arrived at the city of Mul Java, which is the first part of the territories of the infidels' (Lee 2004 [1829]: 201).[2]

---

2   I am grateful to my colleague Johann Heiss (Institute for Social Anthropology at the Austrian Academy of Sciences) who discussed with me Ibn Batutta's account which he can read in the original Arabic version. There Ibn Batutta uses the phrase 'bilad al-kuffar' translated as 'territories of the infidels' for the *Dar al-Harb*. Johann Heiss also informed me that, contrary to what the translator Rev. Samuel Lee believed in 1829, the

Similar to Ibn Batutta, Hadhramis were also producers of texts that comprised itineraries and travelogues of their frontier explorations (Alatas 2005). Ho (2006: 55) has analysed these accounts by pointing to the central role they occupied in the formation of the Hadhrami diaspora:

> For the itineraries that feature so prominently as a basic genre element within these accounts created effects that go beyond the ambitions of positivist historical reconstruction. In telling of the travels of various figures, they created a discourse of frontiers that ultimately transformed landscapes. The discursive effect ... was to transform a place from a destination to an origin.

So when Hadhrami 'travelers open up frontier lands' (ibid.) they transformed those lands through settling and establishing concrete manifestations of Islam such as mosques and graves. And they preferably did so among populations that they saw as having not yet or not yet sufficiently embraced Islam. This brings us to another important difference between Western and Islamic concepts of the frontier, as revealed by Ho (ibid.):

> Unlike the 19th-century American idea of Manifest Destiny, frontiers in Hadhrami sayyid[3] discourses of mobility are not devoid of people but full of them. Newcomers such as the sayyids found places for themselves – as educators – in lands that were already full. This theme has been a constant one throughout the Hadrami diaspora around the Indian Ocean, beginning with Hadramawt itself in the early days.

By travelling along and sometimes transcending the boundaries of the *Dar al-Islam*, Hadhramis were not looking for land but for people. Moreover, their approach suggests that they regarded those they came across as contemporaries and not as representatives of past times. Hierarchy was constructed through stressing noble descent, Islamic knowledge and practice, and not through attaching oneself to a supposedly superior age. In addition to that, reciprocal, more egalitarian relations were established through trade. And when they travelled to 'lands that were already full', for the male Hadhrami migrants[4] this meant that they were also full of women, i.e. of potential marriage partners. These three factors – trade, proselytisation and marriage – can also be discerned in Hadhramis' roles in the Islamisation of parts of Papua, as the next paragraphs give attention to the question of how Papua became an Islamic frontier in the first place.

---

current state of research doubts that Ibn Batutta really visited Java. Rather, it is much more likely that 'the city of Mul Java' refers to a place in Sumatra, an island which was at that time largely inhabited by non-Muslims, whereas the vast majority of its population today adheres to Islam.

3 *Sayyid* (pl. *sada*) is a title for descendants of the Prophet Muhammad.

4 Hadhrami travellers and migrants were almost exclusively men, as Hadhrami society knows heavy restrictions on female mobility (Slama 2012).

Papua as an Islamic frontier

The first contacts between Papuans and Muslim traders must have occurred in the 15th century or even earlier, though this is difficult to determine due to the lack of historical evidence. However, it is clear that in the 17th century two regions in eastern Indonesia became crucial for the spread of Islam to the coastal parts of Papua, i.e. the northern Moluccas with its four sultanates (Ternate, Tidore, Bacan and Jailolo), among which Tidore was most significant with regard to Papua, and eastern Seram and its adjunct Geser-Gorom archipelago from where Muslim traders developed exclusive economic ties with Papuans of the Bird's Head and Bomberai peninsulas. The sultanate of Tidore exemplifies the *Dar as-Salam/Dar al-Harb* frontier pattern of Islamic rulers developing relations with their non-Islamic neighbours eventually resulting in the conversion of the latter. In the 17th century, Tidore increasingly drew its attention towards Papua when the Dutch East India Company (VOC) largely took over its lucrative spice trade. As a sort of compensation, Tidore 'was granted the exclusive right to trade with the "Papuan Islands"' (Warnk 2010: 114). This was a tributary trade in natural goods and slaves, asserting Tidorese authority in the waters east of Halmahera and along the coast of the Bird's Head Peninsula. As a result, as Holger Warnk (ibid. 129) concludes, 'by the mid-17th century the first chiefs in the Raja Ampat Islands had probably been converted to Islam', and, Dutch sources stated, 'in 1705 ... the leaders of Waigeo, Misol and Salawati were Muslims' (ibid. 116).

These Tidore-Raja Ampat ties became particularly pronounced during the revolt of Prince Nuku at the end of the 18th century, when Prince Nuku rebelled against the Dutch and their policy to degrade Tidore to the status of vassalage. He mobilised forces from Raja Ampat, Seram and Halmahera, and diplomatically approached the British. In the course of the conflict, as Muridan Widjojo (2009: 57) has revealed, Nuku was proclaimed 'Sultan Papua and Seram' and called himself 'King of Papua' in a letter to the Dutch. From this strategy of turning tributary trade relations into political support and symbolic power, Widjojo (2009: 215) draws fascinating historical parallels: 'For centuries local ritual and economic ties bound Maluku to Papua. The irony of Nuku's career is that so far nobody has successfully pointed out that, thanks to this Papuan connection, he was able to beat the Dutch at their own game [of playing off powers against each other]. He did so skillfully making use of the English just as the Soekarno Government made use of the United States in 1962 and the United Nations in 1963.'

In the frontier zone of eastern Seram and Geser-Gorom trade with the Papuans from the Bird's Head and Bomberai peninsulas, where conversions to Islam were reported for the mid-17th century (Warnk 2010: 115), were not imbued with sultan-like authority. 'The Serammers were concerned mostly with trading access rather than symbolic power ... they traded rather than raided', as Roy

Ellen (2003: 122) emphasised in his illuminating study of their trading network, which is based on an institution called *sosolot*: 'bays and anchorages in which one polity maintained a recognised monopoly in trade' (ibid. 126). East Seram and Geser-Gorom polities had thus exclusive access to particular trade domains that became increasingly Islamic due to these connections that were further fostered by inter-marriages. Whereas first mosques in the region are confirmed for the 1870s (Warnk 2010: 125), for the 1820s a Dutch expedition reported that the Muslims in the region 'had no mosques or prayer houses and did not fast, they were able to recite the first sura, bury their deceased according to Muslim customs, and did not eat pork or turtle' (ibid. 120). This account of only partial observance of Islamic provisions indicates the ambivalent status of these Islamic pockets of Papua with regard to whether they can be regarded as part of the *Dar al-Islam*, a theme that we will encounter also in today's perceptions of the region.

The sultanate of Tidore also maintained tributary trade relations along the northern coast of Papua, particularly with Papuans of the northern Bird's Head, Biak-Numfor and the Cenderawasih Bay. When Biak seafarers paid homage to the sultan at his court, as Rutherford (2003: 17) has pointed out, they 'claimed that they were absorbing *barak*, the Biak version of the Arabic word for the magical power that pervaded the sultan's person and surroundings'. One can hardly say to what extent these relations also resulted in the conversion of Papuans to Islam, since today the Papuan population of these regions is overwhelmingly Christian. But at least some chiefs converted. According to Warnk (2010: 122), there is evidence for Papuan Muslims in Dorey Bay, close to where Manokwari is now located, before 1850. Ironically, when the German missionaries Ottow and Geissler held their first Christian services in Dore in 1855 in the Malay language, they 'were attended by several local Muslim chiefs who spoke Malay fairly well' (ibid. 124). So what is today celebrated as the coming of Christianity to Papua, also reflected in the adoption of the by-name 'gospel city' (*kota injil*) by Manokwari in post-Suharto Indonesia, was not a coming to a monotheistically 'empty land', but rather to an Islamic frontier where Papuan and Islamic visions had already met before. This earlier religious encounter might have also contributed to the fact that the efforts of Ottow and Geissler were not met with much success, and 'it was not until after 1900 that mass conversions to Christianity occurred in the Cendrawasih Bay and Biak region' (ibid.). This was also the time when Christianity was introduced in Raja Ampat and the Bird's Head and Bomberai peninsulas, the two major regions where Islam has gained a foothold among Papuans. For the latter, Ellen (2003: 144) asserts that with 'the establishment of a Dutch post in Fak-fak in 1898, the influence of Seram Laut traders and Islam declined, and that of Christian missions and the Chinese grew'. However, trade between the Serammers and Papuans went on and only substantially declined after Indonesia's independence when trade between the newly established republic and Netherlands New Guinea was not allowed (see Kaartinen 2010: 59).

With regard to Hadhrami Arabs, as William Clarence-Smith (1998: 43) has argued, they were particularly strong in trade in the Moluccas 'in the third quarter of the nineteenth century, at a time when neither Chinese nor European competitors showed much interest in these distant marches of the Dutch empire' (see also Spyer 2000: 12). Their presence can be understood as a consequence of the overall increase of Hadhrami migration to Southeast Asia fuelled by the opening of the Suez Canal in 1869 and the introduction of steam shipping in the Indian Ocean. From the Moluccas some of them moved to Papua. For the turn from the 19th to the 20th century it is confirmed that Arab traders resided in Kaimana, Fakfak and Kokas (Ellen 2003: 143). Similar to the Serammers, they sometimes took Papuan wives (Warnk 2010: 127). With the Alkatiry and Alhamid as their leading families, Hadhramis had indeed a strong basis among the Muslims in eastern Seram and Geser-Gorom (Ellen 1996, 2003: 253–54). Their influence can be felt until today, especially in the realm of religion, since 'in the Geser-Gorom area we find that families of Arab descent often provide the imam, even if the majority of the population is not ethnically Arab' (Ellen 2003: 265). One of Ellen's Hadhrami interlocutors in Tual who lived for a long time in Geser proudly stated in the 1980s 'that his grandfather was the first to convert Papuans to Islam' (ibid. 238).

Almost 30 years after Ellen's research such narratives are still firmly embedded in Hadhrami family stories in the region. Pak[5] Umar, who is in his fifties, was born and grew up in Seram and resides now in Ambon where he told me of his grandfather who came from the Hadhramaut to the Netherlands East Indies. After a stay in Surabaya his grandfather went to South Sulawesi, then to Ambon and finally to Fakfak, marrying daughters of local leaders (*anak raja*). Especially with regard to Fakfak, he explained that his ancestors contributed to the spread of Islam because 'they married daughters of chiefs that were not yet Muslims; as a consequence, slowly but surely they became Muslims and their people followed them. This was the great way of spreading Islam at that time!'[6] It was Pak Umar's father who married a daughter of a Serammer chief. Being of Arab descent, Pak Umar emphasises his high status in the family of his mother: 'When the chief there [on Seram] wants to do something, he will surely ask me first. There is no difference between us, being of Arab descent, and the local people. Unlike the Chinese, the Japanese or the Dutch who brought their wives with them, we Arabs did not.'[7]

---

5   In Indonesian 'Pak' (short form of 'bapak'), literally 'father', is a respectful form of address for married men.
6   Interview in Ambon, Moluccas, 19 June 2012. All interviews were conducted in Indonesian. All translations are by the author.
7   ibid.

We see here how Hadhramis became highly integrated into the local societies of this Moluccan-Papuan realm without abandoning their Arab identity, which is highlighted through boasting their roles in converting Papuans to Islam. In these accounts, Papua features as a frontier in the sense that it is on the way to becoming, or has already become, part of the *Dar al-Islam*, thanks to the efforts of exemplary Muslims, a status Hadhramis like to claim for themselves. Differing from Western notions of the frontier based on evolutionist/developmentalist discourses, in these accounts, spatio-temporal hierarchies are less pronounced. When Muslim rulers are finally followed by their people, their polities will become part of the *Dar al-Islam* and the 'age of idolatry' immediately ends, regardless of how Papua is perceived from the outside. I want to proceed with examples of such outside perceptions, as they are widespread among Muslims in Indonesia residing west of this zone of close contact and mixing of the Moluccas, the Raja Ampat islands and the Bird's Head and Bomberai peninsulas. An analysis of their discourses will reveal how the frontier status of Papua within the Indonesian nation-state is informed by Islamic views and also how Islamic notions of the frontier can become intertwined with evolutionist/developmentalist ideas. As we will see, one does not have to go too far to the west to encounter such discourses.

'As far as Papua' – Al-Khairaat's frontier and the light of the Prophet

When I did research about eastern Indonesia's biggest Islamic organisation, called Al-Khairaat, which is particularly strong in central and northern Sulawesi and to a certain extent also in the northern Moluccas, 'Papua' frequently popped up in my conversations, i.e. when my interlocutors referred to the high mobility of the organisation's founding father. Al-Khairaat was established in Palu, Central Sulawesi, by Sayyid Idrus Al-Jufri, who was born in the Hadhramaut. In 1925, at the age 36, he migrated to the then Netherlands East Indies. After moving from place to place along the networks of the Hadhrami diaspora in Java and eastern Indonesia, in 1930 he finally settled in Palu where he established the Madrasah Al-Khairaat. Nevertheless, Sayyid Idrus' life was still characterised by a high degree of mobility. He began to build his translocal networks within north-eastern Indonesia by inviting young boys of Hadhrami or local descent to accompany him back to Palu, giving them the opportunity to enroll in the Al-Khairaat school (Azra 2000). These graduates of Al-Khairaat contributed considerably to the spread of the organisation by opening schools in their hometowns modelled after the Palu example. What also informed Sayyid Idrus' popularity was his noble ancestry, since his genealogy goes back to the Prophet Muhammad, which is also indicated by bearing the title *sayyid* (Slama 2011).

Among Al-Khairaat members, the journeys of Sayyid Idrus are considered legendary. I was told that Sayyid Idrus explored villages so remote that no Al-Khairaat member ever visited them again. In these narratives Papua is mentioned frequently. In order to emphasise the achievements of Sayyid Idrus Al-Khairaat members like to employ the phrase that he went 'as far as Papua' (*sampai di Papua*) or 'as far as Irian' (as Papua was called until the end of Suharto's reign). They also like to point out that Al-Khairaat currently runs two branches in Papua, one near Jayapura and one close to Manokwari.

In my conversations with Muslims active in Al-Khairaat we discussed why Sayyid Idrus established his organisation in this remote eastern Indonesian region. It was Ibu[8] Achmisah, the vice chairwoman of the women's division of Al-Khairaat, Wanita Islam Al-Khairaat, who explained that before Sayyid Idrus' arrival the people in Palu 'had no religion' (*tidak punya agama*). Her friend, also an active member of Wanita Islam Al-Khairaat, added that back then 'there was still *jahiliyyah* time' (*masih ada jaman jahiliyyahnya*). 'Yes there was,' the vice chairwoman continued, 'well, there was already Islam, but there was no implementation of the sharia. People were drunk, they gambled. But then Sayyid Idrus settled [in Palu] ... Thank God! From there he spread his wings as far as Irian, as far as Ternate, Ambon, and North Sulawesi.'[9] These accounts by Al-Khairaat members portray the efforts of Sayyid Idrus and his organisation as an attempt to push back the frontier in space and time. Highly mobile ways of proselytising and the opening of Islamic schools in remote areas are aimed at incorporating new territories, eastern Indonesia and especially Papua, into the *Dar al-Islam*, simultaneously leaving behind the *jahiliyyah*. In contrast to the accounts by Hadramis from the Moluccas, who have direct kin and trade relations with Papuans, the discourses I encountered in Sulawesi feature a particular spatial hierarchy with Papua on its furthest and, consequently, lowest end.

Yet, similar to the Moluccas, on Sulawesi one can also find discourses that highlight marriage as a legitimate way to make the Papuan frontier more Islamic. One of my interlocutors, Pak Husein, also a *sayyid* and active Al-Khairaat member, recalled a distant relative of his who had migrated to Papua. He told me that the Prophet Muhammad himself married a woman of dark skin, a rich, 60-year-old widow of high influence, with the motive that the people would follow her in becoming Muslims, which they eventually did. He further pointed out: 'Just like the Prophet we like the Irian people in order that they can become Muslims faster.'[10] And he reminded me: 'The Prophet said that wherever his descendants will live, God willing, there will be light. That means that we don't have to worry in the jungle of Irian. As long as we behave properly, God

---

8   In Indonesian 'Ibu', literally 'mother', is a respectful form of address for married women.
9   Interview in Palu, Central Sulawesi, 8 December 2007.
10   Interview in Tondano, North Sulawesi, 13 April 2008.

willing, there will be light.'[11] By employing the Sufi concept of 'the light of the Prophet' that is said to be handed down from generation to generation among his descendants, Hadhramis can, in this view, even illuminate what is imagined as the dark jungle of Papua. Equating Papua with the jungle and darkness, including dark skin, alludes to the *jahiliyyah* in pre-Islamic Arabia that has been enlightened by the Prophet and, when transferred to other times and places, can have similar effects. Dark jungle and dark skin also evokes Western evolutionist concepts in which the jungle stands for wilderness, where only people of the lowest level of human development live, such as the ostensible Papuan stone-agers.[12] However, the primary concern of Hadhramis from eastern Indonesia is not to advance Papuans' standard of living in a developmentalist fashion, but to marry them and teach them proper behaviour according to Islamic law. In Papua, overcoming the *jahiliyyah* thus means to overcome the darkness of the jungle through prophetic radiance. Although they are deeply entrenched in Islamic theology, these accounts indicate at least a partial convergence of Islamic and evolutionist-cum-developmentalist notions of the frontier where 'the jungle' and the *jahiliyyah* show semantic affinities and where Papua is seen as the furthest-cum-wildest territory that can be reached by Indonesian Hadhramis.

Moving further west to Indonesia's capital Jakarta, but remaining within the networks of the Hadhrami diaspora, reveals further insights into Islamic notions of the Papuan frontier. Such a step evinces aspects of spatio-temporal hierarchisations that again point to entanglements of Islamic and evolutionist/developmentalist notions of the frontier, albeit not in the same variations we have encountered so far.

'No signal': A Jakartan preacher's frontier

In post-Suharto Indonesia, other bearers of the light of the Prophet discovered Papua, most notably Habib[13] Munzir Al-Musawa, a Hadhrami *sayyid* and founder of the Majelis Rasulullah, which is the biggest prayer association in Indonesia's capital, attracting thousands of Muslims to their regular meetings. After the breakdown of the communist regime in South Yemen in 1989, Habib Munzir belonged to the first group of young Indonesian Hadhramis who were given the opportunity to study in the Hadhramaut. He went to the, at that time,

---

11   ibid.

12   In Indonesia, with regard to the ambiguous zone of the forest, evolutionist perceptions resonate with and have probably reinforced indigenous ones; e.g. Dove (1985: 19) asserts for Java: 'Just as cleared land became associated with the rise of the Javanese states and their cultures, so too did the forest come to be associated with uncivilized, uncontrollable, and fearful forces.'

13   'Habib' (literally 'the beloved') is a form of address for descendants of the Prophet Muhammad popular among Hadhramis and their followers.

newly founded and, in the meantime, famous Darul Mustafa boarding school run by Habib Umar bin Hafiz bin Sheikh Abubakar, the leading Sufi figure in the Hadhramaut who is also very popular among diaspora Hadhramis (Alatas 2010). Habib Munzir married a woman from the Hadhramaut, also of Hadhrami *sada* descent, and brought her to Indonesia where she started to preach among women in Jakarta (Nisa 2012). Most importantly in the context of this chapter, Habib Munzir visited Papua several times, in 2007, 2008 and 2010. All his journeys were covered by the popular bi-weekly Islamic magazine Al-Kisah, which is also owned by a Hadhrami *sayyid*.[14] The articles feature diary entries of Habib Munzir as well as direct quotations of what he said with the effect that the reader feels informed about how Habib Munzir personally experienced Papua — through his diasporic Hadhrami and at the same time Indonesian-Jakartan eyes.

Habib Munzir set foot in Papua for the first time on 9 May 2007 in Manokwari where he was welcomed by Ahmad Baihaqi, a preacher and Majelis Rasulullah activist from Jakarta who had expanded his activities to Papua. He was brought to the 'only Muslim hotel in Manokwari', as Habib Munzir laments in his diary, published by Al-Kisah shortly after his visit. In the evening he preached at the mosque of the Indonesian navy where a *maulid*, a ritual celebrating the birth of the Prophet Muhammad, was staged. Around 700 Muslims attended the event, which Habib Munzir found remarkable for such a 'remote town' (*kota terpencil*). The next day, Habib Munzir learned about the difficulties Muslims in Manokwari face if they want to build a mosque, although in Habib Munzir's perception the ratio between Muslims and Christians is already 'fifty-fifty' (English in original). Alluding to the so-called *perda injil*, or Christian by-laws, drafts of which had been discussed in Manokwari prior to Habib Munzir's visit, he expressed his hope that in the future female Muslims could continue to freely wear the veil.[15]

On that second day of his visit, Habib Munzir travelled to an Islamic boarding school located about 65 kilometres outside Manokwari where he found it difficult to find a signal for his mobile phone or to connect his laptop to the internet. This is illustrated with a picture of Habib Munzir sitting on the floor with his laptop put in front of him, holding his mobile phone in his left hand. The caption of this picture reads: 'Habib Munzir Al-Musawa opens his laptop. There is no signal.' From the boarding school, he continued his journey to a 'very remote Muslim area' (*wilayah Muslim yang sangat terpencil*). When they returned to Manokwari in the night, 'the street was very dark and quiet' (*jalanan gelap dan*

---

14 See: Al-Kisah No. 12/4 – 17 Juni 2007, 50–53; Al-Kisah No. 23/3 – 16 Nov. 2008, 38–46; Al-Kisah No. 04/22 Feb – 7 Maret 2010, 52–55; Al-Kisah No. 05/8 – 21 Maret 2010, 70–71; Al-Kisah No. 06/22 Maret – 4 April 2010, 50–53.

15 Al-Kisah No. 12/4 – 17 Juni 2007, 50-51. Similar to the so-called *perda syariah* in other parts of Indonesia, these by-laws have potentially discriminating consequences for those who do not belong to the local religious majority. The draft of the Manokwari by-laws has been heatedly discussed in Papua and in Indonesia at large (ICG 2008). See also the chapters of Myrttinen and Timmer in this volume.

sepi) and Habib Munzir asked his local companions whether this area would be dangerous at night. They explained that the 'Irianese' do not go out after sunset because they believe in a witch that kills people and eats their entrails at night. In consideration of the fact that his journey went according to plan, Habib Munzir expressed his gratitude to his local followers who guarded him and slept in front of his room at night. On the third day, Habib Munzir flew back to Jakarta.[16]

Habib Munzir's second trip in October 2008 also brought him to Manokwari. But this time he travelled further away from the city, 'penetrating the interior of Papua' (*menembus pedalaman Papua*), as the title of the story in Al-Kisah reads, suggesting that Habib Munzir is exploring the real frontier, 'the interior', where he 'has to fight to advance on the muddy roads in the thick jungle' (*berjuang menembus jalan berlumpur di tengah hutan lebat*). The readers of Al-Kisah further learn that Habib Munzir went into the interior to introduce the Islamic confession of faith and that he proselytises not only in 'comfortable areas' (*daerah yang nyaman*) but 'reaches all corners' (*hingga seluruh pelosok*). This narrative is supported by a picture on the first page of the Al-Kisah article depicting Habib Munzir in his long white Arab dress and white turban among Papuans in partly traditional attire with their chests naked, some of them holding bows and arrows. Upon his arrival in Manokwari, he was again welcomed by Ahmad Baihaqi. Ransiki, located about 100 kilometres south of Manokwari, was the first destination of their trip. Baihaqi has good relations to the place since from there he brought young Papuan Muslims to Jakarta to teach them Islam. On the way, Habib Munzir 'was more crying than he was speaking' (*lebih banyak menangis daripada bicara*) because during the three-hour journey he could not spot any Muslims. Instead, he saw 'huge religious buildings of adherents of another religion' (*bangunan besar tempat ibadah penganut agama lain*). Only shortly before Ransiki did he see young men on motorbikes waving the flag of the Majelis Rasulullah, some of them 'indigenous people' (*penduduk asli*), wearing the jackets of the Majelis Rasulullah. He could hardly believe what he saw: Papuan Muslims wearing the *peci putih* (a white cap identified with Islam in Indonesia) and waving the flag of the Majelis Rasulullah in this 'remote area' (*wilayah terpencil*). After Habib Munzir addressed the Muslims of Ransiki, they continued their journey to Bintuni.[17]

On their long way to Bintuni, road conditions deteriorated. The Land Cruiser rented by Habib Munzir's group could hardly get through the mud that is '50cm or more' deep. These road conditions and the 'wild' environment are also illustrated by pictures of which the captions read: 'The car is stuck in the mud. The struggle to proselytise penetrates the interior' (*Mobil terperosok*

---

16   Al-Kisah No. 12/4 – 17 Juni 2007, 52–53.
17   Al-Kisah No. 23/3 – 16 Nov. 2008, 38–41.

dalam lumpur. Perjuangan dakwah menembus pedalaman) and 'Prayer in the middle of the jungle' (*Shalat di tengah rimba*). At half-past eight in the evening Habib Munzir arrived in Bintuni and checked in at 'the only hotel in the town of Bintuni that has air conditioning' (*satu-satunya hotel di kota Bintuni yang dilengkapi AC*). The next morning, 'hundreds of Muslims' were awaiting Habib Munzir in front of the hotel. Some of them were moved to tears, and explained that they only heard about *habib* from their grandfathers and that Habib Munzir's visit is the first one of a *habib* in 'hundreds of years'. Local figures also emphasised that Islam came to Bintuni in the 16th century but then disappeared. In the mosque a *maulid* was celebrated after which Habib Munzir addressed the Muslims. For lunch Habib Munzir asked for local food and was served *papeda* (porridge made of sago flour) with fish. Back in the hotel Habib Munzir had a meeting with local Muslim figures who told him of a village 'close to the beach' where an old copy of the Qur'an was found and the population 'is Muslim, but they don't know Islam, they don't know the confession of faith anymore. They only know that they are not allowed to eat pork. They think that this is traditional law, whereas this is Islamic law'.[18] The locals thus asked him: 'Where are the preachers from Jakarta? How can we know and learn Islam? Where are the rich people of Jakarta? They send a lot of money to Palestine, Bosnia, Afghanistan, but they forget us, whereas we are Muslims of the same nation as they are, the inhabitants of Jakarta.'[19]

On the way back to Manokwari the road conditions were even worse than the day before and the Land Cruiser had to be freed from the 'claws of the mud' (*cengkeraman lumpur*). On the way they met the father of one of Ahmad Baihaqi's students who 'still follows another religion, but apparently is beginning to show interest in becoming a Muslim' (*masih beragama lain, tapi kelihatannya sudah mulai tertarik masuk Islam*). They also passed a small mosque (*mushalla*) that was funded by 'a businesswoman from Jakarta' who once visited the area in the course of her trade activities. Then Habib Munzir fell asleep and dreamt of a young *habib* who told him that he had proselytised here but had died as a martyr. Habib Munzir felt pity for the young *habib* whose 'grave in the jungle of Irian Jaya nobody knows' (*kuburanya tak dikenali orang di dalam*

---

18 Al-Kisah No. 23/3 – 16 Nov. 2008, 44: 'Mereka muslim tapi tak tahu agama Islam, mereka sudah tidak kenal syahadat. Mereka hanya mengenal satu ajaran, yaitu tak boleh makan babi. Mereka menanggap itu hukum adat, padahal itu hukum Islam.'

19 ibid.: 'Di mana dai-dai dari Jakarta? Lalu dari mana kami akan mengenal dan belajar Islam? Di mana para hartawan dari Jakarta? Para hartawan di Jakarta mengirim dana uang banyak ke Palestina, Bosnia, Afghanistan, tapi melupakan kami … padahal kami muslimin saudara sebangsa dengan mereka, penduduk Jakarta.' This can be read as a Muslim Papuan variety of what Stasch calls (in this volume) 'strategies of self-lowering as a way to elicit relations' in the context of the Korowai.

rimba belantaran Irian Jaya), and he was thinking of leaving Jakarta for Papua to proselytise there, perhaps meeting a similar fate as the young *habib* of his dream. Nevertheless, the next day he flew back to Indonesia's capital.[20]

The third trip of Habib Munzir to Papua in January 2010 was covered by Al-Kisah in three subsequent issues. This time he flew not to Manokwari but to Sorong where Ahmad Baihaqi awaited him. They visited a member of the local parliament, whose father and grandfather built mosques in Sorong. They lamented the current situation that the majority of members of parliament are Christians although Sorong's population shows a Muslim majority. They then left for Teminabuan, about 200 kilometres southeast of Sorong, with a 'Mitsubishi Ranger 4 x 4'. On the way they met no Muslims. Instead, they saw only 'non-Muslim villages' with their 'grand religious buildings'. Under the subheading 'The Beauty of Tolerance' (*Indahnya Toleransi*) the story continues with the appearance of a Catholic nun who asked to hitch a ride to Teminabuan. Habib Munzir allowed her to go with them and the nun sat down on the open loading space at the rear of their car. After a while it started to rain which caused Habib Munzir to salute the nun for her fortitude. At the same time he felt ashamed because he was sitting comfortably inside the car. Consequently, he stopped the car and invited the nun to change positions. Sitting in the rain at the back of the car, Habib Munzir began to reflect about his celebrity life in Indonesia's capital, talking to himself: 'You get spoiled in Jakarta. Thousands of people contend to kiss your hand. They glorify and flatter you. Your struggle of proselytisation is only limited to going up and down the stage while being glorified and flattered. Now you deserve to feel proselytisation like this. This is the field for a preacher of the way of Allah. You are too spoiled. You also have to feel proselytisation like this ... Feel the deliciousness of proselytisation, keep sitting here and bear it, oh Munzir you sinner, idler, and spoiled man!'[21]

When they arrived in Teminabuan, Habib Munzir checked in at a 'basic hotel but already equipped with air conditioning' (*hotel sederhana tapi sudah dilengkapi AC*). Then he paid the driver and showed him on the screen of his smartphone an event of his Majelis Rasulullah at the Monas (national monument) in Jakarta. The driver was impressed by the 'hundreds of thousands' of participants and could hardly believe that the man who led this event stood in front of him.[22] The next morning Habib Munzir rented a boat leaving for Kokoda, located on the south coast of the Bird's Head Peninsula. On the way to Kokoda, Habib Munzir

---

20   Al-Kisah No. 23/3 – 16 Nov. 2008, 44–46.
21   Al-Kisah No. 04/22 Feb – 7 Maret 2010, 55: 'Kau di Jakarta dimanjakan. Ribuan orang berebutan ingin mencium tanganmu. Kau dimuliakan dan disanjung. Perjuangan dakwahmu hanya sebatas naik-turun mimbar dalam kemuliaan dan sanjungan. Sekarang patut kau rasakan dakwah yang seperti ini. Inilah medan seorang dai penyeru ke jalan Allah. Kau terlalu dimanjakan. Kau harus merasakan juga dakwah yang seperti ini ... Rasakan lezatnya dakwah, tetaplah duduk di tempat itu dan bertahan, wahai Munzir pendosa, pemalas, dan manja!'
22   Al-Kisah No. 05/8 – 21 Maret 2010, 70–71.

contemplated 'this remote area. Telephone is not yet available, electricity only in Teminabuan and that only at night. There are no Islamic religious teachers or schools in Teminabuan … [but] strong waves of non-Islamic proselytisation and non-Islamic schools'.[23] Kokoda is introduced as 'the third Islamic region [of Papua] that has been penetrated by Islamic scholars from the Hadhramaut' (*wilayah muslim ketiga yang dimasuki ulama Hadhramaut*) with Fakfak and Babo being mentioned as the other two regions. Hadhramis are credited with building the Masjid Annur, the mosque of the light, in Kokoda, alluding to the light of the Prophet Muhammad. In the article it is said that they stated: 'We ignited the light in Kokoda' (*Kami Taruhkan Cahaya di Kokoda*). But after this initial influence from the Hadhrami descendants of the Prophet Muhammad, the area 'was not contacted anymore' (*tidak disentuh lagi*). This is the reason why the five daily prayers were increasingly not practiced and people only gathered for the Friday prayer. Religious life was only revived by Habib Munzir's companion Ahmad Baihaqi, who had visited Kokoda and brought some young men back to Jakarta to study Islam. So when Habib Munzir arrived in Kokoda, he could see the flag of the Majelis Rasulullah. They stayed in a house that was 'good enough for Kokoda standards, but without electricity, no mobile phone signal, let alone telephone' (*cukup bagus untuk ukuran Kokoda, tapi tidak ada listrik, tidak ada sinyal handphone, apalagi telepon*). After the evening prayer, Habib Munzir gave a sermon at the Masjid Annur, when 'many Muslims prayed for the first time, although they were already old' (*banyak orang Muslim yang baru pertama kali shalat, walau mereka sudah lanjut usia*). When Habib Munzir gave his sermon, the Muslims of Kokoda were 'moved to tears'. After the gathering was over, 'their tears were still running down their cheeks. They were contending to greet me, as it happens in Jakarta'.[24] With this emotional account the last of the articles in Al-Kisah ends.

Habib Munzir's engagement in Papua was well-recognised among Majelis Rasulullah members, as it was published not only in Al-Kisah but also on the organisation's website[25] and on YouTube where one can watch shorter videos of his journeys.[26] When Habib Munzir passed away on 15 September 2013 in Jakarta, just having turned 40, his followers came from many places in Indonesia to pay their last respects. Interviewed by Indonesia's popular news portal *detik. com*, a Majelis Rasulullah member from Banjarmasin, South Kalimantan, stated

---

23   Al-Kisah No. 06/22 Maret – 4 April 2010, 51: '… wilayah yang terpencil ini. Telepon belum masuk, listrik baru di Teminabuan, dan itu pun hanya pada malam hari. Pengajar, seperti ulama, atau pesantren tidak ada di Teminabuan … [tapi] hempasan kekuatan dakwah agama non-muslim dan sekolah-sekolah non-muslim.'
24   Al-Kisah No. 06/22 Maret – 4 April 2010, 53: '… air mata masih mengalir di wajah mereka. Mereka berebutan untuk bersalaman dengan saya, sebagaimana juga terjadi di Jakarta.'
25   http://www.majelisrasulullah.org/. See also Warta (2011: 325–329) who interprets the web coverage of Habib Munzir's Papua tours as an Islamic answer to the Christian discourse that depicts Manokwari as 'gospel city'.
26   e.g. see 'Habib Munzir di Manokwari Papua': http://www.youtube.com/watch?v=ZSrysiZ8c_c (accessed 16/09/2013).

proudly that 'friends from Surabaya will come, from Tegal, Sumatra, and also from Papua … He [Habib Munzir] even had students from Papua. He taught them until they were mature, and then sent them back to Papua to proselytise'.[27]

Let me start my discussion of Habib Munzir's account of Papua by contrasting it with the narratives of the eastern Indonesian Al-Khairaat members. Although post-Suharto eastern Indonesia has seen horrible violence along religious lines in Poso (Central Sulawesi) and the Moluccas, Al-Khairaat members who live in provinces with a strong Christian presence are less concerned with Christian activities in Papua than Habib Munzir who, coming from a part of Indonesia with a clear Islamic majority, seems to be shocked by assertions of Christian identity in the places he visited. So, for Habib Munzir, Papua is first of all a land where it can happen that one has to stay in the 'only Muslim hotel', where it can be difficult to build mosques, where one encounters 'huge religious buildings' that are not Islamic and where one can travel for hours without spotting any Muslims. By contrast, the Al-Khairaat members I interviewed, who had never travelled to Papua, one must add, imagine Papua as a place that has the potential to leave behind the *jahiliyyah* and become part of the 'house of Islam' such as other parts of eastern Indonesia. They consider the region where they live to be part of an Islamic frontier with Papua as its remotest and 'wildest' extension where 'the jungle' and 'the primitiveness' of its inhabitants are the greatest obstacles to proselytisation, whereas Habib Munzir's account rests upon a clear dichotomy between centre and periphery, i.e. between Jakarta and Papua, finding its expression in a discourse that is composed of worries about Christian dominance as well as of Hadhrami diasporic and evolutionist/developmentalist perspectives.

Unsurprisingly, the Hadhrami diasporic perspective can be found in the accounts of both the eastern Indonesian Al-Khairaat members and the Jakartan preacher. Both evoke 'the light of the Prophet' that can illuminate the Papuan frontier. Habib Munzir clearly positions himself in a tradition of Hadhrami proselytisation in Papua, as he visits places where Hadhramis are said to have been before and to have left traces, such as the mosque in Kokoda. He even dreams of a Hadhrami who once proselytised in the region and was killed, bemoaning that his grave 'in the jungle' is unknown. This remark must be understood against the backdrop that, as mentioned earlier, graves represent significant sites in the Hadhrami diaspora and grave visits are an important part of Hadhrami religious practice. Habib Munzir thus saw himself on a mission akin to the missions of Hadhramis of former times – such as Sayyid Idrus Al-Jufri, the tireless traveller and founder of Al-Khairaat, one might add – converting locals to Islam or teaching local Muslims how to practice their religion properly.

---

27   http://news.detik.com/read/2013/09/16/005955/2359319/10/pelayat-dari-berbagai-daerah-padati-rumah-duka-habib-munzir (accessed 16/09/2013).

Despite these similarities, the theme of preaching in 'the jungle' features stronger in Habib Munzir's Al-Kisah report than in the accounts of eastern Indonesian Hadhramis, suggesting that as an inhabitant of Indonesia's capital he is more influenced by evolutionist-cum-developmentalist discourses. Apart from the notion of the jungle being part of the semantic field of evolutionist discourses about primitivism and the stone-age (see Stasch's chapter) that he shares with the Al-Khairaat Hadhramis, Habib Munzir's account has a stronger developmentalist emphasis. In fact, he likes to highlight the technological differences between life in 'high-tech' Jakarta and 'underdeveloped' Papua. The reader is thus informed that the hotel where he stayed was basic but 'equipped with air conditioning', if electricity was available and if it was, at which times of day or night. The reader is also informed about road conditions and, most importantly, about the (im)possibility of real-time communication, as it is conveyed to the reader exactly where on his journeys there was 'no signal'. Inspired by Danilyn Rutherford's chapter (in this volume), one can read Habib Munzir's journeys also comprising technology demonstrations, not to demonstrate the stone-age per se as Dutch colonial officials would have done, but to emphasise the differences between 'real-time' Jakarta and 'backward' Papua. Habib Munzir travelled with his laptop and his smartphone, which he also employed to show Muslims in Papua videos demonstrating how he can mobilise the masses in the capital, i.e. how Islam can thrive in a developed and connected place.

Yet the conditions in Papua perceived as deficiencies in both fields, technology and religion, were psychologically straining for Habib Munzir. His encounter with the brave old Catholic nun led to self-criticism of being a spoiled Jakartan who for the first time experiences proselytisation in such an environment, which he perceives as being more authentic than his activities in Jakarta. Papua, not Jakarta, is 'the field for a preacher of the way of Allah'.[28] Moreover, his account comprises not only self-criticism but also accusations of the state of Islamic proselytisation in Indonesia that leaves large parts of Papua abandoned. This is clearly addressed to the readership of Al-Kisah, which is mainly based on Java. Papua is thus portrayed as a region that is not only in need of material but also spiritual development, where people long for receiving money and preachers from Jakarta and like to remind visitors that 'we are Muslims of the same nation'. Thus, enlarging 'the house of Islam' and overcoming the *jahiliyyah* by inflaming 'the light of the Prophet' goes hand in hand with developmentalist agendas of making Papua part of the real-time. In Habib Munzir's account, frontier discourses of various kinds overlap and merge as they are informed by

---

28   In fact, among Indonesian Christian preachers one can encounter similar discourses, as they see working in Papua as both, in most need of their efforts but also as a personal/spiritual trial (Jenny Munro, personal communication).

themes prevalent in Islamic and secular imaginaries of peripheral regions. It is in the conclusion of this chapter where I will come back to the spatio-temporal hierarchies intrinsic to his account.

Hadhramis as Papuans and alternative Papuan imaginaries

In this chapter so far, we followed Indonesian Hadhramis from eastern Indonesia and Java in how they perceive and experience Papua as a frontier region. This discussion would be incomplete, however, if we did not consider those Hadhramis with a longer history in Papua, since the views from Jakarta and parts of eastern Indonesia differ greatly from the views from within Papua, where we can observe today a Muslim Papuan identity in the making as well as alternative Islamic practices and imaginaries.

As outlined above, Arab migration to Papua resulted in trade, intermarriage and the settlement of Hadhramis in the region. For example, a high degree of integration into local society can be observed among Hadhramis in the Raja Ampat islands. Albert Remijsen (2002: 180) writes in his dissertation about clans of non-Raja Ampat origin that have become part of the Ma'ya, as the Muslim population of the islands is called: 'These clans speak Ma'ya and are totally integrated in Ma'ya society.' And among them, Remijsen cites the Alhamid, mentioned previously as one of the major Hadhrami families in the region. In Sorong I was able to interview a representative of this Hadhrami family, Basri Alhamid, the headmaster of Sorong's State Islamic Senior High School (Madrasah Aliyah Negeri) who was born in 1956 on Salawati, one of the Raja Ampat islands. He was quite surprised when I asked him about his Arab descent, as he identifies more with the land where he was born: 'My mother was still of Arab descent, and my father, too. But the mother of my mother was of Raja Ampat origin … and we were born here, grew up here and became Papuans. If I'm called an Arab, it's perhaps just the family name … In Fakfak many Arabs married Papuans. This is a mixing of many layers so that sometimes you can see that they are Arab and sometimes you can't see it anymore … Like me, you can't see that I'm Arab.'[29]

Close identifications with the land where one was born and currently lives are actually nothing special among Hadhramis, as they like to quote the *hadith*, i.e. the saying of the Prophet Muhammad, that reads, 'The love of the fatherland stems from faith' (in Arabic, 'hubb al-watan min al-iman'). For Hadhramis, stressing one's loyalty to Indonesia was particularly important in late colonial

---

29   Interview in Sorong, West Papua, 23 April 2008.

times and after Indonesia's independence when their status as citizens of the new republic was at stake (Jonge 2004). It seems that in post-Suharto, Special Autonomy Papua, in which nationalist and Christian discourses increasingly converge (see chapters by Timmer, Myrttinen, and Richards in this volume), Hadhramis as Muslims are in a familiar situation of having to prove that they are with, and actually part of, the indigenous population.

Given the distinct tendency of Hadhramis in the Moluccan-Papuan region and in Indonesia at large to occupy leading positions in Islamic matters, it does not come as a surprise that Papuan Hadhramis were involved in establishing an organisation for Papuan Muslims in post-Suharto Indonesia, the Papuan Muslim Council or *Majelis Muslim Papua* (MMP). The MMP was formed in 2007 and grew out of the *Solidaritas Muslim Papua* organisation which was founded in 1999 by 47 Muslim figures, including Thaha Alhamid and Sayyid Fadhal Alhamid who are of Hadhrami descent. Thaha Alhamid is a particularly salient figure since he is part of the Papuan nationalist elite, and perhaps the most prominent Muslim Papuan nationalist, serving as the secretary general of the Papua Presidium Council or *Presidium Dewan Papua* (PDP) (Pamungkas 2011: 139, 141; Wanggai 2008: 199–200). According to Cahyo Pamungkas (2008, 2011: 140) the MMP was established in order 'to counter the proposition that Islam is identical with Indonesia', to build a 'communication bridge between Muslim immigrants and Christian Papuan society', to advocate indigenous Papuan rights, human rights and to combat economic inequality, and to counter the influence of Indonesian Islamic organisations that usually focus on Muslim migrants. Its role in bridging interests between Christian and Islamic camps was tested in 2007 in the course of the establishment of the State Islamic Institute Al-Fatah or *Sekolah Tinggi Agama Islam Negeri* (STAIN) *Al-Fatah* in Jayapura. STAIN *Al-Fatah* was protested by the Indonesian Priest Association (*Asosiasi Pendeta Indonesia*) and other groups, and it was Thaha Alhamid who was heavily involved in solving the dispute by convincing the Christian governor of Papua that Papuans will also benefit from the institute (ibid. 147–148). The institute is now headed by another member of the Alhamid family, namely Idrus Al-Hamid, who is a close observer of Christian-Muslim tensions in Papua (Al-Hamid 2013, 2014).

Despite this high level of integration into Papuan Muslim circles and their leading roles in Islamic organisations and institutions, Special Autonomy Papua can haunt Papuan Hadhramis in ways that previously would have been unthinkable. Consider the case of Mohammad Musa'ad, who was one of the negotiators on the Special Autonomy policy, but was rejected as a vice-governor candidate in 2005 because of his Arab ancestry (Pamungkas 2011: 133, 143). The International Crisis Group (2006: 8) also recognised his case: 'Although Musa'ad's mother is a Papuan from FakFak, his father is of Arab descent.' According to the Papuan People's Council (*Majelis Rakyat Papua*, MRP), the body that has the right to screen candidates according to Special Autonomy legislation, 'an indigenous Papuan is a person of the Melanesian race, whose mother and father are Papuan, with patrilineal heritage, and who has a cultural base with a local language, a Papuan tribe, a village to which he or she belong, and a customary tradition (*adat istiadat*)' (ibid.). However, there is also the possibility that one can become a candidate if s/he is 'accepted and acknowledged as an indigenous Papuan by the local customary community' (ibid.: 9), and Mohammad Musa'ad had the support of the Bombarari tribe in the Fakfak region. Yet he was still rejected since, as one member of the MRP explained to the ICG, many MRP members prefer 'full-blooded Papuans, with black skin and frizzy hair' (ibid.) (see also Wanggai 2008: 206).

Despite this trend towards rigid views of who is to be considered a Papuan, Hadhramis with a Papuan background often consider themselves (also) as Papuans and see Papua as the centre of their religious and political activities. They do not share the perspectives of their fellow Hadhramis in other parts of Indonesia that are imbued with Islamic and secular frontier notions. Moreover, as Muslims who have resided in Papua for several generations they not only embody Hadhrami strategies of becoming local, such as intermarrying and identifying strongly with the land where one was born, but are also familiar with interpretations of Islam that follow the logics of Papuan mythology.

These interpretations are particularly widespread in the Bird's Head and Bomberai peninsulas and basically say that Islam, like Christianity, is indigenous to Papua: Papua is the land where Adam and Eve descended, where Noah's ark was stranded, and where all subsequent figures of the holy books lived. A mountain on the land between Arguni Bay and Wondama Bay is known under the name of 'mountain of the prophet' (*gunung nabi*) and some Papuan Muslims like to perform the pilgrimage there instead of travelling to Mecca (Wanggai 2008: 59–60). As an example for such oral traditions I want to refer to a myth that comprises a story of two springs being located close to Fakfak. One is a salt water and the other a sweet water spring. Both are guarded by men who owned books. The guard of the salt water spring owned the Qur'an, whereas the guard of the sweet water spring the Bible. The teachings from the salt water spring were then adopted by the people living on the coast and teachings from the sweet water spring found a following among the people living in the interior, alluding to the distribution of Muslims and Christians in the region (Onim 2006: 53–54; Warta 2011: 334). These narratives are reminiscent of Papuan cosmology, such as Koreri, that identifies Jesus Christ as Papuan (Rutherford 2003, 2012), and denies any portrayal of Papua as an Islamic frontier zone or as an underdeveloped periphery, let alone as the residue of a stone-age. Rather, Papua appears as the centre of all Abrahamic religions, including Islam, wherefrom today's civilizations emanated (see also the chapters by Myrttinen and Timmer in this volume).

Concluding remarks

This chapter has embarked on frontier concepts that rely heavily on evolutionist and developmentalist discourses as they have been – and still are – directed towards Papua and its indigenous inhabitants. These discourses express particular spatio-temporal hierarchisations characterised by a logic of stages of human and societal development, with Papua and Papuans being relegated to the lowest level. As such, it has to be emphasised, they differ from Islamic frontier concepts of the *Dar al-Islam/Dar al-Harb* and the *jahiliyyah* which rest upon a dichotomy between an Islamic and a non-Islamic order. These Islamic frontier concepts do not provide for treating non-Islamic societies unequally by imposing different degrees of devaluation. As a society can be more or less 'primitive', or more or less 'underdeveloped', it cannot be more or less 'un-Islamic', as it is part of the 'house of Islam' or it is not. Enlarging the *Dar al-Islam* and overcoming the *jahiliyyah* is thus the primary goal that can be applied to every community and every human being, including Papuans. And from a Hadhrami diasporic perspective there are different, but combinable, ways to accomplish this, i.e. through trade, proselytisation and marriage.

However, these ideal types (in a Weberian sense) of Islamic frontier concepts can hardly be discerned as such in the narratives of Hadhramis from Sulawesi and Jakarta. Members of Al-Khairaat see themselves situated in a frontier zone of which Papua is its remotest part. Whereas in the Islamic parts of central and northern Sulawesi the *jahiliyyah* has been overcome due to the efforts of the exemplary preacher Sayyid Idrus Al-Jufri, in Papua the bearers of 'the light of the Prophet' still meet the jungle where darkness, and dark-skinned people, prevail. In the strongholds of Al-Khairaat on Sulawesi the *jahiliyyah* has been left behind for several generations now, while remote Papua lags behind these developments. We see here how spatio-temporal hierarchisations that are reminiscent of evolutionist-cum-developmentalist frontier notions inform Islamic depictions of the frontier assigning Papua a particularly lowered place.

Such developmentalist inflections of Islamic frontier concepts can also be discerned in the account of the Jakartan preacher Habib Munzir Al-Musawa, another bearer of 'the light of the Prophet', in which they feature even more strongly. In his account, the Papuan 'jungle' lacks not only proper Islamic proselytisation but also the amenities of the contemporary age, such as good roads, nice hotels, electricity and especially real-time communication. The reader learns about the dominance of Christianity, Muslims who have forgotten how to pray properly, and at the same time, where and when electricity does not work or is not available and mobile communication is not possible due to the lack of signal. Habib Munzir was a bearer of 'the light of the Prophet' who wanted to see Papua being illuminated not only by prophetic radiance but also by the data streams of modern communications. His account suggests that remote Papua lags behind because it is not part of real-time communication circles and of Islamic real-time Indonesia at large. It is even a place where Muslims can be forgotten, where no preachers from Jakarta want to go, and which seems to be farther away than places outside Indonesia such as Palestine.

This stronger emphasis on nationalist-developmentalist themes in Habib Munzir's account, compared to the views of Hadhramis from Sulawesi, corresponds with actual geographic distances and all the more so with an inner-Indonesian centre-periphery hierarchy with Jakarta featuring as the apex of the nation. The (symbolically) closer to the centre the beholder is based, it seems, the more pronounced these nationalist-developmentalist views become and the stronger spatio-temporal hierarchies intrinsic to them inform Islamic frontier notions. Having organised huge prayer meetings at Jakarta's central Monas square, the memory of which he carried with him in digital form on his smart phone, Habib Munzir epitomises the nation's centre, whereas the Hadhramis from Sulawesi live in distance from both Jakarta, the exemplary centre, and Papua, the ultimate frontier.

However, as this chapter also attempts to demonstrate, these frontier notions with their multiple ways of spatio-temporal hierarchisation are not all-pervasive and dominant. In fact, Papuan Muslims, including Hadhramis with a Papuan background, began to challenge discourses that treat Papuan Muslims as mere objects of Islamic and national development. The establishment of the Papuan Muslim Council, in which Hadhramis were heavily involved, provided Papuan Muslims some sort of institutional authority to meet the challenges of Papua's religious and political intricacies. In fact, since the fall of Suharto and the subsequent introduction of Special Autonomy Papuan Muslims have to deal with an increasingly complex religious landscape, including a range of Indonesian Islamic figures and organisations that have discovered Papua as a destination for missionary activities (Noor 2010; Imroatus 2011; Wekke 2013), and with assertions of a heavily Christian-inflected Papuan nationalism. Countering notions that associate Islam with Indonesia and Papua with Christianity, Papuan Muslims try to reposition themselves by refusing to be relegated to the fringes of an Indonesian Islam or a Papuan nationalism, just as Papuan interpretations of Islam put the land of Papua at the very centre of this religion. It remains to be seen to what extent these attempts will be met with success or which new frictions they might generate. This is certainly a dynamic field, but for now, it seems, we should not expect that the spatio-temporal hierarchisations examined in this chapter will fade away too quickly, as they are inscribed in frontier notions that are firmly anchored in the persistent evolutionist-cum-developmentalist discourses so widespread in Indonesia.

References

Ahmad, Aziz 1976. 'The Shrinking Frontiers of Islam'. *International Journal of Middle East Studies* 7(2): 145–159.

Alatas, Ismail Fajrie 2005. 'Land of the Sacred, Land of the Damned: Conceptualizing Homeland among the Upholders of the Tariqa 'Alawiyya in Indonesia'. *Antropologi Indonesia* 29(2): 142–158.

Alatas, Ismail Fajrie 2010. 'A New Resurgence? The Ba'alawi and Islamic Revival in Post-Soeharto Indonesia'. Conference paper 'Islam, Trade and Culture: The Roles of the Arabs in Southeast Asia', National University of Singapore, 10–11 April 2010; http://rihlah.nl.sg/Paper/Ismail%20Fajrie%20Alatas.pdf.

Al-Hamid, Idrus 2013. 'Islam Politik di Papua: Resistensi dan Tantangan Membangun Perdamaian'. *Jabal Hikmah* 6(11): 421–441.

Al-Hamid, Idrus 2014. *Jayapura dalam Transformasi Agama dan Budaya: Memahami Akar Konflik Kristen-Islam di Papua*. PhD thesis, Universitas Gadjah Mada, Yogyakarta.

Azra, Azyumardi 2000. 'Hadrami as Educators: Al Habib Sayyid Idrus ibn Salim al-Jufri (1889–1969)'. *Kultur. The Indonesian Journal for Muslim Cultures* 1(1): 91–104.

Baumann, Gerd 2004. 'Grammars of Identity/Alterity: A Structural Approach'. In Baumann, Gerd and Gingrich, Andre (eds), *Grammars of Identity/Alterity: A Structural Approach*. New York and Oxford: Berghahn Books, 18–50.

Clarence-Smith, William G. 1998. 'The Economic Role of the Arab Community in Maluku, 1816 to 1940'. *Indonesia and the Malay World* 26(74): 32–49.

Dove, Michael 1985. 'The Agroecological Mythology of the Javanese and the Political Economy of Indonesia'. *Indonesia* 39: 1–36.

Dunn, Ross E. 2005. *The Adventures of Ibn Battuta. A Muslim Traveler of the 14th Century*. Berkeley: University of California Press.

Ellen, Roy 1996. 'Arab Traders and Land Settlers in the Geser-Gorom Archipelago'. *Indonesia Circle* 70: 237–252.

Ellen, Roy 2003. *On the Edge of the Banda Zone: Past and Present in the Social Organisation of a Moluccan Trading Network*. Honolulu: University of Hawai'i Press.

Fold, Niels and Hirsch, Philip 2009. 'Re-thinking Frontiers in Southeast Asia'. *Geographical Journal* 175(2): 95–97.

Freitag, Ulrike and Clarence-Smith, William (eds) 1997. *Hadhrami Traders, Scholars and Statesmen in the Indian Ocean, 1750s-1960s*. Leiden: Brill.

Gingrich, Andre 2010. 'Blame it on the Turks: Language Regimes and the Culture of Frontier Orientalism in Eastern Austria'. In de Cillia, Rudolf, Gruber, Helmutm, Krzyzanowski, Michał, and Menz, Florian (eds), *Diskurs-Politik-Identität/Discourse – Politics – Identity*. Stauffenburg: Tübingen, 71–81.

Heiss, Johann and Feichtinger, Johannes 2013. 'Distant Neighbors: Uses of Orientalism in the Late Nineteenth-Century Austro-Hungarian Empire'. In Hodkinson, James, Walker, John, Mazumdar, Shaswati, and Feichtinger, Johannes (eds), *Deploying Orientalism in Culture and History. From Germany to Central and Eastern Europe*. Rochester, New York: Camden House, 148–165.

Ho, Engseng 2004. 'Empire through Diasporic Eyes: A View from the Other Boat'. *Comparative Studies in Society and History* 46(2): 210–246.

Ho, Engseng 2006. *The Graves of Tarim. Genealogy and Mobility across the Indian Ocean*. Berkeley: University of California Press.

Imroatus, Nur 2011. 'Yang Radikal dan Yang Moderat di Papua: Membangun Institusi Perdamaian di Masjid Raya Baiturrahim'. In Al-Makassary, Ridwan, Fauzia, Amelia, and Abubakar, Irfan (eds), *Masjid dan Pembangunan Perdamaian. Studi Kasus Poso, Ambon, Ternate, dan Jayapura*. Jakarta: Center for the Study of Religion and Culture, 273–327.

International Crisis Group 2006. 'Papua: The Dangers of Shutting Down Dialogue'. *Asia Briefing N°47*.

International Crisis Group 2008. 'Indonesia: Communal Tensions in Papua'. *Asia Report N°154*.

Jonge, Huub de 2004. 'Abdul Rahman Baswedan and the Emancipation of the Hadhramis in Indonesia'. *Asian Journal of Social Science* 32(3): 373–400.

Jonge, Huub de and Kaptein, Nico (eds) 2002. *Transcending Borders. Arabs, Politics, Trade and Islam in Southeast Asia*. Leiden: KITLV Press.

Kaartinen, Timo 2010. *Songs of Travel, Stories of Place. Poetics of Absence in an Eastern Indonesian Society*. Helsinki: Academia Scientiarum Fennica.

Kahn, Joel 2012. 'Islam and Capitalism in the Frontiers and Borderlands of the Modern Malay World'. In Mee, Wendy and Kahn, Joel (eds), *Questioning Modernity in Indonesia and Malaysia*. Singapore: NUS Press in association with Kyoto University Press, 21–59.

Khatab, Sayed 2006. *The Political Thought of Sayyid Qutb: The Theory of Jahiliyyah*. London and New York: Routledge.

Kirksey, Eben 2012. *Freedom in Entangled Worlds: West Papua and the Architecture of Global Power*. Durham and London: Duke University Press.

Li, Tania Murray 1999. 'Marginality, Power and Production: Analysing Upland Transformations'. In Tania Murray Li (ed.), *Transforming the Indonesian Uplands: Marginality, Power and Production*. London: Routledge, 1–46.

Li, Tania Murray 2001. 'Relational Histories and the Production of Difference on Sulawesi's Upland Frontier'. *Journal of Asian Studies* 60(1): 41–66.

Lee, Samuel 2004 [1829]. *The Travels of Ibn Battuta in the Near East, Asia and Africa 1325–1354*. Mineola, New York: Dover Publications.

McCarthy, John and Cramb, R.A. 2009. 'Policy Narratives, Landholder Engagement, and Oil Palm Expansion on the Malaysian and Indonesian Frontiers'. *Geographical Journal* 175(2): 112–123.

Nisa, Eva F. 2012. 'The Voice of *Syarifah* on Jakarta's *Da'wa* Stage'. *RIMA: Review of Indonesian and Malaysian Affairs* 46(1): 55–81.

Noor, Farish A. 2010. 'The Arrival and Spread of the Tablighi Jama'at in West Papua (Irian Jaya), Indonesia'. *RSIS Working Paper* No. 191, Singapore: S. Rajaratnam School of International Studies.

Onim, Jusuf Fredrik 2006. *Islam & Kristen di Tanah Papua. Meniti Jalan Bersama Hubungan Islam-Kristen Dalam Sejarah Penyebaran dan Perjumpaannya di Wilayah Semenanjung Onin Fakfak*. Bandung: Jurnal Info Media.

Pamungkas, Cahyo 2008. *Papua Islam dan Otonomi Khusus: Kontestasi Identitas di Kalangan Orang Papua*. Tesis Program Paskasarjana Sosiologi, Universitas Indonesia.

Pamungkas, Cahyo 2011. 'Muslim Papua and Special Autonomy: The Identity Contest in Papua'. *Journal of Indonesian Social Sciences and Humanities* 4: 133–155.

Remijsen, Albert 2002. *Word-prosodic Systems of Raja Ampat Languages*. PhD thesis, University of Leiden.

Rutherford, Danilyn 2003. *Raiding the Land of the Foreigners: The Limits of the Nation on an Indonesian Frontier*. Princeton: Princeton University Press.

Rutherford, Danilyn 2012. *Laughing at Leviathan: Sovereignty and Audience in West Papua*. Chicago and London: The University of Chicago Press.

Slama, Martin 2011. 'Translocal Networks and Globalisation within Indonesia. Exploring the Hadhrami Diaspora from the Archipelago's North-East'. *Asian Journal of Social Science* 39(3): 238–257.

Slama, Martin 2012. '"Coming Down to the Shop": Trajectories of Hadhrami Women into Indonesian Public Realms'. *The Asia Pacific Journal of Anthropology* 13(4): 313–333.

Spyer, Patricia 2000. *The Memory of Trade: Modernity's Entanglements on an Eastern Indonesian Island*. Durham and London: Duke University Press.

Stasch, Rupert 2011. 'Textual Iconicity and the Primitivist Cosmos: Chronotopes of Desire in Travel Writing about Korowai of West Papua'. *Journal of Linguistic Anthropology* 21(1): 1–21.

Tsing, Anna Lowenhaupt 2005. *Friction. An Ethnography of Global Connection*. Princeton and Oxford: Princeton University Press.

Wanggai, Toni Victor M. 2008. *Rekonstruksi Sejarah Umat Islam di Tanah Papua*. PhD thesis, Universitas Islam Negeri Syarif Hidayatullah.

Warnk, Holger 2010. 'The Coming of Islam and Moluccan-Malay Culture to New Guinea c.1500–1920'. *Indonesia and the Malay World* 38(110): 109–134.

Warta, Christian 2011. *Religiositäten in Bewegung: Adat, Schriftreligionen und Nationalismen in Papua, Indonesien*. PhD thesis, University of Vienna.

Wekke, Ismail Suardi 2013. 'Religious Education and Empowerment: Study on Pesantren in Muslim Minority West Papua'. *MIQOT* XXXVII (2): 374–395.

Widjojo, Muridan 2009. *The Revolt of Prince Nuku: Cross-cultural Alliance-making in Maluku, c.1780–1810*. Leiden: KITLV.

Zadeh, Travis 2011. *Mapping Frontiers Across Medieval Islam: Geography, Translation and the 'Abbasid Empire*. London and New York: I.B. Tauris.

www.ingramcontent.com/pod-product-compliance
Lightning Source LLC
Chambersburg PA
CBHW061243270326
41928CB00041B/3393